SOCIAL PROBLEMS: A CASE STUDY APPROACH

SOCIAL PROBLEMS:
A CASE STUDY
APPROACH

Edited By

Norman A. Dolch
Louisiana State University in Shreveport

And

Linda Deutschmann
University of the Cariboo

GENERAL HALL, INC.
Publishers
5 Talon Way
Dix Hills, New York 11746

SOCIAL PROBLEMS: A CASE STUDY APPROACH

GENERAL HALL, INC.
5 Talon Way
Dix Hills, New York 11746

Publisher: Ravi Mehra

LIBRARY OF CONGRESS CATALOG CARD NUMBER: 01-34643

ISBN: 1-882289-72-2 [paper]
      1-882289-73-0 [cloth]

ISBN 1-882289-73-0

Manufactured in the United States of America   9 781882 289738

TABLE OF CONTENTS

PREFACE

This book reflects our many years of teaching undergraduate students. While we have shared with them the research and theory of sociology on various social problems, our students have shared with us experiences with social problems, which they have had, or experiences of acquaintances, family members, and friends. Besides trying to understand social problems, our students often want to know what to do to help persons experiencing the problem. This book attempts to go beyond just discussing theory and research. It attempts to look at interventions – the "what can be done" response which we are often asked by our students.

Since human social life is based on interactions between and among persons, we have chosen to build each chapter around a case study so that students reading the book can readily identify with persons experiencing the social problem studied. Social problems have their basis in the social structure but impact on the lives of people. This book is our attempt to blend theory, research, and pathways to action in an attempt to better understand social problems and to assist students to better respond to social problems if they chose to do so.

There are many persons who we wish to thank for their assistance with this project. We certainly wish to thank our families who have been tolerant and encouraging, especially Norm's wife Cindy and Linda's husband Karl. We thank your students and former teachers from whom we learned much that is reflected in the text. In addition, we especially wish to thank these colleagues and acquaintances for their special role at various stages of the project: Leon Anderson, James McCartney, Tony Orum, Charles Ragin, and Claude Tewells. We extend a special thanks to Larry Reynolds, for his guidance and encouragement. Without the word processing assistance of Nelda Shipp, this volume would not have been possible. Finally, we acknowledge the faith placed in our project by each author who contributed to this edited volume.

CONTRIBUTORS

RONALD L. AKERS is University of Florida Research Foundation Professor of Sociology and Director of the Center for Studies in Criminology and Law. He has conducted extensive research in criminological theory, alcohol and drug behavior, sociology of law, juvenile delinquency, and corrections. He is author of *Criminological Theories* (1997; 2000); *Drugs, Alcohol and Society* (1992); *Deviant Behavior: A Social Learning Approach* (1973; 1977; 1985), *Social Learning and Social Structure: A General Theory of Crime and Deviance* (1998), and numerous articles in criminological and sociological journals. He is former president of the American Society of Criminology and of the Southern Sociological Society.

JEANNE BALLANTINE is Professor of Sociology in the Department of Sociology and Anthropology at Wright State University in Dayton, Ohio. She is active in the American Sociological Association Teaching Program as a department consultant. Among her books are *Sociology of Education, Schools and Society, Sociological Footprints*. She has also authored numerous articles..

CATHERINE WHITE BERHEIDE is Professor of Sociology and former Director of Women's Studies at Skidmore College and a former American Sociological Association Congressional Fellow. Her research focuses the sociology of work, organizations, and gender. Her current research in conjunction with the Center for Women in Government at the State University of New York in Albany is an analysis of top level appointments by the fifty state governors. Among her publications are: *Women, Family, and Policy, Sex and Gender* (a special issue of *Teaching Sociology)*, and *Women Today: A Multidisciplinary Approach to Women 's Studies.*

E. HELEN BERRY is Associate Professor of Sociology at the Utah State University. Her research interests examine the effects of demographic events on social structures. Her current research interests are in rapid population change, teenage pregnancy, and the intersection between social stratification and exercise.

TERRY DANNER is completing a Ph.D. in Sociology at the University of Florida in Gainesville. He has conducted and published research on outlaw motorcycle gangs, female homicide offenders, and the relationship between types of land-use and crime volumes. He is currently chair of the Department of Criminology at Saint Leo University, and is developing a Masters of Science program for Criminal Justice Administrators.

DEBRA DAVID is Professor of Health Science and Director of the Gerontology Program at San Jose State University. Her research interests include ethnicity and aging; ethical issues in later life; long-term care; and reminiscence.

LINDA DEUTSCHMANN, Ph.D. is Associate Professor at the University-College of the Cariboo in central British Columbia. She is the author of *Deviance and Social Control in Canada.* Her current work in progress is a text on criminal careers and a monograph on the reintegration of offenders in the community. She also works with the John Howard Society, an organization devoted to helping those in conflict with the criminal law, their families, and their communities.

NORMAN A. DOLCH is Professor of Sociology at Louisiana State University in Shreveport. He directs the undergraduate American Humanics Program that prepares students for entry level professional positions with youth and human service organizations and also directs the Master of Science in Human Services Administration. Author of numerous articles and chapters in books, he is currently involved in research on nonprofit collaboration and assists many nonprofits with program evaluation and grant writing. He also holds a gratis clinical associate professorship in the Department of Family Medicine and Comprehensive Care at Louisiana State University Medical School in Shreveport.

MICHAEL J. DONNELLY is Professor of Sociology and Chair of the Department of Sociology and Anthropology at the University of New Hampshire. His interests include theory, history of sociology, social thought, and mental health. He has done research and published extensively in these areas.

GWENDOLYN DORDICK is Assistant Professor of Sociology and Social Studies at Harvard University. She recently published *Something Left to Lose: Personal Relations and Survival Among New York's Homeless.* Her current research examines the myth of mobility and limitations of conventional definitions of housing markets as they relate to transitions out of homelessness.

ANTHONY GARY DWORKIN is Professor of Sociology and Director of the Sociology of Education Research Group for the Public Schools at the University of Houston. He is the author of numerous books and articles in the areas of race, ethnic, and gender relations and the sociology of education. Along with Rosalind J. Dworkin, he is the co-author of *The Minority Report: An Introduction to Racial, Ethnic, and Gender Relations,* 3rd edition (Harcourt Brace, 1999). He serves as the editor of the "New Inequalities" book series at SUNY Press

KARL ESCHBACH is Assistant Professor of Sociology and Research Associate in the Center for Immigration Research at the University of Houston. He has published in the areas of race and ethnic relations, demography, and urban sociology.

THOMAS R. HEFFINGTON is a research coordinator with the Department of Family, Youth and Community Sciences and a lecturer with the Center for Studies in Criminology and Law at the University of Florida. He has an extensive background working in the field of alcohol and drug abuse rehabilitation and program development. His recent research has focused on alcohol use among the elderly and social services program evaluation.

EDWARD L. KAIN is Brown Distinguished Teaching Professor in the Department of Sociology and Anthropology at Southwestern University. His research focuses upon a variety of issues related to social change and families as well as the teaching of sociology. His publications include *The Myth of Family Decline* and *Diversity and Change in Families* (ed. With Mark Robert Rank). In 1997 he received the Hans Mauksch Award for Distinguished Contributions to Undergraduate Sociology.

BEBE F. LAVIN, Professor Emerita and past Chairperson of the Department of Sociology at Kent State University, is presently Coordinator for Academic Assessment for Undergraduate Studies at that university. She has completed research and published extensively with Marie Haug in the area of doctor-patient relationships, health and aging, and consumerism in medicine. Her research interests include professionalization of physicians, comparative health care systems, gerontology, and most recently, evaluation of student learning in higher education. Dr. Lavin has received many awards for community work as well as the Exemplary Teaching Award by the American Association of Higher Education and the University Distinguished Teaching Award.

SALLY RASKOFF teaches sociology at the University of Southern California, including courses in work, research methods, and theory. Her current research focuses on teenage volunteering and high school community service programs in an effort to better understand how social problems have been and may be alleviated through civic engagement.

ANN HELTON STROMBERG Is Peter and Gloria Gold Professor of Sociology at Pitzer Collage. Her publications on work include an early text on women and work (*Working Women* with Shirley Harkess) and a co-edited series on Women and Work (with Barbara Gutek and Laurie Larwood). She is very involved in international/intercultural education and regularly directs a summer program in the Central America.

MICHAEL B. TONEY is Professor of Sociology and Director of the Population Research Laboratory at Utah State University. His research has focused on the social determinants of migration in the United States.

RUDI VOLTI is Professor of Sociology at Pitzer College in Claremont, California. His research centers on the social, political, and economic aspects of technological change. His recent publications include *The Facts on File Encyclopedia of Science, Technology and Society,* and the 3rd edition of his widely used textbook *Society and Technological Change.* He serves on the editorial board of Technology and Culture and is a member of the Executive Council of the Society for the History of Technology.

N. REE WELLS is an Associate Professor of Sociology at Missouri Southern State College in Joplin. Her teaching areas and research interests include Social Problems, Social Stratification, Medical Sociology and Gender Studies. She has recently finished a case-study chapter on divorce and poverty for a deviancy textbook.

CHAPTER 1: INTRODUCTION:
WHAT IS A SOCIAL PROBLEM?

At first glance, you may feel that this is a meaningless (or totally obvious) question. Surely everyone sees health care and poverty as social problems? Or do they? Some of you, (mainly those who have health insurance, membership in a health maintenance organization, or supreme confidence in your own health) may not be concerned at all. You may well believe that "anyone" who works hard and plans well can provide for a secure future, and that those who must rely on charity should have simply worked harder and smarter

The assumption in the 60s and 70s was that unequal results were society's fault and that it was society's obligation to address and correct them. We are now moving back toward the traditional American value that people are responsible for their own lives, and that the reality of life is such that there will inevitably be winners and losers. This conception limits the society's moral and legal obligations, but does not rule out compassion (Yankelovich 1998:5). Americans who share this view may see compassion or individual charity as an adequate response to the problems we identify here, and see unemployment, divorce, and other problems as "individual" rather than social concerns. If you do, we hope that you will be willing to consider that there may be limits to this perspective. (There are also limits to the idea that everything bad is "society's fault").

While no one is likely to deny that individual effort will normally have an effect on success and security, we hope that your study of social problems will convince you that some kinds of personal problems are in fact embedded in social conditions. Sometimes the institutions of our society (government, business, schools, health-care systems, civil and criminal justice systems, for example) fail to adapt quickly and adequately to wide scale social changes such as globalization, the march of technology, the introduction of new ideas, or in some cases, war and natural disaster. When this happens, individuals may be squeezed in ways that they could not have anticipated and cannot control. Compassion may not be the best way of ensuring that every citizen has some chance at success, physical and emotional safety, health, and self-respect in their lives.

DEFINING SOCIAL PROBLEMS

THE POPULAR OPINION APPROACH

What are the social problems of our society? One way to identify the problems of our time is to ask a wide range of people about their beliefs and opinions. Each year (since 1935), the Gallup Poll has asked a representative sample of Americans "What do you think is the most important problem facing this country today?" In recent years the top five categories have been the economy (unemployment and jobs), crime, health care, the deficit, and drugs. Other problems that have been identified this way are taxes, the cost of living, welfare, poverty, declining ethical standards, education, teen pregnancy, foreign relations, racism, immigration, AIDS, and abortion. While there is some consistency in these choices, the trend is away from a consensus about what is most important (Gallup 1998). Many other problems are of "most concern" to some Americans. Examples elicited from a first year university class include: wife-battering, pornography, violence by and against children, inner city gangs, sexism, Satanism, suicide, drunk driving, sexual deviance, and surrogate motherhood.

What is your opinion? What do you believe are the most important problems? Try talking to others, perhaps trying to convince them that one problem is more important than another. What happens when you do this? Does everyone agree? What kinds of facts do people use to support their opinions? Your personal ranking of these "problems" will be affected by your general knowledge (Do you know how many babies are born addicted? And what this means for them?) It will be affected by the values that you have acquired as a member of your society (Do you approve of recreational sex? Do you think hard work is good and necessary?) It will be affected by your personal interests (Does supporting environmental causes conflict with your desire for a high paying job in a resource-based industry?) It will also be affected by your exposure to mass media (newspaper and television images of crime, for example). Finally, your feelings may be colored by emotionally-significant events in your life (Have you experienced racism or been harassed out of a good job?) When a great many people agree that something is a problem, it is likely to be recognized publicly as a **social problem.** This does not mean that everyone will agree on the nature of the problem, what causes it, what should be done about it, or even that anything can be done about it.

When Americans perceive that a social problem exists, they often take action to "fix" it. This propensity to take action against perceived ills was noted as early as 1835 by Alexis de Tocqueville, an aristocratic Frenchman, who wrote a perceptive and only mildly critical account of "life among the Americans" based on his experience as a visitor. Americans who see a problem may talk with acquaintances, neighbors, friends, and family in an attempt to define the problem and make others aware of it. The resulting community group may, for example, raise money to provide opportunities for potentially delinquent children, or act to bring Meals on Wheels to those too ill or elderly to cook for themselves. Americans often join together in organizations devoted to a particular cause (such as the reduction of child poverty, or the provision of neighborhood watch programs) and they may lobby government to take action. In comparison with other developed countries, the U.S. relies heavily on volunteerism (grass roots organizations), and shows resistance to the use of government power in the solution of perceived social problems (Roper Center for Public Opinion Research 1998: 35, 80-81).

THE SOCIOLOGICAL PERSPECTIVE

Sociology studies people as "actors" playing social roles. In the course of your day, you play many roles: student, parent, friend, spouse, neighbor, and so on. (You may do this well or badly, conventionally or with inventive flourishes.) Each of these roles "connects" you to other "actors" and to society as a whole. As we interact in these roles, society takes shape, and takes on a reality that is "structural." Thus we create, through interaction, organizations such as colleges, businesses and government agencies. Also, by following the "norms" set for these roles, we maintain and adapt the institutions of society (the family, education, religion, government, and others.) At a fundamental level, we interact with others to produce social definitions and social meanings that guide our actions. (This may not be obvious to you, so take time to think about it a bit.)

THE TOOLS OF SOCIOLOGY: CONCEPTS, METHODS, AND THEORIES

Sociologists use several kinds of tools, the most important of which are concepts, methods, and theories. Let us briefly look at some examples of these tools. **Concepts** are ideas about the common features of things that are observed. They help us to describe and compare the events around us. (Imagine trying to describe and understand a mountain if you had no concept of "size"). The concept of "relative deprivation" applies when people feel that they do not have much compared to others. They may see this "unfair" distribution of reward as a serious problem. Since human beings often compare themselves this way, (choosing to compare ourselves to those who have more) relative deprivation is probably a more common issue than is absolute deprivation (insufficient resources for survival.) Another useful concept is "ethnocentrism." Our early childhood socialization trains us to regard the ways of our own group as best. If the group I belong to thinks bathing twice a day is the only civilized way to behave, my parents will tell me that I am "bad" if I don't meet this standard. As a result, I am likely to regard people who bathe only once a day as bad and less worthy. Ethnocentric people are likely to harbor stereotypes and prejudices against other groups, and may discriminate against them. This can create individual problems for minorities, inefficiencies in the social order (jobs are going to one group, rather than going to the most talented), and conflict and disorder (riots and protests) that undermine the whole system. In this text, you will encounter many useful concepts that help us to understand the nature of social problems.

The second tool that we use is **methodology.** Over time, we have learned that some techniques of data gathering produce reliable and valid information about the world. In public opinion research, for example, it is important to use sampling procedures to ensure that those we question are "representative" of a wider population. Simply talking to the first people who are willing to answer your questions is not a useful way of finding out about public opinion. (If you only interview students in the library, for example, you will likely get different answers than if you only interviewed students in the local bar.) In the study of social problems, many methods are used. We may use participant observation, whereby the researcher takes part in events while recording them. This often shows us that our perceptions (of street people, for example) are stereotypes rather than realities. We may use self-report surveys to identify the victims of crime, illness, or poverty. Secondary analysis of official documents such as government census data can be useful, either alone or in combination with other methods. Methodology answers the question 'how do we know what we know?'

The third tool that we use is theory. A **theory** is an explanation (an answer to the question "why?"). A theory should be logical and testable. In everyday life we resort to many explanations for events without examining them carefully. As an example of this kind of untested explanation, consider the last time someone provided you with an "explanation" for her late arrival, or the last time that you produced such an excuse. Such "explanations" are often inconsistent with known facts and even inconsistent with other explanations given by the same person-unless you and your friends are atypical. These explanations often do not help us to understand the "real" causes of the late arrival, and would be useless in the development of an overall theory of lateness.

A good theory is an explanation that is logically consistent and can be tested by empirical evidence. When a theory is tested, and predictions based on it do not correspond to events, it must be changed, and then tested again. A theoretical perspective emerges when such "explanations" are repeatedly tested. A theory "works" when it can assist us in predicting future events and in helping us to understand how things are related to each other.

Sociology has a variety of theoretical perspectives that reflect the broad paths developed in this testing process. Use of these tested perspectives helps us to avoid "reinventing the wheel" in our efforts to understand the world around us. As you progress through this text, you will become familiar with symbolic interaction, functionalism, and conflict theories, among others.

Let us look at how each of these three major theoretical perspectives helps us to define social problems and to explain them. **Symbolic interactionism** holds that humans do not react to the world directly, but rather to the meanings that they attribute to that world. Social meanings emerge out of interaction with others. The unsocialized infant experiences a tremendous confusion of stimuli (noise, light, wetness, and hunger) which initially have no social meaning for the child. Adults in the environment, however, DO respond in terms of social meanings (whether the child is male of female, contented or fussing), and the child eventually learns this. If male, the child will likely be given more opportunity to explore his environment, and people will praise him for being "a future football player," if female, the adjectives are more likely to be "sweet" and "going to be a heartbreaker." The (initially unsocialized) gestures and (for the child) meaningless gender distinctions are fairly regularly rewarded in particular ways by particular persons. Gradually these gestures become social: that is, they are consciously used as communication, and become part of meaningful interaction between the child and others. Others in the environment act as a mirror to the child (You are wonderful! or You are a nuisance!).

In this interaction the growing child gradually develops a sense of self as well as an awareness of others. The social world gradually expands to include friends and family, lovers and enemies, expectations, values and beliefs. Consider the fact that Americans are typically socialized to place a high value on occupational status (Williams 1970). This long recognized research finding is reflected in our personal experience of meeting new people. These new people may not be much interested or beliefs and opinions, at least not until they have established what it is that we "do", our occupation. When the kind of work that we do is transferred to another country, or made obsolete by technology, our identity is threatened. This personal problem may be an indicator of a potential social problem. *It isn't a "real" social problem (in symbolic interactionist terms) unless it is recognized as a social problem*, and this will depend on the beliefs and values of those who observe it.

Symbolic interactionist theories contribute to our understanding of social problems in many ways. One of these is by highlighting the processes about how we learn to identify one thing rather than another as a problem. Did your high school have programs to teach you about drugs, about family violence, and about sex? What definitions did they provide for you? Did your friends support these "socially constructed definitions?" We find that people are more likely to recognize "drugs" as a social problem if their "significant others" (people they are close to, and care about) constantly make comments and gestures (nonverbal communications) that indicate that drugs are the cause of all sorts of bad behavior. If such a person is then asked about how the rules about drugs should be changed, he or she will be more likely to support relatively extreme solutions. People are more likely to see racism as a problem if racial discrimination violates the values of fair play that they have been socialized to expect and desire. On the other hand, if the most important people in your environment have said that "racialist" thought (race loyalty) is a good thing, and that getting along with other races is a kind of treason, then racism will not seem like a problem. You might very well think that the LACK of racism is a problem.

Another contribution made by symbolic interactionists is the concept of "labeling," which occurs when people acquire a negative (stigmatic) identity as a result of the definitions of others. Labeling can emerge out of malicious gossip (often in a small group) or it can be much more formal (when the courts label a person a convicted felon). One of the things that we learn in our interaction with parents and close friends (significant others) is how our society labels people. Are drug addicts "troubled people" who need support and counseling? Are they "sick" people who should be in medical treatment, or are they "criminals" who need to be locked up and punished? Is "child abuse" a private family matter or a public issue? It is useful to examine the way in which answers to these questions have varied over time. Things that are serious public problems now have frequently been treated quite differently in the past.

The label that we use has a very real impact on the way in which people may be treated, and this in turn may have predictable effects on which people will associate with them, and the social identity that they develop. A "criminal" label will likely keep you out of polite society, and will have a heavy impact on your employment chances. This is true even if your conviction was not justified. Symbolic interactionists often look for evidence that shows how the labeling process works. For example, they would be quite interested in a finding that wealthy shoplifters are often defined as "sick" (kleptomaniacs) while poor ones are treated as "bad" (thieves), and that "white collar offenders" (people who offend in the context of their work, and have respectable positions) are not as heavily stigmatized as "street criminals."

Another idea that is mainly used in symbolic interactionist work is "the self-fulfilling prophecy" or the "social definition of reality." Symbolic interactionists often use concepts such as "the social construction of reality" or "the definition of the situation" to help make clear their model of how meaning is made in the world, and how these meanings guide subsequent actions. As W. I. Thomas (1967) wrote, "If men define situations as real, they are real in their consequences." If I think the stock market is crashing, I may sell all my shares, and thus contribute to a falling market. (Unfortunately, this does not always work in reverse: simply defining something as "not a problem" does not make the underlying reality go away).

You can observe the on-going processes of social definition occurring in your world. At school and on the job (and even in TV sitcoms) people are working out the meaning of ideas such as "workplace harassment," "crimes against the environment" and "acceptable" standards with respect to pornography in public places on the Internet. Other areas where awareness and consensus are incomplete involve issues such as children's access to firearms, the rights of gays and lesbians in jobs and housing, date rape, and the "legalization" of marijuana. Documenting such changes over time is one of the ways in which sociologists from the symbolic interactionist tradition are able to learn a great deal about the processes by which some conditions come to be recognized as social problems.

Another long-standing theoretical tradition is **structural functionalism,** rooted in the work of Emile Durkheim (1987). Functionalism does not totally ignore social interaction, but tends to look at the social system as a **structure** that is above individual interaction. Interaction processes tend to become quite regular over time, and this produces structure. Consider the "structure" of your college. Registration rules are made in interaction, but they come to have a reality that is not unlike a brick wall; they are relatively independent of the will of individual people. Consider the "reality" of entrance policies, for example. Getting in or being excluded are very real, even if the rules are "socially constructed."

Structural functionalism is a way of looking at how the parts of society are related to each other, and to other parts of the whole. Each part contributes to the whole, and when something isn't working properly, the whole system is affected. If there are many drunk drivers on the road, the system is impacted, not just the unlucky individuals who encounter such drivers. A social problem occurs when the system is not getting what it needs to operate at maximum efficiency in a competitive environment (and we are always in a competitive environment). In functionalist terms, the thing that is not working is "**dysfunctional**." Thus, functionalists can look at an issue such as poverty and ask is this situation contributing to the effectiveness of American society? Or is it undermining the survival of this way of life? If some children go to school ill clothed and hungry, is their ability to contribute to society thereby compromised? Often functionalist analysis discovers both functions and dysfunctions. Fear of poverty may motivate many of us to work hard and contribute to the system. People who are poor may be willing to work at jobs that no one else will do, and will buy secondhand and low quality goods, thus contributing to the economy even as they suffer from it. Ghettos, however, are mainly dysfunctional because they provide very few, if any, legitimate opportunities for personal growth or meaningful employment, and become instead places of violence and criminal enterprise. Functionalists rarely suggest radical solutions to social problems. They see the system as needing adjustment rather than replacement.

HOW CLASSICAL FUNCTIONALIST THEORY APPLIES TO TODAY'S PROBLEMS: DURKHEIM'S FUNCTIONALISM AND ANOMIC

Durkheim (1933), one of the founders of sociology, attributed many of the problems of his time to the effects of rapid social change that disrupted the social order. In Durkheim's France, the old feudal order, based on agriculture, had broken down, and the new industrial order was undermining all the old regularities. Durkheim was mainly interested in the way in which social conditions resulted in "rates" of problem events, such as suicides, labor disorder, or trouble in the schools. He noted, in the early societies, almost everyone was engaged directly or indirectly in agricultural production. People's lives were very similar, and their beliefs and values (based on common experience) were very similar too. This produced a strong "common conscience" or "common consciousness" among the people. There was little tolerance for divergence from the common path and individuals had clear guidelines and the confidence that goes with moral certainty. With urbanization and industrialization, however, people's lives became much more diversified. The factory worker not only had little in common with the agricultural worker, but he would also have very different experiences from those of a hospital worker or a deliveryman. The common conscience became weaker, providing less guidance for individuals. This meant more freedom, but also more problems related to a loss of social control. While Durkheim recognized that there was no turning back to the earlier period, he felt that society was in a state of disorganization, or "anomic" (normlessness) and that social problems of the day could be mitigated by reducing this anomic. Society needed new ways of regulation, and new forms of integration. Durkheim's chief proposal for this was the formation of work-based groups. In these groups, persons would talk, share opinions, and as a result, form expectations within the group of what was right, wrong, good, or bad. While various work groups would form different views on morality, the individual in each group would be integrated and regulated in such a way that problems such as suicide and unemployment would be reduced.

Durkheim's insight is just as applicable today as it was over 100 years ago. We can clearly see the process whereby consensus about what is good and bad has broken down, resulting in a society that has few certainties that are widely shared about which things are problems, or certainties about appropriate ways to handle them. Persons living in a community may lose a sense of collective consciousness not only because they lack a common occupation, but because their lives diverge in other ways. People who live in a place only because they can't afford to live elsewhere, or have only stigmatized characteristics in common may fail to identify with each other or with the community as a whole. An organization such as a community health center, for example, could provide at least one focal point in the lives of these citizens, a focal point, which can serve some of the functions that Durkheim thought work groups would meet. It could become a place where individuals would talk, share opinions, and form group expectations about right, wrong, good or bad. The health center could provide its patients, workers, and board members with a sense of belongingness that would make them, and the community, less anomic.

The third major perspective is the structural conflict perspective. **Conflict theorists** focus on the interests of various groups in society (especially their economic interests) and the ways in which groups create social structures as they compete for advantage in society. For Marxist conflict theorists, the only groups that really count are those based on having or not having to sell one's labor to others in order to make a living (being a worker or an owner). If you are an owner, and want cheap labor, having a lot of people out of work (a "reserve army of labor") may be a "good" thing, since fear of unemployment will make your employees willing to work for less reward. If you are a worker, however, this may be perceived as a serious social problem.

Pluralist conflict theorists recognize that there are other bases for group interests, such as gender, age, race, and even sexual orientation. This perspective argues that each group uses the "social resources" that it has (its size, wealth, education, and connections) to enhance its position relative to others. When a group has more power than other groups, it can use this power to help itself do even better, even if this creates "problems" for other groups. Thus, conflict theorists argue that drug laws were made by powerful social groups to regulate the behavior of others (ethnic minorities, workers, and cultural rebels), not themselves. Marijuana legislation, for example, was at least partly motivated by concerns about migrants on the border with Mexico, and later concerns about sailors, jazz musicians, and 1960s "radicals." The legalization gave authorities means of regulating the activities of "deviant" populations. As more and more "respectable" people and children of respectable people are being caught in the use of this drug, the pressure for its legislation (along the lines of alcohol or prescription medicine) has increased.

From a conflict perspective, it is important to identify "who" (which social class or interest group) believes that the situation is a problem. This definition and the proposed solutions to the problem will likely favor this group's economic and political interests. An example of a neoMarxist conflict analysis is Tony Platt (1969) work on the "child-saving" movement's establishment of the juvenile justice system. Although the middle class people (members of the bourgeoisie, the owners of the mans of production) who developed this system were well-intended, and even humanitarian, the actual treatment of wayward youth under the juvenile law was fairly clearly intended to prepare them for lower level employment in the factories. This "rescue of youth" assisted a transformation, which was of most benefit to the class proposing the solution. Marxists are concerned with the elimination of social problems, rather than reforms, and see the role of the researcher as one of "praxis." Praxis means that one studies the world not just to understand it, but to assist the oppressed to take action against their troubles. Pluralists conflict theorists tend to favor interventions only to make the competition between groups fairer.

HOW CLASSICAL MARXIST AND THEORY APPLIES TO TODAY'S PROBLEMS: MARX AND ALIENATED LABOR

Marx (1969), like Durkheim, emphasized social structure and social process in formulating a theory to explain the terrible plight of factory workers in the early stages of industrialization. He did not believe that individual owners of factories caused the suffering of workers out of personal greed or lack of caring for others. Factory owners (members of the bourgeoisie) were competing with each other for a place in the economic order. An owner who did not "exploit" his workers would soon lose his factory to more successful owners, and become a worker himself. All workers and owners were trapped within a system that seemed to be going in the direction of more and more exploitation until it exploded into revolution.

Marx maintained that many problems of his time were due to the alienation of workers, a feeling that they neither controlled the pace of work or the tasks they performed. The alienated worker worked only for survival, finding little satisfaction in the production process, and often not earning enough to buy the products that he has made. The alienated worker would have little satisfaction and little commitment to his work. He might easily become politically radical in ways that would undermine the factory (sabotage) or the system (revolution). Marx felt that the only solution to the underlying problem was the overthrow of capitalism. He predicted that this overthrow would occur in the most industrialized countries, where there were enough resources to support a system of distribution in which all people would have enough, without having to sell themselves for it. Revolutions, however, broke out in places such as Russia and China, where conditions were still largely feudal, and the resulting state was a dictatorship of the party, not a "people's democracy."

What can Marxian theory tell us, when applied to real life experiences? Consider the high unemployment characteristic of many low-income urban areas. Marx would probably maintain that these unemployed persons were being exploited, denied access to the technology and resources to be productive, because the pool of "surplus labor" helps to keep wages down. This is as true today as it was in Marx's time.

Marx predicted that, because work is central to human beings, alienated workers would experience troubles in their lives. The lack of control over the productive aspects of life, for example, could result in severe health problems. An article by Schnall and Kerm (1981) using a Marxian orientation to the study of disease indicates that persons in routine jobs who have little decision-making regarding the type of work and pace of their work are at a greater risk for heart disease. It is possible that much of the sickness experienced by low income agencies is the result of the way in which the capitalist system creates a "reserve army of labor" with little possibility for self-fulfilling productive lives.

Other theories have important things to say about social problems, and will be referred to frequently as we attempt to identify, describe, and explain the problems that are highlighted by each of our case studies. One common element in all of these approaches is "the Sociological Imagination" which understands personal troubles as occurring within a context of social issues.

THE SOCIOLOGICAL IMAGINATION

The term "sociological imagination" was first used by C. Wright Mills, a conflict theorist, in his book The Sociological Imagination (1959). Theorists from other perspectives have expressed very similar ideas, and some would argue that "the sociological imagination" is the central idea in all sociology. In simplified terms, Mills argues that an individual's poverty, or divorce, or experience of racism is felt as a "personal trouble," but that the poverty rate, the rate of family dissolution, or the existence of racial discrimination is a "public issue" or social problem.

Mills defines the **"sociological imagination"** as being the ability to grasp the connection between our personal lives and the larger social forces that shape the conditions that we live in. In living our lives, we shape our world, but the forces that make our place in history also mold our lives, mainly by giving us some choices, and some resources, rather than others. Losing one's job feels like a private issue (we may be personally humbled, embarrassed, or angry) but this lost opportunity may also be an aspect of widespread adoption of new technologies (and thus largely beyond our individual control). The sociological imagination enables us to see and understand the relationship between our personal biographies (the micro level) and larger historical forces (the macro level). Mills' perspective is quite compatible with the ideas of functionalists such as Durkheim (1987), for whom a very private issue such as suicide was to be understood as conditioned by wider forces of disorder and change in society, structural changes which encouraged excessive individualism and a loss of moral bearings at the individual level. It also fits well with the labeling aspect of interaction theory, whereby we become imprisoned in the labels that, whether earned or not, others apply to us.

WHAT CAN BE DONE?

In this discussion of the concepts, methods and theories of sociology, we have identified several different ways in which social problems can be identified and understood. We now turn to the question "What can be done?" and its pessimistic relative "Can anything be done?" Skepticism (show me!) is a natural, and generally healthy, human reaction to new programs and new ideas. Some of the social problems, such as poverty, which are addressed by this book, have existed for centuries, while others, such as the dramatically increasing number of dependent older persons, are phenomena of the last few decades. Are these problems inevitable, immutable, and impervious to our wishes? For long periods in history, the existence of suffering was understood only in religious terms, as a test from God that would ultimately help to save our souls. This changed in the 18th century, challenged by a group of "classical thinkers" called the **philosophes** (see Wallbank, Taylor, and Bailey 1965). They argued that rationality was the highest mode of thought (superior to faith and obedience to authority). Although they were not scientists themselves, they admired the new way of knowing, the "scientific method" which was making great strides in explaining natural phenomena. Many of them (the "utilitarians") argued that the goal of society should be "the greatest happiness for the greatest number." Suffering was no longer seen as a test of one's spirit, but rather as the product of social systems that were not rational and efficient. This active attitude toward identifiable social wrongs has continued to be an influence to the present time, but now involving social scientists, committed to making knowledge a tool for social change.

Sociologists working from a variety of theoretical perspectives have been active as citizens in addressing the problems of their time. Max Weber saw bureaucratization (the dead hand of bureaucracy) as a major source of trouble in the future of his world, and identified "charisma" such as that of Hitler, as an irrational response to such problems. Karl Marx identified many of the problems of capitalist systems, such as worker alienation and its impact on the family and society as a whole. Sociologist-social workers such as Jane Addams of Hull House in the 1900s sought to apply sociological knowledge in ways that would assist immigrants and the poor to "get on board" in American society. While some sociologists have been activists, working with the people they wanted to help, others have contributed to the solution of social problems by serving as disengaged social critics, demystifiers who attack the propaganda of racism, sexism and other "isms," and reporters of the problems that might otherwise be passively accepted as simply individual problems or "necessary costs of doing business." In an overview of this, we can say that sociologists have always challenged the social order to "get smart" about getting tough on social problems. It is not enough to decide that we need a war on poverty or on drugs. We need to decide whether "war" will work, or something else might be better. We can use knowledge of society as we do knowledge about health. We can focus on prevention, solution, and harm-reduction.

HOW THE SCIENTIFIC METHOD CAN HELP

The command of the philosophes that we should be rational has been supported by the application of the scientific method's demand that we test what we assert, and keep on testing it. In everyday life, we often rely upon untested cultural beliefs that we call "common sense." Common sense is sometimes correct (just as a stopped clock is right twice a day). Quite often it is wrong.

Is this true or false? Ask yourself whether (1) The poor in the United States have become a permanent underclass, dependent on handouts and unwilling to change (2) Intelligence is the most important factor in predicting the degree of education each American will attain (3) Persons who were abused when growing up as children are unlikely to abuse their own children (4) The gap between black and white family incomes in the United States has decreased since the 1960s and is clearly becoming a thing of the past? Each of these statements is false, or mainly false.

On Poverty: There are some persons in situations of self-reinforcing poverty, or multiply caused poverty, but on the whole social mobility is more frequent than persistent poverty. The University of Michigan Panel Study of Income Dynamics (PSID) is a major longitudinal study begun in 1968 (Hofferth, Yeung and Stafford 1996). The panel began with 5,000 representative families living in poverty across the nation, and has, due to low attrition rates, expanded over time. Among its findings is the realization that only about one-sixth of those who use welfare at any time still need it after eight or more years. These findings are generally supported by other studies of poverty in America, which show that most people who need welfare remain on it for less than two years, using it to get through a crisis. Less than two percent of those on welfare rolls are "able-bodied" males and many of these are looking for work.

On Education: Education in the U. S. is targeted at the 80% who have average intelligence. Children both above and below this level may fail and drop out, because their needs are not being met. Also, social class has a very large role to play in whether or not a person will achieve post secondary levels of education. This is not just a matter of being able to afford the costs of delayed entry into the labor force, and the price of tuition. It also reflects the values and expectations in the students' backgrounds (see Velez 1994). As for child abuse, a substantial proportion of those who were abused become abusers, possibly because they have accepted this kind of parenting as a model (Gil 1970; Owens and Strauss 1975; and Strauss 1979). Thus, common sense is not always the answer, even if it seems to be logical and obvious.

Science is a method of inquiry that has proven itself superior to other ways of knowing about empirical reality. Science brings together controlled observations of the real world with logical theories about that world. Science is applied to social problems by way of the following sequence of time-tested procedures. (1) We need to specify the problem to be studied. (2) We need to examine previous research which has been done on this problem, both to learn from its failures and to build on its achievements. (3) We need to formulate testable hypotheses. (we assert that two or more things should be connected, identifying them in objective ways.) (4) We design a study that allows us to test the hypotheses we have developed. (5) We use recognized methodology to gather the data. (6) We use appropriate techniques to analyze the data. (7) We draw conclusions from our data analysis, and (8) We share the results, preferably by publishing them. Through this process, we can learn about which aspects of the current reality are contributing to social problems, and which aspects might be manipulated or changed in order to have fewer problems.

THE DESIGN AND EVALUATION OF SOCIAL PROGRAMS: APPLIED KNOWLEDGE

Programs designed on common sense or scientific principles can be tested to see whether they are doing what they say they are doing. For example, one "outreach program" which put social workers out in the streets to "help" street youth actually increased the delinquency of the youths involved. Meeting regularly with the social worker enhanced their ability to organize themselves for making trouble. So much for good intentions.

A program originally designed on the basis of common sense and experience was the Boy Scout program. Founded in Great Britain in 1908 by Lieutenant-General Robert Baden-Powell, it provided group membership, moral leadership, and outdoor skills training for boys from 11 to 15 years of age. Over time, these programs have been extended to younger and older youths. The scout motto "Be Prepared" and its admonition to do a "good deed" each day helped to encourage good citizenship, while its "secret handshake" and regular meetings encouraged a sense of belonging. Scouting quickly spread to other countries, including the United States. In every country the same basic pattern was followed, so that Boy Scouts from many countries had similar experiences and might even meet each other at annual "Jamborees." In part, scouting (with its emphasis on camping and the outdoors and on self-reliance while following orders) was a reaction to the rise of industrialization in Great Britain and the United States. Scouting allowed boys who might otherwise have been delinquent street kids to learn both conformity and leadership skills so that they would become good workers, citizens, and persons.

Although Baden-Powell, as a cavalry officer, was probably more influenced by the military model than by the science of his day, we now know that the essential components of his program are based on recognized scientific principles. For example, youths of scouting age tend to have a strong desire to belong to a group (Hartup 1983). Research by Savin-Williams (1980) indicates that group structures often depend on normative activities such as knowing what to do on a camp-out, and having pride in being able to do these things well. On moral development, Eisenberg (1982) found that, by later elementary and early secondary school, a child helping someone resulted from and confirmed his or her empathy and responsibility toward the other person. Testing of initiatives such as scouting is called program evaluation.

Program evaluation is an extension of scientific research which allows us to fine-tune our efforts at problem solving. Each of the steps of scientific research (as outlined above) has a role in evaluation. Thus we need to be clear about "what" we are evaluating, find out what is already known or suspected about it, formulate clearly testable hypotheses, use reliable methods to test them, and then draw conclusions from our findings. For an organization such as Boy Scouts, it is not difficult to find clear statements of the purpose of the group and of its "target population" of "at risk" youths. The current emphasis in program evaluation, at the testing phase, is "outcome measurement" (see United Way of America 1996). **Outcomes** may be defined as the benefits or changes for individuals or populations during or after participating in program activities. According to a study of the Boy Scouts of America conducted by Louis Harris and Associates the scouting movement has in fact made a difference by reducing the number of youths who "choose to do what is wrong."

If program evaluation can be used to design and test programs in this way, why have we not made more progress? Why are so few programs either evaluated or changed as a result of evaluation? Among the answers to this are a number of constraints. Often, getting people to help fund a program is difficult enough, without asking for resources to evaluate the program. Getting people to put their energy into providing recreation opportunities for youth, counseling for at-risk drug users or pregnant teens, cleaning up a local area or highway, or supporting any other worthwhile initiative is often very difficult. Most Americans have many other "things to do" so that these commitments are hard to sustain over time. Evaluation becomes an afterthought.

THE USEFULNESS OF CASE STUDIES

Case studies have a long, rich and sometimes debated heritage in sociology and the social sciences. A case may be an autobiographical account by a key informant (Nels Anderson's 1928 classic, The Hobo, an in-depth study of a particular community), (Theodore Caplow's 1982 study Middletown Families: Fifty Years of Change and Continuity), or an analysis of organizational change such as Doug Eadie's (1997) Changing by Design which focuses on the stories of nonprofit organization leaders. Feagin, et al. (1991:1) maintain that the study of a single case, or an array of several cases remains indispensable to the progress of the social sciences. Feagin and his colleagues define a case study as an in-depth, multi-faceted investigation, using mainly qualitative research methods, of a single phenomenon. Qualitative methods include in-depth interviews and the analysis of documents such as personal letters, office memos, and other "traces" of the thing or person under study. These methods can be supplemented by other forms of research, but most case studies are very detailed qualitative accounts of particular subjects.

Charles Ragin (Ragin and Becker 1992:4-7) in the book *What is a Case?* discusses the controversy over how a case should be defined. Ultimately, Ragin argues in his introduction to the book that we should follow the stand of Howard Becker in continually asking ourselves, of every study, "What is this a case of?" Ragin and Becker take a very broad view of what can be considered a "case." For them, every study can be seen as a case of some kind of phenomenon: a statewide study of people's feelings on altering IRS regulations would be a "case study" of political opinions, while a study of sexual attitudes in the USA might be considered a "case study" of the industrialized nations of the world. Most observers, however, define a case study in a more limited way. Case studies usually involve detailed qualitative information about individuals or about organizations and individuals, rather than highly abstract quantitative information about large numbers of people or organizations.

"Concocting cases is a varied but routine social science activity" (Ragin and Becker 1992: 217). It is an activity which Ragin calls "casing" and views as a process used throughout research to link ideas and evidence. This social problems text uses this "casing" approach and considers a **case study** to be casing or connecting cases which may be both qualitative and quantitative so that every study is a case of some type of phenomena, which is trying to be understood.

Chapter 2 begins with the case of a manic depressive woman named Joyce. What becomes readily apparent is that the personal trials and tribulations of Joyce are not unique experiences. Other persons share them too. The experiences of Joyce allow the chapter to illustrate problems of diagnosing mental diseases. Various concepts such as egoistic suicide and affective disorder are given reference points. Theories such as the biopsychosocial approach are applied to the case.

Each succeeding chapter in the book begins with a case. Many of these are autobiographical or biographical cases of a person experiencing some aspect of the social problem that is addressed in the chapter. One reason for starting the chapters in this way is to grab your attention as a reader and encourage you to see the human dimensions of the problem being discussed. Social problems impact on the lives of real people who experience hardship, frustration, pain, and hopelessness because they are personally impacted by forces that seem to be beyond their control. A second reason for using cases is that they provide a common reference point for your discussions about theoretical ideas and concepts. A third reason for using cases is to show that the application of sociological tools (concepts, methods, and theories) is useful in taking us beyond unguided "compassion" and into practical modes of problem solving.

USING THIS BOOK

This book is designed with the student in mind, and is intended to be readable and interesting. We are not naive enough to think that you will be constantly on the edge of your seat, but we hope that most of our material will hold your interest, and perhaps stimulate you to do more research on your own. At the beginning of each forthcoming chapter is a case. We encourage you to read the case study carefully and to try to keep it in mind as you read the remainder of the chapter. Is this case an example or illustration of the general points? Is it an exception? In the chapter, key terms and concepts are found in bold type. These are important for understanding and talking about the social problem being examined. Each chapter ends with a summary of its main points, listed in the order of their appearance in the chapter. This should help you to identify the important ideas and to find them in the chapter if you wish to review them. Our hope is that these features will make your reading and learning more enjoyable, especially the cases and we wish to say some more about them.

SUMMARY

1. Some kinds of personal problems are embedded in social conditions.
2. One way to identify problems is to ask people about their beliefs and opinions.
3. Americans often take action to "fix" social problems by forming community groups.
4. A distinctive sociological perspective on social problems is that we interact with others to produce social definitions and social meanings that guide our actions.
5. Concepts are ideas about the common features of things that are observed and they help us to describe and compare events around us
6. Over time, we have learned that some methods produce reliable and valid information.
7. A theory is an explanation that follows rules and should be testable
8. Symbolic interaction holds that humans do not react to the world directly, but rather to the meanings that they attribute to that world.
9. Structural functionalism does not totally ignore social interaction, but tends to look at the social system as a structure that is above individual interaction.
10. Structural conflict theorists focus on the interests of various groups in society and the way in which groups create social structures as they compete for advantage in society.
11. The sociological imagination is the ability to grasp the connection between our personal lives and the larger social forces that shape the conditions in which we live.

12. The use of the scientific method can prove or disprove common sense interpretation of the world.
13. Programs designed on common sense or scientific principles can be tested to see whether they are doing what they say they are doing.
14. Case studies in the text are used as part of Ragin's (1992) "casing" activity to link ideas and evidence.
15. Sociologists have historically challenged the social order to "get smart" about getting tough on social problems.
16. We can use our knowledge of society to respond to social problems and focus on prevention, solution, and harm-reduction.

REFERENCES

Anderson, Nels 1923. *The Hobo: The Sociology of the Homeless Man.* Chicago: University of Chicago Press

Caplow, Theodore 1982. *Middletown Families: Fifty Years of Change and Continuity.* Minneapolis: University of Minnesota Press.

Durkheim, Emile 1987 (1951). *Suicide.* New York: Free Press.
_____.1933. *The Division of Labor in Society.* New York: Free Press

Eadie, Douglas C. 1997. *Changing by Design: A Practical Approach to Leading Innovation in Nonprofit Organizations.* San Francisco: Jossey-Bass.'

Eisenberg, N. 1982. *"The Development of Reasoning Regarding Prosocial Behavior."* Pp.219-249 in N. Eisenberg, ed. *The Development of Prosocial Behavior.* New York: Academic Press.

Feagin, Joe R., Orum, Anthony M., Sjoberg, Gideon 1991. *A Case for the Case Study.* Chapel Hill: The University of North Carolina Press.

Gallup Poll http://198.175.1 40.8/POLL_ARCHIVES/latest.htm.

Gallup, George Jr. *The Gallup Poll: Public Opinion 1998.* Wilmington, Delaware: Scholarly Resources, Inc.

Gil, David 1970. *Violence Against Children.* Cambridge: Harvard University Press.

Hartup, W.W. 1983. *"Peer Relations"* Pp. 103-196 in E.M. Hetherington, ed. Handbook of Child Psychology: Vol.4. *Socialization, Personality, and Social Development.* 4th ed. New York: Wiley.

Hofferth, Sandra, Wei-Jun J. Yeung and Frank P. Stafford 1996. "Panel Study of Income Dynamics" http://www.icpsr.umich.edu/ICPSR/about/Publications/Bulletin/J.

Marx, Karl 1969. "On Class." Pp.14 in Cecelia S. Heller, ed. *Structured Social Inequality.* New York: MacMillan.

Mills, C. Wright 1959. *The Sociological Imagination.* New York: Oxford University Press.

Owens, David J. and Murray Strauss 1975. *"Social Structure of Violence in Childhood and Approval of Violence as an Adult."* Aggressive Behavior. 1:193-211.

Ragin, Charles, and Howard S. Becker 1992. *What is a Case?: Exploring the Foundations of Social Inquiry.* New York: Cambridge University Press.

The Roper Center 1998. "A Roper Center Data Review." *The Public Perspective.* Special Issue on American Opinion in the 1990s. 9(2) February/March: 30-39.

Savin-Williams, R.C. 1980. "Dominance Hierarchies in Groups of Middle in Late Adolescent Males." *Journal of Youth and Adolescence.* 9: 75-85.

Schnall, Peter and Rochelle Kerm 1981. "Hypertension in American Society: An Introduction to Historical Materialist Epidemiology." Pp. 97-122 in Peter Conrad and Rochelle Kern, eds. *The Sociology of Health and Illness.* New York: St. Martin's Press.

Strauss, Murray 1979. "Determinants of Violence in the Family: Toward a Theoretical Integration." In W. Burr, R. Hill, et al., eds. *Contemporary Theory about Families.* New York: Free Press.

Thomas, W. I. 1967. "The Definition of the Situation." Pp. 315-321 in Jerome G. Manis and Bernard N. Meltzer, eds. *Symbolic Interaction.* Boston: Allyn Bacon.

Tocqueville, Alexis de 1935. *Democracy in America.* New York: G. Adlard.

United Way of America 1996. *Measuring Program Outcomes: A Practical Approach.*

Velez, William 1994. "Why Hispanic Students Fail: Factors Affecting Attrition in High Schools." In Leonard Carson and Jeanne H. Ballantine, eds. *Sociological Footprints.* Belmont: Wadsworth.

Wallbank, T. Walter, Taylor, Alastair M., and Nels M. Bailey 1965. *Civilization: Past and Present.* Vol.2, 5th ed. Dallas: Scott, Foresman and Co.

Williams, Robin M., Jr. 1970. *American Society*, 3rd ed. New York: Knopf.

Yankelovich, Daniel 1998. "How American Individualism is Evolving." *The Public Perspective.* Special Issue on American Opinion in the 1990s. 9(2) February/March: 3-6.

CHAPTER 2: MENTAL ILLNESS
CASE STUDY: MANIC DEPRESSION

Joyce's mother kept getting a busy signal on Joyce's telephone. This wasn't unusual because her roommate often took the phone off the hook so Joyce's estranged husband, Harold, could not contact her. According to Joyce, her roommate, Kristi, could not stand Harold. Joyce's mother decided to go to her. When she arrived at Joyce's place, she told Joyce to come over to her house and they would do something together.

Joyce peeked out the window and said, "All right, let me get my bath." Upon her mother's return, Joyce was dressed and ready to go. Arriving at her parents' home, Joyce sat down on the couch in the living room with her mother, who asked how she was doing. Joyce told her that just before her mother's arrival she had gotten undressed, filled the bathtub with water, and thought about getting into the water and cutting her wrists. Joyce said she felt nobody would miss her, she was sick of being sick, she was sick of worrying her mother, and she just did not know when it was going to end. It just was not ending fast enough.

This revelation made her mother quiver. She asked Joyce whether she had taken her antidepressants that day; Joyce replied that she had not. Her mother asked for the keys to the mobile home where Joyce and Kristi lived. She went over to the mobile home, got the medication, and gave it to Joyce.

Joyce is a twenty-four year old Caucasian from a working-class family. Her father is a telephone cable repairman. She works in an office and likes to read, go to the movies, and fish in her spare time. Three months after graduating from college, Joyce had a miscarriage and separated from her husband. Eight months after the miscarriage and separation, she was admitted to the psychiatric floor of a private hospital, suffering from paranoid delusions.

Her family had seen Joyce's hospitalization coming for about six months, but Joyce herself did not realize she was sick. Joyce believed drug dealers were trying to kill her, even though she did not use illegal drugs. She was flighty and could not stay in one place very long. During the six months prior to her hospitalization, Joyce often drove aimlessly around town. She did not live in any one place for more than two months and described her experience during these six months as being hyperactive.

One day Joyce's world collapsed. She was living in a mobile home with a friend and had left for work but returned to get an item she had forgotten. All she can recall of subsequent events is that she spent most of the day driving around town, trying to escape those she thought were after her. Having stopped at her parents' home, Joyce would not let them answer the telephone. When the telephone rang, Joyce lay on the floor so nobody could shoot her through the window. She reported that, while at her parents' she shook with fright and cried.

Joyce arrived at work late in the day and told her co-worker, Kelly that she had to go out of town just to get away. She was going to go fishing. Kelly encouraged her to do just that, because in the past weeks Kelly had watched Joyce busily organize papers and then just sit at her desk, unable to do a thing.

Joyce drove to her Aunt Susan's lake house. On the way, Joyce sang as she drove, because she thought the car was "bugged." When she got to Aunt Susan's, Joyce told her aunt that the telephone was tapped. Her aunt's son, a deputy sheriff, suggested that they take Joyce to a physician, which they did. The physician admitted her to the hospital.

During her first few days in the hospital, Joyce was heavily medicated. She reported falling to the floor and just lying where she fell. Joyce did a lot of hallucinating and thought that she was at the hospital to get away from those chasing her. During her two-week stay, Joyce went to various classes and felt she got some beneficial counseling. The antidepressants she received were very potent, and Joyce spent a lot of time sleeping. The fear of persons chasing her left.

When Joyce was discharged, she went to her parents' home. Unfortunately, her medication dosage was incorrect; she slept a lot and her eyes were dilated. Returning to the hospital was not an option because she had been hospitalized the maximum number of days for insurance coverage. Her psychiatrist wanted to increase her medication and felt that Joyce's problems were the result of a meddling mother. Problems concerning the medication and the psychiatrist continued. Subsequently, Joyce moved out of her parents' home and lived in the homes of two different friends.

During the period between her first and second hospitalizations, Joyce spent a weekend with her estranged husband and became pregnant. She also contemplated taking her own life once during this time, as recounted at the beginning of this chapter. This and other factors led Joyce to be hospitalized a second time and to change psychiatrists. She felt she had a "personality problem" with the original psychiatrist.

Joyce's new psychiatrist used her mother to monitor Joyce's behavior, and his decision to put Joyce on lithium is based on reports that led him to believe Joyce to be manic-depressive. Within two weeks of this treatment, Joyce's symptoms disappeared and her behavior became normal. When she found she was pregnant, Joyce had to stop taking the lithium, but continues to appear normal.

Whether Joyce will suffer another bout of manic depression cannot be predicted. While the birth of her baby did not trigger a return of her illness, some event later in life may do so. Joyce has a tendency toward manic depression and must always remain conscious of the possibility of a recurrence. Her experiences provide an autobiographical case study that illustrates theoretical points and research findings in this chapter on mental illness.

NATURE AND PREVALENCE OF MENTAL ILLNESS

PREVALENCE STATISTICS AND ECONOMIC COSTS

Even though mental illness is one of the oldest maladies known to medical science, many of the mentally ill escape detection. This makes it impossible to determine an accurate count (Cockerham 1992: 140). Some insight comes from the <u>Vital and Health Statistics Series 13, No.129</u>, which indicates that the number of annual office-visits to physicians for mental disorders was 31.7 million in 1995. The total reported visits for schizophrenic disorders was 1.4 million. Schizophrenia is a form of psychosis in which people are out of touch with reality (Walker 1982: 10); they experience things that normal people do not e.g., hearing voices of imaginary beings such as angels or devils. They may laugh or cry inappropriately and sometimes are violent.

Another 5.1 million people were reported to visit their physician for depression and anxiety was reported as a cause for 3.5 million visits to physician offices. Depressed persons and those experiencing anxiety are in touch with reality but experience considerable mental pain.

THEORY BOX by Michael J. Donnelly Chapter 2 Mental Health/Socialconstruction

Children often invent imaginary playmates and whimsical or idiosyncratic names for their toys and other everyday objects. Parents tend to tolerate, even to humor, such behavior, but only up to a point. As the child grows, he or she must eventually learn to distinguish clearly between "make-believe" and the "real world." One of the parents' and other adults' tasks in socializing children is to steep them in their own (adult) sense of reality.

But what constitutes our "sense of reality?" It is, of course, conditioned by our physical environment, by the world of nature. "Reality" as we know it is also, however, work of culture. The names we apply to things, for instance, do not inhere in the nature of those things; names are social conventions that we agree upon and use. We call a certain object "chair," but there is nothing in the nature of a chair that makes that acoustic image (sound) uniquely appropriate and "right" as its name. Indeed, in other languages different sounds substitute for our sound/name "chair." Our sense of reality, similarly, is at least partly a convention, something we have to agree upon, maintain, and enforce. It may sound odd to say, but keeping our sense of reality takes effort, indeed joint, concerted effort, even if we are not aware of it at all that that is what we are doing. On a small-scale individuals do something similar all the time. We know the difference between daydreaming (and the fantasies of idle reverie) and what actually happens and can happen. If we are having trouble remembering just what occurred on such and such a day, we are liable to turn to a trusted friend to confirm, validate, or complete our own memories. When an individual begins to have problems maintaining the boundary between fantasy and reality, we are likely to infer that this person is "out of touch with reality"-one of the signs most of us would immediately recognize of mental disorder or mental illness.

The "reality checks" that individuals perform on themselves have a broader social counterpart. A lot of what happens in everyday interactions and conversations serves indirectly as a kind of collective "reality check." We keep each other in line, not coercively but for mutual convenience, by playing out social conventions. If we were to stop and think about it, those conventions might seem simply arbitrary. But in so far as the conventions hold (people conform to them in their behavior), conventions make the world a more predictable place, and allow our interactions to flow more smoothly and effortlessly. This is one of the senses in which human groups jointly construct their social realities; moreover, the orderliness of the world as we know it depends on maintaining and enforcing that jointly constructed sense of reality.

Insight into the considerable cost of mental illness is provided by the work of Rice and Miller (1992). More than $150 billion each year is spent on treatment, which includes the costs of social services to patients and their families, disability payments to patients, lost productivity, and premature death. Direct costs including care in mental specialty institutions, hospitals, nursing homes, professional services, and prescription drugs amounted to $67 billion in 1990. Lifetime earnings of those who died due to mental disorders amounted to 11.8 billion in 1980. These statistics objectify the personal experiences of persons like Joyce. Joyce became a statistic, but she also remained a person with a family who struggled with mental illness.

RELATIONSHIP TO THE SOCIAL STRUCTURE

Social structure is defined most simply as "the patterned relationships that exist among people as they interact," and sociologists refer to these relationships as "normative behavior."

Class gender, and race are aspects of the social structure selected for this discussion, but there are others, such as marital status and urban versus rural living.

Class. Faris and Dunham's (1939) pioneering study on social class and mental disorder in Chicago found that schizophrenia occurs most frequently in the center of the city while manic depression is systematically distributed throughout. As Gordon (1958) points out, these areas were delineated on the basis of economic position. Low-status areas were located near the center of Chicago with high-status areas on the periphery. This indicates that schizophrenia is more strongly related to class position than is manic depression.

Eleven years later, sociologists, and psychiatrists explored the relationship of mental illness to social class in New Haven, Connecticut. The chief investigators, Hollingshead and Redlich (1958:212), found a significant difference in the incidence of mental disorder in various social classes: rates of psychosis (delusional disorders) were highest in the lowest class but did not differ among the other classes. Neurosis (less serious illnesses, such as psychosomatic complaints), however, showed no relationship to social class. Hollingshead and Redlich also measured the prevalence of mental disorder- that is, all the cases of mental disorder active during a given period (1953; 1958: 235-36). For both neuroses and psychoses, they found a significant difference between classes even when the rates were adjusted for sex and age. Neuroses were more prevalent among the four higher classes, whereas psychoses were more prevalent in the lowest class.

Another group of researchers under the direction of Rennie and Srole were examining social class and mental health in midtown Manhattan (Srole, Langner, Stanley, Opler, and Rennie 1962). The intriguing aspect of the midtown study was its attempt to deal with the prevalence of mental illness in a non-hospitalized population. Srole et al. (1962: 216) found that respondents' socioeconomic status (SES) was related inversely to their mental health.

In addition to incidence and prevalence rates, these researchers also dealt extensively with the relationship between social class and type of treatment received. Hollingshead and Redlich (1958: 253-303) found that upper- and upper middle-class persons tended to use private psychiatrists on the first visit. Lower middle-class individuals were likely to go to a private practitioner or a particular clinic. Working-class persons went to a Veterans Administration hospital if they were veterans; otherwise they visited a private practitioner or a particular clinic the first time and a state hospital on their second visit. Lower-class persons went wherever they could get treatment-whether a private practitioner, a clinic, or a state hospital.

Hollingshead and Redlich (1958:253-303) examined not only the relationship with social class but also the use of facilities and the patient's social status. In addition, they looked at the principal form of therapy prescribed for patients. Among private practitioners and private hospitals, they found no significant differences between social class and the principal forms of therapy; almost all the schizophrenic patients received psychotherapy. In public hospitals, they found that only a small percentage of schizophrenic patients received psychotherapy, and those were concentrated in the upper social levels. Hollingshead and Redlich (1958: 300) concluded that treatment for mental illness depends not only on medical and psychological considerations but also on powerful social variables.

Myers and Schaffer (1954) examined differential value orientations of psychiatrists and their patients in relation to mental health treatment. They observed that treatment was not recommended for 66% of lower-class patients, 20% of working-class patients, and only 10% of upper middle-class patients. Medical students (rather than doctors) treated the patients of the lowest social class. In their 10-year follow-up to the New Haven study, Myers and Bean (1968: 211) concluded that as social class position decreases, psychotic patients appear more frequently in the hospital; as class position increases, neurotic patients are found increasingly in outpatient clinics. All of these studies indicated that the poor receive the most serious diagnoses of mental illness but receive the least high quality professional care.

Cockerham (1990), in examining the relationship of socioeconomic status to psychological stress, reports that persons with low socioeconomic status have significantly greater tendencies toward psychological stress. Other researchers, such as Gallagher (1987) and Kessler (1979), also report a relationship between class considerations and mental illness, and studies outside the United States confirm the relationship (e.g., Mirowsky, and Ross 1983). Explanations for this relationship, as reported by Cockerham (1992:159-166), include the following: (1) Genetics. As a result of genetic inheritance, there is a greater disposition toward mental illness among the lower class. (2) Social stress. Members of the lower class are subjected to greater stress and have fewer resources for coping with life. (3) Social selection. Mentally ill persons drift downward in the social structure and mentally healthy persons experience upward mobility. Cockerham suggests that the best explanation is probably a combination of genetics and stress.

Gender. A large body of knowledge has emerged regarding the influence of gender differences on mental health, and the literature on depression is illustrative of these differences. One set of studies uses records of persons treated for various forms of depression (e.g., Lemkau, Tietsze, and Cooper 1942; Faden 1977; Williams and Spitzer 1983). The mean male to female difference in a diagnosis of depression in these three studies is 1:53. Community studies using questionnaires and interviews also show a higher ratio of females experiencing depression than men (Radloff 1975; Myers, Weissman, Tischler, Holzer, Lend, Ovaschel, Anthony, Boyd, Burke, Kramer, and Stoltzman 1984). There also is evidence that male and female differences in depression exists in other industrialized countries, such as Australia (Byrne, 1980).

The possibility that this gender difference is related to socioeconomic status or to the expression of symptoms is not supported by the literature.

Ensel (1982) found no difference in mean scores on the Center for Epidemiological Studies Depression Scale (CES-D) for men and women while controlling for income, education, and occupation. On the issue of expressing symptoms, King and Buchwald (1982) found men as willing as women to discuss symptoms in both private and public.

Two prominent psychosocial explanations are the sex role theory of depression and learned helplessness. McCoby and Jacklin (1974) report that, even though females describe themselves as more socially oriented in comparison to men, there are no actual behavioral differences, and their research discounts this explanation. Other researchers have suggested that the female role contributes to greater feelings of lack of control and helplessness (Radloff 1975). Nolen-Hoeksema (1987) suggests that the differences stem from socially learned response sets. Women are more likely to dwell on their depressed state of mind, whereas men are more likely to turn to activities to relieve their depression.

Race. Racial differences in mental health rates are well-documented (Dohrenwend and Dohrenwend, 1969; Steinberg, Pardes, Bjork, and Sporty, 1977). When controls for socioeconomic status are introduced, these differences tend to disappear, but Kessler and Neighbors (1986) have demonstrated that racial discrimination exacerbates the health-damaging effects of poverty among Blacks. They analyzed eight epidemiological surveys and found Blacks to be more distressed than Whites at low levels of income. Ridley (1984) provides an alternative explanation of differences on the basis of race; he suggests that paranoid tendencies among Blacks are a healthy response to a paranoid society.

The relationship of race/ethnicity to the amount and type of psychiatric treatment received is complex (Flaskerund and Hu 1992). It involves a consideration of race/ethnicity as well as the patient's diagnosis, socioeconomic status, other personal characteristics, and the characteristics of treatment. In a study of Whites, Blacks, Latinos, and Asians in Los Angeles, Flaskerund and Hu found that Black race/ethnicity patients had fewer sessions with a primary therapist and more treatment with medication. They also found that low socioeconomic status was related to fewer sessions with the primary therapist and less use of treatment with medication. These researchers also report that, whereas Blacks over-utilized the county mental health services, Latinos, and Asians were under-utilizing them and Whites were utilizing them in proportion to their percentage standing in the general population. They ask whether some racial/ethnic groups use alternative, informal sources of care. This question currently is being explored, as researchers continue to investigate the relationship of race/ethnicity to mental health.

Relationship to Case Study. What clues regarding social structure can we find in the case study of Joyce? She was separated from her husband, White, 24 years old, and an office worker. Joyce had grown up in a working class family, but her college degree gave her upper-middle class standing, and persons of higher SES are less likely to be diagnosed with a serious mental health problem. Joyce received treatment at a private hospital, which is consistent with her personal SES. Her aunt and cousin took her to the family physician, who placed her in a hospital with a mental health unit. Even so, we must keep in mind that studies of mental health and the social structure are based on groups and populations. Their findings predict behavior at the societal and group level, and are not totally consistent with the behavior of individuals in particular circumstances.

MENTAL ILLNESS AS MYTH

Psychiatrist Thomas Szasz (1960) believes that mental illness is a myth. He maintains that it is a concept that has outlived whatever usefulness it might once have had. One of his arguments is that mental illness makes sense only when behavior reflects organic damage. An example is the "senility" of advanced syphilis, in which persons exhibit disorders of thinking and behavior. From his perspective, mental illnesses are viewed as diseases of the brain in which some neurological defect ultimately will be found to explain mental illness. According to Szasz, mental illness is the result of such a defect, analogous to cancer or to a breakdown in the immune system.

A second argument made by Szasz is that persons are diagnosed as mentally ill when they are not coping well with problems in living. In this case, the term illness is used by mental health professionals to imply a deviation from some clearly defined norm not an organic illness. Szasz says that behavior leading to "excessive repression" and the "acting out of an unconscious impulse" are examples treating maladaptations to problems of living as symptoms of mental illness, when the diagnosis is really a normative judgment by mental health professionals. Situations such as chronic hostility or divorce, according to Szasz, also illustrate the application of mental illness definition to problematic normative behavior. As for the idea that only mentally ill persons would commit homicide, the concept of mental illness is used once again to explain a problem involving deviation from the norms of society.

Szasz makes a third argument regarding mental health as myth. This argument centers on the psychiatrist and is tied much more closely to problems of ethics than to medicine. Szasz declares that the psychiatrists' socioethical orientations are critical because they influence ideas regarding the patient. Psychiatry deals with problems in human relations; psychiatrists may apply norms and values from their own life situation, religious orientation, or social class to their patients, rather than considering the individual patient's cultural values.

Szasz (1960) has raised some thought-provoking points about mental illness in American society (also see Szasz, 1974). Joyce's case seems relatively non-problematic. Most individuals would conclude that someone who thinks imaginary drug dealers are chasing them is mentally ill. They would probably encourage a family member who had seriously considered committing suicide to at least see a medical provider, just as Joyce's aunt did. In the next section, we explore the diagnosis of mental health.

DIAGNOSTIC DEFINITIONS

Hughes (1991: 4) defines mental illness as disorders of mood, perception, thought volition, memory, or cognition developing in subjects whose psychological functioning previously was normal. Professionals from earlier times and lay people use two outmoded terms, psychosis, and neurosis. Psychoses tend to be severe illnesses in which patients lose touch with reality. As mentioned earlier, these patients have experiences that others do not have-for example, hearing voices of imaginary persons or harboring delusions that they are someone like Napoleon. Neuroses perhaps are understood most accurately as exaggerations of moods or overreactions to normal stress. Although you are likely to hear lay people use these terms, they are Freudian in origin and have been replaced in professional usage by more specific categories, as found in the American Psychiatric Association's Diagnostic and Statistical Manual of Mental Disorders, Fourth Edition (*DSM-IV*). The *DSM-IV* p. 25) states that it uses a multi-axial (multifaceted) system of evaluation to ensure that evaluation takes into account various mental conditions, psychosocial and environmental problems, and level of functioning that might be overlooked if a single presenting problem were the sole focus. There are five axes: Axis I-Clinical Disorders and Other Conditions That May Be a Focus of Clinical Attention, Axis II-Personality Disorders and Mental Retardation, Axis III-General Medical Conditions, Axis IV-Psychosocial and Environmental Problems, Axis V-Global Assessment of Functioning.

While *DSM-IV* is praised for resolving problems of diagnostic reliability for psychiatrists and other health professionals, diagnosis may be viewed as socially constructed. Brown (1987) found that diagnostic work was full of conflict and contradiction. Although diagnosis is the core of medicine, Brown says that it serves different functions for the different parties involved. For the practitioner, it provides a means of communicating the cause, nature, onset, and prognosis of a disease. Institutions may use diagnosis to make staffing plans and to allocate financial resource; insurers use the diagnostic codes to determine reimbursement. These functions often are at odds with one another. The main problem identified by Brown is that the inaccuracy of diagnosis throughout the mental health fields calls into question the validity of diagnosis and produces uncertainty, ambivalence, and conflict among the different parties. This problem, illustrated by Joyce's experience, has no simple solution.

Joyce was hospitalized twice during her illness. During her initial hospitalization, the psychiatrist believed her to be overly dependent on a meddling mother. Joyce reported a personality conflict with her first psychiatrist, and her mother said he would not answer any of her questions. This first psychiatrist treated Joyce only by increasing her medication and would talk only with her, not with her mother. On her second hospitalization, Joyce had a different psychiatrist. Whereas the first would listen to Joyce and say that her thoughts were not important, the second listened and responded in a way that she considered meaningful. This second psychiatrist also used Joyce's mother to observe and report on Joyce's behavior. Joyce's experiences with psychiatric diagnosis clearly call into question the validity of diagnosis and illustrate its variability.

FOCUSING ON DEPRESSION AS A DIAGNOSTIC CATEGORY

Depression, is one of the most pervasive mental health disorders. The National Institute of Health indicates that schizophrenia and major depression account for the greatest number of persons with severe mental disorders (See *http//www.Nimh.nih.gov/research/sc593 6.htm*). As we continue our inquiry, we may be able to understand why Joyce, the woman in the case study at the beginning of the chapter, would be diagnosed as manic-depressive.

DEPRESSION

Depression is classified in the *DSM-IV* as a mood disorder. In the earlier version of the diagnostic and statistical manual of the American Psychological Association, *DSM-III,* depression was classified as an affective disorder. *Affective* is a word traditionally used by philosophers and psychologists as denoting emotion, mood, or spirit (Papolos and Papolos 1987:3).

Frequency and population distribution. The lifetime prevalence rate of depression in the United States is estimated by Boyd and Weissman (1981) to be 8 to 12% for men and 20 to 26 % for women. The duration of depression varies from 4 to 8 months (Winokur 1978); 70 to 90% of patients recover in a few months, even without treatment (Hughes 1991: 43), but the rest (10 to 30%) have chronic cases that may last for years. Mirowsky and Ross (1992) found that the frequency of depression was high among persons in early adulthood and reached its lowest level in persons in middle adulthood-about age 45. Depression increased in occurrence during late adulthood and reached its highest level in adult's age 80 and older. Joyce belonged to an age group considered to be at high risk.

Gender and age are not the only characteristics associated with the risk of depression (Hirschfield and Cross 1982). Depression rates vary by marital status; separated and divorced persons have the highest rates, while the never married and the married have the lowest. The few studies on rural-urban differences suggest that no differences exist. Racial differences usually disappear when social class is taken into account. Religion has no relationship to depression, but class and measures of socioeconomic status (SES) have a strong inverse relationship. The lower the SES or social class, the higher the prevalence of depression. In view of her divorce and early adult age, Joyce, the woman in our case study, was at high risk.

Types of Depression. Three types of depression are distinguished by Walker (1982: 40-44). One type results from the reaction to a stressful event or significant loss: divorce, loss of a job, birth of a child, death of a family member, or a similar occurrence. The second type has no apparent cause and seems to be spontaneous. Unlike the first type, it usually cannot be identified with a psychosocial factor. A chemical imbalance is believed to cause this type of depression. In such cases, medication with tricylic antidepressants such as Elavil alleviates symptoms, and a low maintenance dosage prevents their return. The third type of depression is associated with mania, which includes elated or euphoric moods. A person with this type of depression may feel on top of the world for awhile, and then may slip into a prolonged period of depression, only to return eventually to euphoria. Such individuals also are known as manic-depressive; their condition often is difficult to diagnose because usually they seek treatment only when they feel depressed. The care provider may not see the mania without prolonged, regular contact.

In Joyce's case, it was believed that she was so busy while in college that the highs and lows of her manic depressive condition were not visible as problems. When she left that highly structured setting, the problems became more visible. One psychiatrist thought she was depressed because her mother was domineering. It was the second psychiatrist, who used her mother to track Joyce's behavior, which diagnosed her as manic-depressive. Prolonged and regular contact with Joyce, careful observation, and knowledge of the symptoms of manic depression were essential to this diagnosis.

Clinical Diagnostic Criteria. Depression manifests itself differently in different persons, but mental health professionals focus on periods of both depression and hypomania to diagnose depression (APA, 1994; Papolos and Papolos 1987: 7). Periods of depression are characterized by: (1) poor appetite and weight loss or the opposite (increased appetite and weight gain); (2) sleep disturbances-sleeping too little or sleeping too much in an irregular pattern; (3) loss of energy, excessive fatigue, or tiredness; (4) change in activity level, either increased or decreased; (5) loss of interest or pleasure in usual activities; (6) decreased sexual drive; (7) diminished ability to think or concentrate; (8) feelings of worthlessness or excessive guilt that may reach grossly unreasonable or delusional proportions; and (9) recurrent thoughts of death or self-harm, wishing to be dead or contemplating or attempting suicide.

Periods of hypomania are characterized by: (1) persistently "high" euphoric, or irritable mood states; (2) decreased need for sleep; (3) appetite disturbances; (4) increased activity, sociability, and sexual drive; (5) pressured speech; (6) racing thoughts; and (7) loss of self-control and judgment

Unfortunately, only 1 person in 3 suffering from serious mood disorders seeks care, and only 1 in 10 seeks care from a psychiatrist (Papolos and Papolos 1987: 8) Joyce was fortunate to receive care, and we recall that only careful observation resulted in her diagnosis

Causes of Depression. The causation of depression is currently explained most effectively as multifaceted, except possibly in the case of bipolar disorder, which may be influenced by a single gene (Paykel 1989: 774). Even where there is a genetic aspect, stress from the social environment often works as a trigger. A disease with such a multifaceted etiology would seem an unlikely candidate for treatment from any single theoretical approach. Social, biological, and psychological considerations are all important, and an eclectically oriented treatment professional will assign importance to all three. The best current explanation may be the biopsychosocial approach of Engel (Engel 1980, Jeffrey 1983), whereby an individual's biological functioning is related closely to psychological and social functioning.

Joyce evidently had a biologically based chemical imbalance, because the salt lithium completely alleviated her symptoms of depression within two weeks. Why did the chemical imbalance develop? Current thinking, based on the biopsychosocial approach, is that stress from social relationships triggered a biologically based tendency or weakness. In Joyce's case, the stressors seem to have been marital problems and changing from a student life to a working life. In all probability, the marital problems, which included abuse, were the key stress factors in her social environment. These socially based stresses triggered the salt deficiency and resulted in her psychological depression. To alleviate the depression, psychotherapy addressed both psychological and sociological factors, while the biological salt factor was addressed through medically administering lithium. The treatment of Joyce's depression serves as an excellent example of the application of the biopsychosocial approach.

Suicide. Walker (1982: 47-48) points out that approximately 25,000 suicides occur per year, and that probably twice that number are either misclassified or unreported. The French sociologist Emile Durkheim ([1897]1951) established a relationship between suicide and social structure. After plotting the suicide rates in France by parish on a map, Durkheim realized that the rates were higher in predominantly Protestant areas of France. He postulated that this might be related to Protestant beliefs regarding suicide, in which God's judgment is not to be second-guessed, whereas the Catholic church of the time dogmatically proclaimed that persons taking their own lives assuredly would be condemned to hell. Also significant, in Durkheim's account, was the degree of regulation (supervision, accountability) and integration (strong common values) characteristic of Protestants and Catholics of his time. Durkheim highlighted four kinds of suicide: anomic, egoistic, altruistic, and fatalistic. Anomic Suicide occurred when the values/norms where loose enough to condone suicide or when the individual recognizes no restraints. Examples of this in modern times might include individuals in groups which condone the suicide of Alzheimer's patients, or in the face of severe economic difficulties. Anomic suicide might also occur, though, when a sudden increase in wealth and power freed the individual from society's restraints (e.g. Cockerham 1992:106)

Egoistic Suicide was a reflection of a society in which there was an excess of individual freedom and self-regulation. Both anomic and egoism were problems of modern societies in which the old ways were breaking down and new forms of integration and regulation had not taken hold.

Altruististic Suicide is the opposite of egoistic suicide. It is the suicide of the individual who lays down his life to support his group or honor. For example, Japanese kamikaze pilots in World War II were expected to die on their missions; some crashed their planes into U. S. destroyers in the Pacific to sink them. The expectation in society is that persons will sacrifice their own lives for a greater cause; usually failure to do so results in disgrace and sanctioning of the individual. A kamikaze pilot who returned was shunned. No one would have anything to do with him, and the only way honor could be restored to his family was through hara-kiri, a ceremonial self-disemboweling. Finally, fatalistic suicide was the opposite of anomic suicide. This suicide occurs when the structure is rigid but meaningless, (in prisons, for example). Thus, Durkheim saw the social problem of suicide as one caused by excesses in regulation and integration, rather than purely psychological, in origin.

Treatment. Treatments of depression range from the use of psychopharamceuticals (drugs) to psychotherapy, electroconvulsive therapy, and institutionalization. Because the most effective treatment currently is a multifaceted or biopsychosocial approach, practitioners generally will utilize simultaneous biological, psychological, and social interventions. During the last thirty years, a number of drugs have proven extremely effective in the treatment of depression; these are likely to be used to reverse physiological changes in the brain's neuron functioning. Psychotherapy often is used along with drug treatment to alleviate mental anguish and pain and to help persons deal with the day-to-day problems of living that depressed persons often find so difficult. Because depressed individuals usually live in families, sometimes the family members are included in therapy. Electroconvulsive therapy generally is used only in cases that are nonresponsive to drug therapy and psychotherapy. Persons are institutionalized (hospitalized) for a variety of reasons, such as supervising the start of medication or providing a protective environment for someone who has indicated suicidal thoughts.

Depression is an easily treated disease (Walker 1982: 54-8). The problem is that only 15% of depressed persons receive treatment. Joyce was indeed fortunate to have been under psychiatric care.

Children and Older Adults. Abrupt demographic changes over the past several decades have resulted in a declining child population and an increasing adult population. While the expectation was that this type of rapid change would have favorable consequences for children and negative consequences for the elderly, Preston (1984) points out that this has not been the case. A reduced suicide rate among the elderly seems to reflect better overall psychological well-being, and is indicated by decreasing anxiety scores when compared with scores of twenty years ago. This may be partly attributable to increased Social Security benefits and Medicare.

Among children, suicide is rare, but the trend is upward and a comparison of results from the U. S. Health Examination Survey in 1965 and 1976 indicate a 10% increase in parental reports of serious disturbance or upsets of their children. Zill and Peterson (1983) conclude that childhood stress has increased primarily because of the rise of family disruption, which greatly increased between 1965 and 1976. Recent research by Cherlin, Chase-Lindsdale, and McRae (1998) indicates that family disruption, divorce, and its aftermath may have mental health effects, possibly including depression, that persist into adulthood. In fact, the effects may not emerge until adolescence or young adulthood.

A Recapitulation. Depression is a pervasive problem; it affects many people and ranges in severity from mild dysthymic disorder to severe depression and manic-depressive disorder. Depressed people fell "blue" all the time; their mental pain is as real as the pain you feel if you hit your thumb with a hammer. Symptoms include inability to make decisions, changes in sleep patterns, and lack of appetite. The increase in depression among children and its decrease among older adults is related to structural changes in society.

If you know of someone who seems to be manifesting signs of depression, encourage them to seek treatment. You may want to consult a mental health professional to see how you might encourage him or her to seek care.

INTERVENTIONS

When individuals suffer from depression, or other types of mental illness, what can be done? This section focuses on commonly used interventions such as; psychotherapy, psychopharmaceuticals, electroconvulsive therapy, institutionalization, and community treatment.

PSYCHOTHERAPY

Psychotherapy, commonly known as "therapy," is a household word (Hirschfield 1991: 155-159), but persons who have not experienced it often suffer some fear and confusion. Therapy, like all psychiatric treatment, begins with an evaluation, which includes a thorough medical history, a detailed family history, and relevant information about the present difficulties. Three basic forms of therapy exist: individual, group, and couple. In individual therapy, the patient and the therapist form a relationship to reach the common goal of resolving the problem for which the patient is seeking help. The patient honestly verbalizes inner thoughts, feelings, and concerns. The therapist requests information, helps the patient to understand the problem from a more objective perspective, and guides the patient in changes in attitude and behavior.

Group therapy is similar to individual therapy, except that it is conducted in a small group of persons, with one or more therapists present. Group therapy provides patients with an opportunity to view others more realistically, to receive feedback from others about their behavior, to practice social skills, and to gain insight from listening to others discuss their problems.

Couple therapy is sometimes recommended. In this treatment, marital couples attend therapy jointly with a therapist or as part of a group. This can help to address family problems related to the illness.

Therapy is difficult to evaluate with objective measures because it is a subjective experience. Does it really make a difference? Many patients and practitioners maintain that it does. Do persons sometimes continue therapy for years? Some do, but others may see a therapist for only a very limited period. In fact, the therapist and the patient often set time limited or progress limited goals. Patients often develop a very trusting, emotional relationship with their therapists and occasionally, may want to stay in contact with that person after termination of therapy, just as anyone might wish to continue to see a very good friend.

In evaluating therapy, probably the best question is simply whether the patient feels that it is helpful and whether the patient's family and friends are aware of changes in the patient. Joyce reported that therapy with her first psychiatrist was worthless because he just would not listen. Her second psychiatrist not only listened to Joyce, but also to her parents, particularly her mother. It is not definitely known whether therapy cures people who are mentally ill, but it is believed that therapy considerably lessens the mental anguish for patients and for persons involved with them. Patients, family, and friends often say that they feel better because the patient is receiving therapy. Perhaps sociologist W. I. Thomas was right in saying that if persons perceive something as real, then it is real in its consequences.

PSYCHOPHARMACOLOGY

The use of psychopharmaceuticals also may be referred to as drug therapy. John F. Cade (see Lickey and Gordon 1983:3), an Australian psychiatrist, began the drug revolution in psychiatry when he found that lithium tamed otherwise wild and fearful guinea pigs. In an experiment that would not be permitted today, Cade gave lithium to 10 hospitalized patients with manic and agitated symptoms. They exhibited much more normal behavior. Several groups of psychiatric drugs have emerged from this pioneering work. The group of drugs used frequently in treating schizophrenia and the mood disorders will be discussed, and some general observations will be made about the use of drugs in mental health treatment.

One group of drugs is used frequently in treating schizophrenia, and three in treating mood disorders. The first group consists of the antipsychotic medications, also known as neuroleptics or major tranquilizers. These are the drugs of the psychiatrists' choice for 90% of schizophrenics (Hughes 1991: 30). A second group, consisting of the tricylic antidepressants, is used most widely in treating depression. Drugs in a third group, the monoamine oxidase inhibitors, are used when the tricyclics have failed. Finally, lithium is used in treating both schizophrenia and manic-depression, a mood disorder (Hughes 1991: 3; Walker 1982: 222).

Antipsychotic drugs, developed in France, were subsequently introduced in the United States. The original drug, known as chlorpromazine, was marketed in the United States in 1954 by Smith, Klein, and French, and was known as Thorazine (Lickey and Gordon 1983: 77). Thorazine, like other drugs in the antipsychotic group, suppresses psychotic thoughts and behaviors. The use of these drugs makes many schizophrenic patients appear healthy. Their behavior is said to change dramatically over several weeks of hospitalization and treatment.

The crucial question is the long-term effect of antipsychotic drug intervention. In 10% of patients, these drugs do not work; however, 30% are enabled to remain outside hospitals and to be employed at least some of the time. Another 30% do not recover, but are not obviously ill. The remaining 30% appear to recover completely; they stay out of institutions, are employed, and sometimes marry (Lickey and Gordon 1983: 90).

Tricyclics are the drugs of choice for depression. They help the nerve synapses to function properly. According to Lickey and Gordon (1983: 180), a group of researchers at the National Institute of Mental Health believe that tricyclics combined with psychotherapy are more effective than either therapy alone. When the tricyclics do not work, monoamine oxidase inhibitors (MAOIs) often are used. Just as the body produces chemicals to foster neurotransmitter activity, it also produces enzymes that remove the neurotransmitter-enhancing chemicals to prevent "overload." The MAOIs metabolize these enzymes. A lack of neurotransmitting chemicals is thought to cause depression. Generally, MAOIs are weakly selective for anxiety and for reversing physical complaints such as headaches, backaches, and constipation. Patients treated with MAOIs require dietary care and periodic check-ups for possible medication interactions (Walker 1982: 221; Paykel 1989: 756).

Lithium is the drug of choice for mania (Lion 1978: 86), but because it may require several days to take effect, it is often used in combination with antipsychotic medications in the initial stages of treatment. Although not an antipsychotic, lithium induces remission in manic-depressive mood disorders, particularly those of the bipolar type. Lithium does not eliminate moods, but it limits the extent of oscillation in moods (Lion 1978: 94-90). A salt, lithium treatment is analogous to insulin treatment for diabetics; this knowledge sometimes helps patients to understand its use more fully.

Because of toxic reactions related to its use, establishing the correct dose of lithium for individual patients entails monitoring serum blood samples and constant medical supervision. Patients with a history of noncompliance with medication regimens may not do well on lithium. Although some patients may receive lithium for extended periods, need for this drug decreases with the patient's age. Patients who experience only one manic or depressive episode a year may be candidates for lithium-free periods if they notify their clinicians when they start to experience mood swings. In Joyce's case, her symptoms disappeared after two weeks, and she is now off lithium because of pregnancy.

Selection of the appropriate prescription medication for individual patients is the domain of psychiatrists. In our current understanding of most types of mental illness, clear biochemical changes occur in brain functioning; thus psychopharmaceutical drugs are an important intervention for those types. According to Weissman (1974), studies by a National Institute of Mental Health group show that combined drug therapy and psychotherapy are more effective than either intervention used alone. When the two were used in combination, drug therapy had a more immediate effect on sleep disturbances and appetite, while psychotherapy improved social adjustment in terms of work performance and interpersonal communications (Weissman 1974: 771-778). From a sociological perspective, this finding reinforces both the sociobiological and the biopsychosocial approaches to mental health.

Drug therapy may bring about distinct social changes, as documented by Kramer (1993). Allison is a good example from his book (Pp. 204-208). She often had feelings of fear and sadness, and felt physically weak, intellectually second-rate, and socially awkward. On Prozac, an antidepressant, Allison reported no longer feeling second rate when visiting a cousin she adored. She became confident, energized, and assertive. Allison's "self" changed and so did her relationship with persons around her. Other individuals taking Prozac are reported by Kramer to have asked for raises, while others became leaders rather than the followers they always had been. Drug therapy can transform a person's social life.

Compliance issues surround drug therapy, just as they do with the taking of any other medication. Patients sometimes stop taking the medication as soon as the symptoms subside, while others cease their medication for cost reasons. People often are concerned about taking medication. Many drugs have at least some unpleasant side effects. It is helpful to remember that the only medication, which cures a condition, is an antibiotic for a bacterial infection.

Other drugs merely <u>treat</u> conditions such as blood pressure and glaucoma, just as neuropharmaceuticals treat mental disorders. Patients, family members, and friends should discuss medication concerns frankly with trained health professionals. Other people probably have asked them similar questions. Accurate knowledge can help us to cope with mental health problems. As stated by George Herbert Mead, founder of the symbolic interactionist perspective in sociology, we think because we are cognitive beings.

ELECTROCONVULSIVE THERAPY

Although electroconvulsive therapy (ECT) has been and remains one of the most important advances in treatment in our time, its use as an intervention of choice has been declining worldwide for more than 20 years. The status of ECT as an intervention is discussed in extensive review articles by Kendell (1981) and Weiner and Coffey (1991). The main reason for its decline is the advance in neuropharmaceuticals, which has reduced ECT to an intervention of last resort.

The use of ECT has been affected not only by the development of the neuropharmaceuticals, but also by public attitudes. Electrical shock deliberately given to human beings is often equated with torture at best and with execution at worst. During the 1970s several states passed restrictive legislation regarding ECT, partially because it was thought that this treatment was used to subdue difficult patients and was given without patients' and relatives' consent. Although these beliefs no doubt have some validity, severely depressed patients often cannot make decisions regarding their treatment. It is also documented that patients who initially refuse ECT often are frightened and change their minds when given an opportunity to talk with relatives and friends. ECT is not an intervention of choice, but it may be recommended under certain circumstances.

INSTITUTIONALIZATION

In spite of neuropharmaceutical drugs and the availability of therapy from various community-based mental health professionals, some patients still require hospitalization for a variety of reasons. Some simply are exhausted emotionally and psychologically, and need a rest. This is sometimes true as well for their families. At other times, patients are afraid of hurting themselves or others, and need the security of hospitalization. Also, the practitioner may want the patient to begin drug therapy in a supervised setting or may wish to place the patient in an intensive psychotherapeutic setting. All of these are legitimate reasons for hospitalization; undoubtedly there are others.

Some observers, such as Townsend (1976), maintain that it is unclear whether patients enter mental institutions because they become convinced that they are sick or because they cannot cope with the real world. Regardless of the explanation, the decision to undergo hospitalized care should be made carefully with a trained mental health professional, such as a psychiatrist or social worker. In Joyce's case, the decision was made by her physician.

Institutionalization for psychiatric care may take place at a specialty or a general hospital. In Joyce's case, she was admitted to the psychiatric floor of a general hospital. The classic research on mental hospitalization was conducted by Erving Goffman (1961), who identified the following six characteristics of total institutions, including mental hospitals. First, role differentiation must exist between the staff and inmates. One of Goffman's observations in this report was that low-level employees are the carriers of tradition because the high-level employees such as psychiatrists and nurses have a fairly high rate of turnover. Second, Goffman noted that "recruits" are either involuntary, semivoluntary, or voluntary. In the case of mental hospitals, very few patients arrive voluntarily.

The third characteristic of a total institution is staff members' desire to see self-regulated change among inmates. Goffman believed that the staff looked for evidence of emotional and attitudinal changes among mental hospital inmates. Fourth, mental hospitals and other total institutions have some degree of permeability: the standards inside the institution are influenced by those outside the institution, such as the customary manners of the society. A fifth characteristic identified by Goffman was that the admissions procedures of mental hospitals and other total institutions strip away the patient's or client's former self and place him or her on the same level as others. The use of an institutional uniform is a good example; it removes any status differences that might exist in the type or brand of clothing. Goffman's sixth characteristic of total institutions was the varying fate of its "graduates." Whereas asylum inmates generally avoid contact with each other and with the hospital after discharge, some prep schools maintain very active "old boy" networks.

Goffman was concerned not only with the characteristics of mental hospitals but also with the careers of mental patients. He viewed patients as going through three phases: pre-patient, inpatient, and ex-patient. In the pre-patient stage, a few persons may be relieved to be taken in to a hospital because they regard themselves as unbalanced. The majority of patients, however, develop feelings of abandonment, perceptions of disloyalty by others, and embitterment when they encounter problems in face-to-face living that results in actions to hospitalize them. Joyce thought the craft classes and other such activities were stupid, but she ultimately realized that her "time out" had been helpful.

During the inpatient phase, Goffman says that patients usually desire anonymity; they may not want others to know who they are. Eventually patients settle down and enter the regimen of the hospital and its system of operation. Goffman describes the regimen and the system in public mental hospitals as involving stark accommodations such as wooden benches and group sleeping quarters under the worst of conditions and one's own room, ground privileges, and recreational facilities under the best of conditions. Goffman found that inmates of public hospitals were punished for disobeying rules but rewarded with taken for granted aspects of life outside the institution when they behaved obediently.

Goffman's observations correspond well with Joyce's experiences. She stated that the nursing staff told her just to do what she was told. In addition to the regimen and the system of the hospital, the patient as inmate is also subject to direct and blatant attacks on his or her view of self. Goffman believes that this is particularly true of the more medical and more "progressive" hospitals because inmates in such hospitals are confronted more often by high-ranking staff members who argue that the inmates' past outlook and behavior were a failure. Success and cure or healing are defined by patients' acceptance of these redefinitions and of the hospital regimen. Then, at some point, they become ex-patients.

Rosenhan (1973) studies the process of becoming an ex-patient. His research used pseudopatients - persons without mental health problems who faked problems in order to be hospitalized. When the pseudopatients began to act normally and told patients and staff that they really were normal, nobody, except some of the other patients, believed them. Although this study raises diagnostic questions, the factors leading to discharge are the important consideration here. The patients advised the pseudopatients to tell the staff that they were still sick but were getting better. If the pseudopatients said they were well, the patients said the staff would discount them totally. The staff wanted to hear that the patients recognized change; such recognition hastened the likelihood of discharge.

Hospitalization is an important topic because inpatient care consumes 70% of the dollars spent for mental health care (Kiesler 1991). Although the number of residents in public mental hospitals declined sharply between 1965 and 1980, the proportion of mental patients in general hospitals was rising dramatically. Kiesler has documented that, in 1980, 1.7 million patients were treated in general hospitals and about two thirds had a primary diagnosis of mental disorder. Specialty hospitals accounted for 13% of mental illness hospitalizations; 9.5% of patients were treated in scattered beds in hospitals with psychiatric units. Hospitals without any specialty unit treated 28.6% of patients with a diagnosis of mental illness. General hospital treatment is delivered outside psychiatric units for plausible clinical reasons, not merely because patients are placed there for referral. Even so, 71% of all general hospital patients are treated in psychiatric units. Joyce was treated in a general hospital.

DEINSTITUTIONALIZATION AND COMMUNITY TREATMENT

Largely because of the introduction of neuropharmaceuticals, many patients who previously required hospitalization can now function in the community, although they often need organizationally provided services such as day care and sheltered homes (Gloag 1985). In fact, a combination of neuropharmaceutical drugs and litigation resulted in the deinstitutionalization of many mental patients. Two key court cases were Baxstrom v. Herold (1966) and Dixon v. Attorney General of the Commonwealth of Pennsylvania (1971), both of which were heard before the United States Supreme Court.

In Baxstrom v. Herold, the court ruled that Baxstrom had been confined beyond the maximum sentence in violation of his civil rights and those of the class he represented, namely inmates serving criminal sentences who had been placed in a New York State hospital for the criminally insane. The ruling ended the practice of extending institutionalization because inmates were judged still to be mentally ill. Dixon v. Attorney General of the

Commonwealth of Pennsylvania challenged the use of "dangerousness" as the most important criterion for long-term forensic institutionalization. According to French (1987), the deincarceration of mentally ill offenders was expanded to include voluntarily committed mentally ill and mentally retarded patients, especially those in state hospitals and schools. Advocates of this movement based their actions on the legal concept of providing the least restrictive environment for treatment of patients.

Besides the courts, the most dramatic development in regard to deinstitutionalization was President Kennedy's personal involvement in obtaining congressional passage of the Community Mental Health Centers (CMHC) Act of 1963, which funded community-based mental health centers. Unfortunately, however, deinstitutionalization was not matched by the growth of the community-based system of mental health care envisioned by President Kennedy (Kennedy 1990). A shift from federal to state funding for mental health services occurred during the Reagan presidency. Although this shift was intended to give states more freedom to work out local problems in their own way, the result was a reduction in treatment of about one-third (Goplerud, Walfish, and Broskowski 1985).

One way of viewing the current turmoil in the care of the mentally ill is that mental health care is moving from an era of institutional and facility-based thinking to one in which patients are seen as service recipients in need of professional support (Blanch, Carling, and Ridgeway 1988). The problem, according to Torrey (1989), is that many people are not receiving the care they need. This point is illustrated dramatically by the homeless, who number between 350,000 and 600,000 persons. According to the most recent estimates, one-tenth to one-third of the homeless are mentally ill (Snow, Baker, and Anderson 1986; Rossi 1991). To this number Torrey would add 5 to 20% of the nation's 750,000 prisoners, and additional 37,500 to 150,000 mentally ill persons. Torrey believes that the problem is not being resolved but that the public mental health system has grown more ineffective over the past 30 years. He states that the lack of care for mentally ill homeless persons is extraordinary in a country that spends at least $17 billion annually in public funds for mental health programs.

Cockerham (1992: 295-297) indicates that the fundamental shift to community based care was undertaken to avoid the depersonalizing and dehumanizing aspects of mental hospitalization. The shift also implied a belief in using the community as a therapeutic tool and a view that poverty, racism, and inequality were pathogenic and contributed to mental disorder. As a result mental health workers engaged in activities previously not recognized as their domain, with the intent of improving the general community mental health. Hammer and Cockerham (1992:305) maintain that the original vision of institutionalization and community care has not been national because it never was adequately funded, and the debate will continue (Cockerham 1992: 305)

SUMMARY

In the case study at the beginning of the chapter, Joyce exhibited somewhat bizarre behavior. She had periods of hyperactivity. She drove aimlessly around town. Joyce believed her car was "bugged" and her aunt's telephone tapped. It was a cousin, a deputy sheriff, who suggested that Joyce be taken to a physician, who admitted her to a hospital.

For Joyce, her diagnosis was problematic. The first psychiatrist believed her to be depressed and had her heavily medicated. Because Joyce had been hospitalized for the maximum number of days covered by her insurance, returning to the hospital for further treatment was not an option. Problems around the medication and the psychiatrist continued until Joyce moved out of her parents' home. During this period, Joyce spent a weekend with her estranged husband and also contemplated taking her life. Eventually she was hospitalized a second time and changed psychiatrists. The new psychiatrist used Joyce's mother to monitor her behavior and placed Joyce on lithium when her mother's reports led him to believe that Joyce was manic-depressive. Joyce's symptoms disappeared within two weeks, and her behavior became normal. Subsequently Joyce discovered she was pregnant as a result of the weekend with her estranged husband and had to stop taking the lithium.

Joyce's current mental health is fine. The birth of her baby did not trigger a return of Joyce's manic depression, but a future life event may. Joyce must always remain conscious of the possibility of a recurrence. Among the theoretical points and research findings illustrated by this case study are the following:

1. Although suicide often is perceived as an individual act, it is influenced by social factors.
2. Gender differences exist in the prevalence of mental illness.
3. The cost of mental health care is increasing, as is the number of professionals delivering mental health care.
4. A relationship exists between social structure and mental illness
5. Szasz believed that mental illness was a myth. Mental illness is diagnosed according to *DSM-IV* categories. Research shows, however, that diagnosis is sometimes problematic, in part because of social influences on the health professionals who make the diagnosis.
6. Depression is a pervasive problem that may strike both the old and the young.
7. The three types of depression are reactions to stressful events, depression with no apparent cause, and depression associated with mania.
8. Depressed persons may exhibit any number of characteristics, including poor appetite, loss of energy, and diminished ability to think or concentrate. A trained mental health professional such as a psychiatrist or clinical social worker can and should make the assessment.
9. The causation of depression is explained most accurately as multifaceted; it includes a combination of biological, psychological, and social factors.
10. Some depressed persons attempt suicide, usually to escape mental pain and anguish.
11. Interventions for mental illness include psychotherapy, chemotherapy and psychopharmacology, electroconvulsive therapy, institutionalization, and deinstitutionalization.

SUGGESTED READINGS

Coate, Morag. 1964. *Beyond All Reason*. London: Constable.

Cockerham, William C. 1996. *Sociology of Mental Disorder, Fourth Edition*. Englewood Cliffs: Prentice-Hall.

Goffman, Erving. 1961. Asylums: *Essays on the Social Situation of Mental Patients and Other Inmates*. Garden City: Doubleday Anchor

Greenberg, Joanne (Hannah Green). 1964. *I Never Promised You a Rose Garden*. New York: Holt, Rinehart, and Winston.

Papolos, Demitri F. and Janice Papolos. 1987. *Overcoming Depression*. New York: Harper and Row, Publishers.

REFERENCES

American Psychiatric Association (APA) 1994. *Diagnostic and Statistical Manual of Mental Disorders (Fourth Edition)*. Washington, D. C.: American Psychological Association.

Andreasen, Nancy C., and Scott Olsen 1982. "Negative v. Positive Schizophrenia." Archives of *General Psychiatry*. 39: 789-794.

Beers, Clifford W. 1970. *A Mind That Found Itself An Autobiography*. Garden City: Doubleday and Company.

Blanch, A. K., P. J. Carling, and P. Ridgeway 1988. "Normal Housing with Specialized Support: A Psychiatric Rehabilitation Approach to Living in the Community." *Rehabilitation Psychology.* 32:47-55.

Bleuler, Eugene 1950. *Dementia Praecox or the Group of Schizophrenia.* (Joseph Zinkin, Trans.) New York: International Universities Press.

Boyd, J. and M. Weissman 1981. "Epidemiology of Affective Disorders," *Archives of General Psychiatry.* 38: 1039-1045.

Brown, Phil 1987. "Diagnostic Conflict and Contradiction in Psychiatry." *Journal of Health and Social Behavior.* 28: 37-50.

Byrne, D. G. 1980. "The Prevalence of Symptoms of Depression in an Australian General Population." *Australian and New Zealand Journal of Psychiatry.* 14: 65-71.

Carling, Paul J. 1990. "Major Mental Illness, Housing, and Supports: The Promise of Community Integration." *American Psychologist.* 45: 969-975.

Cherlin, Andrew. P, Lindsay Chase-Lindsdale, and Christine McRae 1998. "Effects of Paternal Divorce on Mental Health Throughout the Life Course." American Sociological Review. 63: 239-249.

Cockerham, William C. 1990. "A Test of the Relationship between Race, Socioeconomic Status, and Psychological Distress." *Social Science and Medicine.* 31: 1321 -1326.

_____. 1992. Sociology of Mental Disorders, Third Edition. Englewood Cliffs: Prentice-Hall

Dassori, A. M., J. E. Mezzich, and M. Keshavan 1990. "Suicidal Indicators in Schizophrenia." *Acta Psychiatrica Scandinavica.* 81: 409-413.

Dennis, Deborah L., John C. Buckner, Frank R. Lipton, and Irene S. Levine 1991. "A Decade of Research and Services for Homeless Mentally Ill Persons." *American Psychiatrist.* 46: 1129-1138.

Dohrenwend, Bruce P., and Barbara S. Dohrenwend 1969. *Social Status and Psychological Disorder: A Causal Inquiry.* New York: Wiley-Interscience.

Durkheim, Emile. (1897)1951. *Suicide: A Study In Sociology.* (John A. Spaulding and George Simpson, Trans.) New York: Free Press.

Engel, George L. 1980. "The Clinical Application of the Biopsychosocial Model." *American Journal of Psychiatry.* 137: 535-544.

Ensel, W. M. 1982. "The Role of Age in the Relationship of Gender and Marital Status to Depression." *Journal of Nervous and Mental Disease.* 170: 536-543.

Faden, V. B. 1977. *Primary Diagnoses of Discharge from Nonfederal General Hospital Psychiatric Inpatient Units.* U. S. 1975. (Mental Health Statistical Note 137). Rockville MD: Department of Health, Education, and Welfare.

Faris, Robert E. L., and H. Warren Dunham 1939. *Mental Disorders in Urban Areas: An Ecological Study of Schizophrenia.* New York: Hafner Publishing Company.

Flaskerund, Jacquelyn and Li-Tze Hu 1992. "Racial/Ethnic Identity and Amount and Type of Psychiatric Treatment." *American Journal of Psychiatry.* 149: 379-384.

French, Laurence 1987. "Victimization of the Mentally Ill: An Unintended Consequence of Deinstitutionalization." *Social Work* 32: 502-505.

Gallagher, Barnard J. 1987. *The Sociology of Mental Illness.* Englewood Cliffs, NJ: Prentice-Hall.

Gloag, Daphne 1985. "Rehabilitation in Psychiatric Conditions: 1-Community and Residential Care." *British Medical Journal.* 290: 981-984.

Goffman, Erving 1961. *Asylums: Essays on the Social Situation of Mental Patients and Other Inmates.* New York: Anchor Books.

Goldstein, Michael J. 1987. "The UCLA High Risk Project." *Schizophrenia* Bulletin. 13(3): 505-514.

Goplerud, E. N., S. Walfish, and A. Broskowski 1985. "Weathering the Cuts: A Delphi Survey on Surviving Cutbacks in Community Mental Health." *Community Mental Health* Journal 21: 14-27.

Gordon, Milton M. 1958. *Social Class in American Society.* New York: McGraw-Hill.

Hirschfield, Robert M. A. 1991. *When the Blues Won't Go Away: New Approaches to Dysthymic Disorder and Other Forms of Chronic Low-Grade Depression.* New York: Macmillan.

_____. and Christine K. Cross 1982. "Epidemiology of Affective Disorders." *Archives of General Psychiatry.* 39: 35-46.

Hollingshead, August B., and Frederick C. Redlich. 1958. *Social Class and Mental illness: A Community Study.* New York: John Wiley & Sons.

Hughes, Jennifer 1991. *An Outline of Modern Psychiatry.* Chichester: John Wiley & Sons.
Jeffrey, Ina A. 1983. "The Biopsychosocial Model: An Interdisciplinary Alternative." *Journal of Social and Behavioral Sciences.* 29: 15-21.
Keith, S. J., and S. M. Matthews 1982. "Group, Family and Milieu Therapies and Psychosocial Rehabilitation in the Treatment of Schizophrenic Disorders." *Psychiatry 1982, Annual Review.* Washington, D. C.: American Psychiatric Press, Inc.
Kendell, R. E. 1981. "The Present Status of Electroconvulsive Therapy." *British Journal of Psychiatry.* 139: 265-283.
Kennedy, Edward M. 1990. "Community-Based Care for the Mentally Ill: Simple Justice." *American Psychologist.* 45:1238-1240.
Kessler, Ronald C. 1979. "Stress, Social Status, and Psychological Distress." *Journal of Health and Social Behavior.* 20: 259-272.
_____ and Harold W. Neighbors 1986. "A New Perspective on the Relationships Among Race, Social Class, and Psychological Distress." *Journal of Health and Social Behavior.* 17: 107-115.
Kiesler, Charles A. 1991. "Changes in General Hospital Psychiatric Care, 1980-1985." *American Psychologist.* 46: 416-421.
King, D. A., and A. M. Buchwald 1982. "Sex Differences in Subclinical Depression: Administration of the Beck Depression Inventory in Public and Private Disclosure Situations." *Journal of Personality and Social Psychology.* 42: 963-969.
Kramer, Peter D. 1993. *Listening to Prozac.* New York: Penguin Books.
Leff, Julian, and Christine Vaughn 1985. *Expressed Emotions in Families: Its Significance for Mental Health.* New York: The Guilford Press.
Lemkau, P., C. Tietsze, and M. Cooper 1942. "Complaint of Nervousness and the Psychoneuroses: An Epidemiological Viewpoint." *American Journal of Orthopsychiatry.* 12: 214-223.
Lickey, Marvin E., and Barbara Gordon 1983. *Drugs for Mental Illness: A Revolution in Psychiatry.* New York: W.H. Freeman and Company.
Lion, John R. 1978. *The Art of Medicating Psychiatric Patients.* Baltimore: Waverly Press.
McCoby, E. E., and C. N. Jacklin 1974. *The Psychology of Sex Differences.* Stanford, CA: Stanford University Press.
Mechanic, David 1989. *Mental Health and Social Policy.* Englewood Cliffs: Prentice Hall.
Mirowsky, John, and Catherine E. Ross 1992. "Age and Depression." *The Journal of Health and Social Behavior.* 33: 187-205.
_____.1983. "Paranoia and the Structure of Powerlessness." *American Sociological Review.*
Myers, Jerome K., and Lee L. Bean 1968. *A Decade Later: A Follow-Up of Social Class and Mental Illness.* New York: John Wiley and Sons, Inc.
_____ and Leslie Schaffer 1954. "Social Stratification and Psychiatric Practice: A Study of an Out-Patient Clinic," *American Sociological Review.* 19: 307-310.
_____., M. M. Weissman, G. L. Tischler, C. E. Holzer, P. J. Lend, H. Ovaschel, J. E. Anthony, J. H. Boyd, J. D. Burke, M. Kramer, and R. Stoltzman 1984. "Six-Month Prevalence of Psychiatric Disorders in Three Communities." *Archives of General Psychiatry.* 41: 953-967.
Nolen-Hoeksema, Susan 1987. "Sex Differences in Unipolar Depression: Evidence and-Theory." *Psychological* Bulletin. 101: 259-282.
Papolos, Demitri J., and Janice Papolos 1987. *Overcoming Depression.* New York: Harper & Row.
Paykel, E. S. 1989. "Treatment of Depression: The Relevance of Research For Clinical Practice." *British Journal of Psychiatry.* 155: 754-763.
Peterson, Dale 1981. *A Mad People's History of Madness.* Pittsburgh: University of Pittsburgh Press.
Preston, Samuel H. 1984. "Children and the Elderly: Divergent Paths for America's Dependents." *Demography.* 21: 435-476.
Radloff L. 1975. "Sex Differences in Depression: The Effects of Occupation and Marital Status." *Sex Roles.* 1: 249-265.
Rice, D. P. and Miller, L. S. 1992. "Costs of Mental Illness." In Hu The-Nei, A. Rupp eds., *Advances in Health Economics and Health Services Research: Research In the Economics of Mental Health.* Vol. 14 New York: JAI Press

Ridley, Charles R. 1984. "Clinical Treatment of the Non-Disclosing Black Patient: A Therapeutic Paradox." *American Psychologist.* 39: 1234-1244.

Rosenhan, David L. 1973. "On Being Sane in Insane Places." *Science.* 179: 250-258.

Rossi, Peter H. 1991. *Down and Out in America: The Origins of Homelessness.* Chicago: University of Chicago Press.

Scheftner, W. A., L. Fogg, and D. C. Clark 1990. "Time-Related Predictors of Suicide in Major Affective Disorders." *American Journal of Psychiatry.* 147: 1189-1194.

Snow, David A., Susan G. Baker, and Leon Anderson 1986. "The Myth of Pervasive Mental Illness among the Homeless." *Social Problems.* 33: 407-423.

Srole, Leo, Thomas S. Langner, T. Stanley, Marvin K. Opler, and Thomas A. C. Rennie 1962. *Mental Health in the Metropolis: The Midtown Manhattan Study Volume 1.* New York: McGraw-Hill.

Steinberg, M. D., H. Pardes, D. Bjork, D. and D. Sporty 1977. "Demographic and Clinical Characteristics of Black Psychiatric Patients in a Private General Hospital." *Hospital and Community Psychiatry.* 28: 128-32.

Szasz, Thomas S. 1960. "The Myth of Mental Illness." *American Psychiatrist.* 15: 113-18.

_____.1974. *The Myth of Mental Illness.* New York: Harper & Row..

_____.1997. *Psychiatric Slavery.* New York: The Free Press.

Torrey, E. Fuller 1989. "Thirty Years of Shame: The Scandalous Neglect of the Mentally Ill Homeless." *Policy Review.* 48: 10-15.

Townsend, J. Marshall 1976. "Self-Concept and the Institutionalization of Mental Patients: An Overview and Critique." *Journal of Health and Social Behavior.* 17: 263-371.

Walker, J. Ingram 1982. *Everybody's Guide to Emotional Well-Being.* San Francisco: Harbor Publishing.

Warstadt, G. M., R. A. Nemiroff, and R.C. Fowler 1991. "Suicide, Stressors, and the Life Cycle." *American Journal of Psychiatry.* 148: 524-527.

Weiner, Richard D., and Edward Coffey 1991. "Electroconvulsive Therapy in the United States." *Psychopharmacology* Bulletin. 27: 915.

Weissman, M. M. 1974. "Treatment Effects on the Social Adjustment of Depressed Patients." *Archives of General Psychiatry.* 39: 771-778.

_____ 1978. "Psychotherapy and Its Relevance to Pharmacotherapy of Affective Disorders: From Ideology to Evidence." In M. A. Lipton, A. DiMascio, and K. F. Killam, eds., *Psychopharmacology: A Generation of Progress.* New York: Raven Press.

_____ and J. Myers 1978. "Affective Disorders in the United States Urban Community: The Use of Research Diagnostic Criteria in an Epidemiological Survey." *Archives of General Psychiatry.* 35: 1304-1311.

Williams, J. B., and R. L. Spitzer. 1983. "The Issue of Sex Bias in *DSM-III.*" *American Psychologist.* 38: 793-798.

Winokur, G. 1978. "Mania, Depression: Family Studies, Genetics, and Relation to Treatment." In M. A. Lipton, A. diMascio, and K. Killam, eds. *Psychopharmacology: A Generation of Progress.* New York: Raven Press.

Zilboorg, Gregory 1941. *A History of Medical Psychology.* New York: W.W. Norton.

Zill, Nicholas and James L. Peterson 1983. "Marital Disruption and the Child's Need for Psychological Help." Report prepared for NIMH.

COURT CASES CITED

Baxstrom v. Herold [legal reference details] (1966)

Dixon v. Attorney General of the Commonwealth of Pennsylvania [ref. details] (1971)

CHAPTER 3: SEXUAL BEHAVIORS
CASE STUDY: WHAT SHOULD NICOLE DO?

Nicole loves her job as a computer consultant; she is enthusiastic about her career and confident in her abilities, especially since receiving a promotion last month. At 36, Nicole is energetic and physically fit, and is considered to be sexually attractive. Though she realizes it's not easy being a single woman today, she has an interesting and active social life, with a handful of close friends and many acquaintances. On the surface, Nicole's life is rich and rewarding, but she speaks of an emptiness in her life - the longing for a child. She feels that her "biological clock" is ticking and wants to be pregnant. Nicole has been dating Matt, a software designer, for nearly two years. They are happy together and describe their relationship as "fulfilling." As both have been previously married (and divorced), neither is in a rush to remarry. Although each maintains a separate residence, they often spend nights together.

Matt has two children from a previous marriage who live with their mother in an adjacent state. His children visit four or five times each year. Nicole loves these interactions and when the children return to their home, she misses them. Her closest married friends, Sarah and Marshall, have a beautiful baby daughter and Nicole shares many events in their lives. Thus, Nicole is realistic about the potential responsibilities and joys of having a child, and is willing to change her life in the very significant ways that a baby would require.

Years before Nicole and Matt began dating, he had a vasectomy. They discussed the topic recently, and although a surgical reversal is technically possible, he doesn't want any more children. Among other concerns, he feels financially burdened by monthly child support payments and with the prospects of putting his two children through college over the next decade. Even so, Matt loves Nicole and understands her desire to experience parenthood. Although Nicole would be responsible for the child's financial needs, she is aware that it would be extremely difficult to raise a child on her own. Matt says that he is willing to help her in whatever capacity he can, during a pregnancy or adoption, and would play a role in the child's life. Although Nicole strongly desires to mother a child, various factors - including her sexual history, her age and current medical condition, and the force of traditional gender roles (especially social norms about being single) - may interact to prevent this from happening.

NICOLE'S SEXUAL HISTORY

When she was 17 years of age, Nicole had unprotected sexual intercourse with Scott, her high school sweetheart. They had been dating for over a year and wanted to be married. Although many of their peers were also having sex, she felt guilty and worried about getting pregnant. She went to a gynecologist listed in the phone book, who wrote her a prescription for birth control pills. Within days, however, she suffered a serious side effect of the hormones: blackouts. Nicole stopped taking the birth control pills and within two months became pregnant.

She had heard about abortion counseling and after discussing the matter with Scott, called for an appointment. Although she and Scott wanted to remain together, they had serious doubts about their abilities to parent a child properly. The counselor was a Methodist minister in a local church; during their meeting, he asked a question that would haunt her for the next 20 years: "What if this is the only chance you are given by God to have a baby? Do you still want an abortion?" Under the circumstances, she felt that abortion was the best decision.

On the day of Nicole's appointment, her mother and Scott accompanied her to the abortion clinic, so she felt supported in her abortion decision. Soon after, she and Scott renewed their engagement plans and within three months were married. They remained together for ten years, during which time neither chose to speak much about having children. They stayed very busy during their marriage, enjoying friends, developing hobbies, pursuing education, and establishing careers. Still, their lives gradually grew separate and at one point Scott had an extramarital affair. The disclosure of his sexual infidelity became too much for Nicole; she no longer trusted Scott, and eventually, they divorced.

NICOLE'S MEDICAL HISTORY

During the decade after her divorce, Nicole had intimate relationships with three or four men, none of who were seriously interested in marriage or in creating a family with her. These sexual experiences influenced her physical and emotional health.

Genital Warts. One of Nicole's relationships became a source of extreme physical and emotional distress for her. Although they had discussed sexual histories, this partner did not feel it necessary, since he did not have any visible symptoms, to disclose that his previous sexual partner had genital warts. When Nicole developed symptoms, he became remorseful, but it was too late. She regretted her decision not to insist upon using a prophylactic for protection against STDs. This initial onset of genital warts was the worst, and since that time, Nicole has managed this viral condition with adequate rest, regular exercise, and a nutritious diet. It takes a healthy outlook on life to overcome the negative stigma of having a STD. Although she has not had a symptom for over three years, she informed Matt before they became intimate and they always use a condom during sexual intercourse.

Endometriosis. About two years ago, Nicole noticed illness symptoms around the time of her period, including much heavier flows, fatigue, and chronic lower back pain. She had heard of a condition that affects many women – endometriosis[1]. This painful condition is often misdiagnosed, which is significant in that it is associated with infertility. Over the past few years, Nicole has relied on a female gynecologist for most of her medical needs[2]. Her gynecologist suggested outpatient surgery, which is necessary both to detect and to treat endometriosis. The physician performed a laparoscopy (using a fiber optic viewing device) and treated her mild case of endometriosis. During the treatment, the physician also noticed an anomaly in her left fallopian tube. When she discussed it with Nicole later, they decided to conduct a hysterosalpingogram (an X-ray of the pelvic organs using a radio-opaque dye). The test results showed that one fallopian tube was blocked.

THEORY BOX by Michael J. Donnelly Chapter 3 Sexual Behavior Symbolic Interaction

The term "symbolic interaction" may seem high-falutin'; actually what it refers to is not all-difficult to grasp. It provides one of sociologists' basic frames of reference for understanding how humans create symbolic worlds and how those worlds in turn shape our behavior.

Imagine that you and a friend have plans to go to the movies this evening. You are going to see a film that you've wanted to see for ages. Shortly before you're about to go out, you get a call from your friend, in tears, who tells you that she's just had bad news from home. How would you likely react to that phone conversation? You might immediately feel a twinge of regret about having to postpone your film date (part of you still wants to see the film). But you'd probably also be moved by your friend's sorrow and conclude that what you ought to do is to go console her.

This sort of situation is not at all hard to imagine. All of us have had moments in life like this, when we experience a conflict between two possible actions which we might take-one which is basically egoistic (what **I** want do to) and another which follows an opposing voice, like the voice of conscience (which tells **me** what I should do in the situation). The simple everyday situation is a good way to begin thinking about what sociologists call symbolic interaction. In a sense the interior dialogue between the **I** and the **me** in this example is an interaction, and one which highlights the significance of our human capacity to use symbols in dealing without our environment. How so? Sociologists who focus on symbolic interaction think of the bold as something like the voice of society within us. How did it get there? Symbolic interactionists don't think of it as innate but as acquired, during the course of the infant's and the child's socialization through interactions with its significant others. The child learns to interpret his or her parents, through the signs, gestures, and eventually words the parents use. Part of becoming a conscious individual is learning to anticipate the effect of our actions on others, and to anticipate others' likely response. When the child begins to accomplish this, it is as if the child could examine his or her behavior through the eyes of the parents; by taking their point of view and anticipating their reaction, the child is looking upon itself as if from the outside, as an object (note that, grammatically, while "I" is the subject of an action, "me" is an object). The self formed in this matter is likely to deliberate - to weigh what the "I" wants to do against the point of view of the social "me." Initially, the "me" represents the parents' point of view; as the child develops, however, the "me" comes to encompass an entire group. The individual is said then to be able to "take the role of the generalized other;" in other words, self-conscious individuals can interpret the reactions of others from the vantage point of societal norms.

This is a powerful way of thinking about how individuals learn and internalize the social norms of their groups. It may also be a fruitful way of thinking about certain internal conflicts individuals experience. If the self is made of an **I** and of a **me** which retains a record and memory of its past interactions, in various situations the **I** and the **me** are likely to collide; or the **me** may in a sense speak with conflicting voices, representing the plural or complex social norms which the modern individual tends to encounter in the course of life. Think of the experience of a young person raised in a conservative religious household who comes to college and discovers freer or more liberal attitudes towards sexual behavior; the voice of one's parent's morality may be at odds with the norms prevailing among one's peers.

Infertility. Nicole went to see a local fertility specialist. Expensive tests (not covered by her health insurance company) were conducted to determine ovulation dysfunction, but these were not conclusive. Nicole was warned that because of her age, the probability of having a child with Downs Syndrome is increased. Also, because of the blocked tube and the endometriosis, it would be very difficult for her to get pregnant "the old fashioned way." He suggested a regimen of drugs to stimulate ovulation, coupled wit AI (artificial insemination), as a possibility. However, when the fertility specialist realized that Nicole wasn't married, and that her current partner had a vasectomy, he instructed his nurse to inform Nicole by phone that they did not provide AI (with purchased donor sperm) for unmarried women at his clinic. Nicole was shocked; when she pressed for an explanation, the nurse tried to avoid an

answer, but then replied, "We believe that every child should have a father."
End of conversation.

SOCIAL NORMS

As in earlier life experiences - when Nicole felt the pressure of conflicting
social norms concerning teenage pregnancy and abortion, infidelity and
divorce, and sexually transmitted diseases – she now faces social forces that
inhibit her mothering a child. In addition to the unsympathetic treatment she
experienced at the fertility clinic, she heard that informal mechanisms of
adoption tend to favor married couples over single people (even though it is
legal for a single person to adopt a child). She explored the topic on the
Internet, and discovered that the costs of adoption typically run between
$15,000 and $20,000.

Nicole believes she has the maturity, love, and commitment necessary to
parent a child properly. Further, Nicole has the financial resources to maintain
a middle-class lifestyle for herself and a child. Her mother, her best friend,
and her boyfriend all are supportive of her becoming a single parent. She is
growing frustrated with the "system" that she sees as promoting prejudice and
discrimination against single women who wish to become mothers. It is the
same system that discourages any deviations from "normal" sexual behaviors
and traditional gender roles. What should Nicole do?

SEXUAL BEHAVIOR: PERSONAL, BUT PROFOUNDLY SOCIAL

Like most of us, Nicole has made decisions regarding her sexuality based
on a personal set of values or moral guidelines. And yet, her sexual values are
based on behavioral expectations from the larger culture of which she is a part.
Thus, although many of us assume that sexual behaviors are the most personal
or private of all-human activities, they are also profoundly social. Human
sexuality obviously has a biological base, but it is also socially constructed.
Social norms - folkways, mores, and laws - shape our ideas about what is
erotic, who are appropriate sexual partners and what sexual activities are taboo
(Eitzen and Baca Zinn 1997). Various social institutions - including the
family, church, school, the media and the medical community generally
interact to reinforce "appropriate" sexual behaviors, as well as to define the
sexual behaviors that deviate from norms or otherwise constitute a social
problem.

In this chapter, we explore several types of sexual behaviors and the social
norms associated with those behaviors. Eitzen and Baca Zinn (1997:11)
define one type of social violation of the values expressed by the fertility
Clinic represents this type of social problem. In addition, Coleman and
Cressey (1993:2) note a related type of social problem: "when there is a
sizable difference between the ideals of a society and its actual achievements."
The fact that many people, like Nicole, have new standards of behavior that
are widely shared, but differ from some "ideals" of the larger society,
represents the second type of social problem.

Most of the topics in this chapter illustrate the pervasiveness of conflicting
values within North American society. There are conflicts among the sexual
norms held by various social groups and actual behaviors of group members,

conflicts within individual relationships and even conflicts within an individual's own psyche. The conflict of values is both cause and consequence of many individual (i.e., physiological and psychological) and social problems that form around contemporary experiences of sexuality; this is especially the case for sexuality that deviates from powerfully supported norms. Some of these "problems" are reflected in Nicole's story, including premarital and extra-marital sex, sexually transmitted diseases, unplanned pregnancies and abortion, and infertility options. Other important "social problem" aspects of sexual behavior include the issues of sexual orientation (homosexuality, bisexuality, and divergent sexuality) and the commodification of sex, as illustrated by pornography and commercial sex. Solutions will not be easy to come by, but there are ideas, strategies, and programs that can reduce the amount of social harm and personal unhappiness associated with these social problems.

COMING OF AGE: TEENAGE SEXUALITY

Social norms regarding the sexual behaviors of teenagers vary in different cultures. The Marquesans in Eastern Polynesia, for example, tend to encourage premarital sexual explorations for both boys and girls beginning around ten years of age; members of this society insure proper sexual instruction by elders in the tribe and parents take pride in their children's sexual development (Knox and Schacht 1994:119). In sharp contrast, the Kenuzi Nubians living along the Nile River in Egypt strictly forbid premarital intercourse; the penalty for some females caught engaging in premarital sex has been death (p. 119)[3]. Most societies have norms against premarital sex, especially for girls, however, the negative sanctions for violating such norms are generally less severe than for Nubians.

According to Knox and Schacht (1994:119), premarital sex in the U.S. is generally tolerated, although expressions of family and community disapproval for teenage coupling are common. The negative stigma and sanctions for teenage sexuality, however, vary considerably across groups-by gender, social class, race, religiosity, and region of the country. Sexual activity among adolescents has increased since the 1970s and more than half of U.S. teens engaged in coitus in the 1990s (Rathus et al. 1997:388). Even so, there remains a double standard: teenage boys are encouraged to experiment with numerous sexual partners, whereas girls and young women are encouraged to remain virgins, at least until they are in a loving relationship or engaged to be married.

AVERAGE AGE AT FIRST INTERCOURSE

In many cultures, a person's first intercourse is considered a rite of passage and there are subtle norms about the timing of this rite. For example, Nicole's first experience of intercourse at 17 was not unusual for young women in the 1980s. For many adults, sexual intercourse first occurred after high school or while in college. However, young people are now engaging in intercourse at earlier ages, and the average age at first intercourse is 16 for girls and 15.5 for boys (Rathus, et al. 1997:389). The timing of first intercourse also varies by racial background, although the U.S. pattern suggests that young men have first intercourse earlier than young women, regardless of racial-ethnic identity. Black youth generally have intercourse earlier than their white counterparts, who generally have intercourse earlier than their Hispanic counterparts (Day 1992). By the age of 19, 86% of boys and 78% of girls in metropolitan U.S. had engaged in sexual intercourse (Zeman 1990).

There are various factors associated with premarital intercourse, including dating age: beginning to date at a younger age may increase the likelihood of progressing towards sexual intercourse (Rathus et al. 1997:389). Gender also influences premarital intercourse; for example, most (51%) of the men in a national study reported that the primary reason for their first coital experience was curiosity, or "readiness for sex," whereas the most frequent response for women was "affection for their partner," reported by 48% of the women (Michael et al. 1994: 93).

Many adolescents experience peer pressure to engage in sexual intercourse and often the pressure comes from their dating partners. For example, in a national study, 24% of the sampled women reported their first intercourse was "only" for the sake of their partners, suggesting a degree of coercion (Rathus et al. 1997) Adolescents with friends who are sexually active are more likely to engage in intercourse themselves (Coles and Stokes 1985). And yet, many young people abstain from sexual intercourse for religious or other reasons. For example, some youth groups have made contracts with themselves and their churches to abstain from sexual intercourse until marriage. Further, fears of being caught, contracting a disease or getting pregnant may also restrict the sexual behaviors of some adolescents.

TEENAGE PREGNANCY

Each year, over 1 million teenagers (15-19 years of age) in the U.S. become pregnant (Ahlburg and DeVita 1992), and most of these pregnancies (90%) are unplanned) (Hatcher et al. 1990). Unplanned teenage pregnancies may be explained, in part, by conflicting values: since "nice" girls are not supposed to plan to have sex, they have accidents instead. Though nearly 40% of teen pregnancies end in abortion (Rathus et al. 1997:391), over one-half of pregnant teenagers give birth to their baby (Ahlburg and DeVita 1992). For these teenagers, there are major life-changing consequences of having a baby. Common consequences for teenage mothers include dropping out of high school and trying to raise a child while living in poverty. Some consequences for their babies include lower birth weights and poorer health than for babies with older, financially secure parents.

There are racial differences in teenage pregnancies: Blacks are more likely than Whites to be unmarried while pregnant and are less likely than Whites to end the pregnancy by abortion. Some of the factors associated with the higher rate of births to black teenagers include earlier and higher levels of sexual activity and less frequent use of effective contraception; further, black unmarried mothers tend to experience lower social stigma than their white counterparts) (Knox and Schacht 1994:521).

Like other social problems that vary by race or ethnicity, these differences in rates of pregnancy may best be explained by socio-economic status differences. Generally, the lower the social class positions of families, the higher the rates of reported teenage pregnancy.

There are also significant international differences in the rates of teenage pregnancy. The current rate of births to teenagers in the U.S. is as much as five times higher than for other post-industrial societies in Europe (Knox and Schacht 1994:521). Research findings do not show that U.S. teens are more sexually active than their European counterparts; rather, other countries tend to provide higher levels of sex education, and contraception is generally more available to sexually active teens in Europe (Ahlburg and DeVita 1992). Again, the point is not that teens in this country are having sex more frequently than their European counterparts; the difference lies in how other societies handle information about sexuality and protection against unwanted pregnancies.

The debates about whether or not to provide contraception and how much sex education should be presented to teenagers involve a values conflict. There are opposing political and religious views between conservative and liberal factions concerning the best way to handle teenage sexuality. On the one hand, conservatives tend to believe that we would send the "wrong message" to our youth if we provide sex education and especially if we distributed contraceptives. On the other hand, liberals tend to acknowledge the European research that found sex education in the school and providing contraceptives for sexually active teens decrease the negative consequences of teenage sexuality.

Most U.S. schools are characterized by an **"evaded curriculum,"** whereby students do not receive adequate education on sexuality, teen pregnancy, the HIV/AIDs crisis and the increase of sexually transmitted diseases (STDs) among adolescents (Eitzen and Baca Zinn 1997:264) to prevent them from being trapped by uninformed choices. Consider the specific issue of providing condom machines in schools, a strategy of the "harm reduction" approach. Does this tell students that sex is permitted or even expected? Or, given the reality that a large proportion of students are at risk for pregnancy or sexually transmitted diseases, is it immoral <u>not</u> to provide access to condoms and the encouragement to engage only in "safe sex"?

SEXUALLY TRANSMITTED DISEASES

The high rates of teenage pregnancy suggest that many teenagers are engaging in sexual intercourse **without** the effective use of contraception and protection against sexually transmitted-diseases (STDs)[4]. STDs are diseases that are passed from one person to another by vaginal, oral or anal sexual activity. Records dating thousands of years ago document descriptions of sexually transmitted diseases (Coleman and Cressey 1993:291). Unlike other common, but non-sexually transmitted diseases, there is a negative social stigma attached to people who contract a STD. The fear of this stigma, which might prevent unwary sexual activity, is commonly reduced by denial - "It won't happen to me[5]." The following section will discuss contemporary STDs in two categories: common STDs, such as genital warts (in Nicole's case study), and HIV/AIDS, the most recent and feared form of STDs.

COMMON STDS

Bacterial Diseases. In recent decades, the most commonly recognized STDs have been those caused by bacteria - **syphilis** and **gonorrhea**. The agency collectively known as Centers for Disease Control (CDC) is charged with collecting data on these STDs. Each year, about 1 million cases of gonorrhea are reported, with most new cases contracted by people between the ages of 20 and 24 (Rathus et al. 1997:476). Although the incidence of syphilis (about 50,000 cases reported in 1990) is lower than for gonorrhea, the consequences of non-treatment are more severe. Possible long-term effects of syphilis include heart disease, blindness, gross confusion and in the final stages, death (p. 482). **Chlamydia** has been recently added to the list of STDs caused by bacteria; this condition is more prevalent, and usually less devastating, than either syphilis or gonorrhea, with estimates of 4 million cases annually in the U.S. (p. 483). Of further importance is the fact that chlamydia infections are very common among college students.

Viral Diseases. The viruses that are transmitted sexually include genital herpes, genital warts, and HIV. **Genital herpes** is caused by the herpes simplex virus type 2 (HSV-2). Approximately 500,000 new cases of herpes occur each year (Rathus et al. 1997:489). **Human papillomavirus (HPV)** is the cause of genital warts. This virus is extremely widespread; estimates suggest that between 20% to 30% of sexually active people in the U.S. carry HPV (p. 492). In the case of Nicole, she became infected because her partner was asymptomatic and they did not practice "safe sex." Once infected with HSV-2 or HPV, the host carries the virus for life and may pass it along to subsequent sexual partners.[6] The **Human Immunodeficiency Virus (HIV)** is a newly discovered virus that usually leads to **Acquired Immune Deficiency Syndrome (AIDS).** AIDS is the most serious and life-threatening condition that is transmitted sexually, and demands further discussion.

HIV/AIDS

The first reported case of AIDS was recorded in 1981 and the devastating effects of this disease have been followed by social epidemiologists. There have been about 175,000 reported cases of full-blown AIDS in North America; however estimates at the beginning of the 1990s suggested that up to 1.5 million people in this population are infected with HIV (Coleman and Cressey 1993:291). In 1985, national headlines revealed that Rock Hudson, a movie star with a strong, heterosexual image, was dying of AIDS. Since that time the public has been informed about other prominent figures in entertainment and sports who were infected with HIV, including Magic Johnson (who tested positive in 1991). Initially, most people erroneously thought that casual social contact would put them at risk (Zastrow 1996:363). Public fear and ignorance surrounding AIDS generated a type of hysteria among some groups. One consequence was that some parents refused to send their children to the same school with an HIV-positive child.

By the early 1990s, medical research had confirmed the patterns of transmission. In addition to sexual contact with an infected person, HIV may be transmitted by intravenous drug use (sharing equipment), by infusion with contaminated blood during transfusions, organ or tissue transplants, through donor semen for artificial insemination, and through the placenta of an infected pregnant woman to her unborn baby. Thus, HIV enters the bloodstream by way of body fluids (blood or semen) from an infected person. Worldwide, the most common means of transmission is heterosexual intercourse, though in the wealthy industrial nations, AIDS is more prevalent among gay men than among the general population. In the U.S., for example, 84% of AIDS cases in 1993 were male (Anderson 1997) and homosexual transmission is the primary mode of transmission among U.S. men. We find a different pattern for U.S. women for whom heterosexual contact and sharing drug injection equipment are the primary modes of transmission. The incidence of female cases of AIDS is on the rise; in fact, 45% of all new AIDS infections in adults worldwide have been in women (Anderson 1997:202). Consequently, the incidence of infant cases of AIDS is also on the rise. About one-third of pregnant women with HIV pass the infection to their fetus and it is also possible for an infant to be infected during breast-feeding. Most infected babies die within three years of birth (Holzman and Rinehart 1995:188).

Once in the body, HIV attacks the white blood cells (T-lymphocytes), lowering immunity and a carrier's ability to fight other diseases, and leaves the person susceptible to harmful infections, such as Kaposi's Sarcoma or pneumonia. Until recently, when an HIV-positive person came down with one of these complications, he or she was said to have AIDS (Holzman and Rinehart 1995:188). Since 1992, the Centers for Disease Control (CDC) has broadened its definition of AIDS to include anyone who is HIV positive and has a T-cell count of 200 cells per cubic millimeter of blood or less, suggesting an advanced stage of the disease. During the early stages of HIV infection, most people are asymptomatic. Even without observable symptoms, however, infected people transmit the disease during further sexual contacts. Because the HIV virus may be dormant for up to a decade after the carrier is first exposed, many people carry the disease - and infect others - without knowing that they are HIV positive. Nearly everyone who is infected with HIV eventually develops AIDS. The mortality rate for AIDS has been nearly 100%, although with medical treatments HIV-infected people are now living longer.

Unlike other contagious diseases, AIDS carries a severe stigma of shame - suggesting that those who are infected are to blame. It is typical to feel that something that is morally wrong should also be harmful, and that, in reverse, harm be evidence of wrongdoing. Some fundamentalist religious groups have claimed that the outbreak of AIDS among gay men was a form of judgment and punishment by God for what they see as immoral behavior. We do not, however, see similar claims by moral authorities that lung cancer or heart disease (both influenced by behaviors) is a punishment from heaven. Also, many victims of AIDS acquired it through blood transfusions and not as a result of sexual or drug-related behaviors. As a result of the negative stigma, most people with AIDS are additionally victimized by discrimination: they are likely to be shunned and risk losing their jobs. Some are abandoned by family members and friends, and some experience mistreatment in their contacts with the medical community.

SYMPTOMS AND TREATMENT

Although most STDs produce symptoms, such as burning urination, vaginal, or penile discharge, chancre sores or skin irritations it is of vital importance for sexually active people to know that many infected men and women are asymptomatic. Table 3.1 includes some of the symptoms associated with common STDs and the typical strategies of treatment. As with most communicable diseases, early detection and treatment of symptoms decreases the likelihood of contagion.

Table 3.1: Common Sexually Transmitted Diseases, Symptoms and Treatments.

STDs:	SYMPTOMS:*	TREATMENTS:**
BACTERIAL		
1. CHLAMYDIA	Women: vaginal discharge, painful or frequent urination, pelvic pain (most are asymptomatic) Men: penile discharge, burning or painful urination (most are asymptomatic)	Antibiotics
2. Gonorrhea	Women: vaginal discharge, minor genital irritation, pain and fever (most are asymptomatic) Men: penile discharge, burning urination	Penicillin; Antibiotics
3. Syphilis	Primary stage: painless, round chancre or sore within 2-4 weeks of infection	Penicillin
VIRAL		
1. Genital Warts	Women: appearance of painless warts on vulva, labia vagina or cervix (internal) Men: appearance of painless warts on penis, scrotum or urethra (internal)	Freezing, burning, surgical removal
2. Genital Herpes	Painful, reddish bumps that become blisters around the genitals, thighs or buttocks; fever, aches and pain	Antiviral drug; Acyclovir
3. AIDS	Initially, HIV infection is asymptomatic or mild, flu-like symptoms. AIDS symptoms-fever, weight loss, fatigue, diarrhea and opportunistic infections	Antiviral drug: AZT

* Note: for many of these condition there may be no observable symptoms, especially in the early stages of infection.
**Note: for viral diseases, there are no cures, only treatments for some of the symptoms

Associations Between STDs And Health. There are two noteworthy associations between the presence of STDs and health: infertility, especially for women, and compromised health status for infants of infected women. Chlamydia and gonorrhea may cause Pelvic Inflammatory Disease (PID), and this has been associated with infertility (Holzman and Rinehart 1995:185). HPV infection (genital warts) has been linked too higher rates of cervical cancer and possibly to infertility, as well (p.186). With regard to infant health, some of the bacterial and viral diseases may be passed from mother to newborn during delivery, as the baby passes through the birth canal (for example, with gonorrhea, chlamydia and herpes) or from the mother to fetus during pregnancy (in the case of AIDS). Further, newborns may develop additional health problems, including eye infections (in the cases of chlamydia and gonorrhea), blindness or mental retardation (with herpes), warts on the vocal cords in early adolescence (with genital warts) or death (in some cases of herpes and AIDS). In order to avoid some of these serious consequences associated with STDs those who are sexually active should use the information in Table 3.1 to guide their interpersonal behaviors.

PREVENTION STRATEGIES

There are various prevention strategies that can lower the risk of contracting a STD. At the micro or interpersonal-level of analysis, the most effective prevention strategy is abstinence; short of this, maintaining a monogamous sexual relationship with an uninfected partner is the best prevention. It's prudent to incorporate a variety of strategies to remain STD-free. Yet, notoriously, in moments of passion, many individuals do not stop to consider the risks associated with "unprotected" sex.

In addition to (1) undergoing testing before initiating a sexual relationship, (2) using latex condoms and (3) regular inspection for discharge, odor or sores, prevention involves avoidance of high risk sexual behavior.

Avoid High-Risk Sexual Behaviors. An individual's vulnerability to contracting a STD is increased by having multiple sexual partners and by not discussing and practicing "safe sex" with his/her partner(s). Some behaviors are considered of "higher risk" than heterosexual intercourse with a known partner[7]. For example, prostitutes and people who frequent prostitutes are at an increased risk for contracting a STD. Another high-risk category is intravenous drug addicts who share hypodermic needles. Because alcohol and drug use increase the likelihood of engaging in risky sexual behaviors (Rathus et al. 1997:496), remaining sober (and drug-free) may be life-saving advice for college students.

Anal penetration by a penis is considered a very high-risk behavior because tears in the anal lining are a port of entry for microorganisms entering the bloodstream. This is, in part, why homosexual males are considered a high-risk group. However, homosexual males are not the only group to engage in anal sex. During a campus HIV/STDs task force meeting I attended, one student commented that anal intercourse among young, heterosexual couples was on the increase. He provided two explanations: 1) with anal intercourse, couples engage in sexual intimacy without the risk of pregnancy, and 2) some young women believe that without vaginal coitus, they may still consider themselves a "virgin." Thus, heterosexual anal intercourse presents a risk factor, as well.

HIV prevention efforts are being made at the macro-level in the U.S., with scientists working to develop a vaccine that prevents AIDS, and with mass media and educational programs to inform people about the behavioral risks so that they may make safer choices. Some European countries and cities have decriminalized drugs (making drug trafficking less profitable) and provided clean needle exchanges for drug addicts. These strategies, like distributing condoms to sexually active youth, have not been popular in the U.S., especially among political conservatives and fundamentalist religious groups. In this values conflict, feminists and political liberals ask, which is worse - to potentially send the "wrong message" or to miss the opportunity to reduce human suffering and save lives?

PROBLEMS ASSOCIATED WITH PROCREATION

In modern, post-industrial societies like the U.S., various issues associated with procreation have become part of social discourse and are particularly tied to values conflicts, especially the attitudes (and behaviors) surrounding abortion and the medical technologies emerging to deal with infertility. Although neither of these topics are sexual behaviors per se, they both deal with potential consequences of sexual behaviors - unwanted versus desired pregnancies.

ABORTION

The purposeful termination of a pregnancy is called an induced abortion; decisions to abort usually come into play when other birth control strategies have failed. More than 1.5 million abortions are performed in the U.S each year (Rathus et al. 1997:360).

Sociodemographic information concludes that (1) nearly 90% of these abortions occur during the first trimester of pregnancy, when they are least costly and safest to the woman, and (2) nearly 80% of women who have abortions are not married (p.360). More than half (55%) of these women are in their twenties and 25% are teens between 15 and 19 years of age; many already have another child and substantial family obligations (p. 360)

A national controversy over abortions has emerged over the past decade or so, and involves a value conflict between two distinct groups, commonly referred to as "pro-choice" and "pro-life." The pro-choice movement contends that the government shouldn't interfere with a woman's right to control what happens to her own body, including terminating a pregnancy. The pro-life movement is decidedly anti-abortion and asserts that abortion is murder of an unborn child (Sagan and Dryan 1990). The moral concerns voiced by the pro-lifers concentrate on when human life begins; they believe it occurs at the moment of conception. The controversy has played out via large public marches and demonstrations and in recent years by extreme acts of violence, such as fire-bombings of abortion clinics and murder of physicians who perform abortions (Rathus et al. 1997:360).

Like other social norms, attitudes about abortion have varied across cultures and over time. In the U.S., for example, during colonial times women were permitted to terminate a pregnancy up to the "quickening" or point when the woman could feel the fetus move (Sagan and Dryan 1990). Abortion laws changed after the American Civil War, corresponding to political strategies to increase the population, and abortion was banned. In 1973, in the *Roe v. Wade* decision, the U.S. Supreme court legalized abortion during the first trimester, holding that a fetus is not a person and is not protected by the Constitution. Since 1973, most states have enacted laws that require parental consent before a minor may obtain an abortion (Carlson 1990). Even without such laws, most pregnant teenagers consult their parents before they seek an abortion.

Even though abortion is considered a "women's issue" a majority of the U.S. population -both men and women - want to keep abortion legal (Rathus et al. 1997). People from the pro-choice movement are concerned that the controversy has led to a decline in the numbers of abortion providers, and that women who seek abortions often must pass a line of pro-life picketers at most abortion clinics. The Hyde amendment, enacted by Congress in 1997, denies Medicaid funding for abortions, except to protect the women's life. Further barriers include bans on abortion by public employees or in public facilities; these barriers make it difficult for poor women to safely obtain an abortion.

The decision to have an abortion is typically a thoughtful, if not painful, one. Even women, who believe that it is the best choice under current circumstances, may respond later with remorse or sadness. Data suggest that women who have the support of their parents or male partners tend to show a more positive emotional reaction afterwards (Armsworth 1991). This was certainly true for Nicole, in the case study, who had the support of both her mother and her fiancé. Like Nicole, some women may have regrets about an earlier abortion if they later experience difficulty becoming pregnant (Rathus et al. 1997:369).

INFERTILITY AND MEDICAL TECHNOLOGIES

That medical technology has influenced attitudes and sexual behaviors is especially evident with birth control and abortion technologies. Less clear is how emerging medical technologies will influence reproduction options for individuals or couples with fertility problems. **Infertility** is defined as the failure to conceive after one year of unprotected intercourse. Current knowledge about conception is limited (Robin 1993:16) and even when problems can be identified; physicians can't always "fix" the situation. Doctors often disagree about diagnosis and treatments, and even with extensive treatments, a "favorable outcome" (that is, a pregnancy) is not guaranteed. There is not enough clinical research to suggest that these treatments are especially effective, and fertility treatments are incredibly expensive, especially considering that few insurance companies cover these costs. Also, fertility clinics are only available in major metropolitan areas.

The *Wall Street Journal* highlighted that infertility is big business, costing consumers about $2 billion a year (Robin 1993:91). Expensive tests and procedures are often necessary to treat infertility. One typology identifies three treatment levels: conservative, moderate or aggressive; these levels are based on the problems identified, the degree of treatment options available, and the level of participation of the infertility patients (p. 186). Conservative-to-moderate treatments for infertility may include drug therapies (e.g., to stimulate ovulation or the production of sperm) and surgery (e.g., laparoscopy to correct endometriosis). **Assisted Reproductive Technologies** (ARTs) are an "alphabet soup" of moderate-to-aggressive strategies (p.257). IUI stands for intrauterine insemination also called artificial insemination (AI), which places the sperm into the woman's uterus without sexual intercourse (p.259). IVF stands for in vitro fertilization, which involves fertilization of a surgically obtained egg in a glass lab dish and the implantation of a pre-embryo in the mother or surrogate mother's womb (p. 266). GIFT is gamete intra fallopian transfer and ZIFT is zygote or fertilized egg intra fallopian transfer (p. 271). A single attempt at IVF, GIFT or ZIFT may run between $5,000 and $12,000;

since these procedures are not covered by most health insurance policies, they represent choices for the middle- and upper-classes only.

Whenever we start interfering with the "natural process" by which other human beings are created a range of ethical issues and considerations are raised (Robin 1993:293). Several controversies have emerged concerning the use of donor sperm, donor eggs, host uterus, and/or surrogate mothers. For example, are current laws sufficient to protect all of the participants? What happens when a surrogate mother changes her mind and decides to keep the newborn child? What happens to the fertilized eggs that aren't implanted? And who is responsible if the resulting baby has severe deformities? Like other value conflicts discussed in this chapter, competing values between various social groups are represented, in this case, among religious fundamentalists, feminists, medical researchers, and infertile people. Further, these controversies cut across various social institutions, including the family, the church, medicine, and politics. Thus, although infertility problems are experienced on the micro-, or interpersonal-level, the influence of macro-level constraints and opportunities remains.

HOMOSEXUALITY: SEXUAL ORIENTATION OR SEXUAL PREFERENCE?

Knox and Schacht (1994:248) define homosexuality as "the predominance of cognitive, emotional and sexual attraction to those of the same sex." Thus, the primary distinguishing factors of sexual orientation are "cognitions (thoughts or fantasies), emotions (feelings) and sexual attraction (desire to touch/enjoy physically)." Of course, preferred sexual behaviors also delineate a person's orientation.

There is a continuing debate about how homosexuality should be defined and labeled; both "sexual orientation" and "sexual preference" are terms used to describe homosexuality. Whereas sexual preference implies a sense of choice regarding the subjects of one's sexual attractions, sexual orientation implies a characteristic that is innate and not changeable. This debate is tied to the larger questions of nature vs. nurture, and the focus becomes, which is relatively more important in determining the origins of homosexuality - biology or the social environment? Although the theory that homosexuality is biologically based is receiving growing support in the scientific community, the genetic arguments are not conclusive (Eitzen and Baca Zinn 1997:297). It is probably more accurate to acknowledge that there is an interaction of both genetic and environmental factors.

There are policy implications to each of these approaches. If we assume that homosexuality is a choice, then opponents may feel justified in punishing or forcing deviants of the norm of heterosexuality to change. If we assume that homosexuality is not chosen, but is an illness, then opponents may feel justified in "treating" the condition. And if we argue that homosexuality is innate, then opponents may either consider homosexuality an acceptable deviation or argue for genetic control of the condition. According to Eitzen and Baca Zinn (1997:296), most homosexuals define sexuality in terms of sexual orientation, whereas heterosexuals tend to view homosexuality as a matter of sexual preference. Most of the gays and lesbians I have encountered in university settings ask: "why would anyone choose this orientation and lifestyle, given the extremely negative stigma associated with this status?"

PREVALENCE OF HOMOSEXUALITY

It is difficult to estimate the prevalence of homosexuality. Given the negative stigma attached to this status, many who are predominantly or exclusively homosexual have not come "out of the closet" or are not willing to disclose this type of information to researchers. Based on earlier research (e.g., Kinsey 1948), about 10% of the population were estimated to be predominantly or exclusively homosexual. Current estimates generally find slightly lower percents of gay and lesbian people. For example, Janus and Janus' (1983) longitudinal study found that 9% of men and 5% of women may be considered homosexual in orientation. Diamond's (1993) cross-cultural study found that only 5% of men and 3% of women have engaged in homosexual experiences at least once since adolescence, and that fewer people report a bisexual orientation than a homosexual one.

A CONTINUUM OR SEPARATE DIMENSIONS?

Sexologists have suggested that sexual orientation may be understood as a continuum; Kinsey's (1953) rating scale assumes that the single dimension of sexuality may be viewed on a continuum from exclusively heterosexual to exclusively homosexual.

This seven-point scale classifies people according to their sexual behavior and the magnitude of their sexual attractions to and experience with members of their own or the other sex. A person who rates a "0," or is exclusively heterosexual; has fantasies, feelings and desires for members of the opposite sex only, and has engaged in heterosexual behaviors only; most of the people Kinsey (1953) surveyed report this rating. Likewise, a person who rates a "6" may be considered exclusively homosexual in cognitions, emotions, sexual attractions and sexual behaviors. People could also self-report between 1-5, reflecting that they have had some sexual fantasies, feelings or desires for members of the same sex, and for the higher scores, that they have acted on those desires.

An alternate view is that hetero-erotic interests and homo-erotic interests are separate, independent dimensions (Storms 1980). Thus, an individual may be low or high on both dimensions at the same time. Although most people are high on one dimension (with predominantly homosexual or heterosexual interests), a bisexual person or transsexual may be high on both dimensions. A person low on both dimensions may be considered relatively asexual.

HOMOPHOBIA

Rathus et al. (1997:273) define homophobia as a "cluster of negative attitudes and feelings toward gay people, including intolerance, hatred and fear." Thus, homophobia, which has a long tradition in western society, includes a loathing of homosexual behaviors and an intolerance of their lifestyles. The expression of homophobia may take a variety of forms, such as the use of derogatory names (e.g., "queer" or "dyke"), the telling of disparaging jokes, and discrimination against gays and lesbians in housing or employment opportunities.

Eitzen and Baca Zinn (1997:315) state that "variance from the societal norm of heterosexuality is not a social problem; the societal response to it is." In other words, homosexuality is not, in itself a social problem, but the reactions of those who feel entitled to demean or punish gays and lesbians are. Such reactions include the public expression of prejudiced attitudes or stereotyped images in the media, discrimination against homosexuals in the workplace, and hate crimes in the community.

Anderson (1997:90) suggests that interpersonal relationships are influenced by heterosexism, or "the institutionalized set of behaviors and beliefs that presume heterosexuality to be the only acceptable form of sexual expression." For example, heterosexual behaviors, such as a couple holding hands or kissing in public, and symbols of heterosexuality, such as wedding rings and family pictures on one's desk, are proudly displayed. On the other hand, a heterosexist system negatively sanctions those who act or are presumed to be homosexual. For example, most employee health care plans do not include a provision for spouse equivalents or significant others, as they do for married couples. And yet, over one-third (36%) of the public think that homosexual relations between consenting adults should be legal (Anderson 1997:83). Thus, even in the social context of homophobia and heterosexism, many people seem to take the attitude "Live and let live." Of the general population who favor legal rights for homosexuals, women are more supportive than are men, and Whites are slightly more supportive than are Blacks and Latinos (p. 83).

SEX FOR SALE: PORNOGRAPHY AND PROSTITUTION

In a capitalist economy, various forms of sex become commodities to be bought and sold. Some of these sexual commodities are sold in the open market and some are restricted to the black market or underground economy. The following discussion is organized around two types of sex for sale: pornography and prostitution.

PORNOGRAPHY

Pornography has been defined as written or visual material that is sexually explicit and produced for the purpose of eliciting or enhancing sexual arousal; in other words, it has prurient intent (Rathus et al. 1997: 612). It is big business, with nearly 20 million pornographic magazines sold each month (p. 611); however, this business is controversial. Rarely are people "neutral" about the subject[9]. Although the viewing of pornography appears to be a popular pursuit for a segment of the U.S. population, there are many opponents of pornography.

Both fundamentalist religious groups and feminists have been united in the effort to control the escalation of pornography in the U.S. Although these two groups represent different values with regard to women's rights, they both align against commercial efforts to produce and distribute pornography. Fundamentalists tend to fear the effects of such material on family values and personal morality, whereas feminists tend to oppose the sexual objectification of women, the effects of viewing pornography on violence against women, and the exploitation of sex workers. On the other hand, proponents of pornography defend it as a first amendment right of free expression and oppose efforts that would censure its production or distribution. Thus, efforts to restrict pornography have been met with resistance by both producers and consumers of this commodity, who feel that their constitutional rights are being threatened.

Throughout much of human history - and prehistoric times - people have sought to depict and comment on human sexuality (Scarpitti et al. 1997:268). Depictions of sexuality have ranged from paleolithic fertility images, to the Kama Sutra and to contemporary advertisements in the media (p. 268). However, some groups believe that recent pornography has reached new levels of degradation of women and children; further, it has been associated with increased rates of violence against women (p.268). The clash of values surrounding pornography has resulted in extensive public debate with political implications. This debate raises questions about "the definitions of obscenity, the relationship of pornography to violence, and the degradation of women in the manufacture of pornography" (p.268). Each of these questions will be briefly addressed.

Obscenity. Historically, U.S. laws have been concerned about "obscenity" rather than pornography, per se (Scarpitti et al. 1997)[10]. In 1957, the U.S. Supreme Court established guidelines concerning **obscenity**: material is considered obscene and subject to legal action if "to the average person, applying contemporary community standards, the dominant theme of the material taken as a whole appeals to prurient interest" (p. 269), and is totally without socially redeeming value[11]. However, these guidelines are too vague to end controversy; what may be a violation of "contemporary community standards" in a small, Midwestern town may not be in Los Angeles or New York City. And some may argue that "soft" pornography has cathartic value.

Congress created the Commission on Obscenity and Pornography in the 1960s to examine the effects of pornography. The Commission, relying on research of the day, was unable to find clear evidence that pornography led to violent crimes or sexual offenses; thus, it was deemed essentially harmless (Rathus et al. 1997:616). Given this conclusion, the Commission recommended that legislation should not interfere with the rights of adults who wish to participate in this industry. The issue, however, did not go away. Two decades later, President Reagan appointed a federal Commission on Pornography to reexamine the effects of pornography[12].

The Meese Commission's 1986 report acknowledged a substantial increase in the proliferation of violent pornography since the earlier Commission's report and pornography that involves children (Scarpitti et al. 1997:269). Recent research had confirmed a causal relationship between certain types of pornography and acts of sexual violence against women (p.269). The panel presented extensive suggestions for curbing the availability of pornography and making child pornography a felony[13]. Thus, the panel's interpretation of the 1957 ruling by the Supreme Court was that the first amendment does not protect obscene material and that judges may apply community standards to determine what is or is not obscene.

Research On The Effects Of Pornography. The Meese Commission's report generated academic critique by two researchers who argued the findings were overgeneralized and that exposure to nonviolent, sexually explicit materials is not statistically associated with sexual aggression (Donnerstein and Linz 1987). In their research, Donnerstein and Linz (1987) found that exposure to **violent** pornography does increase male aggression against females and influences men to be more accepting of the use of violence in interpersonal relationships; further, men who view violent pornography tend to be more accepting of rape myths and less sensitive to women who are victims of rape. They concluded that it is the viewing of violence, and not of sexually explicit materials, that leads to increased violence in male subjects.

According to Zastrow (1996:167), frequent exposure to pornographic materials will have an effect on viewers; to argue otherwise would be asserting that experience does not affect human development. Further, the viewing of violent pornography appears to have a "triggering effect," as viewers display more aggressive attitudes and behaviors compared to non-viewers (p 169). Research has found that viewing violent rape scenes where the woman is portrayed as enjoying or becoming "aroused" by the rape increases male viewers' acceptance of rape myths and violence against women (Hyde 1990:511). Thus, the inclusion of this common theme in pornography - that women enjoy being overpowered sexually - may be socially irresponsible, with dangerous interpersonal consequences.

When Canadian serial killer Paul Bernardo was arrested on multiple rape and murder charges, a police search of his home found a library of pornography, some of which came close to describing Bernardo's behavior. Police have often reported finding such collections in the homes of sex offenders of varying kinds. At the most extreme end of violent pornography are "snuff" films, appearing in the mid-1970s, where pornographic actresses were actually murdered during the production of the sex scenes (Zastrow 1996).

The Degradation Of Women. Even nonviolent pornography typically depicts women in "degrading dehumanizing roles - as sexually promiscuous, insatiable and subservient" (Rathus et al. 1997:618). Although research on the effect of viewing nonviolent pornography on violence against women is not conclusive, studies have found that male viewers' attitudes towards women become less sensitive and more callous (p.619). Do such pornographic portrayals of women reinforce negative stereotypes of women as sex objects?

The pornographic depiction of a woman having sex with numerous men in a short period of time is an example of degrading sex (Coleman and Cressey 1993:295). Repeated exposure to nonviolent pornography that projects casual sexual encounters between strangers has been found to loosen traditional values concerning family obligations and responsibilities (Zillmann 1989). This raises concerns about how men who regularly use pornography view women both their partners (in particular) and women in general.

PROSTITUTION

Prostitution involves accepting money in exchange for impersonal sexual activities. Most prostitutes throughout history have been women. Although it is socially normative to ostracize prostitutes, in some cultures and at some points in time they have been held in high esteem. And yet, even with high status, these were women whom respectable men didn't marry. According to Scarpitti et al. (1997:272), prostitutes were an integral part of U. S. history, especially west of the Mississippi River during the second half of the 19th century[14]. Most frontier prostitutes were poor white women who were engaged in "the world's oldest profession" out of economic necessity, servicing the large number of single men (p.272). Some prostitutes sought economic security through marriage; however, the men who married prostitutes were "among the most disreputable on the frontier" (p.273) and rarely brought these women honor or security.

Although prostitution was illegal one hundred years ago, it was still widespread in North America (Coleman and Cressey 1993:293). Most prostitutes worked in brothels concentrated in the "red-light" districts of larger cities and were rarely disturbed by police, who were paid by "Madams" to leave their "girls" alone. In the early part of the 20th century, this arrangement was altered by a "wave of vice crusades" (p. 294). The YMCA, for example, mounted a successful campaign to close down most of the red-light districts. However, an unintentional consequence of these actions was an increase in the number of "streetwalkers," who pose a more serious social problem than do "house girls" (p.294).[15]

Prostitution declined dramatically in the second half of the 20th century. One sociological explanation is that as social norms favoring sexual freedom have increased, the demand for prostitution has decreased. For example, the stigma attached to premarital sexual relations has been greatly reduced; so more young men are having their first sexual experience with girlfriends rather than with prostitutes. Further, since there are greater educational opportunities and more employment options available to young women now, fewer enter the sex trade. A recent explanation for the decrease in prostitution has been the fear of contracting AIDS. Streetwalkers generally service numerous clients every day, some of which refuse to wear condoms, and these practices increase the likelihood of HIV transmission.

Even with decreasing numbers, approximately 500,000 prostitutes currently work in the U.S. (Scarpitti et al. 1997:274). Although most prostitutes are female, the proportion of males arrested for prostitution has increased. In 1994, for example, there were 86,816 arrests for prostitution and nearly 39% of those arrested were male (p.274). This may be explained, in part, as an increase in the visibility of homosexual prostitution and efforts to control it (p.274). Further, arrest rates vary by race; while only 40% of street prostitutes are women of color, they are more likely than their white counterparts to be arrested and jailed for prostitution (Scarpitti et al. 1997:274). In contrast, the clients of female prostitutes, referred to as "johns" or "tricks," are typically white middle-class, middle-aged men. Unless caught in the act, as popular actor Hugh Grant recently was, the "johns" are not arrested. According to the "sexual politics" explanation, prostitution is primarily a crime where the person who offers to deliver sexual services is targeted for arrest, while the person who is purchasing the illegal services is not; also, where the gender, sexual orientation, race, and social class status of the prostitute influences arrest rates (Anderson 1997).

Female prostitutes are usually classified according to the settings, in which they work, and include streetwalkers, brothel or "house" prostitutes, and call girls. The following paragraphs provide a brief description of each type, along with a profile of male prostitutes.

Streetwalkers. Most prostitutes are streetwalkers, located in the lowest strata of the prostitution hierarchy. They earn the smallest incomes and run the highest risks for abuse by customers and the male pimps who serve as their agents. Although some pimps provide streetwalkers with "protection," jail bail and accommodations, they charge a very high premium for their services, usually more than 90% (Rathus et al. 1997:603). Some streetwalkers literally walk the streets or cruise bars for local "tricks"; the latter often have to pay bartenders a percent of their take. Other streetwalkers work out of hotels and at conventions, where most of the "tricks" are from out-of-town.

The careers of streetwalkers tend to be short. The lifestyle is dangerous and is associated with drugs, physical abuse, STDs, and suicide. Since most "tricks" prefer younger prostitutes, those who are older or less attractive have less bargaining power or may be forced to engage in sex with clients who are clearly dangerous. In part because of their visibility, streetwalkers run the highest risks for arrest by the police.

Brothel Or "House" Prostitutes. Many of my students believe that prostitution is illegal in the U.S., and it is against the law **except** in some Nevada counties where there are state-licensed brothels (Rathus et al. 1997:600). Most women in this type of prostitution, however, work in "massage" parlors or for an escort service (p.603). Although most massage parlors and licensed masseuses/masseurs are legitimate, some parlors serve as "fronts" for prostitution rings. "Escort" services are listed in the telephone directory of every major U.S. city and present themselves as legitimate business enterprises. Prostitutes who work for escort companies are generally better educated and come from middle-class backgrounds. With regard to social status, these prostitutes fall in the middle - they do not make as much money as call girls, but their circumstances are not as degrading as are those of streetwalkers.

Call Girls. These women (not "girls") occupy the highest status of female prostitution and charge the most for their services. They arrange for customers by telephone; the "call' refers both to telephoning and to being "on call" (Rathus et al. 1997:605). Further, these women demand more money because they are usually very attractive and well educated. In addition to providing sex, call girls are often expected to be charming and engaging; they work to make the client feel attractive and important. Although most work out of their apartments and do not split their incomes with a pimp, brothel or massage parlor, they often incur expenses for clothes, furnishings, answering services and laundry services, and they sometimes pay bribes to doormen in order to protect their cover (p.605).

Myths about the glamorous lives of call girls abound (Scarpitti et al. 1997:274). The box office hit *Pretty Woman,* for example, depicts a beautiful prostitute who is rescued by a rich, handsome and caring man. Similar myths surround Heidi Fleiss, the "Hollywood Madam" who has made millions of dollars running a prostitute service exclusively for the rich and famous (p.274). The reality for most, however, is far from these portrayals. Most prostitutes have a history of sexual and/or physical abuse (as a child) and are currently living in poverty. The typical biography is one of family abuse and instability. They are young women with children, who "drift" into this lifestyle after a series of causal sexual relationships. Since many are poor, they "choose" prostitution as a means of economic survival (p.274).

Male Prostitutes. Some male prostitutes provide sexual services to female clients; however, most of their business is solicited by other men (Coleman and Cressey 1993:293). Even so, many of these men are not gay; they are engaged in survival sex. Male prostitutes may be classified according to the clients they service. Those who service gay men are called "hustlers" while their patrons are called "scores" (Rathus et al. 1997). The few male prostitutes, who service female clients are called "gigolos" and their clients are typically older, divorced or widowed women who are financially secure.

There are similarities between men and women in this business: like female prostitutes, most male prostitutes come from troubled families and are survivors of sexual abuse. Also, the primary motive for both male and female prostitution is the same - money. Finally, like their female counterparts, many male prostitutes in the U.S. and Canada are initiated as teenage runaways. Since most teen prostitutes were sexually abused as children, this factor "pushes" them out of the home and into the streets. Teenage runaways may engage in survival sex; given their homelessness, young age, and limited work skills, many find few viable alternatives to prostitution (Rathus et al. 1997:606).

Prostitution As A Social Problem. From a religious perspective, prostitution is immoral; it violates norms of sexual monogamy and fidelity in marriage and encourages sex for recreation, rather than for procreation. From a public health perspective, street prostitution facilitates the spread of STDs and is associated with drug addiction and violence. From a police perspective, prostitution commands resources and is associated with other types of crime (including organized crime). From a community perspective, open prostitution is a social problem because it negatively affects the value of housing and the peace and safety of their streets. Is prostitution anything but a social problem?

Because relationships with prostitutes are defined by the participants as commercial, they do not threaten family breakup the way that extramarital sex between social equals can. Davis (1937, citation in Zastrow 1996:166) took the position that prostitution is functional for society. Here's how his argument went: single, divorced and widowed men have no socially approved sexual outlet. Some married men are members of the armed forces or are salesmen - both occupations that require extended periods away from home - or report unfulfilled sexual relations with their wives and the desire for sexual variety[16].   Davis neglected to attend to the distinctions of prostitution, however, such as its negative personal and social consequences.

Prostitutes often argue that they are performing "social work" and that making a living in some of the low-wage jobs that are "legitimate" would be even more demeaning.   There is a small social movement to decriminalize adult prostitution comprised, in part, by organized groups of prostitutes, such as COYOTE (Cast Out Your Old Tired Ethics), established in San Francisco in 1972 and PONY (Prostitutes of New York).   Proponents claim that decriminalizing prostitution would save public resources: in San Francisco, for example each arrest of a prostitute costs the city more than $1000 and the prostitutes are usually back on the street by the next night (Kornbulm and Julian 1992).   Legalization also has its proponents: this would make prostitutes' income taxable, providing a new source of tax revenue, and reduce the involvement of organized crime.   For example, a 1971 Nevada statue provided the right for counties to license houses of prostitution; licensing fees provide a source of revenue for the state government.   Prostitutes are required to obtain regular medical exams, which have reduced the spread of STDs, and overall, the system in Nevada appears to be working well.   Still, there is substantial opposition to legalizing prostitution and the values conflict is not likely to be resolved quickly.   According to Zastrow (1996:162), two current trends surrounding prostitution are noteworthy: (1) a decline in the number of full-time and an increase in the number of part-time prostitutes and (2) advertising for prostitution services seems to be more conspicuous.   The first trend is very hard to document, given this occupation's illegal status.   Typical examples of the second trend include "escort" listings in U.S. phone books and advertisements in magazines.   An extreme example has been observed in international publications that advertise the availability of children, who are ostensibly AIDS-free, for sex.   These trends require further sociological attention.

THE SEXUAL REVOLUTION AND SEXUAL POLITICS

The final section of this chapter explores the sexual revolution of the 1960s and some of its remaining ideological traces.   Also, the explanatory framework of sexual politics is presented in order to illuminate some of the causes and consequences of contemporary sexual attitudes and behaviors.

THE SEXUAL REVOLUTION

Various historical influences, including Judeo-Christian values, the Puritan influence and rigid sexual codes dating back to the Victorian period have generally functioned to repress sexual expression in modern times (Scarpitti et al. 1997:251; Zastrow 1996:179).   Over the past few decades, however, our society has witnessed a "revolution" in sexual values and behaviors. Beginning in the 1960s, mainstream attitudes began to reflect an increase in premarital and extramarital sexual activities.   In the 1970s, sexual experimentation was encouraged by the media.   This, combined with greater availability of effective birth control technology, contributed to the view of sex as a recreational activity, rather than strictly for procreation.

In the 1980s, there was substantial publicity and growing concern about sexually transmitted diseases, especially the new epidemics of genital herpes and AIDS (Zastrow 1996:148). Concerns about increasing rates of teenage pregnancy, abortion, and divorce emerged and specific solutions were voiced by members of the "moral majority." By the early 1990s, many people were reconsidering the attitudes and behaviors encouraged by the sexual revolution. For example, some tenets, such as recreational sex without consequences, have been rejected and replaced with more conservative attitudes (p. 148). The sexually permissive contexts of the 1970s have been altered by a current emphasis on long-term relationships and fewer sexual partners. This has resulted in an increasing instance of serial monogamy - one partner at a time, but many partners over a person's lifetime.

On the other hand, examples of socially permissive attitudes toward sexuality remain; nudity is displayed more frequently and sexual topics are explored more fully now, in both print and visual media, than in the past. Partial nudity and sexual appeal is frequently used by advertisers to sell products, from designer jeans to soft drinks. Previously, this strategy had been reserved for automobile and beer commercials targeting adult male consumers. With regard to media coverage of sexual topics, daytime television is filled with talk shows and people disclosing information about their sexual relationships. And the periodical stands are full of articles about how to improve one's sex life.

Premarital Sex And Sexual Fidelity. More than half of the U.S. public approves of premarital sexual relations (Zastrow 1996:258). Of those who don't approve, women are more likely than men and the old are more likely than the young to think that premarital sex is wrong (Anderson 1997). The negative stigma previously attached to women who have engaged in premarital sex has lessened considerably; they are no longer considered "unfit" for marriage (Zastrow 1996:149). Although traces of the double standard of sexuality for men and women still remain, young women in serious relationships are less likely to abstain because of social pressures. Recent studies of young adults have found that over 70% of young women and over 80% of young men engage in sexual intercourse prior to marriage (p.258). Nevertheless, current norms do not suggest that promiscuity is acceptable, especially in the age of AIDS.

Generally speaking, there is a more supportive social environment for premarital sex than there is for extramarital sexual activities. Though a recent study found that approximately 25% of married people have had extramarital affairs (Laumann et al. 1994), and the likelihood of infidelity increases with age, infidelity, as Nicole's case study suggests, is correlated with marital disruption. Although having an extramarital affair does not cause divorce, it may be a significant contributing factor.

Traditional Gender Roles. Even with more permissive social attitudes, sexuality continues to be patterned by traditional gender roles and definitions of masculinity and femininity. For example, female sexuality is generally defined as passive, whereas male sexuality is defined in terms of achievement and performance (Anderson 1997:81). Further, men are stereotyped as having a stronger sex drive than women, while women are stereotyped as needing a man's penis for sexual arousal and orgasm (also known as phallocentric thinking). When women's sexuality is viewed by men as out of control, women have been labeled as witches, whores or lesbians, and their sexuality is depicted as evil and dangerous (Anderson 1997:81). Again, cultural assumptions about gender influence social attitudes toward sexuality.

SEXUAL POLITICS

A final type of social problem to be explored is "societally induced conditions that cause psychic and material suffering for any segment of the population" (Eitzen and Baca Zinn 1997:11). In the context of sexual behaviors, this includes the conditions of patriarchy or male dominance, sexism and racism. Anderson (1997:14) described the presence of a "**matrix of domination**," whereby the "particular configuration of race, class, and gender relations in society is such that together they establish an interlocking system of domination." This system causes suffering for significant segments of the population, especially racial-ethnic minorities, the poor, and women.

The matrix of domination is closely tied to sexual politics, whereby "sexuality and power are linked through the intersection of race, class and gender oppression" (Anderson 1997:84). Numerous examples of sexual politics have been presented throughout this chapter; it was noted that women, not men, are typically arrested for prostitution. Black streetwalkers are targeted more than are white streetwalkers by the police. Poor and working-class women are more likely to have to "sell" their sexuality in the open market (as prostitutes or pornography models) than are middle-class or elite women (p.80). In these examples, sexual politics are enacted through the systematic domination and social control of women, racial-ethnic minorities, and the poor.

White men accused of rape are less likely than black men to be prosecuted; even when they are convicted, white men serve shorter sentences than do black men convicted of rape (Anderson 1997:84). Despite laws and organizational policies that make sexual harassment illegal, many businesses and universities have "protected" their senior white male employees who have sexually harassed female workers or students (Anderson 1997:84). When a wealthy, white woman is raped, it is taken more seriously by the authorities than when a poor, black woman is raped. A final example of sexual politics is that white middle-class married couples are more likely to receive infertility therapies than are white working class single women. In all of these examples, sexual politics are enacted through the advantages of a more powered social group, often at the expense of a less powerful one.

CONCLUDING COMMENTS

Most young adults go through the process of developing a personal code of sexual behaviors. Although we are influenced by social norms (via the various agents of socialization), and by institutional constraints or opportunities, we make a series of personal choices in response to our unique biographies. As for Nicole's case study, it may be helpful to incorporate C. W. Mills' (1959) "sociological imagination"; that is, an ability to see the interplay between biography (or personal troubles) and history (or social problems). Many of the sexual situations that Nicole experienced as "personal" were in fact, influenced by social structures. For Mills, the task of sociology was "to understand the institutional arrangements of society and their effect on the social problems we face" (Scarpitti et al. 1997:3).

Social problems associated with sexuality, including teenage pregnancy, pornography and abortion, are "debated with intensity because they tap sexual value systems that are contested areas of public opinion" (Anderson 1997:84); these values conflicts show "the extent to which sexual meaning systems are socially constructed; they are not merely inherent in human nature." Although sexuality is often experienced as physical pleasure, it is as much a social construction as are other features of identity (Anderson 1997).

Social problems are conditions originating in the structure of social institutions that have a negative effect on individual and group well being (Scarpitti et al. 1997:4). Since many of the social problems discussed in this chapter have their origins in the conditions of society, they may be altered through social policy and social change. Given that human sexuality is in large part socially constructed, social problems associated with sexuality must be addressed at both the micro- and macro-levels, and solutions must emphasize changing the social conditions from which the problems emerged.

SUMMARY

1. Human sexuality has a biological base, but is also socially constructed because social norms (folkways, mores, and laws) shape our ideas about what is erotic, who are appropriate sexual partners, and what sexual activities are taboo.
2. Social norms regarding the sexual behaviors of teenagers vary in different cultures.
3. Various factors are associated with premarital intercourse including dating age, gender, and peer pressure.
4. The debates about whether or not to provide contraception and how much sex education should be presented to teenagers involve a value conflict.
5. STDs are diseases that are passed from one person to another by vaginal, oral, or anal sexual activity.
6. Prevention strategies that can reduce the risk of STDs
7. In modern, post-industrial societies like the U.S., various issues associated with procreation have become part of social discourse and are particularly tied to value conflicts, especially abortion and the medical technologies emerging to deal with infertility.
8. The decision to have an abortion is typically a thoughtful, if not painful one
9. Although infertility problems are experienced on the micro- or interpersonal-level, the influence or macro-level constraints and opportunities remain.
10. Sexologists have suggested that sexual orientation may be understood on a continuum from exclusively heterosexual to exclusively homosexual (Kinsey) or as separate dimensions, with predominately hetero-erotic or homo-erotic interests (Storms).
11. Homophobia, a cluster of negative attitudes and feelings toward gay people, has a long tradition in western society; yet, over one-third of the public think that homosexual relations between consenting adults should be legal.
12. The clash of values surrounding pornography has resulted in extensive public debate with political implications. Research indicates that the inclusion of the theme that women enjoy being overpowered sexually may be socially irresponsible with dangerous interpersonal consequences.
13. Prostitution has dramatically declined in the last half of the 20th century. Explanations range from norms favoring sexual freedom to fear of contracting AIDS.
14. The sexually permissive context of the 1970s has been altered by a current emphasis on long-term relationships and fewer sexual partners. On the other hand, examples of socially permissive attitudes towards sexuality remain exemplified by the more frequent displays of nudity and exploration of sexual topics in the media.

15. Sexual politics are enacted through the advantages of a more powerful social group, often at the expense of a less powerful one.

ENDNOTES

[1]This occurs when the endometrial cells lining the uterus implant themselves on abdominal organs, instead of exiting the body as menstrual blood.

[2]Like many women, Nicole feels more comfortable talking with another woman about her health problems. However, in most communities, female gynecologists are simply not available: either there are none present or they tend to carry full patient loads and rarely accept new patients.

[3]Futher, the Nubians practice female genital mutilation, including sewing up the vagina of young girls (Knox and Schacht 1994).

[4]Short of abstinence, the proper and consistent use of latex condoms is probably the single most important barrier to contracting an STD (Rathus et al. 1997).

[5]Furthermore, the fear of this stigma may interfere with timely and appropriate treatment that would reduce the rates of transmission.

[6]When considering viruses, it is important to remember that modem medicine has not yet found a cure for them, though some viruses may be treated.

[7]However, this may be misleading because heterosexual intercourse with a known partner, in and of itself, is **not** protection against STD transmission. For protection, partners must incorporate "sex safe," practices, such as the use of a condom, that prohibit the exchange of body fluids.

[8]Pornography's prurient intent has been contrasted to that of erotica or books and pictures that have to do with sexual love; erotica includes sexual materials that are artistically produced or are motivated by artistic, rather than prurient, intent (Rathus et al. 1997:612).

[9]For example, I am personally offended by the euphemism "adult" or "mature" to describe pornography; most of the popular magazines, such as *Playboy* or *Penthouse,* seem "adolescent" and sexually "immature" to me.

[10]For example, federal laws were enacted during the 19th century to prohibit the transportation of obscene publications and their dissemination through the U.S. mail (Scarpitti et al. 1997:269). Obscene materials are considered offensive to accepted standards of decency or modesty.

[11]The Supreme Court has had a difficult time defining obscenity and determining applications that do not jeopardize the Bill of Right's guarantee of free speech (Rathus et al.1997:612).

[12]This commission was headed by then Attorney General Edwin Meese and became known as the Meese Commission.

[13]In fact, 92 recommendations were issued, including tighter enforcement of obscenity laws and greater restrictions applied to the dissemination of pornography.

[14]In some of those communities' prostitutes performed important non-sexual functions, such as nursing the sick and other charity work.

[15]Such problems may include violence by customers and pimps, the intrusion of sex and drugs into residential communities, condoms left where children play, increased noise levels and an exodus of respectable homeowners or businesses from the areas where streetwalkers are picked up.

[16]According to Davis' (1937) logic, without prostitution, many more men would leave their marriages to seek sexual satisfaction and variety; as the number of divorces increased, there wouldn't be an effective means of socializing children, and society would collapse.

[17]These topics were addressed under the headings "Homosexuality: Sexual Orientation or Sexual Preference?" and "Sex for Sale: Pornography and Prostitution."

[18]However, studies of rapists in prison are not representative, since less than 4% of rapists are caught and eventually imprisoned (Gibbs 1991).

[19]According to Powell (1991), if this doesn't stop a persistent harasser, victims should file a formal complaint with their organization and/or seek legal remedies to the problem.

REFERENCES

Ahlburg, D. A and C. J. DeVita 1992. "New Realities of the American Family" *Population Bulletin.* 47:1-44.

Anderson, Margaret L. 1997. *Thinking About Women: Sociological Perspectives on Sex and Gender.* Boston: Allyn and Bacon.

Armsworth, M.W. 1991. "Psychological Response to Abortion." *Journal of Counseling and Development.* 69:377-379.

Burgess, A. W., and L. L. Holmstrom 1974. "Rape Trauma Syndrome." *American Journal of psychiatry.* 131:981-986.

Calhoun, K. S., and B. M. Atkeson 1991. *Treatment of Rape Victims: Facilitating Social Adjustment.* New York: Pergamon Press.

Carlson, M. 1990. "Abortion's Hardest Cases." *Time,* July 9:22-26.

Coleman, James William and Donald R. Cressy 1993. *Social Problems, fifth* ed. New York: Harper Collins College Publishers.

Coles, R. and G. Stokes 1985. *Sex and the American Teenager.* New York: Harper and Row.

Day, R. D. 1992. "The Transition to First Intercourse Among Racially and Culturally Diverse Youth." *Journal of Marriage and the Family.* 54: 749-164.

Diamond Milton 1993. "Homosexuality and Bisexuality in Different Populations." *Archives of Sexual Behavior.* 22: 291-310.

Donnerstein, E. J., and D. G. Linz 1987. *The Question of Pornography.* New York: The Free Press.

Eitzen, D. Stanley and Maxine Baca Zinn 1997. *Social Problems,* 7[th]ed. Boston: Allyn and Bacon.

Finkelhor, David 1984. *Child Sexual Abuse.* New York: Free Press.

Gibbs, N. 1991. "When is it Rape?" *Time,* June 3:48-54.

Groth, A. N. and H. J. Birnbaum 1979. *Men Who Rape: The Psychology of the Offender.* New York: Plenum.

Groth, A. Nicholas 1982. "The Incest Offender." In Suzanne M. Sgroi, ed., *Intervention in Child Sexual Abuse.* Lexington, MA: Lexington Books.

Holzman, Gerald H. and Rebecca D. Rinehart, eds. 1995. *Planning for Pregnancy, Birth, and Beyond,* second edition. The American College of Obstetricians and Gynecologists.

Hyde, Janet S. 1990. *Understanding Human Sexuality,* 4th ed. New York: McGraw Hill.

Janus, Samuel S. and Cynthia L. Janus 1993. *The Janus Report on Sexual Behavior.* New York: John Wiley.

Kinsey, A. C., et al. 1948. *Sexual Behavior in the Human Male.* Philadelphia: W. B. Saunders Co.

Kinsey, A. C., et al. 1953. *Sexual Behavior in the Human Female.* Philadelphia: W. B. Saunders Co.

Knox, David and Caroline Schacht 1994. *Choices in Relationships: An Introduction to Marriage and the Family.* Fourth ed. St. Paul: West Publishing Co.

Kombulm, William and Joseph Julian 1992. *Social Problems* 7[th]ed. Englewood Cliffs, NJ: Prentice-Hall.

Laumann, E.O., et al. 1994. *The Social Organization of Sexuality: Sexual Practices in the United States.* Chicago: University of Chicago Press.

Michael R. T., et al. 1994. *Sex in America: A Definitive Survey.* Boston: Little, Brown.

Powell, E. 1991. *Talking Back to Sexual Pressure.* Minneapolis: CompCare Publications.

Rathus, Spencer A., Jeffrey S. Nevid, and Lois Fichner-Rathus 1997. *Human Sexuality in a World of Diversity* 3rd ed. Boston: Allyn and Bacon.

Sagan, C. and A. Dryan 1990. "The Question of Abortion: A Search for Answers." *Parade Magazine,* April 22:4-8.

Scarpitti, Frank R., Margaret L. Anderson and Laura L. O'Toole 1997. *Social Problems, third* ed. New York: Addison-Wesley Educational Publishers.

Schafran, L. H. *1995.* "Rape is Still Underreported." *The New York Times,* August 26:A19.

Storms, M. D. 1980. "Theories of Sexual Orientation." *Journal of Personality and Social Psychology.* 38:783:792.

Tedeschi, J. T., and R. B. Felson 1994. *Violence, Aggression and Coercive Actions.* Washington, D.C.: American Psychological Association.

Weinberg, T. 1987. "Sadomasochism in the United States: A Review of Recent Sociological Literature." *Journal of Sex Research. 23:50-69.*

Zastrow, Charles 1996. *Social Problems: Issues and Solutions* 4th ed. Chicago: Nelson-Hall Publishers.

Zeman, N. 1990. "The New Rules of Courtship" (Special Edition) *Newsweek,* Summer/Fall, Pp. 22-24.

Zillman, D. 1989. "Effects of prolonged consumption of pornography." In D. Zillman and J. Bryant, eds., *Pornography: Research Advances and Policy Considerations.* Hillsdale, NJ: Erlbaum.

CHAPTER 4: ALCOHOL AND DRUGS IN AMERICAN SOCIETY
CASE STUDY: AN INSTANCE OF DRUG ADDICTION

Sixteen-year-old Naomi had been born to nearly-well-to-do parents whose commitment to Christian missionary work in east Africa had allowed the family to avoid the intemperate drug use that rocked the U.S. throughout the late '60s and '70s. By the time they returned to the U.S. in 1981, she had only vague memories of kindergarten at a public school near Macon, Georgia. The "drug wars" were just gearing up when Naomi entered the 11th grade at a small public school just outside Atlanta, Georgia near the church where her father had been appointed pastor. Her parochial education served her well in this new academic setting and her slim figure, pleasant features, and smart, conservative dress allowed her to fit in with some of the more popular students. It was exciting and refreshing to be away from the discipline of her father's tutoring. There were no threats of "damnation and perdition" or slaps on the cheek for botching bible verses.

At first, she was perplexed by the ease that her new schoolmates would discuss matters which at home would have inspired a blistering tirade of rebukes and chastisements. She had long been warned of the "depraved," "godless," and "shameless" youth she would find on her return to public schools in the U.S. Her trepidation was gradually replaced with enough composure to chat cautiously about dating, sex, and drugs with the girls who had, she felt, so genuinely accepted her as one of their own. When she finally admitted she had never been on a "date" or drunk a beer, they had tenderly chided her about living a "sheltered life." She was often taken aback with the casual exchanges between boys and girls and within a month of her return she realized that a handsome boy in her clique was becoming increasingly flirtatious with her. Her sudden recognition of his interest was startling and caused her to flush crimson at his every glance. After a week of chitchat during the break before math class, punctuated with regular encouragement from their mutual friends, he invited her on her first date.

Her excitement about this comely, interested boy turned instantly to humiliation when her parents prohibited the date. She was forced to call the boy and cancel the date and apologize for "leading him on." Her father began questioning her about the character of her new friends at school and promptly restricted her extra-curricular activities to church and certain school-sponsored events.

She continued to maintain many of the friendships she had established. Her friends were incredulous at her father's behavior and designated him the "toad." A reference that Naomi herself eventually began to use when with them. By the end of the 11th grade, the creativity of her friends had allowed her to sneak away about once a month to some clandestine party where she could drink beer or wine coolers, laugh, listen to "Satan's music," and deride the "toad." She would smoke marijuana with her friends when offered, but found its subtle effects only mildly attractive. On sporadic occasions, one of her friends would manage to obtain some LSD or "speed" (amphetamines) which she described as an 'unusually entertaining" experience. However, what she really enjoyed were the wine coolers. She felt that drinking made her more confident and less self-conscious in the company of friends. Her friends eventually began to light-heartedly refer to her as the "wild preacher's kid." A reference she believed signified a niche for her among her friends.

Her relationship with the boy from math class continued. They met at basketball games in the fall, baseball games in the spring and the various parties she would sneak away to with friends. Naomi found that the wine coolers and beer not only enlivened the parties she would attend, but eased the awkwardness and embarrassment she felt from his attention. Her first sexual experience occurred during spring break that year after a night of heavy drinking. The next day, her guilt for what she had done was almost overwhelming. It was only after they had all started drinking again that she discovered that her religious injunctions against fornication were abating.

The summer before her senior year, her father was relieved of his responsibilities with his congregation. The reason for the dismissal was what she would later described as an "affaire d'amour" with a prominent member of the congregation. Naomi was enraged that he could be so sanctimonious after the way he had treated her. She left home before her senior year, moved in with a beloved aunt in the panhandle of Florida, and enrolled in school to finish her senior year. Shortly after the school year was underway, she discovered a three-year-old bottle of Percodan® (see Appendix) in her aunt's medicine cabinet. She was awed by the effect of the drug and she reported a sense of relief she had not felt in years. Much better than the wine coolers and beer. She described her first experience with narcotics as "almost spiritual."

Naomi recounted this story years later while in therapy for drug abuse following an arrest for forging prescriptions for narcotics. She had gone on to finish high school and eventually obtained a B.S. degree in Nursing at a nearby university. She tried a variety of drugs during her college years-- marijuana, alcohol, amphetamines, cocaine--but none were more appealing to her than the prescription narcotics. There were no other drugs that offered the releasing euphoria she felt when using them. In her job as a nurse she found a plethora of drugs available to her. She was surprised at the ease with which one could divert drugs. Initially she would simply palm a pill or two when setting up the medications for distribution to the patients. After a few years of working in different hospitals, she had become quite adept at diverting drugs from either the secure narcotics cabinets or from patients. As time passed, her aptitude for obtaining narcotics expanded and became more sophisticated. Under the pretense of a variety of ailments, primarily migraine headaches, she would visit numerous physicians for treatment. Not only did the treatment generally consist of various analgesics, but a few minutes alone in the examination room would, more times than not, yield a few blank prescriptions. For a time she had extensive dental work done, mostly cosmetic, and her exaggerated and loud complaints of pain could get her a nice supply of analgesics. She had also managed to unearth a few discrete drug dealers who could occasionally supply her with narcotics. When narcotics were not available, which was rare, she would sometimes drink as much as a half-gallon of wine a day.

She eventually married and had a son. In retrospect, she was amazed that she had managed to avoid drugs and alcohol during the course of her pregnancy. She had seen enough babies delivered addicted to cocaine or narcotics or, worst yet, victims of Fetal Alcohol Syndrome to frighten her into staying clean and sober during the pregnancy. By all accounts, her husband never knew of her drug use, she often said that hiding it from him was really quite easy. Except for her pregnancy she wasn't sure he had ever seen her quite straight or sober and his graduate studies had always kept him somewhat preoccupied. She recalled being quite cranky toward him during the course of her pregnancy but even he had written off her moodiness to her condition. She had a nagging craving for drugs almost continually during the pregnancy. Within two weeks after the birth of her son, she had scheduled an appointment for a recurrence of her "migraine headaches" and reestablished her routine of loud, exaggerated complaints of pain.

One week after their son's first birthday, her husband learned about her drug problem when she called him to bail her out of jail. She had been arrested while sitting in her car in an empty parking lot, doped up and virtually incoherent, with half-a-dozen blank prescriptions and 80 Percocet® in her purse that had been prescribed to another name. Although the police were not privy to all the names she had used with pharmacists and physicians, their investigation still resulted in seven counts of forged prescriptions for various narcotics. Upon threat of divorce, loss of contact with her son, loss of her nursing license, and six months in jail, she elected to get involved in a treatment program.

After 18 months of intensive therapy, regular involvement in Alcoholics Anonymous, random drug testing, a year of probation, and a short stint of aftercare counseling she said that the craving for drugs finally ceased. Three years later she had added a daughter to the family, completed her graduate studies in counseling psychology and entered into private practice as a family therapist. She considers herself one of the fortunate few who actually managed to benefit from treatment for drug addiction. She continues to attend Alcoholics Anonymous meetings the first day of every month.

INTRODUCTION

In the United States the term "drug" conjures up a number of separate and distinct images. On one hand there is the therapeutic connotation associated with the positive effects of drugs used in medical arenas for the treatment of physical and psychological problems. On the other hand, there are the more negative connotations associated with the illegal recreational use and abuse of drugs which can result in various social harms and tragic personal outcomes. This chapter focuses on the problem of drug and alcohol use, as it could affect any of us directly and personally at some point in our lives, and as a social issue which indirectly affects all of us daily.

While this distinction between therapeutic and problem use definitions of a drug may be useful in some regard, it is inconsistently maintained in practice. On one hand, some mood altering drugs are socially accepted, while others are demonized and criminalized.

A recent break for a prime time television sitcom epitomized this inconsistency by running a popular commercial comparing drug use and its effects on the brain to an egg in a frying pan, which was immediately followed by another showing a group of young men surrounding a campfire, drinking a popular beer and commenting that "life doesn't get any better than this." It is clear that the legality and illegality of mind altering substances has been based on social acceptance factors rather than on the intrinsic harmfulness or usefulness of the drugs in question. Despite statistics showing hundreds of thousands of tobacco-related deaths in the U.S., the federal government has only recently classified nicotine as an addictive drug. With respect to illegal drugs, the cocaine and heroin epidemics of the 1990's seem to be a repetition of the cocaine and opium epidemics of the 1890's, showing that, as a society, we have never achieved the capacity to use psychoactive drugs in a responsible manner, or respond strategically to the ensuing problems.

By all indications, no society has adequately deterred the efforts of humans to alter their consciousness or perceptions via mood altering drugs without resorting to oppressive tactics. Societies differ, however, in their designation of "which" drugs to treat as problems. In North America, there is considerable tolerance of alcohol, tobacco, and even marijuana, although they are perceived as increasing the likelihood that their users will try other drugs. Clearly, a significant portion of people who use drugs and alcohol (legally and illegally) do so to the extent that they risk their health, jobs, families, freedom and sometimes their very lives as did Naomi in the opening case study.

Estimates for 1996 indicate that over 13 million Americans over the age of 12 have used illicit drugs (drugs other than alcohol and tobacco) in the previous 30 days. An estimated 11 million of these are marijuana users; approximately 1.7 million have used cocaine, 1.3 million have used hallucinogens, and about 216,000 have used heroin. In addition, the illicit use of psychotherapeutic drugs is estimated at approximately 3.1 million. Of course, these figures pale in comparison to the approximately 109 million who drink alcohol and 62 million who smoke tobacco (SAMHSA 1997). Socially and personally, the variety of problems associated with alcohol and drug use are well documented in both the professional literature and popular media. The use of alcohol and drugs has been associated with employment problems, legal entanglements, marital disruption, spouse and child abuse, and a variety of psychiatric problems. For example: (1) Drug Abuse cost American businesses $166 million a year in lost workdays and disabilities. Hospital treatment for victims of crime by street level drug dealers is estimated at $1 billion per year. (2) Court costs associated with drug trafficking cases are about $30 billion per year (Forbes 1994: 94). (3) Between 2000 and 3000 deaths per year are attributed to cocaine or heroin use. 100,000 deaths per year are associated with alcohol use. (4) Cigarettes are linked to 400,000 deaths per year (Lazare 1990:24). (5) In 1991 one-fifth of children in Oakland, California, were being raised by grandparents due to their parent's drug involvement (New York Times 7/23/90:A-1)

There is a wide range of drug use patterns that can be observed in virtually any modern society. At one end of the spectrum there is *abstinence* from drug or alcohol use and at the other end there is what is often referred to as *addiction (from* the Latin *addicere,* meaning to be bound to something). Drug addiction is indicative of a state of chronic physical and/or psychological dependence. In between there are categories typically referred to in the literature as light or social use, moderate use, and heavy use which can occur with or without attendant problems. For example, a physical dependence on opium or an addiction to cocaine can be manifested quite easily within a period of five to ten days, perhaps even more quickly in some individuals. Certain drugs, such as marijuana and inhalants, have a more moderate potential for addiction. Although many would argue that marijuana is not addictive, most treatment programs have admitted a small proportion of patients for problems associated with its use. Regardless of the categories used, problems do occur with the use of any and all drugs, including alcohol, and these problems are often tragically disruptive to individuals and families.

THEORY BOX by Michael J Donnelly Chapter 4 Drug Use/Social Learning

One of the early ways psychologists began to study learning was through experiments on laboratory animals (rats, pigeons, sometimes-human subjects). The experiment would present a stimulus and record the animal's response. By varying patterns of stimuli, for instance by presenting positive (rewarding) stimuli or other negative (punishing) stimuli, the experimenter could try to mold, or "condition," the animal's response-to select for, and reinforce, some desired target behavior. Pavlov, for instance, taught dogs to salivate upon hearing a bell ring; his dogs had "learned" to associate the bell with an imminent feeding. Such experiments illustrated teaching and learning of a fairly rudimentary sort. The animal would "learn"-acquire an appropriate response to a given stimulus-through trial and error, guided by the experimenter's selected reward of desired behavior. Laboratory protocol required that the experimenter record only observable data (stimuli and responses) and refrain from speculating about inner states of the animal, which were described as hidden, as if closed "within a black box."

Such experimental studies had some, but only fairly limited, applications to understanding how humans learn, and what variety of influences shape our behavior. Social learning theory was developed explicitly as a reaction against unduly reductive models of human behaviors through observation of others' behavior and the positive or negative consequences it brings. Moreover, social learning theory introduces a significant cognitive, or deliberative, element into explaining behavior (Akers, 1992). Individuals tend to deliberate before putting in motion their learned behavior, calculating what subsequent reward of punishment they may receive. Altogether this suggests quite a different image of human nature than that of the behaviorists; as Albert Bandura, one of the theory's major proponents, puts it: "human nature is characterized as a vast potentiality that can be fashioned by direct and vicarious experience into a variety of forms within biological limits" (1977:13). A good way to capture the force of social learning is to think of the human capabilities it involves and enables; a capacity to process experience into models which can guide future behavior; a capacity for forethought, which allows us to anticipate consequences and form goals; and a capacity to reflect on our own experiences and gain understanding of our thought processes, adapting our goals and purposes accordingly.

BRIEF HISTORY OF ALCOHOL AND DRUGS IN AMERICA

Americans have been relatively heavy users of alcohol since the first settlers arrived in the Colonies. Initially beer, wine, and liquor (primarily rum) were imported by the settlers of the New World. Drinking was integral to colonial life and the Puritans consumed alcohol as the "Good creature of God" (Rorabaugh 1991). By 1770 per capita consumption was about three and a half gallons of alcohol per year, almost double the current rate of consumption in the U.S. The Revolutionary war brought British blockades and American taxation, which prompted Scottish and Irish immigrants to begin the production of American whiskey. The Corn Belt farmers of Ohio and

Kentucky quickly discovered that there was more profit in distilling their corn into spirits and transporting it to market than shipping the grain itself. By 1820 corn liquor was cheaper than beer, wine, coffee, tea, or milk in the retail market. By 1830 the consumption of alcohol had risen to more than seven gallons a year (about three times the current rate of use). If there were problems associated with this (such as violence in the family or the streets), there were no alarms raised. An agricultural society, lacking automobiles and heavy machinery, could tolerate higher rates of intoxication, and there was less awareness of the family and health costs of such abuse. Over time, however, there did emerge a growing opposition to alcohol use by the upper classes (such as New England aristocrats) aimed at maintaining social order in the growing urban areas. This was quickly followed by various Protestant temperance preachers vilifying those who drank, swore, and neglected their work. By 1840 the temperance movement was well underway in the U.S. By 1850, 13 of 40 states had passed legislation prohibiting alcohol distribution. These legal changes continued pressure from the temperance movement, and increasing numbers of religiously oriented "teetotalers," who took the pledge to abstain, cut alcohol consumption in half. It didn't last, and by the decade of the 1870's the public sentiment shifted and the "liquor was flowing freely again" (Mustos 1996: 78).

This resurgence was not without opposition. Led by the Women's Christian Temperance Union, the Anti-Saloon League, and the Methodists' Board of Temperance, the prohibition movement re-emerged and boomed at the end of the 19th century. The temperance message, aimed primarily at the new immigrants, was quite simply to stay sober, work hard and become a member of the middle class. An appealing goal for some segments of the working and lower classes caught in the industrial revolution taking place in the U.S. (Gusfield 1962).

Temperance efforts culminated in 1920 with the ratification of the Eighteenth Amendment to the Constitution, which prohibited the manufacture, sale, and transportation of intoxicating liquors. Initially, prohibition was viewed as quite successful, particularly in small towns and rural areas. Unfortunately, for law enforcement agencies, the Eighteenth Amendment did not expressly forbid the consumption of alcohol. For those willing to break the law, this loophole neatly dovetailed with Canada, which had outlawed drinking alcohol, but not the manufacture of it. This legal inconsistency and the enhanced profits of illegal trade was a boon to those willing to break the law. The competition between criminal gangs for control of the illegal alcohol business was regularly punctuated by violence, bribery, and extortion. As organized crime emerged, the power gained through the illegal liquor industry expanded into other areas of the government and the economy. Large cities saw the wholesale importation of illegal liquor, the decline of the all-male saloon which was replaced with the speakeasy that catered to both men and women, and the rise of political and law enforcement corruption. In Chicago, Al Capone was grossing $200 million a year with a reported 400 police officers accepting bribes for turning a blind eye to alcohol manufacture, distribution, and consumption.

By the late 1920's, Prohibition was recognized as being largely unenforced, and perhaps unenforceable, and public sentiment shifted to establish a repeal movement. Prohibition was argued to be a violation of personal rights, corrupting of law enforcement, and a major cause of crime. On December 5, 1933 Prohibition was repealed with the ratification of the Twenty-first Amendment to the Constitution. Although Prohibition was quite successful in reducing alcohol consumption, alcohol related illnesses and hospital admissions, and deaths due to liver disease, it came to be widely perceived as a failure; a "noble experiment" but a catastrophic failure of public policy nonetheless (Siegal and Inciardi 1995: 49).

From the end of prohibition through the 1970's alcohol use rose steadily eventually returning to the rates similar to those seen prior to Prohibition. In 1971, the Twenty-sixth Amendment to the Constitution lowered the voting age in the U.S. to 18. This was almost immediately followed by a reduction in the drinking age by most states to 18 to coincide with the newly established voting age. In 1980, however, states had begun to increase the drinking age to 21. This reflected increased public attention to highway fatalities and problems associated with drinking and driving. The federal government, in 1984, established a policy to withhold federal highway funds to any state which did not increase the drinking age to 21. All states have since complied with this requirement for receiving highway funding (Musto 1996:78).

This pattern of shifting public sentiment concerning alcohol use has, since the early 1800's, been complicated by the popularity of other substances used by various groups for their mood altering effects. The natural forms of opium, cocaine, and marijuana have been used throughout history. In 1806 the relatively new science of organic chemistry allowed for morphine to be synthesized from raw opium and in 1874 diacetylmorphine (later named Heroin by the Bayer Company) was synthesized from morphine. Cocaine hydrochloride, currently referred to as "powder cocaine," was synthesized in 1859. Both heroin and cocaine were initially touted for their beneficial effects. Morphine was liberally used on the battlefield during the Civil War and its use continued to rise in the public sector until the turn of the century. As little was known of the notion of cross-addiction (the mutual and interchangeable dependence that occurs with drugs in the same pharmacological category), heroin was initially thought to be a "cure" for morphine addiction (Mustos 1991). Sigmund Freud concluded that cocaine was a "magical drug" and encouraged its use to his family, friends, and colleagues. Cocaine was argued to be helpful for everything from alcoholism and opium addiction to venereal disease. Opium, morphine, heroin, and cocaine solutions were readily available in various over-the-counter tonics, elixirs, and hypodermic kits until the late 1890's. Pharmacists (sometimes in back-alley operations), dispensed cocaine in substantial quantities (Spillane 1994). By the early 20th century, amid growing concern of the addiction potential of these drugs, the Pure Food and Drug Act of 1906 was passed and cocaine and heroin use began declining (Inciardi and McElrath, 1995: xii). In 1914 the Harrison Tax Act was passed in response to international pressure to restrict the world trade of opium. This act effectively prohibited the distribution of opium and coca products by requiring strict accounting procedures and a tax on each transfer required to move the drugs from the U.S. point of entry to the end user. In effect, these rules were applied in a way that made legal transfers virtually impossible. This resulted in the rapid decline of cocaine and heroin use in the general population and drove their use underground.

Unlike heroin and cocaine, the use of marijuana was initially the activity of minority groups and emerged most prominently during the drug intolerant period of the 1920's. Its use by blacks, Latinos, jazz musicians and certain avant-garde social circles prompted a number of states to pass anti-marijuana laws, fearing that its use would spread to white youth. By the mid-1930's a number of political conservatives and the media had labeled marijuana as the "killer weed" and the "assassin of youth" and argued that it was the cause of murderous rampages and permanent insanity by its users. Since taxation had worked well with the Harrison Act and also with restricting the transfer of fully automatic weapons, the same approach was applied to marijuana. In 1937 the Marijuana Tax Act was passed requiring the purchase of a transfer tax stamp to distribute marijuana. Since the government would not (and never intended to) issue the required stamp, marijuana was added to the list of dangerous and essentially illegal drugs (Mustos, 1991).

From 1920 until the late 1950's drug use was generally renounced by the public and use remained relatively low. During the late 1950's this temperance posture began changing considerably. While alcohol use was steadily on the rise, drug use had remained fairly low during the 1950's. A resurgence of tolerant attitudes concerning drug use coupled with the introduction of new varieties of drugs and the coming horde of baby boomers set the stage for the "hippie" movement of the 60's and the proliferation of drug use in the U.S. throughout the 1970's reaching a peak of use in 1979 that has yet to be equaled. The federal government stepped up efforts to control drug use with new legislation and stiffer penalties for drug violations.

The connection between social change and drug use is no more clearly exemplified than with the introduction to the U.S. of lysergic acid diethylamide (LSD) in 1949. It had been synthesized in 1938 by Albert Hoffman who experienced the "world's first LSD trip" in 1943 (Neill 1987). It was brought to the U.S. for experimental purposes by psychotherapists interested in its utility as a treatment for mental illness. Psychologists Timothy Leary and Richard Alpert had established the "Psilocybin Project" at Harvard University to examine the utility of hallucinogenic mushrooms (Psilocybin), LSD, and the peyote derivative mescaline as adjuncts to psychotherapy. While the experiments were originally focused on criminal inmate volunteers, by the early 1960's Leary was encouraging the use of and providing these "psychedelics" to his graduate students, colleagues, artists, alcoholics, drug addicts, and assorted intellectuals. He envisioned that these drugs would one day be integral to the education process from kindergarten to graduate school (Weil 1972,1986). In 1962 new legislation was enacted by congress expressly giving the Food and Drug Administration control over experimental drugs. Leary left Harvard, moved to Arizona, and began an evangelical movement to "turn on America." His connections with Harvard and his message of using LSD to "turn on, tune in, and drop out," captured the attention of the national media. His "mission"'' coupled with support from leading authors of the day (Aldous Huxley, Ken Kesey, Hermarm Hesse and the "beat" poet Allan Ginsberg) and the new "acid rock" music of the Beatles, Jefferson Airplane, and Donovan, came to epitomize the drug culture of the 1960's and 1970's.

Although drug use remained relatively low during the 1960's, the variety of drugs available proliferated in subcultural settings and in the youth culture surrounding schools, as was the case for Naomi, in our introductory example. By the early 1970's it was well known, even in the general population, that marijuana use did not result in "murderous rampages" or insanity, as had previously been claimed, and its use began to increase dramatically as the federal government lost any sense of credibility as a source of accurate information concerning the effects of drugs (Musto, 1991). A literal smorgasbord of drugs were readily available to youth and young adults including marijuana, cocaine, amphetamines, various hallucinogens and a host of drugs which had previously been used in the medical arena (barbiturates, benzodiazipines, sedatives/narcotics). Drug trafficking cartels formed in South America, Mexico, and Asia to supply the increasing world demand for illegal drugs. Motorcycle gangs in North America and Europe had become well entrenched in the manufacture and distribution of amphetamines and the diversion of pharmaceutical drugs for recreational consumption became a lucrative activity. At the height of drug use in 1978-79 "roach clips" were common trinkets on keychains and "coke spoons" were popular pieces of jewelry.

By the early 1980's drug use in the U.S. was on the decline. Nonetheless, the reports of addiction, overdoses, and the devastating effects of drugs on families, work, and social life were legion in the popular media. The fear of drug use, and the effort devoted to preventing it, rose just at the time that actual use was declining. Sexual promiscuity, crime, venereal disease, the arrival of AIDS (Acquired Immune Deficiency Syndrome) and a variety of physical and psychological problems were all tied, either directly or indirectly, to drug and alcohol use. By the mid-1980's the "war on drugs" was well underway, focusing on interdiction and drug abuse prevention campaigns. All drug and alcohol use continued to decline through the decade with one exception. A relatively inexpensive, smokeable form of cocaine, referred to popularly as "crack", had been rediscovered and its use became epidemic in inner-city slums. By the mid-to-late 1980's all metropolitan areas of the U.S. and many small municipalities were reporting problems with "crack."

In the early 1990's, after a decade of declining use, rates of use for virtually all drugs began increasing. By the mid-1990's it had become evident that we were in the midst of another pendulous shift in drug use patterns in the U.S. Numerous surveys of the late 1980's and early 1990's had already shown that proscriptive attitudes among the young were not as prevalent as they had been a decade before. In addition, the large distribution cartels and drug smugglers had learned in the early 80's that it was much more lucrative to traffic in cocaine than in marijuana or other drugs and had shifted their product emphasis. In the 90's drug distributors had recognized an increased demand for heroin and had again shifted their product emphasis. Opium, which had historically been imported from Mexico and the notorious Golden Crescent and Golden Triangle of Asia, is now being produced in South America and production in Mexico has recently increased to accommodate the increased U.S. demand.

It has become obvious that we are currently experiencing a period of increased drug tolerance in the U.S. A recent referendum in California approved the use of marijuana for medical purposes. Arizona voters took the matter a step further by approving the medical use of a variety of drugs including, but not limited to, marijuana, LSD, and amphetamines for medical purposes. Despite a rather dubious connection between the medical use of substances and more general recreational use, both of these events were seen as a victory for anti-prohibition advocates. These more liberal attitudes, coupled with increased availability have some costs. Overdoses and deaths associated with heroin use have been increasing steadily since 1992. On August 26, 1997 a 20-year-old student was found dead at a Louisiana State University fraternity house and three others were hospitalized for alcohol poisoning. Unfortunately such events are not particularly surprising in the U.S. There is little doubt that regular reports of overdoses on drugs or alcohol will continue to make the headlines.

THE INTEGRATION OF DRUGS

Problems associated with drug and alcohol use have attracted considerable research attention. As a result there has emerged a body of knowledge aimed at specifying the social factors which contribute to the problems of drug and alcohol use. One set of social factors, demographic characteristics, offers considerable general information concerning the social characteristics of those people who use alcohol and drugs and subsequently increase their risk of experiencing problems or addiction. Characteristics related to age, gender, race, and social status offer important information concerning general patterns of use and the structural integration of drugs in U.S. society.

Legally obtained drugs and alcohol are, and always have been, used by a majority of U.S. citizens. While the use of over-the-counter and prescription drugs is of concern to many, the integration of illegal drugs in our society has pervaded the media and has been blamed for many of the social problems of our society. An important question rising from the opening case study is how social conditions contribute to the emergence of problem drug use with particular individuals and how do we respond socially to those problems? The examination of illicit drug and alcohol use problems can be approached by understanding: 1) the extent to which drugs are integrated into the very culture of our society as a whole; 2) how drugs are integrated into the social groups and relationships that we participate in, and; 3) how drugs are integrated into the personal lifestyles of individuals. An analysis of the integration of drugs offers a framework for describing and understanding drug use behavior.

Cultural Integration. The issue of cultural integration focuses on the extent to which illicit drug use has become tolerated or even openly accepted in our society. The underlying assumption of this perspective is that the more culturally integrated and less socially disapproved a drug is, the more likely people are to come into contact with it. For example, the cultural integration of alcohol would be considered very high in our society. It is readily available, generally accepted, and the vast majority of our citizens have tried alcohol. There are three factors which indicate the extent of cultural integration. These factors--perceived availability of drugs, perceptions of risk associated with drug use, and lifetime prevalence (proportion of the population who have ever used drugs)--combine to provide information concerning the general availability of drugs and offer indications concerning the willingness of individuals to try certain drugs. Since the statistical tendency to use drugs is highly associated with age, we have drawn information from the Monitoring The Future survey of high school seniors (University of Michigan, 1997). The perceptions of this particular age cohort provide a window into the level of cultural acceptance of drug use in the U.S. High school seniors are at the beginning of the age range in which we find the peak use rates for many drugs. Since young people are often on the cutting edge of social change, particularly regarding drug use, the patterns of use for this group are critical for anticipating the dimensions of future prevalence.

From the Monitoring the Future Study survey, it can be seen that 12th graders demonstrated a relatively low perception of risk associated with marijuana during the late 1970's and early 1980's. During the course of the 1980's there was an increase in the perception of risk associated with marijuana use which peaked in 1991 with 27.1% of seniors reporting significant risk associated with using marijuana once or twice. This was up from the low perceptions of risk reported in 1978 (8.1%). Other drugs were perceived to be more risky especially cocaine and heroin. This perception of risk associated with cocaine greatly increased around 1987 when the problems with "crack" cocaine became apparent. Concerning the availability of drugs to high school seniors, the Monitoring the Future study found that over the last two decades marijuana has been consistently the easiest drug to obtain. Heroin has been the most difficult drug to obtain. As for lifetime prevalence of use by high school seniors reported in this study 60.4% of seniors in 1979 had tried marijuana but this dropped to 32.6% by 1992 and similar declines are seen with the other drugs.

Collectively these trends indicate the degree of cultural integration of particular drugs into this cohort of students. Among the illicit drugs, marijuana use appears to be the most integrated into our culture, as this drug is reported to be readily available to over 80% of seniors. Seniors report other drugs such as cocaine, LSD, and heroin are more available at the present than was reported during the late 1970's. All in all, the perceptions of risk associated with using drugs appear to have been declining since 1990 and the lifetime prevalence has been increasing since 1992. What is important to note in the Monitoring of the Future study is that the perceptions of risk, perceptions of availability, and the lifetime prevalence of drug use for high school seniors are all highly correlated with each other. As the perceptions of risk decline then drugs are seen as more available and subsequently the lifetime prevalence increases.

While the prevalence, availability and perceived risk associated with drugs rise and fall as the result of numerous influences, what is striking is the degree to which certain drugs appear to be widely accepted in our culture by our youth. Averaged over the last two decades only 52.9% of seniors report a perception of risk associated with experimental use of heroin. Only 43.9%, of seniors perceive a significant risk associated with experimental use of cocaine and 43.3% perceive significant risk associated with LSD use. Less than 30% of seniors perceive significant risk associated with experimental amphetamine use. Only 16.1% of seniors since 1975 perceive any significant risk associated with experimental marijuana use. Coupled with the perception that these drugs have been readily available to seniors over the last two decades (marijuana 86.3%, LSD 38.3%, Cocaine 47.1%, Heroin 25.2%, and amphetamines 63.2%) this perceived lack of risk no doubt contributes to the average lifetime prevalence rates seen since 1975. On average, since 1975, 49.4% of seniors report having used marijuana, 21.9% report using amphetamines, 12% have used cocaine, 9.3% have used LSD, and 1.3% have used heroin.

The attitudes, availability, and use rates of high school seniors are indicative of the degree of the general cultural integration of drugs in our society. Marijuana is, by all indications, readily available, perceived as having little risk, and therefore widely use. Amphetamines, which can be quite dangerous physiologically, also appear to be readily available, widely used, and having a relatively low perception of risk. The risks associated with cocaine since the advent of "crack" have dampened its popularity, but nonetheless it is more popular than LSD, perhaps because of its availability and the consistency of the effects. Heroin, despite the recent media attention, remains the least culturally integrated drug of those listed. What appears to be most disconcerting about heroin use is reflected both in the recent changes in the proportions of users and the estimated number of users. The lifetime prevalence of heroin use for 18-25 year olds increased from 0.7% in 1995 to 1.3% in 1996. While this remains a relatively small proportion of the population, it represents an increase from an estimated 208,000 users to 365,000 in a single year (SAMHSA, 1997). Such increases are ominous for the criminal justice system, educational institutions, and the medical establishment.

Social Integration. The matter of social integration focuses on the extent to which the use of particular drugs have become acceptable practice within certain social groups. Lifetime prevalence rates, discussed above, include all users regardless of the frequency of use. Both experimental drug use and chronic drug use, which have quite different implications, are captured in the same rate with no distinction. The issue of social integration focuses on social group characteristics which circumscribe the degree of illicit drug and alcohol use. Specifically, the age, race, gender, location, and socio-economic status of one's social group are factors which influence the degree of illicit drug and alcohol use.

The demographic characteristics associated with the prevalence of alcohol, marijuana, and any illicit drug use in the past 30 days are reported in the

National Household survey on drug abuse (SAMHSA 1997). This survey specifies the different characteristics of "current" users, those who have consumed the substance within the past month. The past-month prevalence shows the magnitude of consistent use. Individuals who have used drugs or alcohol within the past 30 days are more likely to participate in social groups where drug use is either tolerated or approved outright, and therefore there is an increased likelihood of drug abuse in these groups. Data from the National Household Survey on Drug Abuse also reflects that alcohol use is relatively highly integrated culturally into our society. In addition, comparison of the category "Marijuana Use" to the category "Illicit Use of Any Drug" shows that the bulk of illicit drug use occurring in the U.S. is marijuana use.

Age. The peak years for alcohol use begin in the late teen years following high school and continue through the young adult years, remaining relatively high until about 30 to 35 years of age. Following this initial crescendo, the rates of alcohol and drug use tend to decrease as age increases. In the National Household Survey on Drug Abuse indicates that 60% of 18-25 years old and 61.6% of 26-34 years old report using alcohol in the past 30 days. For those aged 35 and older the alcohol use rates drop. For those age 35 and older the rate of alcohol use drops off gradually. The overwhelming generalization that emerges from the research is that moderate alcohol use, heavy drinking, problem drinking, and alcohol abuse tend to decrease with age (Heffington 1997)

Rates of marijuana and other illicit drug use show a slightly different pattern. While 13.2% of 18-25 years old report using marijuana in the past 30 days, the rate for 26-34 years old is half of that (6.3%) and drops to 2% for those 35 and older. Just as with alcohol use there is perhaps no single characteristic that is more highly correlated with illicit drug use than is age. While there are many people of various ages who use illicit drugs, drug use is primarily an activity of youth. Few people are attracted to drug use after the age of 30 (Kendel, Yamaguchi, and Chen 1992; SAMSHA 1997). Some of the explanation for this is found simply in the types of activities individual are involved in as they age. By age 30 most individuals have shifted their interests and focus from planning to the actual achievement of social goals. They have a stake in establishing their career, have married, and are starting families. By age 35 or 40 individuals have completed the transition from the young adult who is establishing a social niche to a social level where the priorities have shifted to an emphasis on economic stability, child rearing, and planning for future needs (children's college, retirement, etc.). The social cost of illicit drug use and excessive alcohol use becomes increasingly threatening to careers, child rearing, and family life. The physical and psychological problems associated with continued use, especially when it progresses to abuse, are added to the negative social consequences of use and the positive benefits of discontinuing drug consumption. In addition, the public attention to the problem of alcohol and drugs in the workplace, in the last decade, has given rise to the popularity of drug testing of employees, random drug testing in some companies and specific occupations (i.e., truck drivers) and drug testing associated with employee related accidents. Such programs have spread to college athletics and high schools and resulted in many individuals ceasing marijuana and other drug use because they perceive that they will be held accountable for illicit drug use.

Age is also an important variable in the onset of substance use. In 1963, for those using marijuana, the average age of initial use was almost 20 years old. By 1978 the average age had dropped to just over 18. After a period of increase in the average age to just over 19 in the early 1980, the average age of initial use of marijuana has steadily declined. At present the average age of first use for those who use marijuana is quite low at around 16.5. These changes in the average age of first use are important in that the younger people begin to use drugs, the greater the tendency for that use to escalate to higher levels of use and a greater variety of drug use. This is not to say that anyone who uses marijuana will necessarily use other types of drugs. However, there is a statistical tendency for individuals who use any type of drug, including tobacco, to have a greater risk associated with the use of other drugs. Keeping in mind that only a small proportion of those who use illicit drugs experience problem or subsequent addiction, a typical progression for those who do would be starting tobacco use at 14, using marijuana, alcohol, or inhalants by 17, followed by cocaine, heroin, or hallucinogen use by 17 or 20 years old. The younger the initial use, the younger such a progression would occur coupled with a greater likelihood that a progression to problem use will occur (Kendel, Yamaguchi and Chen 1984).

Race. Overall, whites show higher annual and daily alcohol use rates than blacks and Hispanics across all age categories. Whites also show the highest rates of use of marijuana and other drugs up to about age 25, thereafter blacks tends to have the higher rates of marijuana and other illicit drug use. Regarding alcohol, there are indications that the drinking behavior among blacks is quite different than it is for whites. Black men are generally characterized by a tendency to either abstain from alcohol use or to drink heavily (Harper and Saifnoorianm 1991; Brown and Tooley 1989): Black women on the other hand tend to show some of the lowest rates of alcohol use. Explanations for this trend have generally focused on economic limitations, family responsibilities, and various social restrictions (Harper and Saifnoorianm 1991). Considering the low socio-economic status experienced by many members of racial minority groups in the U.S., low rates of drinking associated with relatively high rates of problems would be consistent with those use patterns related to socio-economic status. These same socio-economic conditions would also contribute to the higher levels of drug use seen with blacks after age 25.

Gender. It has been well established that men, regardless of age, use alcohol and illicit drugs at higher rates and in larger quantities than women do. The National Household Survey on Drug Abuse indicates that the difference between men and women in drinking and drug behavior is especially noticeable among those over the age of 18. However, in the 12-17 year old age group, the proportions of males and females reporting the use of alcohol and drugs are virtually identical. Some of this can be attributed to the changes that have occurred with adolescent peer groups in the last two decades.

During the 1970's adolescent peer groups became increasingly gender mixed groups. In the 1950's and throughout the 1960's women, especially adolescent girls, did not enjoy many of the freedoms their male counterparts were allowed. The introduction of the birth control pill, increasing labor force participation of women, and increased rights for women between 1960 and 1980 changed this pattern of differential treatment and subsequently access to drugs. The clique that Naomi was a member of at her high school allowed for males and females to interact freely in a variety of activities, including alcohol and drug use.

Population Density and Region. There are relatively stable patterns of alcohol and drug use associated with population density and region in the U.S. With the exception of alcohol use for younger age groups, the general trend regarding population density is that urban areas tend to have higher rates of both alcohol and drug use. This distinction becomes particularly more pronounced with age. As age increases the rate of alcohol consumption also becomes lower in less densely populated areas than in metropolitan communities (SAMHSA 1997). The greater the degree of urbanization, the greater the likelihood of easy access to drugs and exposure to liberal attitudes regarding drugs and alcohol, particularly for youth.

Alcohol use is typically higher in the Northeast and North Central U.S. than in the South and the West. Regarding drug use, higher rates are typically found in the West and North Central U.S. In general, the North Central U.S. has the highest rates of alcohol, marijuana, and illicit drug use. However, for adolescents the highest rates of marijuana and illicit drug use are found in the West. The South, the region which Naomi was located, has relatively high rates of alcohol and marijuana use for those aged 12-17.

SOCIO-ECONOMIC STATUS: EDUCATION AND EMPLOYMENT

Contrary to popular opinion, depressed socio-economic circumstances and low education are not typically associated with high levels of alcohol consumption (Molgaard, et al. 1990; La Greca and Akers 1991; Cahalan, et al. 1968, 1974). Despite mixed and inconsistent findings concerning socio-economic factors and alcohol use rates, the trend appears to be a positive relationship--as social status increases, so does the use rate (Akers 1992). The National Household Survey on Drug Abuse indicates that rates of consumption increase significantly as educational levels and employment stability (and hence income) increase. Those men and women who have less than 12 years of education and who are unemployed or employed part-time report the lowest rates of alcohol consumption. Those with college degrees and full employment report the highest rates of alcohol use for all age groups shown. The general trend is that those with the most education and highest income tend to have the highest levels of alcohol use.

There is however a general tendency for those with relatively high socio-economic status, despite high rates of use, to experience fewer problems associated with drinking than those of lower socio-economic status. While a high socio-economic status may be related to higher rates of drinking, it is not related to heavy drinking or problem drinking behavior. On the other hand, those with a lower socio-economic status, while having relatively low rates of use, tend to experience relatively more problems associated with alcohol use (Goode 1993:177).

The opposite of this is seen with regard to marijuana use. In general, marijuana use is more closely associated with lower levels of education with rates decreasing as education increases. Contrary to popular opinion, college students show slightly lower rates of drug use than seen in similar aged cohorts not attending college. It is interesting to note that for persons 26-34 years old the rate of "Illicit Use of Any Drug" is higher for those with higher levels of education. These higher rates are associated with the increased likelihood for post-college adults to have access to marijuana and a greater variety of other drugs.

It is important to keep in mind that these variables collectively, along with other demographic variables (i.e. religion, marital status, and ethnicity) contribute to the likelihood of alcohol and drug use. The structural position which individuals occupy and their various group associations influences the degree of social integration of drugs and alcohol in their immediate environment. While there has been some variation in the patterns in the National Household Survey on Drug Abuse these generalizations about drug and alcohol use have been relatively stable since the mid 1970's. Naomi's return to the U.S. found her amidst a white, relatively high status, high school group located in a small metropolitan, southern community. At the time of her return to the U.S. the nation was experiencing high rates of drug use, with high school seniors reporting relative ease in accessing drugs and alcohol. Naomi's association with drinking, drug using friends in this context combined with her increased alienation from her family, motivated her toward use and eventually abuse of alcohol and drugs.

PERSONAL INTEGRATION

The Monitoring of the Future Study provides information concerning daily use rates of alcohol and marijuana for high school seniors since 1975. While much of this use may indeed be non-problematic, it is reasonable to conclude that the daily use of marijuana or alcohol contributes to a number of problems associated with education and juvenile crime. The highest rates of daily marijuana use for high school seniors were seen in 1978-79 with over 10% reporting daily use of marijuana. This rate declined to a low of around 2% in 1991-92. Rates of daily use have been increasing since then with daily use rates of marijuana at 5% in 1996. Alcohol use also declined for seniors during this same period; however, the decline was not as dramatic as that seen for marijuana. Prior to 1983 a higher percentage of seniors were using marijuana on a daily basis than those using alcohol. That same situation has arisen again since 1994. The findings indicate that these substances are becoming integrated into the daily lives of a small, but significant, proportion of American adolescents, just as alcohol and drugs became an integral part of Naomi's life each day.

The Monitoring of the Future Study does not show trends for other drugs that contribute to the drug abuse problems in the U.S. These other drugs-- cocaine, heroin, LSD, and amphetamines--are used by much lower percentages of the population than are marijuana and alcohol. The proportion of seniors using these drugs on a daily basis has remained below 1% since 1975. While the use of these drugs is not as well integrated into adolescents' personal lifestyles, even sporadic use of some of these drugs can lead to significant problems. For example, certain drugs, (i.e., heroin, and cocaine) are particularly dangerous due to the tendency to lead to physical and psychological addiction. While the initial motivation for use may be the euphoric effects, continued use may be motivated by intense drug cravings and various withdrawal symptoms. This happens even with the kind of prescription narcotics that Naomi preferred to take. And as we saw in Naomi's case this can lead to deviant drug-seeking behavior which can include involvement in other types of criminal activity. Use of these drugs, tend to result in a "sinister" loyalty. On the other hand, some drugs tend to have a low potential for addiction. For instance, the daily use of LSD or other hallucinogens is relatively uncommon even among regular users. Hallucinogens tend to have inconsistent effects, rather harsh physiological effects and tolerance develops quite rapidly. In effect, they typically do not provoke a high degree of user "loyalty" and as such tend to have relatively low rates of use.

THE FORMAL AND INFORMAL SOCIAL CONTROL OF DRUG AND ALCOHOL USE

The official U. S. response to the problems associated with the abuse of drugs has primarily been two-pronged. On one hand, there are legal efforts aimed at interrupting the international and domestic production and trafficking of illicit drugs, and on the other applying legal penalties for the possession of illicit drugs. These legal efforts are aimed at deterring the use and distribution of illicit drugs. While it is known that illicit drugs will, in all likelihood, never be completely eliminated, these efforts do serve to keep the overall use and, more importantly, abuse rates down. Public policies aimed at controlling alcohol use revolve around (1) regulating the sale, distribution, and consumption in the general population (age, place, and hours), (2) enacting and enforcing laws against drunk driving, and (3) arresting persons for public drunkenness and disorderly conduct. Tobacco consumption is also restricted in the general population by controlling (1)) cigarette advertising, (2) sales to minors, and (3) places where smoking is allowed. Tobacco companies have also been sued by state governments and individuals to re-coup costs associated with loss of health and life due to smoking.

Primary and secondary prevention and education programs have also been established for alcohol, tobacco, and other drugs. Primary prevention programs are aimed at anticipating drug use problems and stopping them before they start. Nancy Reagan's "Just say no" campaign of the 1980's, school based drug education programs, community policing prevention programs, and various community-based diversion programs have all been focused on warning youth of the dangers of drug and alcohol use and attempted to discourage the drug use (Akers 1992).

Secondary prevention programs focus on stopping drug use after individuals have been initiated into drug use and a subsequent habit or addiction has been established. Most of these programs follow the disease model of addiction, which has been influenced by the American Medical Association, social work perspectives, and legal decisions over the past 60 years. In the public discourse taking place in the popular media, the "disease of addiction" as (a mental disorder or biologically based condition) is readily recognized as the cause of many of the personal and social problems we experience in the U.S. with regard to alcohol and drug use. This disease model is expressed in the individual in primarily two forms. First, there is the genetic mold which places the cause of addiction at the level of the individual as a biological organism. Addiction is located at the molecular level of the individual's DNA. Those individuals who are prone to addiction either metabolize drugs and alcohol in a different way than normal people do, (perhaps requiring higher doses of the drug to get its euphoric effects) or they undergo metabolic changes at the onset of drug or alcohol use that require continued use in much the same way as a diabetic needs insulin. The second aspect of the disease model focuses on addiction as an emotional disease. This approach is rooted in psychoanalytic theory which presupposes that drug addiction is the result of psychological inadequacies in coping with the rigors of daily living or, more simply put, an "addictive personality." Such individuals tend to exhibit low self-esteem, low self-control, tendencies toward depression, and a limited ability to defer gratification (Stephens 1992:15-18).

Against the backdrop of these biological and emotional concerns there has emerged four basic types of programs aimed at returning alcoholics and addicts to abstinence, or, more rarely, to moderate and responsible use. Collectively detoxification, residential treatment, outpatient treatment, and self-help groups constitute the treatment strategies employed in the U.S. and other industrial societies. While usually rooted in social service agencies and a medical context, these programs are currently being integrated into a number of rehabilitation programs tied to the corrections component of the criminal justice system.

DETOXIFICATION

These programs are usually considered to be short-term treatment programs. Typically a hospital-based, three to 7-day program detoxification is aimed at managing the health risk associated with the cessation of alcohol and/or drugs. Patients are usually prescribed tranquilizers in decreasing doses over several days. The intent is to avoid the danger, discomfort and cravings associated with withdrawal and establish a plan for subsequent treatment focusing on the permanent cessation of drug or alcohol use.

RESIDENTIAL TREATMENT

These programs are found in two basic forms. First there are hospital-based inpatient treatment programs typically lasting from 10 to 30 days. They typically have a well-established curriculum based in psychotherapeutic models, which emphasize behavioral, cognitive, and affective issues. Patients are involved in both individual and group counseling activities, a variety of therapeutic strategies and (usually) self-help groups.

Second are the therapeutic communities. Evolved from the now defunct Synanon programs, these programs emphasize individual and group counseling and typically employ a confrontational approach. Many therapeutic communities focus on younger individuals with limited education and few marketable skills in conjunction with a significant drug abuse problems. As such, many have fairly well established educational and vocational training programs. These programs are considered long-term programs with typical duration of 6 months and sometimes lasting as long as 18 months. In recent years the therapeutic community model has become quite popular in the prison setting and many state correctional facilities have incorporated these models into their rehabilitation curriculum.

OUTPATIENT TREATMENT

Outpatient programs are often modeled either directly or indirectly on the approaches and curriculum used in residential programs. Typically they involve educational programs and individual and group counseling. There is considerable variety in the structure of these programs. Many times, treatment consists of weekly individual or group meetings with a therapist. Other programs can be quite elaborate, with well-established and intensive curriculum, meeting several times a week and providing drug education and family counseling.

SELF-HELP GROUPS

While technically not a treatment program, self-help groups are a prominent feature in the treatment of alcoholics and drug addicts. All of the various self-help groups available to alcoholics and drug addicts evolved from Alcoholic Anonymous. Typically referred to as Twelve-Step groups--a reference to their program of recovery--they are unaffiliated with any official entity and are always freestanding groups. Since their inception in the 1930's, other groups have borrowed their tenets and a variety of other Twelve-Step based programs have emerged. Cocaine Anonymous, Alanon, Gamblers Anonymous, Narcotics Anonymous, and various other recovery groups have formed over the years. Other programs using their basic format but emphasizing different therapeutic philosophies or material concerns (i.e., Rational Recovery groups, Alzheimer Support groups, Adult Children of Alcoholics) have also emerged in recent years. Twelve-Step groups remain the most popular and probably the most widely used approach. Although no official statistics are maintained because of the traditions of the program, estimates suggest that there are literally thousands of Twelve-Step groups throughout the world, primarily in the U.S., and perhaps 5 million participants at any given time. Since Alcoholic Anonymous readily accepts the disease model of addiction, Twelve Step groups, in some form, are invariably suggested and often required for those participating in detoxification programs, hospital-based programs, therapeutic communities and outpatient treatment programs.

WHICH INTERVENTION?

While no particular approach is considered better than another, these types of programs are considered alternatives for individuals pursuing cessation of alcohol and drugs. For Naomi, the combination of short-term residential treatment, outpatient counseling, and attendance at Alcoholic Anonymous meeting was instrumental in getting off alcohol and drugs. Long-term residential treatment and methadone maintenance programs have been shown to be quite successful for other individuals.

A FINAL THOUGHT

The level of alcohol and drug use in society, however, "may be the result of changes in social norms and the informal control system unrelated to conscious and deliberate parenting, treatment, or law enforcement" (Akers 1992: 183). There are a number of social factors, which contribute to the personal integration of drugs and alcohol into individual lifestyle. As we have seen in Naomi's case, being a member of a social group whose members use and condone alcohol and drugs is the most powerful predictor of an individual's alcohol and drug use (Forney, Forney, and Ripley 1989; Swaim 1991; Kitano, et al; 1992, Akers 1992). Naomi felt acceptance and found a niche for herself with friends who drank alcohol, smoked marijuana, and used other drugs. They provided substance using role models, encouraged her rejection of the religious values of her family, and socially rewarded her drinking and drug-taking behavior.

However, membership in a group which approves of drugs and alcohol use does not necessarily mean that individuals will abuse drugs. Naomi's life demonstrates that socialization in the family also can contribute to enhancing or controlling drug and alcohol abuse. For instance, lower rates of alcoholism are associated with the following family characteristics (1) Abstinence or moderate alcohol use is integrated into the context of strong family life, moral values, or religious orientation (2) Low-alcohol-content beverages--beer and wines--are most commonly used (3) Alcoholic beverages are ordinarily consumed at mealtimes (4) Parents typically provide an example of abstinent, light, or moderate drinking behavior rather than heavy or abusive drinking (5) Drinking is not a moral question, merely one of custom (6) Drinking is not symbolic of attaining adulthood (7) Drunkenness is not socially acceptable (8) Alcohol is not a central element in social activities (i.e., cocktail parties) (9) There are clear and consistent expectations regarding what is proper and what is improper in drinking alcohol. (adapted from National Institute on Alcohol Abuse and Alcoholism 1975:21-22)

Since the degree of cultural and social integration concerning alcohol is quite high in our society, these family characteristics influence attitudes and behavior concerning alcohol use and subsequently other drugs as well. Although it is quite possible for alcohol and drug abusers to come from abstinent families as did Naomi, generally children whose parents have a history of alcohol or drug abuse are more likely than other children (who came from the kind of family in which Naomi was raised) to abuse alcohol and use drugs (Glen and Parsons 1989, Cumes-Rayner, et al.1992). The pattern of drug and alcohol behavior by parents strongly influences the behavior of their children both as youngsters and adults. Rates of involvement with drugs, alcohol, and tobacco are higher in single-parent households than in two-parent households (Flewelling and Bauman 1990). But the family does not have to be disrupted; drug and alcohol abuse is associated with troubled relationships even within intact families. Those youths who report unhappy parental marriages, parental aloofness, and conflicts with parents have higher rates of heroin and marijuana use (Simcha-Fagan, Gersten, and Langner 1986). Parental expression of open hostility toward adolescents, severe family conflicts, and verbal aggression between parents and children are all associated with problem drinking among adolescents (Tubman, 1993; Smith, Rivers, and Stahl 1992). It is quite possible that the conflicts Naomi had with her parents, especially her father, and the hypocrisy and inconsistencies in his own behavior played an important role in her turning to alcohol and drugs

SUMMARY

1. The legality and illegality of mind-altering substances has been based on social acceptance factors rather than the intrinsic harmfulness or usefulness of the drugs in question.
2. The abuse of drugs, including alcohol, is by and large non-problematic in the U.S. and other modern societies. Societies' psychiatric problems differ, however, in their designation of "which" drugs to treat as problems.
3. The problem of alcohol and drugs has been associated with employment problems, legal entanglements, marital disruptions, spouse and child abuse, and a variety of psychiatric problems.
4. Patterns of drug use range from abstinence to addiction, and this is reflected in the history of drug use in America.
5. The cultural integration perspective says that the more culturally integrated and less socially disapproved a drug is, the more likely people are to come in contact with it.
6. The social integration perspective focuses on the extent to which the use of particular drugs has become acceptable within certain social groups.
7. Besides age, other factors such as race, gender, population density and region, and socio-economic status are important social group characteristics circumscribing the degree of illicit drug and alcohol use.
8. The official response to the problems associated with the abuse of drugs has been a two pronged approach in the U.S.: 1) interrupting the international and domestic production and trafficking of illicit drugs, and 2) applying legal penalties for the possession of illicit drugs.
9. Primary prevention programs are aimed at stopping drug use before it starts, such as Nancy Reagan's "Just Say No" campaign of the 1980s.
10. Secondary prevention programs focus on stopping drug use after individuals have been initiated into drug use and a subsequent habit or addiction has been established.

REFERENCES

Akers, Ronald L. 1992. *Drugs, Alcohol, and Society.* Belmont, CA: Wadsworth Publishing Co.

Akers, Ronald L., and Anthony J. La Greca 1991. "Alcohol Use Among the Elderly: Social Learning, Community Context, and Life Events." Pp.242-262 in David J. Pittman and Helene White eds. *Society, Culture. And Drinking Patterns Re-examined.* New Brunswick, NJ: Rutgers University Press.

Brown, F., and J. Tooley 1989. "Alcoholism in the Black Community." Pp.115-130 in Lawson and Ann Lawson eds. *Alcohol and Substance Abuse in Special Populations.* Rockville, MD: Aspen Publishers.

Cahalan, Don, Ira Cisin, Helen Crossley 1974. *American Drinking Practices.* New Brunswick, NJ: Rutgers Center of Alcohol Studies.

Cumes-Rayner, D. P., J. C. Lucke, B. Singh, B. Adler, T. Lewein, M. Dunn, and B Raphael 1992. "A High-Risk Community Study of Paternal Alcohol Consumption and Adolescents' Psychosocial Characteristics."

Flewelling, R. L. and K. E. Bauman 1990. "Family Structure as a Predictor of Initial Substance Use and Sexual Intercourse in Early Adolescence." *Journal of Marriage and Family.* 52 (February): 171-181.

Forney, M. A., P. D. Forney, and W. K. Ripley 1989. "Predictor Variables of Adolescent Drinking." *Advances in Alcohol and Substance Abuse.* 8(2): 97-117, Forbes, 1994. (October 10): 94.

Glen, S. A., and O. A. Parsons 1989. "Alcohol Abuse and Familial Alcoholist: Psychosocial Correlates in Men and Women." *Journal of Studies on Alcohol.* 50(2): 116-127.

Goode, Erich 1993. *Drugs in American Society.* Fourth ed. New York, NY: McGraw-Hill, Inc.

Gusfield, J. R. 1962. "Status Conflicts and the Changing Ideologies of the American Temperance Movement." In D. J. Pittman and C. R. Snyder, *Society, Culture, and Drinking Patterns.* New York, NY: John Wiley and Sons.

Harper, F. D. and E. Saifnoorianm 1991. "Drinking Patterns among Black Americans," Pp.327-338, in David J. Pittman and Helene White, eds. *Society, Culture, and Drinking Patterns Re-examined.* New Brunswick, NJ: Rutgers University Press.

Inciardi, J. A., and K. McElrath, 1995. *The American Drug Scene.* Los Angeles, CA: Roxbury Publishing Co.

Heffington, T.R. 1997. *Social Learning Theory and Elderly Drinking: A Longitudinal Structural Equation Model.* Dissertation. University of Florida, Gainesville, Florida. 1997.

Kendel, D. B., K. Yamaguchi, and K. Chen 1984. "Patterns of Drug Use from Adolescence to Young Adulthood." *American Journal of Public Health.* 74 (July): 677-81.

Kendel, D. B., K. Yamaguchi, and K. Chen 1992. "Stages of Progression in Drug Involvement from Adolescence to Adulthood: Further Evidence for the Gateway Theory." *Journal of Studies on Alcohol.* 53 (September): 447-57.

Kitano, H. H. L., I. Chi, S. Rhee, C.K. Law, and J.E. Lubben 1992. "Norms and Alcohol Consumption: Japanese in Japan, Hawaii, and California." *Journal of Studies on Alcohol.* 53 (January): 33-39.

Lazare, D. 1990. "The Drug War is Killing Us." *Village Voice.* (January 23): 22-29.

Molgaard, Craig A., Chester M. Nakamura, Percil E. Stanford, Michael Peddecord, and Deborah J. Norton 1990. "Prevalence of Alcohol Consumption Among Older Persons." *Journal of Community Health.* 15(4): 239-251.

Mustos, David F. 1991. "Opium, Cocaine, and Marijuana in American History." *Scientific American.* July 1991:40-47.

_____.1996. "Alcohol in American History." *Scientific American.* April 1996:78-83.

National Institute on Alcohol Abuse and Alcoholism 1975. *Facts About Alcohol and Alcoholism.* Rockville, MD: National Institute on Alcohol Abuse and Alcoholism.

Neill, J. R. 1987. "'More Than Medical Significance': LSD and American Psychiatry 1953-1966." Pp.214-216 in J. A. Inciardi and Karen McElrath, eds. *The American Drug Scene.* Los Angeles, CA: Roxbury Publishing Co.

Rorabaugh, W. J. 1991. "Alcohol in America." *OAH Magazine of History.* Fall 1991:17-19.

SAMHSA 1996 "Percentages Reporting Past Month Use of Alcohol or Drugs by Age and Demographic Characteristics." *Office of Applied Studies, National Household survey on Drug Abuse.*

Siegal, H. A., and J. A. Inciardi 1995. *The American Drug Scene.* Los Angeles, CA: Roxbury Publishing Co.

Simcha-Fagan, O., J. C. Gersten, and T. S. Langner 1986. "Early Precursors and Concurrent Correlates of Patterns of Illicit Drug Use in Adolescents." *Journal of Drug Issues.* 16(Winter): 7-28.

Smith, P. D., P. C. Rivers, and K. J. Stahl 1992. "Family Cohesion and Conflict as Predictors of Drinking Patterns: Beyond Demographics and Alcohol Expectancies." *Family Dynamics of Addictions Quarterly.* 2(2): 61-69

Spillane, Joseph 1994. "Cocaine Before Prohibition: The Social Control of a Legal Drug." Presented at the American Society of Criminology Meeting November, Miami, FL.

Stephens, R. C. 1992. "Psychoactive Drug Use in the United States Today: A Critical Overview." Pp.1-31 in Thomas Mieczkowski, ed., *Drugs, Crime, and Social Policy.* Needham Heights, MA: Allyn and Bacon.

Substance Abuse and Mental Health Services Administration (SAMHSA) 1997. "National Household Survey on Drug Abuse (NHSDA), 1996. Preliminary Data," Rockville, MD: Substance Abuse and Mental Health Services Administration, Office of Applied Statistics. (Internet: www.health.org/pubs/nhsda).

Swaim, R. C. 1991. "Childhood Risk Factors and Adolescent Drug and Alcohol Abuse." *Educational Psychology Review.* 3(4): 363-398.

Tubman, J. G. 1993. "Family Risk Factors, Parental Alcohol Use, and Problem Behaviors Among School-age Children." *Family Relations.* 42 (January): 81-86.

University of Michigan 1997. "The Monitoring the Future Study." Ann Arbor, MI (Internet: www.isr.umich.edu/src/mft).

Form No. 2033

UNPACK
DATE __16-16-0109__   QTY. __31__

SB/SS/SRSER S# _____

SERIES TITLE _____

**S# _____ Vol. _____

ST# _____

PO # _____

PUB _____

INT _____

AD _____

PI _____

PO _____

CP _____

LP _____

V _____

R# _____

TOC   CIP   NO

REC.
DATE __54-417-02__

QTY. __31__   LOC.

CHAPTER 5: CRIME AND DELINQUENCY
CASE STUDY: JOE, A SADISTIC SERIAL KILLER

He was his mother's eleventh child, the unwanted product of a temporary relationship. His mother's most frequent partner was physically violent and sexually abusive. Joe was small in size, possibly due to poor nutrition or his mother's chain smoking. While some social work visitors reported that Joe's mother was "asking for more help than she needs," others reported that the home was filthy, there was no food in the kitchen, and no appropriate toys or facilities for small children. At the age of four, after an "accident" in which Joe received head injuries, Joe was placed in a foster home. During this period (1950s), it was held that children in foster care should be moved frequently, so that they would not form undue attachments that would interfere with a later adoption. At first Joe was moved from one home to another on the basis of the "undue attachment" policy. Later moves, however, were precipitated by Joe's behavior. A chronic bed wetter, Joe also liked to set fires and torture animals. Over a period of eleven years, Joe was placed in eleven foster homes.

A teacher described Joe as "Quite bright, but a devious manipulator. When Joe was eleven, he committed a serious assault on a fellow student, and was placed in an institution. There, he received little education or personal attention.

At age 16, Joe was transferred to an adult mental institution. Here he was exposed to various treatments inspired by the pharmaceutical advances of the 1950s and the psychiatric ideologies of the 1960s. He was given a powerful hallucinogenic drug cocktail that was supposed to make him more dependent on others, and therefore more willing to get along with them. Another (ineffective) treatment involved chaining psychopaths (such as Joe) with schizophrenics (people with a poor connection to reality), in the hope that the psychopaths would become more empathetic, and the schizophrenics would become more organized.

Up until the mid 1970's, most patients such as Joe were never released. But during the 1970s there was increased pressure from patients' rights groups, and new legislation made it more difficult to hold mentally ill persons for indefinite periods. At the same time, there was increased government enthusiasm for cost cutting "deinstitutionalization" of mental patients. Thus, Joe was released.

Almost immediately he was involved in a violent assault on two children, and he was arrested. Joe's institutional record of assaults was not admissible evidence in the court. Despite this, he was convicted. He was sent to a sex offender program, where he rejected all attempts at change. Here he was diagnosed as a sadistic psychopath (a person with no conscience who derives pleasure from inflicting pain on others) with high pedophilia (attraction to children as sex objects) and high probability to re-offend. This prediction was confirmed as soon as Joe was released.

When arrested for an assault on a child, Joe explained "I wanted to tell him that I loved him, but I didn't think he'd understand." The prosecutor was forced to offer Joe an advantageous plea bargain in order to spare the victim the pain of facing his abuser. A psychiatrist who examined Joe at this time warned that Joe was capable of murder, both in view of his sadism, and in view of his desire to avoid being caught again.

Two years later, Joe was released to a halfway house. This was the only positive phase in his life. He was introduced to the wonders of shopping malls, buying Christmas presents for the first time, owning an aquarium, making up his own mind about his clothes and meals. Under the conditions of his parole, he was expected to participate in a drug program to control his sexual drives, and also expected to participate in a psychiatric support group. He was not to associate with people under 16 unless supervised, and not to frequent places where there were young people. He was supposed to meet with a parole officer twice a month.

But Joe was not well supervised. He found the drug therapy had unpleasant side effects, so he dropped it. He did not attend his support group. After many other unreported violations of his parole, Joe kidnapped a ten-year old boy at knifepoint, assaulted and killed him. When Joe was arrested, he burst into tears, saying, "He was such a nice kid. Why did he have to die?"

Joe's lawyer opted for an insanity defense, arguing that Joe did not have the mental capacity to be criminal. Joe took the stand in his own defense and asked to be sent back to the mental hospital "where they have excellent programs." The jury, however, found Joe guilty of first degree murder, and he was sentenced to life imprisonment. A year later he was murdered by "regular cons" who broke into his cell in order to mete out their own "justice."

CRIME DELINQUENCY AND SOCIAL PROBLEMS

The sadistic pedophile is one of the most horrifying of criminals and the least amenable to treatment or correction. Fortunately they are also the most rare of criminals. The greatest number of criminals are in fact nonviolent property offenders, who are simply appalled at having to share a prison courtyard with men like Joe. What Joe has in common with many career criminals, however, is a life that got off to a "wrong start" very early, and was characterized by "help" that was ineffective and inappropriate.

There are two main questions that criminologists ask about the social problem of crime: first, why are some people labeled "criminal" or "delinquent"; and second, why do some people commit the acts that put them at risk for being called criminal? The answer to the first question is that the criminal law and the criminal justice system combine to certify crime and delinquency. The answer to the second lies in the application of theories such as symbolic interactionism, functionalism, and conflict theory to the available data on criminal careers.

DEFINING CRIME

The most commonly cited definition of crime is that given by Paul Tappan: "Crime is an intentional act or omission in violation of criminal law,...committed without defense or justification, and sanctioned by the state as a felony or misdemeanor" (1960)

When Joe was charged with "first degree murder," he was accused of committing a specific prohibited act (the actus reus) while having the awareness of "a reasonable man" (intentionality or mens rea). Joe's behavior was neither justified (for example, by being a police officer apprehending an offender) nor covered in the acceptable criminal defenses (such as insanity, duress, or necessity). The fact that Joe came from a highly disturbed background was not, in the view of the court, sufficient to take away this assumption about his ability to think reasonably. If they had decided otherwise, Joe would have again evaded the definition of criminal, despite his confession to the killing

DEFINING DELINQUENCY

Delinquency involves offenses by a juvenile that if committed by an adult would result in criminal prosecution (Butts 1996:2), and it may also involve "status offenses." Examples of status offenses are truancy, incorrigibility, underage liquor law/smoking, law/curfew violations, and underage sexual activity. In juvenile court, offenders are not found guilty of crimes, but are "found to be delinquent" because they committed a crime (Greenwood 1995:102). On the whole, delinquents are those over 10 and under 18 at the time of their offense, although some states have a lower limit of 12, and some have an upper limit as low as 15 (Champion 1997:70, Butts 1996:11).

CRIME AND THE STATE

In early England, crimes were violations of the "King's Peace" (Chambliss and Seidman 1982). The current justice system in the U.S. maintains the position that the state (now represented by each state government rather than by a king) is the offended party. Reflecting the role of the state as accuser in a criminal trial, the case is called: U.S. v. JONES (1997), i.e. The United States versus Jones (the accused person, the defendant in the case), in the year 1997.

Since the state is the official "injured party" in the criminal trial, the person who was hurt is often "used" in the court process or left out of it completely. Such victims rarely feel that the system has done them justice. On the other hand, the defendant seems to have all kinds of rights. There are elaborate protections for the accused, (collectively called "due process") developed over the centuries to prevent the abuse of state power. One example of this is the Fifth Amendment right to silence. These rights sometimes interfere with convictions, and we often hear that "the accused are being given too many rights," or "got off on technicalities."

CRIMINAL AND CIVIL LAW

Not all law is criminal law. In the O. J. Simpson case, Simpson was the defendant in a criminal trial when he was charged with the murder of his ex-wife. He was found not guilty on this charge. This simply means that the prosecution was unable to prove its case. Following this, Simpson was sued in civil court for the tort of wrongful death (Dershowitz 1997). In a civil suit, the court decides between two citizens. While the standard of proof in a criminal case is "beyond a reasonable doubt," the standard in a civil case is the "balance of probabilities." Also, in a civil case, many more kinds of evidence are "admissible" to be heard by the court. Thus, it is possible to be found liable for damages in civil court while being found "not guilty" with respect to the same incident in criminal court

DETERMINING WHO WILL BE CERTIFIED AS CRIMINAL

Criminal law is not equal in its impact. Anatole France (in The Red Lily, 1984) observed that the law equally forbids both the rich and the poor to sleep under the bridges of Paris. The process whereby laws are made and enforced produces a very select group of "criminals" who are disproportionately from the lower classes and minorities. It is interesting, and worth your attention, to look closely at this process of crime definition. Here, we will look at two aspects of this: first the fact that law does not simply reflect the common culture of a nation; and second, the "crime funnel" effect whereby some cases are rejected or diverted out of the system, while an increasingly homogeneous group stays in it.

CRIMINAL LAW AND COMMON VALUES

Many criminal laws reflect the working out of public fears (moral panics), and the beliefs and understandings of earlier times. They reflect the decisions of particular governments in particular time periods, often after these governments had been strongly lobbied by special interest groups (usually those with power in the community). Because of this, the criminal code of each state is somewhat unique. Is prostitution a crime in your state? Can a man be convicted for raping his wife? What about legal access to marijuana? Your answer to each of these questions (and many similar ones) will depend largely on which part of the country you live in.

On the other hand, many harmful and distressing kinds of behavior are very rarely treated as criminal. In the case of Joe, his mother's neglect was not treated as criminal. No policeman intervened to protect him from the adults in his life. Joe's antisocial and destructive behavior was not initially treated as criminal, first because of his age, and then because of his protection under mental health legislation. At the other end of the social scale, we see harmful acts by persons with money and power are not treated as criminal. It is quite rare for company officials to be charged over the deaths of workers, even when such deaths were foreseeable consequences of company policies (Sutherland 1940; Conklin 1972).

THE CRIME FUNNEL – WHICH PEOPLE REMAIN IN THE SYSTEM?

There is no automatic translation of a forbidden act into a criminal label. The "crime funnel," described as follows, is a model which illustrates the loose fit between the operation of the criminal justice process and the actual use of the term "criminal" in social life:

(1) The space above of the funnel represents the "dark figure" of crime: all actions that violate a criminal law. Most of these actions will not even be noticed. Did your wallet get stolen, or did you just lose it? Is the broken window the sign of an attempted break-in, or was it wind damage? Even when potentially criminal actions are noticed it is possible that nothing will be done about them.

(2) When offenses are reported to police (reactive policing) or discovered by the police (proactive policing) cases begin to enter the system (move down the funnel). The police may make an effort to keep the event within "the funnel" by documenting it, and by locating the perpetrator(s). Or they may

decide that it wasn't really a crime, or that there's not enough evidence for conviction, and classify it as "unfounded." If unfounded, it is treated outside the funnel.

(3) If an offender is identified, charges may be laid. Generally, if a case is not winnable on the available evidence, the prosecutor will drop it. The accused person may choose to plea bargain (plead guilty in exchange for some form of leniency, or just to get it over with) or fight the allegations. Those with more resources are more likely to fight, regardless of the evidence against them, and more likely to escape the funnel.

(4) At the trial stage, the weight of the evidence will be extremely important, but the way in which the courtroom drama unfolds can also have a profound influence on the outcome. Factors such as the competence and preparedness of the prosecutor and defense lawyer, the effect of publicity on the judge, or the concern of the jury over "going home to the community" may all have their impact.

(5) If the case results in conviction, offenders move to the bottom of the funnel and may spend some time under the supervision of the correctional system, as prison inmates or as probationers, serving supervised release in the community.

In the process from detection to incarceration certain kinds of cases stay in the system, while others are filtered out. <u>Criminals are the people who have been kept in the system.</u> Criminals in this sense are mainly lower class and often members of minority groups (Sulton 1996:22). The generalization of the idea of "any crime" to "violent crime" to "dangerous-looking people" is sometimes called categorical contagion (Zimring and Hawkins 1966:61). Categorical contagion ensures that people who "look like criminals" will be more readily convicted if they are charged.

PERVASIVENESS OF CRIME

Thousands of activities, some trivial, some very serious, are legally defined as "crimes." Most of us break some of these laws. Over 90% of drivers exceed the speed limit some of the time and over a third of us cheat a bit on our income tax. Failure to make an honest declaration of our purchases when crossing a border (smuggling) is often a matter of humor and pride (Gabor 1994). Student life often includes activities that could be considered criminal, such as defacing public monuments or disturbing the peace, not to mention offenses of interpersonal violence. Despite this pervasive low-level criminality, relatively few citizens have a criminal record, think of themselves as being criminal, or are treated as "criminals" (Gabor 1994:15 Snyder and Sickmund 1996:49)

What about "serious" offenses? Are these frequent and pervasive? Consider the people around you. Have any of them ever tried to kill another person? Have they used physical threat or a weapon to force another person to give money (or sex)? Have any of your friends set up an elaborate scheme to siphon off funds from their college? Less than 5% of citizens are involved in this sort of criminality. An even smaller number, less than a 10th of 1%, have committed random acts of violence against strangers.

MEASURES OF CRIME (UCR& NVCS)

There are two nation-wide programs that report on the nature and magnitude of crime in America: the FBI's Uniform Crime Reporting (UCR) Program and the Bureau of Justice Statistics' National Crime Victimization Program (NCVS) (FBI 1996:378). The UCR program collects crimes recorded by police. It reports on a narrow group of eight "index crimes" which are meant to convey the overall crime situation. This system is gradually being replaced by a more sophisticated program, the National Incident-Based Reporting System (NIBRS). This incident-based reporting system collects information about 57 types of crimes (Greenfeld 1997:11), and gives researchers much more information about each offense. The second major program, the NCVS, represents the victim perspective. It is conducted by the Bureau of Justice Statistics in conjunction with interviewers from the Census Bureau. The NCVS is based on interviews with a nationally representative sample of households. Neither program catches all crime, and neither of them report crimes such as political corruption, violations of human rights or environmental offenses. The emphasis on "index crimes" contributes to the public conception that most crime is "street crime."

When we put the UCR and the NCVS together, we find that rates of crime reported by victims are very much higher than the rates of crime reported by police. Victims often fail to report victimization. They may refrain from reporting, for example, if the perpetrator is someone who cannot be avoided in future. Over time, the two sources of information about crime are becoming more alike, with the rate of victimization dropping, and the rate of crime known to police becoming stable after a long rise. This seems to mean that crime is stabilizing or dropping, and that victims are becoming more willing to trust the police and courts to provide them with help. In other words, some of our crime-related social problems are actually becoming less serious.

EXPLAINING CRIME: WHY DO OFFENDERS DO IT?

Genetics and biology may sometimes load the gun for crime, but the environment pulls the trigger. We know, for example, that children such as Joe, who come from chaotic and violent backgrounds, suffer frontal lobe brain damage, and show sadistic tendencies at an early age are at much greater risk for serious and repetitive adult offending than children who lack this background. We can even say that Joe's criminality was "over determined" in that there are many explanations, each of which would be sufficient in itself to explain why Joe became such a defective piece of humanity. Theories that you are now familiar with, namely symbolic interactionism, functionalism and conflict theory all have useful things to say about the origins and shaping of criminal careers and criminal events.

SYMBOLIC INTERACTION THEORY

Making Criminal Identities. How are some events recognized as criminal, and some people are labeled criminal? Being labeled criminal can cause people to lose their legitimate employment prospects, thus making them more vulnerable to criminal opportunities, more likely to adopt a deviant identity, more likely to associate with other "criminals" and more likely to commit more offenses. (Symbolic Interaction Theory helps to explain why "being born again" is such a potent way of coping with a deviant identity once this process has begun). Symbolic interactionism can help us to understand how small quarrels in the family or the local bar, can "get out of control" when people see trivial insults as serious threats to their self image, and use violence to regain control and respect. It also helps to make sense of the cultivation of a protective "mean and hard" identity among ghetto gang members and their wannabe (want-to-be) followers (Katz 1988)

FUNCTIONALISM: SOCIAL DISORGANIZATION, STRAIN, AND CONTROL

Functionalism points to the fact that crime serves certain purposes for society. It is like a vaccination: it challenges the social body to protect itself and this may make the system stronger. In Durkheim's terms, even a society of saints would have some crime, since crime is "needed" by the system. If there is not enough crime, we invent some, as happened with the witchcraze in medieval Europe (Deutschmann 1998:91-103). More recently, it has been argued that crime that is more than the system "needs" will be "defined down" (Moynihan 1993). We will not react to it as we did in less criminal times. Crime is certainly functional for some parts of our system. The "crime control industry" (catching, prosecuting and incarcerating criminals) is one of the most rapidly expanding parts of the economy (Christie 1994) and both politicians and the media would be severely impacted if crime were suddenly eradicated.

As an explanation for why particular people commit crime, functionalism takes three main forms: social disorganization, strain theory and control theory. The **theory of social disorganization** (based on Durkheim) argues that, people commit offenses when social regulation (clear rules and supervision) and integration (belonging and sharing common values) have been disrupted by social change. Signs of disorganization are high rates of divorce, out-of-wedlock births, unemployment, mental illness, and, of course, crime. People commit offenses because they are anomic (not guided by common values) and because they are not held accountable by strong institutional controls.

Strain theory (based on the work of Robert Merton) argues that, while all Americans are exposed to cultural goals of the "American Dream," many poor and minority Americans are not positioned to have access to the legitimate institutional means necessary for this. While the young woman from a wealthy family may experience little strain as she acquires education and job experience to meet her goals, the equally intelligent ghetto youth, especially if also handicapped by racial discrimination and poor local economy, may see no legitimate path to success. In Merton's terms, the strain between cultural goals and blocked opportunities provides an incentive for crime. The person experiencing strain may *innovate,* (by choosing criminal enterprise, for example) or engage in *ritualism* (going through the motions, but not trying to get ahead). He or she may *retreat* (by escaping into drugs, for example). Another way to deal with the strain is to *reject and replace* both the cultural goal and the institutional means (becoming a revolutionary, for example). Thus, Merton's theory holds that the cause of crime is the combination of two factors: first, many people in American society experience blocked opportunities, so that they cannot legitimately attain their goals and second, Americans tend to respect material success without being too concerned about how that success was attained, so that "cheating" is often an effective way of resolving the strain.

Control theory, an outgrowth of disorganization theory, argues that, when it comes to motivation, most of us are potentially criminal. Criminality is often fun and, in the short-term, rewarding. Cheating is "easier" than working, and a lot faster. So, what we need to explain is why most of us are not criminal, not why some of us are. Travis Hirschi's control theory argues that there are four main social bonds that hold us to the straight and narrow. These are attachment, commitment, involvement, and belief. If we are *attached* to law-abiding parents and friends who care about us and observe our behavior, we are unlikely to jeopardize the relationship by breaking the rules. If we are *committed* to certain goals, such as getting a bonded job in industry or a position in the military, risk of a criminal conviction will be avoided. When we are *involved* in many legitimate activities, we will not be available for other kinds of action. Finally, if we believe in the rules of our society, and respect those who enforce them, we will likely be law-abiding citizens. Control theory argues that the solution to crime is the strengthening of institutions such as the family and the school, and the provision of meaningful career paths that will induce commitment and involvement.

THEORY BOX by Michael J. Donnelly Chapter. 5 Crime and Delinquency/Differential Association

Differential association theory treats crime and delinquency basically as learned phenomena. What people do in general is learned through their associations with others, particularly in our primary groups, with those we encounter while we are young, with whom we interact with over a long period, and whom we admire and care about. When individuals live in environments in which criminality is approved and favorably defined, they will be prone to commit deviant acts themselves; this is especially likely when the individual encounters deviant orientations at an early age and in long-term interaction with admired role models. Hence, the likelihood that an individual will engage in crime or delinquency. Associating principally with criminals tends to distort an individual's perception of proper behavior; or to put it otherwise, the individual who associates principally with criminals learns to act in ways appropriate and approved by, that group. It is not difficult to think of applications of this approach. Think of two American high schools: one in a prosperous suburb where a majority of students are in a college-preparatory track; the other in an impoverished inner city, where drop out rates are high and gangs a feature of everyday life in the surrounding neighborhoods. Such schools would offer dramatically different possibilities for "differential association," different role models, different values, rewards for different sorts of (locally judged) achievement and success.

Differential association is a thoroughgoing sociological approach. It was developed as an alternative to explanations of crime and delinquency rooted in biological predisposition or in aberrant psychological states. One typical criticism of differential association is that it may be more useful for explaining some varieties of deviancies than others-petty theft, for instance, rather than crimes of passion or mental illness.

CONFLICT THEORY

Crime is the product of intergroup conflict. Conflict theory, like functionalism, takes many forms, but one common feature is the argument that the powerful set the rules that others must live by, and enforce them most strongly on those with less power. Conflict theory does not agree with the view that criminal law represents a true consensus about right and wrong. Conflict theorists, for example, point out that mood enhancers (such as alcohol) used by the powerful are legal, even if regulated, while those used mainly by the less powerful are criminalized. The "war on drugs" enables authorities to put far more surveillance on youth and minority populations than would be possible without it, so that they are more likely to be caught and held in the crime funnel. In this way criminal law can be a tool used to maintain the advantages of some and the disadvantages of others.

There may be many roads to crime (Nettler 1982:6). An arsonist, for example, may arrive at the point of lighting the fire by many different routes: he or she may be a child expressing feelings about divorce, a pyromaniac who gains sexual pleasure from the fire, an organized crime enforcer or terrorist sending a "message", a hired "torch" helping a businessman collect insurance money or even a person who hopes to find employment in the clean-up after a fire (Deutschmann 1998:43). Some of these paths are more commonly followed than others. When this is understood, we can work on ways of preventing people from starting on them, or **target-hardening** the things they attack. As we look at different kinds of crime, you may wish to consider which theories are most useful in explaining them.

CRIME CATEGORIES I: CRIMES AGAINST PERSONS

The UCR classifies murder, rape, assault, and robbery as "crimes against persons." These four index crimes together constitute about 12% of reported crime (FBI 1996:8). It is in these categories of crime, especially homicide, which the United States stands out among the industrialized western nations (Reiss and Roth 1993). As noted by Siegal (1995:6) "If the United States had the same murder rate as England's, it would experience 2,500 homicides a year instead of 24,000; if it had Japan's robbery rate, 4,500 robberies would occur annually instead of the actual number of more than 600,000." Americans are aware, possibly over aware, that they have a problem with violent crime.

MURDER

The FBI's list of index crimes (crimes included in the UCR) begins with murder and non-negligent homicide. These crime categories includes willful killing of one human being by another, but excludes deaths occurring due to negligence, suicide, or legitimate police work. Homicide rates in the United States rose sharply in the 1960s through 1980, and again between 1985 and 1990, a fact usually explained by the explosion of armed drug trafficking and gang warfare in the inner cities (Barkan 1997:258). According to recent research the recent decline in the homicide rate may be mainly due to the provision of trauma centers in nearly all major urban areas, so that many victims enter into the aggravated assault statistics instead of the homicide category (FBI 1996: 276). Homicide is a major public health problem; it is the 10th leading cause of death overall and the 2nd leading cause of death in males aged 15 - 34 years (Hutson, et al. 1995). The United States has an overall rate of 8 murders per 100,000 population (FBI 1996:14, Parker 1995). Other industrialized nations range between one and three homicides per 100,000 population (Barkan 1997:256).

EXPLAINING AMERICA'S HIGH RATE OF HOMICIDE.

Are Americans more violent than other people? Could the high rates of violence mean that more Americans are badly raised, brain damaged, or subjected to stress than people of other nations? Could all the violence in the media be teaching them to be criminal? Is America's involvement in recent wars a factor? Is racial conflict the explanation? While possible, none of these explanations is supported by convincing evidence. One controversial explanation that we can propose here is that the availability and widespread cultural acceptance of firearms in the U.S. has escalated the consequences of violence, rather than the amount of violence. Not only are people who have been shot more likely to die than people who have been stabbed or beaten, but firearms also raise the "rate" of violent crime in a strictly technical sense. The thief who carries a gun may well find himself charged with robbery (classified as violent) rather than burglary (classified as a property offense), even if there is no other difference in the actual offense. The high rates of violence that are reported as "gun-related" tend to support this view. Seven out of 10 murders and almost half of robberies in the U.S. involve firearms (FBI 1996:17,274)

Americans are much more likely than Asians or Europeans to carry guns (legally or not) and to keep them in their vehicles and their homes (Van Dijk et al. 1991, Barkan 1997:277, and Kopel 1992). There is also a huge surplus of illegally acquired guns (Siegal 1995:297). A majority of youths currently in correctional facilities apparently carry a gun almost always when they are free, and over 80% of them own a gun (Sheley and Wright 1993). Criminals and many regular citizens share the belief that guns are an appropriate form of self-defense (Kleck and Gertz 1998, Decker, Pennell and Caldwell 1997:1).

Is intervention possible? While firearm availability is a factor in the high rates of homicide in the U.S., (and also in the high costs of trauma center medical care), it is not clear that there is any simple way of resolving the problem (Kopel 1992). Sudden changes in legislation could simply create a lucrative black-market for guns. There is little evidence that Americans are willing to give up their constitutional right to weapons, especially if this means that the law-abiding are disarmed before the criminal population is (Barkan 1997:281).

Regional Variations in Murder.

Urban areas average about nine victims per 100,000 persons, while rural areas report about five per 100,000. The South tends to have higher rates, at 10 murders for every 100,000 people, compared with only six per 100,000 in the Northeast. However, even in high crime states, the incidence of murder is highly localized, reflecting inner city conditions in major urban areas (See the discussion of juvenile homicide, below). Some theorists have tried to explain the high rates of interpersonal violence in the south as a cultural phenomenon, arguing that men in the south are raised to a code that makes them more likely to resort to weapons in defense of their women and their honor.

EXPLAINING HOMICIDE AMONG FRIENDS AND FAMILY.

While homicides by strangers have increased, it is still largely true that unless you hang with a criminal gang in a violent area, your nearest and dearest are most likely to do you in. Roughly 80% of homicides are committed within the circle of friends, relatives and acquaintances (Decker 1993, Dawson and Langan 1994). The remaining 20% are predominantly the product of drug wars and robbery rather than the actions of serial killers (Craven 1996:2). The stereotype of the "predatory stranger," as the main source of danger is not well supported.

Personal Homicide. Symbolic interactionists have highlighted the kind of "personal homicide" (sometimes called "victim precipitated homicide") that emerges when people believe themselves to have been intolerably insulted by another person, especially someone very close to them. They may respond with escalating insults and violence (Luckenbill 1977, Wolfgang 1958). Especially when heavy use of alcohol is involved, and knives or guns are close by, "silly" arguments can escalate, with the result that one partner will be killed (Luckenbill 1977:185, Parker 1995; Katz 1988). Roughly half of known homicides are personal homicides (Felson and Steadman 1983).

Feminist conflict theorists have highlighted another angle on personal homicide. They argue that the ingrained notions of patriarchy (whereby dominant roles are played by men) make men particularly vulnerable to perceived slights to their manhood. Unrealistic expectations for constant respect and deference can lead to homicide. With these ideas in mind, consider the following evidence on homicide in the U.S.

Murderers and their victims are mainly male, and under 25 years of age. 9 out of 10 female victims were killed by males, 1 in 4 by a spouse or boyfriend. In contrast, only 3% of the male victims were killed by wives or girlfriends (FBI 1996:17). Females tend to kill people they know well, sometimes turning on an abusive partner, or killing children in their care (Saltzman and Mercy 1993). Nonetheless, all but 3% of offenders who committed violent crimes against children in 1995 were male (Greenfeld 1996:1).

In incidents with one victim and one offender, 84% of White murder victims were killed by Whites, while over 90% of Black murder victims are killed by Black offenders. The problems of "Black on Black" homicide and interpersonal violence has received considerable high-level attention within the Black community. In 1994, African-American politicians, entertainers and civil rights leaders announced a new "moral offensive" to combat this phenomenon (Barkan 1997:259).

Other Kinds of Killing. Several infrequent kinds of murder attract a disproportionate amount of attention both in the media and the public imagination. Examples of this are thrill killing (killing for the experience of doing the forbidden), cult killing (killing in the context of religious beliefs), mass murder (killing of many people in one incident) and serial murder (killing of many people in a sequence).

Intervention to prevent these other forms of killing is hampered by the fact that they are so rare that few police agencies have developed methods of recognizing the problem before it happens. Children such as Joe in our case study will continue to fall through the cracks of social support systems until they have become truly dangerous. The main efforts at this time are concentrated on improving police work, so that in the future, these killers will be quickly identified.

Poor communication and lack of cooperation between rival law enforcement agencies have sometimes hampered investigations. This problem is being met with new systems of police reporting (such as the Violent Criminal Apprehension Program (VICAP) and the development of "profiling systems" that give police clues about the characteristics of the offender they are looking for (Holmes 1989, Egger 1990, Douglas et al. 1997). Geographical mapping procedures are also improving police performance in catching serial killers, by pinpointing their range of activity.

RAPE AND SEXUAL ASSAULT

Definitions. Forcible rape, according to the UCR, is "the carnal knowledge of a female forcibly and against her will." Unlike the UCR, the NCVS recognizes the possibility that males may be victims of rape (Barkan 1997:289). Early rape laws assumed that the female victim was the property of her father or husband, and that rape took value away from him (Siegal 1995:299). Rape is still frequently misunderstood by the public as a predominantly sexual act, a "normal" act of male mastery incited by female behavior (as presented in mass-produced pornography). This widely shared cultural viewpoint provides a neutralization that helps rapists to feel "normal" and sometimes makes the courts treat them with more leniency. While rape is often sexually gratifying to the offender, it is rarely committed by people who lack outlets for consensual sex, who are "oversexed," or who are responding to a woman's actual sexual signals (Groth and Birnbaum 1979). Rape has more to do with psychopathy, anger, and/or cultural scripts for dominance than with sex (Henslin 1996:155).

Campuses and Rape. A great deal of sexual coercion occurs in the context of ordinary college and university dating and group activities, particularly when alcohol is also present. Gang rapes have occurred on at least five campuses, and it has been estimated that 15 to 20% of college women have experienced rape or attempted rape (Siegal 1995:300). The recent advent of an odorless, tasteless "date rape" drug called Rohypnol (street names include Roofies, Rib, Rope, Mind-Eraser and others) has caused alarm in Europe as well as America. The drug is virtually undetectable in a drink, and it can render the victim unable to resist and unable to remember what happened in the incident. The symptoms of this drug resemble extreme drunkenness, which adds to the likelihood that the victim will not be helped.

Police, prosecutors and judges are now somewhat more likely to view rape as "real crime." Nonetheless, because "lack of consent" must be proven in court, the victim is often on trial as well. Many victims feel twice victimized, first by the perpetrator, then by the system. Willingness to convict is increasing, and the number of prisoners sentenced for sexual assault during the 1990s has increased at 15% per year, a rate only exceeded by the increase in drug related incarcerations (Greenfeld 1997:vi).

Rape and Sexual Abuse of Children. Sexual abusers who target children are called **pedophiles**. Almost all known pedophiles are men. Most seduce their young victims, but others use threats and force. Most violent offenders, like Joe in our case study committed many offenses prior to their first conviction, and many although not the majority, had been violently abused themselves (Greenfeld 1997:vi, 2). The pedophile typically preys on his own child (or stepchild), or the child of a close acquaintance (Greenfeld 1996:2).

Interventions with pedophiles have a poor reputation overall, partly, perhaps, because nothing less than a perfect cure is acceptable to us. In fact, many offenders are quickly shamed or frightened away from this activity, especially those that sought out children mainly because they were immature themselves. Some youths are labeled criminal sex offenders because they had consensual sex with an underage girlfriend. Some offenders, however, (and these are the minority that we hear the most about) are violent predators. They are extremely resistant to treatment of any kind. They are masters of denying that they have done anything wrong, and rather good at manipulating "experts" into believing a cure has been made. Some current treatment programs are producing evidence that they can "reduce the rate of offending" for people of this kind (Marshall and Barrett 1990). This reduction, although in some cases is quite impressive, gives little reassurance to the public.

Communities are increasingly demanding long-term supervision of all sex offenders. Some states are experimenting with indefinite "involuntary commitment" of sex offenders, even after they have served their sentences, as "mentally abnormal" even if not "mentally ill" under civil mental health laws. More controversial are "Megan's Law" community notification provisions. These allow people in the community to be notified about the names and addresses of any sex offenders living near them or near the school that their child attends. There are three main dangers to this well-intended solution. First, it tends to include a wide range of "sex offenders," most of whom have a minimal chance of re-offending; second, it may well encourage neighbors to take the law into their own hands (vigilantism); and third, it may make people careless about the many uncaught potential offenders in their children's circle of family friends, relatives and acquaintances.

AGGRAVATED ASSAULT

According to the UCR, "aggravated assault is an unlawful attack by one person upon another for the purpose of inflicting severe or aggravated bodily injury" (FBI 1996:31). The rates of assault in the U.S. are comparable to those of other democratic countries. When asked "Have you been personally attacked or threatened by someone in a way that really frightened you..." about 13% of Americans agreed, in comparison with 12% of Australians, 9% of Canadians, 7% of French citizens and 5% of the English (Van Dijk et al 1991:174-175, cited in Barkan 1997:256).

Family Violence. Assault in the home has always been underreported. Family loyalty, dependence, fear, and ignorance of the law combine to ensure silence. It was estimated in the 1970s that almost 1 million children were being abused by their parents each year. There is no reason to suppose that this abuse has declined, and authorities continue to discover very high rates of sustained abuse (Siegal 1995:324). Abused children are at increased risk for physical and mental problems, and sometimes, like Joe, become criminals themselves.

Spousal abuse is widespread (Siegal 1995:351) reports 70% of evening calls to police involve domestic disputes. The Conflict Tactics Scale (CTS), a widely used measure of spousal violence, has led to assertions that women are just as violent as men, and that women's violence against men is a major social problem (Straus 1993). The CTS, however, ignores the context of the violence and does not effectively measure how serious it is. Women are much more frequently seriously injured in marital violence than men are, and victimization studies such as the NYCS show that as much as 90% of all intimate violence is experienced by women (Barkan 1997:301-2). Academic studies of interpersonal violence (in and outside the family) also confirm the higher rates by which "big people hit little people" and women are victimized (Felson 1996). Violence by women against men may be a social problem, but it is not nearly on the same scale that violence by men against women is.

There are many myths about spousal abuse. One is the myth of women's "masochism," the idea that women like to be hurt (Caplan 1993). Another myth holds that, if women don't leave the situation, the battering can't be too bad. In fact, many battered women attempt to leave, but find insufficient resources for the support of themselves and their children. Shelters are often filled to capacity or offer only extremely short-term help. Leaving, or attempting to leave, may lead the batterer to stalking, harassment and even murder. Many women who kill their husbands have done so after they were unable to get help from either the welfare system or the law to escape him (Karmen 1995, Browne 1995). While arresting the abuser can be useful in conveying social disapproval of the batterer, it is too clumsy to work well with respect to complex family dynamics, and it rarely does anything to help the victim in the long term (Barkan 1997:303).

ROBBERY.

The UCR defines robbery as "the taking or attempting to take anything of value from the care, custody or control of a person or persons by force or threat of force or violence and /or by putting the victim in fear" (FBI 1996: 26). Robbery is considered to be a violent crime. Some robberies, however, are almost indistinguishable from (nonviolent) theft. The shoplifter who brushes by a store employee in order to slip away, or who is carrying a weapon, will very likely be charged with robbery.

While some robberies are carefully planned team events showing considerable advance preparation and thought, these "project crime" robberies are quite rare. Most modern armed robbers are youths with guns seeking the easiest available target. They are repeat offenders, but not skilled professionals. More than half of reported robberies are "muggings" that occurred in the street (FBI 1996).

OTHER CRIMES AGAINST PERSON

CARJACKING.

Carjacking is quite rare, amounting to only about 2% of cars stolen in the course of a year. The public generally sees Carjacking as a crime in which young hoodlums force a woman onto the street and drive off with her infant in the back seat. Cases that look at all like this get dramatic coverage in the news media. In fact, both victims and offenders tend to be young Black men, and the crime tends to occur in parking lots rather than on the road (Siegal 1995:341)

HATE OR BIAS CRIMES.

Hate crimes are defined as "crimes that manifest evidence of prejudice based on certain group characteristics" (BJA 1997). These characteristics include race, religion, sexual orientation, ethnicity, and most recently added, disability. Attacks have been made on people who are vagrants, mentally ill, elderly, gays, (or apparent gays), Blacks in "White" areas, immigrant workers, and visa students. Even when the crimes themselves are not violent (hate graffiti, for example) their effect in raising levels of fear, mistrust, and anger within a community can be very serious.

CRIME CATEGORIES II: CRIMES AGAINST PROPERTY

The three property offenses of larceny, burglary, and motor vehicle theft together comprise 90% of the total of index crimes and are declining (Voigt et al. 1994:72). These are crimes of stealth rather than violence, force or threats. Nonetheless, burglary can make the victim feel violated and unsafe.

LARCENY-THEFT.

Larceny-theft is defined by the UCR as "the unlawful taking, carrying, leading or riding away of property from the possession or constructive possession of another." It includes crimes such as shoplifting, pocket-picking, purse-snatching, thefts from motor vehicles, thefts of motor vehicle parts and accessories, and bicycle thefts, in which no use of force, violence, or fraud occurs (FBI 1996:43). Larceny-theft is one offense in which women have a substantial share, mostly in the form of shoplifting. This is the most common offense among women arrestees although male shoplifters still outnumber them 2 to 1.

Larceny is very often not recorded, partly because it isn't recognized at the time of the offense, and partly because clearance rate for this offense (only 20%) is so low that many victims do not think reporting is worthwhile. Modern merchandising and the increasingly portable nature of high priced items have contributed to the problem of larceny (Siegal 1995:338).

Storeowners are now fighting larceny not only with video cameras (Kockeisen 1993) but also with the use of civil damage laws. When shoplifters are apprehended they may be required to compensate store owners not only for the value of the goods they attempted to steal, but also for costs incurred to catch them, and punitive damages (Davis, Lundman and Martinez 1991). While this saves time and money for the store and for the courts, it can result in a double standard of justice: poorer people are turned over to the criminal justice system, while wealthier ones are invited to "buy" their way out.

BURGLARY

The Uniform Crime Reporting program defines burglary as "the unlawful entry of a structure to commit a felony or theft." Burglary, lower in the U.S. than in many other countries, appears to be declining, possibly due to the "fortressing" of America. This offense is often reported, probably for insurance purposes (FBI 1996). Burglars are usually nonviolent offenders who not only avoid occupied buildings but also choose 'easier' targets rather than richer but well-defended ones (Siegal 1995: 343, FBI 1996). Often a known target is preferred over an unfamiliar one (Bastian and DeBerry 1994). It is not unusual for burglary victims to become angry, fearful or depressed, and to feel less safe in their environment (Shover 1991, Rountree and Land 1996).

MOTOR VEHICLE THEFT

This UCR offense category includes the stealing of automobiles, trucks, buses, motorcycles, motorscooters, and snowmobiles. Motor vehicle theft comprises about 2% of property crime (FBI 1996:34). Many nations have higher rates of vehicle theft than does the U.S.

Vehicle theft takes several different forms. Joyriding is done mainly by youths that desire to experience the power, prestige, and potency that the car seems to offer. Cars may also be "borrowed" when a taxi is too expensive, or an untraceable vehicle is needed in order to commit another crime. At the other end of the scale are professional theft-rings, which steal cars for resale (often overseas) or run "chop shops" where cars are stripped for parts.

Manufacturers have introduced locking steering columns and other theft deterrents, which have had some impact on "which " cars get stolen (mainly a displacement effect). Recently, sticker/decal programs have been introduced. Owners can use a decal to indicate to police or border guards that "this car is not in use between 1and 5 a.m. and to permit police to make an investigatory stop. Some cars are now equipped with hidden radio transmitters that give off a tracking signal (Siegal 1995:341).

ANOTHER PROPERTY CRIME: FRAUD

Although fraud is not treated separately in national crime statistics, it is a significant crime problem. Fraud occurs when a victim suffers loss of money or property as a result of believing and acting upon an intentionally untrue representation of an important fact or event (Simmons 1998).

While a very common form of fraud is "paperhanging" (i.e. writing a check for an amount greater than is in your account or on a false account), there are many more inventive forms of fraud. Confidence games usually offer a "get-rich-quick" scenario that is literally too good to be true. "You have won a new car, just send us the money to complete the paper work and pay the transportation." No car comes, or it is a toy. The victim (mark) is often too embarrassed by the situation to report it. Fraud can occur when we are unable to evaluate what we pay for. Medical frauds prey on people who have incurable diseases; "repair" frauds deceive those who have little knowledge of engines. Securities frauds take advantage of peoples' ignorance about the investment market. Religious swindles take advantage of trust in religious leaders. Fraud also occurs when advertising misleads us into dangerous or useless purchases. Much of this crime is undetected. Also fitting the description of fraud are numerous practices such as coupon fraud, welfare and tax fraud, insurance fraud, and health care fraud (Barkan 1997:330-353).

Embezzlement is a form of fraud that involves using one's position to divert company property for one's own use. Companies are often quite unwilling to report this when they discover it, since it indicates their failure to hire an honest person, and the weakness of their accounting systems. A major incident of collective fraud occurred in the Savings and Loan Industry, where top executives abused their position of trust and ultimately caused the failure of more than 650 savings and loans institutions. The ultimate cost of this scandal to American taxpayers may top $1 trillion and the effects will be felt well into the new century (Barkan 1997:352)

CRIME CATEGORIES III: JUVENILE DELINQUENCY
CRIME ATTRIBUTABLE TO JUVENILES

What is the proportion of crime that is attributable to juveniles? In 1995, youths under age 18 accounted for: 9% of murders, 15% of forcible rape clearances, 20% of robbery clearances, 13% of aggravated assault clearances, 25% of property crime clearances, 21% of burglary clearances., 26% of larceny clearances.

Demographic change in the number of teenagers as a proportion of the population is a major variable affecting the contribution of juveniles to overall crime figures. When there are more juveniles relative to adults in the society, they will contribute more to the crime statistics, even if their rate of offending is low (Barkan 1997:259).

NUMBER OF DELINQUENTS.

Some 30 to 40% of all boys growing up in urban America will be arrested before their 18th birthday. In any one year, though, relatively few juveniles are arrested and very few of these are arrested for something serious (Greenwood 1995:105). FBI figures for 1992, for example, show that of all juveniles ages 10 to 17 in the United States in that year only 5% were arrested for any offense, and of this number, only 9% were arrested for a violent offense (FBI 1993). The vast majority of juvenile offenders are not arrested again (Greenwood 1995:91). They may well become respected citizens who brag about their wild days, or politicians who claim to have smoked marijuana without inhaling it. Despite this, public stereotypes of wayward youths have become increasingly modeled on the idea of the psychopathic, drug-crazed, gun toting "super predator" (Gluck 1997). It is true that the most dangerous offenders in the system are those who "started early"(Greenwood 1995:99, Blumstein et al. 1986) and also true that many "street elite gang members" portray themselves in this way. It is untrue, however, that most juvenile offenders are like this, or that a significant proportion of juveniles are offenders at all. While the incidence of juvenile crime may be high in some areas, this crime is being committed by a relatively small number of high rate offenders, not by juveniles as a whole.

WHERE IS DELINQUENCY OCCURRING?
HOW WIDESPREAD IS IT?

Although national violent crime rates are sinking, juvenile rates for serious and violent crime are rising, largely fed by the inner city gang situation.

Juvenile homicide is highly site-specific. Although Los Angeles, New York, Chicago, and Detroit account for 5.3% of juveniles in the U.S., these four cities experience one third of the nation's youth homicides. On the other hand, more than 80% of America's counties report zero known juvenile homicide offenders each year (Lotke 1997, Lotke and Schiraldi 1996).

GROUPS AND GANGS

The group character of much youth crime has been recognized at least since the 1930s (Warr 1996). Young teenagers tend to commit their crimes in a group context: "solo offending does not become the model form of offending until the late teens or early 20s"(Reiss 1986:152, Greenwood 1995:103). Youth gangs take many forms (informal groups, street gangs, skinhead gangs, organized crime gangs). They are rarely restricted to youth under 18 and vary from criminal organizations to simple friendship groups

There are many reasons for joining gangs. The attraction is particularly strong for youths that are alienated from school, lack strong family support, and are unlikely to develop meaningful work skills in their current environment. Gangs provide, (or promise to provide), belonging, protection, status, adventure, and sometimes access to moneymaking opportunities. They seem to solve the short-term dilemmas of young adults. If this means a short life (and it often does), it may seem better than coping with hopelessness and disrespect (Lattimore, Linster and MacDonald 1997). Gang membership can also become a **"master status"** that creates further negative pressures on the youth in the form of negative community expectations and police attention (Miethe and McCorkle 1997).

CRIME AND INTERVENTIONS: PUBLIC OPINION AND SUPPORT FOR TRADITIONAL AND ALTERNATIVE CRIME CONTROL MEASURES

The dominant form of intervention in the control of crime is still "fortification", and use of the traditional criminal justice system (police, courts, corrections). This system is now seriously overloaded, very expensive to run, increasingly exposed as ineffective, and possibly even a cause of crime.

Conventional wisdom holds that the American mood at the present is rigidly punitive, favoring a rhetoric of "law and order" and "throw away the key" (e.g. Sasson 1995). Certainly many politicians believe that taking a "get-tough" stand on crime (and criminals) is a safe way to get re-elected. The result has been what Clear has called "the great punishment experiment" (Clear 1994). Survey data indicate that most American citizens do not support a vindictive view of criminal justice (Flanagan 1997; Sasson 1995). On the other hand, there has been little support for the development of a crime control policy based on research and guided by theory, rather than one based on fear and anger (Gottfredson and Hirschi 1995). Getting smart is harder than getting tough.

The goal of the existing justice system is not simply to "correct" those who have gone astray. It is also largely to mete out revenge or retribution, and to "send a message" to potential offenders. Other goals may include restitution (making the offender return value for what was done), and reform and rehabilitation through therapy, training and support. It is difficult to imagine any correctional program that could accomplish all of these goals at the same time. Correctional work has instead become narrowly focused on the administrative goal of running the institutions more efficiently, without regard to any longer term goals.

PRISONS

A prison is a state or federally operated facility designed for offenders serving incarcerative terms of one or more years. The President's Commission on Law Enforcement and Administration of Justice, released in 1967, documented an overreliance on the **prison system.** The situation has worsened since then, as an increasing number of states have opted for **"three strikes"** legislation and other forms of **mandatory minimum sentencing** (Clark, Austin and Henry 1997, Blumstein 1995:413-416). An estimated 1.7 million persons were incarcerated in prisons and local jails the United States in 1997, a figure that rose by 6.8% during the year (Gilliard and Beck 1996:1) This amounts to 1 in every 167 Americans.

Although America's crime rates (other than gun-homicide) are very similar to the rates of other nations, the U.S. locks up 5 times as many people per capita than Canada, and 7 to 16 times as many as most European democracies (Sentencing Project 1997). The U.S. also spends a great deal more on courts and prisons, even though it spends on average nearly $20,000 less per year per inmate than neighboring Canada does.

The perception that crime stops during imprisonment is misleading. In our case study, for example, Joe committed assaults on weaker inmates, and later became a victim of numerous violent incidents culminating in his murder. The overcrowding and understaffing of many institutions mean that there is either a jungle kind of order (in which the real power holders are violent criminals) or a rigid militaristic one in which prisoners are given no chance to practice responsible decision-making. Many prisons operate as schools for the transmission of criminal skills, ideas and connections rather than places in which inmates can acquire positive social attitudes or useful civilian skills.

In recent years, the perception that prisons are "country clubs" has driven policies for the reintroduction of deprivation and pain. This "country club" idea has been likened to the Loch Ness monster: Many people believe in it, but no one has ever seen it (Levinson 1988, cited in Johnson 1996:1). Prisons are places of meaningless, debilitating idleness and occasional violence (Johnson 1996:3). There is increased public support for chain-gang labor and decreased support for academic upgrading, despite evidence that the later is more effective in transforming inmate attitudes and behavior (Gilligan 1998:34). The problem is not really that we are too cruel (though we may be): the problem is that this cure is expensive and ineffective (Zimring and Hawkins 1997).

It can be suggested that incapacitation could be reserved for violent, offenders (Blumstein 1995). Serious violent offenders amount to no more than 10 % of the current prison population, so that overcrowding could be eliminated, and programs could be specifically directed to this one group. Nonviolent property offenders might be more effectively and less expensively managed through alternative forms of justice, methods which are not always "softer" or easier than doing a prison sentence. Sometimes having to make things right is a lot harder (emotionally and physically) than sitting out a prison sentence. Substance abusers might better be handled through the health system (Erickson, Riley, Cheung and O'Hare 1997). At an average direct imprisonment cost of $20,000 per year per prisoner, (as well as related costs, such as welfare for the prisoner's family, lost wages and the cost of appeals) we have an incentive to find better ways of handling crime.

BOOT CAMPS

In 1983, the Juvenile Justice and Delinquency Prevention Act provided for conversion of military bases into boot camps (also known as "shock incarceration programs") for youth offenders (Reid-MacNevin 1997:159). Boot camps provide alternative sanctions "with teeth" intended to relieve pressure on overcrowded prison facilities. They are based mainly on the intuitive notion that what young offenders need are a dose of discipline and hard work (Correia 1997:96). There is high public support for this as a solution for youth crime (Reid-MacNevin 1997).

Thirty-six states had **boot camps** by 1994 (Mackenzie 1994:1). Canada also has three programs and is planning more (Reid-MacNevin 1997:155). Boot camp programs normally include military drill, hard labor, and physical training. Unlike prisons, they allow very little, if any, idle time. **Sentences** last from 3 to 6 months on the average. **Boot camps** vary in the extent to which academic education and life-skills counseling are offered, but most of them offer greater access to rehabilitative programs than traditional prisons (Clark et al. 1994). A controversial aspect of many of these programs is that they accept only youths convicted of nonviolent crimes and without prior record of imprisonment (Mackenzie 1994). Such offenders generally are not sent to prison, so that the effect of the camps on reducing prison populations is dependent upon their deterrent effect (Clear and Braga 1995). Some critics believe that these camps are an example of **net widening,** whereby people are needlessly drawn into programs, just because the programs exist. Ethridge and Sorensen (1997:139) suggest that boot camp should be used only for those who "are truly prison bound"(139; also Mackenzie and Souryal 1994, Cowles, Castellano and Granski 1995).

Findings at this point are mixed, but so far they suggest that programs that work are not those with the most punitive or military regimes, but those with the best continuing supervision in the community following release (Mackenzie 1995, Mackenzie et al. 1995). Similar findings apply to other short term "shock" programs such as wilderness programs and "scared straight" projects. Some work, many do not. Overall they are not more effective than traditional incarceration (Parent 1989).

CAPITAL PUNISHMENT

A controversial aspect of American justice is the use of the **capital punishment,** which has been abandoned by most European nations and by Canada. Sixteen U.S. states executed 56 prisoners in 1995, and by year-end there were 3,054 prisoners under sentence of death (Snell 1996). The main argument that supports this intervention is that death is suitable as payment for taking life. It is also clear that those who are executed will not offend again.

Those who oppose the death penalty often cite its unequal application. Wealthy people (Black or White) with good legal representation are rarely found on death row. Blacks, who were 14% of the population in 1996, were 44% of the death row population (Miller 1996). Others argue that, when civil rights are fully respected, execution costs more than life imprisonment, and has a **brutalization effect** on society. Finally, it is indisputable that the death penalty cannot be revoked if a mistake has been made.

RESTORATIVE JUSTICE

The idea of restorative justice has several different roots. One lies in the historical practices of aboriginal societies and another is found in the religious message shared by many groups such as the Mennonites and the Quakers. In restorative justice, offenses are viewed as a disruption of the harmony of social life (rather than insults to the state). The response is to seek restoration of the balance in the community, not just between the offender and the victim(s), but for the community as a whole. The offender is treated as a basically good (or at least salvageable) person who has made a mistake. He or she is encouraged to do whatever is possible to "make good" the damage that has been done. The offender must not only "fix" or replace damaged property but must also acknowledge and respect the feelings of those who have been injured, and the community as a whole. In return, when reparation and apology has been done, the offender is reintegrated into the community (Umbreit 1994; Ness and Strong 1997).. In criminology, this form of justice is recognized in the idea of "reintegrative shaming" (Braithwaite 1989).

SUMMARY

1. Crime is widespread in America, but only some of it is recognized and treated as a social problem.

2. Crime is a kind of social problem that is "claimed" by the state, and dealt with by formal agencies such as the police, courts, and prisons. This method of dealing with offenses does not give the victim much satisfaction, and often puts strain on society's support for the individual rights of defendants.

3. Much of the current rhetoric about crime may be considered evidence of moral panic about disorder in society.

4. The working of the criminal justice system results in some crimes and criminals being kept in the system and labeled "criminal," while others are not retained.

5. Offenders who remain in the system are disproportionately youthful "street offenders" rather than mature White-collar offenders. Official criminal statistics also reflect this perception of who the "problem" criminals are.

6. Symbolic interactionism, functionalism and conflict theory all help us to understand the environmental aspects of crime and criminals, and to suggest the characteristics that effective interventions might have.

7. Crime in America occurs at about the same rate as crime in other western industrialized countries, with the exception of crimes committed with increasingly lethal kinds of firearms.

8. The homicide rate, which is more than double that of Canada and other western countries, creates an impression urban American as a crime-ridden "wild west". In fact, over 80% of crime in America (as in other countries) consist of nonviolent property offenses.

9. Delinquency, roughly 25% of each violent crime category, attracts concern mainly because violence seems to be increasing, even though it is concentrated among a relatively small number of offenders.

10. Most youth offenders however are arrested only once.

11. Crime intervention proposals are often related to assumptions about the causes of crime. In this chapter, we have outlined some traditional and new intervention tactics.

12. Unfortunately, most efforts to control crime fall into the "band-aid" category. They do not systematically use our cumulated theoretical and experimental knowledge to attack the fundamental roots of offending behavior.

REFERENCES

Bastian, Lisa D and Marshall M. DeBerry Jr., eds. 1994. *Criminal Victimization in the United States* 1992. Washington, D.C.: U.S. Department of Justice, Bureau of Justice Statistics.

BJA (Bureau of Justice Assistance) 1997. *A Policymaker's Guide to Hate Crimes.* Washington: Bureau of Justice Assistance NJC 162304 (http://ncjrs.org.txtfiles/ 162304.txt)

Blumstein, Alfred 1995. "Prisons" Pp. 387-420 in James Q. Wilson and Joan Petersilia, eds. *Crime.* San Francisco: Institute for Contemporary Studies.

Blumstein, Alfred, Jacqueline Cohen, Jeffrey Roth, and Christy Visher, eds. 1986. *Criminal Careers and Career Criminals.* Vol. 2 Washington, D.C. National Academy Press.

Bonczar, Thomas P. and Allen J. Beck 1997. "Lifetime Likelihood of Going to State or Federal Prison" *Bureau of Justice Statistics Special Report.* Washington, D.C.: U .S. Dept of Justice Office of Justice Programs Bureau of Justice Statistics.

Braithwaite, John 1989. *Crime, Shame, and Reintegration.* Cambridge: Cambridge University Press.

Browne, Angela 1995. "Fear and the Perception of Alternatives: Asking "Why Battered Women Don't Leave?" is the Wrong Question." Pp.228-245 in Barbara Raffel Price and Natalie J. Sokoloff, eds. *The Criminal Justice System and Women: Offenders, Victims and Workers.* New York: McGraw Hill.

Butts, J. 1996. *Offenders in Juvenile Court 1993.* Juvenile Justice Bulletin. Washington, D. C.: Government Printing Office.

Chambliss, William and Robert Seidman. 1982. *Law Order and Power.* Second ed. Reading, MA: Addison-Wesley.

Champion, Dean J. 1997. *The Roxbury Dictionary of Criminal Justice: Key Terms and Major Court Cases.* Los Angeles, CA: Roxbury.

Christie, Nils 1994. *Crime Control as Industry. Towards Gulags Western Style.* Enlarged second ed. NY: Routledge.

Clark, Cheryl L., David W. Aziz, and Doris Layton MacKenzie 1994. *Shock Incarceration in New York. - Focus on Treatment.* Washington, D.C.: National Institute of Justice.

Clark, John, James Austin and D. Alan Henry 1997. "Three Strikes and You're Out': a Review of State Legislation" *Research in Brief- National Institute of Justice.* Washington, D.C.: U.S. Department of Justice Office of Justice Programs.

Clear, Todd R. 1994. *Harm in American Penology: Offenders. Victims and Their Communities.* Albany: State University of New York.

Clear, Todd R. and Anthony A Braga 1995. "Community Corrections." Pp.421-444 in James Q. Wilson and Joan Petersilia, eds. *Crime.* San Francisco: Institute for Contemporary Studies.

Conklin, John 1972. *Illegal But Not Criminal.* Englewood Cliffs, NJ Prentice Hall.

Correia, Mark E. 1997. "Boot Camps, Exercise and Delinquency: An Analytical Critique of the Use of Physical Exercise to Facilitate Decreases in Delinquent Behavior." *Journal of Con temporary' Criminal Justice.* 13(2) May: 94-113.

Cowles, E. T. Castellano, and L. Granski 1995. *"Boot Camp" Drug Treatment and Aftercare Interventions. - An Evaluation Review.* Washington, DC: Department of Justice, National Institute of Justice.

Craven, Diane 1996. *Bureau of Justice Statistics Selected Findings Female Victims of Violent Crime.* Washington, D.C.: Office of Justice Programs, Bureau of Justice Statistics.

Curry, G. David, Richard A. Ball and Scott H. Decker 1996. *National Institute of Justice Research in Brief Estimating The National Scope of Gang Crime from Law Enforcement Data.* Washington, D.C.: National Institute of Justice. U.S. Department of Justice.

Davis, Melissa, Richard Lundman, and Ramiro Martinez 1991. "Private Corporate Justice: Store Police, Shoplifters, and Civil Recovery." *Social Problems.* 38:395-408.

Dawson, John M. and Patrick A. Langan 1994. Murder in *Families.* Washington, D.C.: U.S. Department of Justice, Bureau of Justice Statistics.

Decker, Scott H. 1993. "Exploring Victim-Offender Relationships in Homicide: The Role of Individual and Event Characteristics." *Justice Quarterly.* 10:585-612.

Decker, Scott H., Susan Pennell and Ami Caldwell 1997. *Research in Brief. Illegal Firearms; Access and Use by Arrestees.* Washington, D.C. U.S. Dept of Justice National Institute of Justice.

Dershowitz, Alan M. 1997. *Reasonable Doubts: The Criminal Justice System and the O. J Simpson Case.* Second Ed. New York: Touchstone.

Deutschmann, Linda 1998. *Deviance and Social Control.* Second ed. Scarborough, ON: ITP Nelson Canada.

Douglas, John E, Ann W. Burgess, Allen G. Burgess and Robert Ressler 1997. *Crime Classification Manual.* San Francisco: Jossey Bass.

Egger, Steven A. 1990. "Taxonomy of Law Enforcement Responses to Serial Murder." Pp.177-200 in Steven A. Egger, ed. *Serial Murder: An Elusive Phenomenon,* New York: Praeger.

Erickson, Patricia, Diane M. Riley, Yuet W. Cheung and Patrick O'Hare, eds. 1997. *Harm Reduction: A New Direction for Drug Policies and Programs.* Toronto: University of Toronto Press.

Ethridge, Philip and Jonathan R. Sorensen 1997. "An Analysis of Change and Community Adjustment Among Probationers in a County Boot Camp." *Journal of Criminal Justice.* 13(2) May 139-154.

FBI (Federal Bureau of Investigation). 1996 Annual. *Crime in America: Uniform Crime Reports.* Washington, D.C.: U.S. Government Printing Office.

FBI (Federal Bureau of Investigation). 1993 Annual. *Crime in America: Uniform Crime Reports.* Washington, D.C.: U.S. Government Printing Office.

Felson, Richard B. 1996. "Big People Hit Little People: Sex Differences in Physical Power and Interpersonal Violence." *Criminology.* 34(3) 433-452.

Felson, Richard B. and Henry A. Steadman 1983. "Situational Factors in Disputes Leading to Criminal Violence." *Criminology.* 21:59-74.

Flanagan, Timothy J. 1997. "Public Opinion and Public Policy in Criminal Justice." *The Public Perspective.' A Roper Center Review of public Opinion and Polling.* 8:4 (June-July) 1-2.

Gabor, Thomas 1994. *Everybody Does It.' Crime by the Public.* Toronto: University of Toronto Press.

Gilliard, Darrell and Allen J. Beck 1996. *Prison and Jail Inmates, 1995.* Washington, D.C.: Bureau of Justice Statistics, U.S. Department of Justice

Gilligan, James 1998. "Pictures of Pain." in *Behind the Razor Wire: Portrait of a Contemporary American Prison System.* New York, NY: New York University Press.

Gluck, Stephen 1997. "Wayward Youth, Super Predator: an Evolutionary Tale of Juvenile Delinquency from the 1950s to the Present." *Corrections Today.* 59(3) June: 62-66.

Godwin, Tracy M. 1996 *Office of Juvenile Justice and Delinquency Prevention Fact Sheet #45 August. A Guide for Implementing Teen Court Programs.* Washington, D.C.: Office of Justice Programs APPA. OJJDP Juvenile Justice Clearing House.

Gottfredson, Michael R. and Travis Hirschi 1995. "National Crime Control Policies." *Society.* 32(2): 30-37.

Graham, Hugh D. and Ted R. Gurr, eds. 1969. *Violence in America.* Washington, D.C.: U.S. Government Printing Office.

Greenfeld, Lawrence 1996. *Bureau of Justice Statistics Executive Summary Child Victimizers: Violent Offenders and Their Victims.* Washington, D.C.: U.S. Department of Justice Bureau of Justice Statistics.

_____.1997. Sex Offenses and Offenders: An Analysis on Rape and Sexual Assault. Washington, D.C.: Bureau of Justice Statistics, U.S. Department of Justice

Greenwood, Peter W. 1995. "Juvenile Crime and Juvenile Justice." Pp. 91-120 James Q. Wilson and Joan Petersilia, eds. *Crime. San* Francisco: Institute for Contemporary Studies.

Groth, A. Nicolas and Jean Birnbaum 1979. *Men Who Rape.* New York: Plenum Press.

Gurr, Ted Robert 1980. "Development and Decay: Their Impact on Public Order in Western History." Pp. 31-52 in James Inciardi and Charles E. Faupel eds. *History and Crime.* Beverly Hills, CA: Sage.

Henslin, James M. 1996. *Social Problems 4th ed.* Saddle River: Prentice Hall

Holmes, Ronald M. 1989. *Profiling Violent Crimes: An Investigative Tool.* Newbury Park: Sage.

Homey, Julie and Cassia Spohn. 1996. "The Influence of Blame and Believability Factors on the Processing of Simple Versus Aggravated Rape Cases." *Criminology.* 34(2): 135-162.

Hutson, H. Range, Dierdre Anglin, Demetrios N Kyriacon, Joel Hart, Kelvin Spears. "The Epidemic of Gang Related Homicides in Los Angeles County from 1979 through 1994." *JAMA.* (Journal of the American Medical Association). Oct 4 1995.1031-1035.

Johnson, Robert 1996. "Humane Prisons: A Call for Decency in Conservative Times." *Corrections Today. 58(4)* July 130-133.

Karmen, Andrew 1995. "Women Victims of Crime: Introduction." Pp.181-196 in Barbara Raffel Price and Natalie J. Sokoloff, eds. *The Criminal Justice System and Women: Offenders, Victims and Workers.* New York: McGraw Hill.

Katz, Jack 1988. *Seductions of Crime: Moral and Sensual Attractions in Doing Evil.* New York: Basic Books.

Keckeisen, George 1993. *Retail Security versus the Shoplifter.* Springfield, IL: Charles Thomas.

Kleck, Gary and Marc Gertz 1998. "Carrying Guns for Protection: Results from a National Self-Defense Survey." *Journal of Research in Crime and Delinquency.* 35(2) May: 193-224.

Klein, Malcolm W. 1997. *The American Street Gang: Its Nature, Prevalence and Control.* New York: Oxford University Press.

Klein, Malcolm W. 1995. "Street Gang Cycles." Pp. 217-236 in James Q. Wilson and Joan Petersilia, eds. *Crime.* San Francisco: Institute for Contemporary Studies.

Kopel, David B. 1992. *The Samurai, the Mountie, and the Cowboy: Should America Adopt the Gun Controls of Other Democracies?* Amherst, NY: Prometheus

Lattimore, Pamela K., Richard L. Linster, and John M. MacDonald 1997. "Risk of Death among Serious Young Offenders." *Journal of Research in Crime and Delinquency.* 34(2) 187-209

Levinson, R.B. 1988. "Try Softer." In R. Johnson and H. Toeh, eds. *The Pains of Imprisonment.* Prospect Heights: Waveland Press.

Lotke, Eric 1997. "Youth Homicide." *Valparaiso Law Review.* 31(2) Spring. (http://www.ncianet.org/ncia/casey.htlm)

Lotke, Eric and Vincent Schiraldi 1996. "An Analysis of Juvenile Homicides: Where They Occur and the Effectiveness of Adult Court Intervention." (http//www.ncianet.org/ncia/waiver/html)

Luckenbill, David F. 1977. "Criminal Homicide as a Situated Transaction." *Social Problems.* 25:176-186.

Mackenzie, Doris Layton 1994. *Multi-Site Evaluation of Shock Incarceration: Executive Summary.* Washington, D.C.: National Institute of Justice.

Mackenzie, Doris Layton, Robert Brame, David McDowall and Claire Souryal 1995. "Boot Camp Prisons and Recidivism in Eight States." *Criminology.* 33(3): 327-358.

Marshall, W. L. and Sylvia Barrett 1990. *Criminal Negligence: Why Sex Offenders Go Free.* Toronto: Doubleday.

Martin, Patricia Yancy 1997. "Gender, Accounts and Rape Processing Work." *Social Problems.* 44(4) November: 464-482.

Martin, Susan F. 1995. "'A Cross-Burning is not just an Arson': Police Social Construction of Hate Crimes in Baltimore County." *Criminology.* 33(3): 303-326.

Miethe, Terance D. and Richard C. McCorkle 1997. "Gang Membership and Criminal Processing: A Test of the Master Status Concept." *Justice Quarterly.* 14(3): 407-427.

Miller, Jerome G. 1996. *Search and Destroy: African American Males in the Criminal Justice System.* Oxford: Cambridge University Press

Moynihan, Daniel Patrick 1993. "Defining Deviancy Down." The American Scholar 62(1): 17-20.

Nelson, Steve and Menachim Amir 1975. "The Hitchhike Victim of Rape: A Research Report." In Israel Drapkin and Emiho Viano, eds. *Victimology: A New Focus.* Vol. III Lexington Mass: Lexington Books.

Nettler, Gwynn. 1982 *Explaining Criminals.* Criminal Careers. Vol. I. Cincinnati, OH Anderson.

Parent, D., ed. 1989. *National Institute of justice: Issues and Practices.* Washington, D.C.: Government Printing Office.

Parker, Robert Nash with Linda-Anne Rebhun 1995. *Alcohol and Homicide: A Deadly Combination of Two American Traditions.* Albany: State University of New York Press.

Reid-MacNevin, Susan A. 1997. "Boot Camps for Young Offenders: A Politically Acceptable Punishment." *Journal of Contemporary Justice.* 13(2): May 155-171.

Reiss, Albert J. Jr. 1986. "Co-Offender Influences on Criminal Careers." In Alfred Blumstein, Jacqueline Cohen, Jeffrey Roth, and Christy Visher, eds. *Criminal Careers and Career Criminals* Vol. 2. Washington, D.C.: National Academy Press.

Reiss, Albert and Jeffrey Roth 1993. *Understanding and Preventing Violence.* Washington, D.C.: National Academy.

Rountree, Pamela Wilcox and Kenneth C. Land 1996. "Burglary Victimization, Perceptions of Crime Risk and Routine Activities." *Journal of Research in Crime and Delinquency.* 33(2): 147-180

Saltzman, Linda and James Mercy 1993 "Assaults Between Intimates: The Range of Relationships Involved." In Anna Victoria Wilson, eds. *Homicide: The Victim/Offender Connection.* Cincinnati: Anderson.

Sasson, Theodore 1995. *Crime Talk: How Citizens Construct a Social Problem.* New York: Aldine de Gruyter.

Schaffner, Laurie 1997. "Review of *No Matter How Loud I Shout. Contemporary Sociology A Journal of Reviews.* 26(1) January: 86

Schlesinger, Philip and Howard Tumbler 1994. *Reporting Crime: The Media Politics of Criminal Justice.* New York: Oxford U Press

Sentencing Project (The) 1997 *The International Use of Incarceration.* (http://*www.*sproject.com/press- 12.html).

Sheley, Joseph and James Wright 1993. *Gun Acquisition and Possession in Selected Juvenile Samples.* Washington, D.C.: National Institute of Justice.

Shover, Neal 1991. "Burglary." Pp. 73-113 in Michael Tonry, eds. *Crime and Justice A Review of Research.* Chicago: University of Chicago Press.

Siegal, Larry J. 1995. *Criminology: Theories, Patterns and Typologies.* Fifth ed. Minneapolis/St. Paul: West.

Simmons, Mark R. c1998. *Recognizing the Elements of Fraud.* (http//www.echotech.com/elfraud.html).

Snell, Tracy L. 1996. *Capital Punishment 1995.* Washington, D.C.: Bureau of Justice Statistics, U.S. Department of Justice.

Snyder, Howard N. and Melissa Sickmund 1995. *Juvenile Offenders and Victims: A Focus on Violence. Statistics Summary.* Washington, D.C.: Office of Juvenile Justice and Delinquency Prevention, Office of Justice Programs, U.S. Department of Justice

Straus, Murray A. 1993 "Physical Assaults by Wives, A Major Social Problem." Pp. 67-87 In Richard J Gelles and Donileen R. Loseke, eds. *Current Controversies on Family Violence.* Newbury Park, CA: Sage.

Sulton, Anne T., ed. 1996. *African-American Perspectives on Crime Causation, Criminal Justice Administration, and Crime Prevention.* Boston: Butterworth-Heinemann.

Sutherland, Edwin 1940. "White Collar Criminality." *American Sociological Review.* 5:2-10

Tappan, Paul W. 1960. Crime Justice and Correction. NY: McGraw-Hill.

Van Dijk, Jan J. M., Pat Mayhew and Martin Killias 1991. *Experiences of Crime Across the World: Key Findings from the 1989 International Crime Survey.* Duventer: Kluwer Law And Taxation Publishers.

Voigt, Lydia, William E. Thornton, Jr., Leo Barrile, and Jerrol M. Seaman 1994. *Criminology and Justice.* New York: McGraw-Hill.

Warr, Mark 1996. "Organization and Instigation in Delinquent Groups" *Criminology.* 34(l): 11-37.

Wolfgang, Marvin E. 1958. *Patterns in Criminal Homicide.* Philadelphia: University of Pennsylvania Press.

Zimring, Franklin E. and Gordon Hawkins 1996. "Is American Violence a Crime Problem?" *Duke Law Journal.* 46(1): 43-72.

Zimring, Franklin E. and Gordon Hawkins 1997. *Incapacitation: Penal Confinement and the Restraint of Crime.* New York: Oxford University Press.

CHAPTER 6: GENDER INEQUALITY
CASE STUDY: EMMA AND THE GLASS CEILING

Emma Anthony, with an MBA in Public Administration and several years of experience as a professional staff member in the State Legislature, had recently been hired to head the Office for Public Relations of the state's Department of Energy. From the very first meeting of Department executives, at which she was one of two women - the other being the Director of Personnel-she realized that personnel and public relations were not terribly important concerns of the agency leaders. Such work carried less prestige than did that of regulating industries and building plants, enterprises involving complex negotiations and heavy spending, that is the type of activities in which men were thought to excel naturally, in contrast to the "people work" for which women were assumed more suited. Buildings and contracts were 'hard," complaints by clients and employees were "soft stuff." While the percentage of women employed in professional and managerial positions in the Department of Energy had grown over the past 5 years, women were still not equally represented across the hierarchical levels and programmatic divisions at the agency. Even when women did have the same type of job and the same amount of experience, the Director of Personnel told top management that women earned almost $4,000 less than men did.

Emma expected to see women equally represented throughout the various levels of the organization, especially since over half of its employees were women. They were not, however. In the past 5 years, the lower ranks had become more female dominated while the upper levels had made some progress toward gender integration, most notably by hiring Emma. Women were still underrepresented, however, especially at the highest, policy-making levels of the Department of Energy. As a result, Emma found that women had limited input into department policy and decision-making.

Emma found there was a sharp distinction between "professional" and administrative support staff (secretarial and clerical workers). Women employees who had been promoted out of clerical titles into professional ones complained to Emma that their secretarial past followed them. Emma overheard a male manager say, "Well, there are two former secretaries, they can help with the typing."

Working in a male-dominated agency, Emma had problems not being taken seriously, not being listened to, being judged by her appearance rather than accomplishments, and sexual innuendoes. From her days at the Legislature, Emma was fairly inured to the cascade of vulgarities and dirty jokes that dominate the men's informal conversations, and even spill over to formal meetings, but she was surprised when top management ignored the sexual harassment that was occurring in one unit.

Emma had intentionally chosen government employment because it was regulated by Civil Service rules that, she thought, would protect her from the kind of arbitrary behavior that often characterize employers in the private sector. Emma and the other women managers found, however, that upper management in the department was a "boys club" that was closed to them.

The "sticky floor" held most of the Department's women employees in the lowest civil service ranks, while only 6% were able to reach the top ones. Emma soon realized that having evaded the sticky floor, she had hit the "glass ceiling" after only 10 years in government employment.

Now that Emma is married and established, she wants to have children. Unfortunately she finds that the Department of Energy no longer seems as willing to accommodate employees' family responsibilities as in the past. The agency in general and certain managers in particular seem less open to job-sharing, voluntary work reductions, part-time work, and flextime. Some flextime options have been taken away or have not been applied uniformly across units. Staff members who share a job do not seem to get promoted and are particularly vulnerable during layoffs. For a woman to take reduced hours at the Department of Energy is to risk loss of her job loss of prestige, and loss of the benefits or of being taken seriously as an employee.

Emma has observed that the Department seems to judge commitment by how early and late workers stay at the office. Those who regularly leave because of childcare or car pooling schedules are perceived as less dedicated and loyal to their jobs, even if they take work home. The Department has an "after hours" work culture that women with families cannot be part of.

At an earlier time, Emma would probably have blamed herself for the problems she faced, asking "what am I doing wrong?" and trying to adapt to the conditions of her workplace by being more compliant, less angered by unwanted familiarities, and lowering her ambitions. This is the avenue still taken by the great majority of employed women. In other words, personal troubles were just that - personal. Emma, however, is aware that the difficulties are not mainly of her own making, and that her success (and that of other women) will depend on her ability (along with the cooperation of others) to transform the conditions of women's work in general and in the Department. This will be difficult: those who have privileges usually see them as justified, and rarely surrender them, and those who have few privileges may be afraid to take the risks required for change. In Emma's case, awareness of the women's movement has helped her to acquire the "sociological imagination," so that she can better understand and cope with the prospects and problems of her career choices.

A SOCIAL STRUCTURE PERSPECTIVE

The Department of Energy is a social system. To understand Emma Anthony's experience we must shift our focus from individuals to the organization itself, its culture and the patterning of interactions and role performances that we call **social structure.** From this perspective, the most important fact about any organization, even today, is that men dominate it and that its processes are deeply gendered (Acker 1990; Reskin 1988). That is, the way in which the workplace is defined and organized reflects a masculine (androcentric) worldview. This reinforces the power of men over women, as well as that of some men over other men. In the extreme (but hardly unknown) case men of lower status become honorary women and are spoken of in feminized terms (think of the demeaning words your classmates have used for unathletic men who avoid contact sports). The executive office and shop floors alike are arenas for displays of maleness that define the relationships of employers to employees and of employees to one another. Blue-collar workers, for example, emphasize their physical masculinity as a means of gaining respect from colleagues; white-collar executives engage in power plays that humiliate the losers (Acker 1990).

Similarly, politics is a highly masculinized arena in which men play to win at all costs because defeat is a loss of manliness. This was clearly displayed in the reasons given by Presidents Lyndon Johnson and Richard Nixon and Secretary of State Henry Kissenger for continuing the war in Vietnam (Dallek 1998). Gender assumptions are an unspoken underlayer of all legislation that has any effect on women, especially welfare programs. For example, girls in the Job Corps were taught how to do household tasks while the boys received training in skilled trades (Quadagno and Forbes 1995).

Emma Anthony's personal troubles, therefore, do not reflect only or even mainly her own shortcomings but are products of the organizational environment itself affecting all its workers, male and female. Until women realize that the troubles they have are not just personal problems but are features of gendered organizational life, little can be done to change their situation. This realization is made difficult by the idealized images and abstract concepts that present each of us as a bodiless worker in a desexualized workplace, and the dominant ideology that our success or failure is entirely due to individual effort. In C. Wright Mill's (1959) terms, improvements for women like Emma require that the accumulation of individual troubles reach a threshold level whereby they are recognized as a public issue. Change is more likely if this public issue is also defined as a social problem, a condition that negatively affects the well being, and life chances of a sizable number of citizens, and which therefore requires a societal response. The inequality must be perceived as **inequitable**, as unfair, before it is transformed into a social problem. Even today many Americans do not see gender inequality as unfair because they believe that men really are naturally superior to women by virtue of their size, intellect, aggressiveness, historical dominance of social life, or any other trait that men are presumed to possess that can be considered of greater value than that associated with women. If men dominate, it is because they deserve to. This chapter primarily focuses on the concerns of girls and women, but the student should be aware that many men (and transgendered persons) also suffer from the dominance of men.

The essential first step in reducing inequality is to redefine personal troubles as public issues that rise to the level of a social problem. This redefinition occurs only when the affected population has a voice loud enough to bring the issues to public attention, typically through the creation of a broad-based **social movement.**

THE NEW FEMINIST MOVEMENT

In the case of American women, the turning point was the mid-1960s when a new Feminist Movement emerged from the turmoil generated by the Civil Rights and Anti-war Movements. Young activists, who found that their interests were ignored by the male leadership of these causes, joined in the late 1960s with older women, who had been unable to break into the higher levels of politics and business, to form several national organizations and local groups with the goal of equality for women (Lipetz and Berheide 1980; Ferree and Hess 1994). Although women had won the right to vote in 1920, following decades of activism by the first wave of American feminists, they were still barred by law and/or convention from many of the benefits of citizenship - inheritance rights, the ability to secure credit in one's own name, protection from interpersonal violence, educational access, military service, and reproductive control, to name only a few. Women in the labor force experienced widespread discrimination in wages and job placement, while those who remained at home performing labor that went without pay or recognition found themselves relatively powerless, dependent on a male breadwinner. One of the first and most important accomplishments of the New Feminist Movement was to raise public consciousness of the system-wide nature of women's inequality - that the personal was actually political in its origins and solutions - and to insist that this was unfair.

Whether or not Emma Anthony describes herself as a feminist, the Women's Movement has deeply and indelibly touched her life. Inequalities that had for so long been taken for granted were now a matter for debate. This second wave of feminism has ultimately affected women throughout the world, generated a new vocabulary and field of study, changed the composition and nature of every academic discipline, and altered the operation of every social institution in modern societies. This is no small achievement for a social movement that has recently been proclaimed "dead" by its critics. As the ideology, if not the practice, of women's rights spreads to other parts of the world, to more traditional, less industrialized societies, it is no exaggeration to say that a concern for gender equality today is a global phenomenon. In the United States, ironically, the movement's achievements have become the new taken-for-granted reality, so that many younger women fail to realize how very recent is their access to credit, education, and well-paying jobs, or how many barriers still remain.

Gender is not a social problem, but gender inequality is. Women and men are not equals anywhere in the world. Women perform more of the work, yet earn less than men and own little land across the globe. Women are more likely than men to be illiterate. Women face discrimination and even physical violence throughout the world. Women's movements and other social changes, however, mean that these differences in the life experiences of women and men are less likely to be taken for granted as natural and more likely to be regarded as social problems today.

This chapter explores the social problems associated with gender today. Men and women act differently and others act differently toward them depending on their gender. Social problems arise out of these different patterns of behavior. These differences exist at the macro level of social institutions, such as the economy and the political order, as well as at the micro level of interpersonal relationships between individuals.

In this chapter, we will discuss the causes and consequences of gender inequality and the outlook for a more egalitarian future. Although gender inequality as a social problem is universal, our focus will be largely on the

United States. We will examine the social structural conditions of gendered inequality at the macro level (e.g. the economy, polity, or family system) and the mesolevel (e.g. the organization, household, or school), and how these are reinforced, reproduced, and resisted at the microlevel (e.g. in face-to-face interaction). But first, we must define "gender."

THEORY BOX by Michael J. Donnelly Chapter 6 Gender Critical Theory

Most sociologists set out to describe and explain the social world as it is. They want to get the 'facts" right; indeed, much of what constitutes sociology as a formal discipline is concerned with training and tools designed to discipline observation of the social world. Of course, like other humans, sociologists are also political animals; they see right and wrong, justice and injustice, and good and bad in our social arrangements. Sociologists have been traditionally trained, however, to keep value judgments as separate as possible from getting, first of all, to the facts of the matter.

Sociologists who characterize themselves as "critical" have a different agenda and a different sense of their role as social observers. They are critical to begin with of the very goal of objectivity – objectivity, in their view, figures as an obstacle to a genuine engagement with the social world. Objectivity may well be warranted in the natural sciences, but when social scientists adopt the same detached attitude (as if they too were observing facts in nature), the perverse result is to make what happens in society appear as if it were "second nature."

Critical sociologists, by contrast, try not just to observe but to judge, often taking a social institution's avowed purpose as a value standard against which to evaluate its performance. If the American system, for instance, claims and has long claimed to provide "liberty and justice for all," why then did African-Americans continue to suffer systematic discrimination a century after Emancipation? The point of making such value judgments is to induce new attitudes, critical attitudes toward existing social arrangements not as how things are (and need to be), not as second nature, but as a historically contingent result of human agency and human choices. Things could be different; alternative (and better, more just and equitable) arrangements are possible. The critical sociologist's task is to restore to social actors their sense of agency and efficacy, and to develop knowledge of the social world that can help emancipate people from unduly restrictive, unfair, or unjust institutions. Hence, critical, "emancipatory" sociology targets the varied forms of oppression under which individuals labor.

GENDER

Gender is related to but not the same as sex. **Sex** refers to the biological difference between males and females. This biologically based difference has made gender differences seem "natural." However, gender is not biologically based. It is socially constructed.

Women are not the only ones who have gender, although we usually focus on them when we talk about gender issues because they are often the ones experiencing the negative consequences of gender differences. Men have gender too. Men's lives are as affected by their gender as women's lives are affected by theirs. Taking men as the norm, it is easy to see how women are disadvantaged compared to them. Yet not all men are privileged and not all women are disadvantaged. Other factors, such as race, class, sexual orientation, and disability, can disadvantage a man and privilege a woman. Thus, there are important differences among men and women, especially race and class differences.

When first used by feminist social scientists, the term gender was intended to distinguish the biological categories of male and female - sex - from the socially constructed and culturally variable traits of femininity and masculinity. Volumes of new research had thoroughly demonstrated that behavioral and psychological traits long assumed to be determined by biological sex were neither innate nor "natural." Rather, most such characteristics are historically, culturally, and personally variable. Gender differences in behavior are produced in part by **socialization**, the process of learning the culture and its expectations of girls and boys. But the cultural values placed on sex-typed behaviors tend to reflect the actual distribution of power in the society, so that the most valued traits are typically those associated with maleness. Then, because they do not possess or demonstrate these virtues, girls and women are assigned less important roles. Thus the differential placement of females and males in various social systems generates and reinforces gender inequality.

Yet, when carefully measured, the distribution of presumably sex-linked traits such as intelligence, assertiveness, sensitivity, and so forth, is not as highly gender differentiated as might be expected from the way in which they are usually described. All boys do not punch and all girls do not hug. Rather, the data show much more within group than between-group variation; that is, the range of differences is greater within all-male or all-female groups than between the group averages for males and females. The overlap in scores is considerable, with the bulk of cases clustering around the mean. In other words, boys and girls and women and men are more similar than different along most dimensions of thought and behavior, with the differences largely due to gender socialization and social statuses; that is, the desire to perform according to expectations derived from the gender expectations of one's class and racial/ethnic locations. But systems of inequality depend on finding differences not similarities, so it is in the interest of the dominant group to emphasize whatever differences can be found and to attribute these to all members of a given sex category.

Gender, however, is not simply a set of personal traits. Over time, the concept has been both increasingly refined and broadened until most sociologists now conceptualize **gender** as a set of social relationships (an institution) that "establishes patterns of expectations for individuals, orders the social processes of everyday life, is built into the major social organizations of society and is also an entity in and of itself" (Lorber 1994). Gender is not a quality of individuals, but of the relational fields in which they interact, from a conversation around the water cooler to the organization of the school or of a religious denomination.

In addition, sex itself is not as simple and clear a characteristic as commonly assumed. Maleness and femaleness are not absolutely dichotomous; many people have characteristics of both sexes. What is considered "biological" or not is a matter of social definition. In this view, both sex and gender are <u>mutually constituted</u> in that each defines the other. The newly-minted category of **transgendered** suggests the range of variation -- from persons who have undergone surgical transformation to those who have assumed the outward characteristics of the opposite sex to individuals who move freely from one type of sexual display or relationship to another. Which of these is considered "normal'" or "abnormal" is clearly a matter of societal norms. Such 'gender bending" is disturbing precisely because of the powerful pressures toward assigning people to one distinct sex category. Think of your original responses to the character of Pat on *Saturday Night Live* or to any other person whose sex and gender identity was ambiguous.

The only constant in all of this appears to be that whatever traits are thought to characterize males are accorded higher social approval than are those that describe females. It is this differential evaluation of people on the basis of observed sex and assumed gender that constitutes the sex/gender system of inequality (Rubin 1975)

THEORY BOX by Michael J. Donnelly Chapter. 6 Gender Feminist Theory

The contemporary feminist movement has raised three sorts of challenges to sociology and the knowledge it produces about society. Most fundamentally, feminists have asked, where are the women? There is little question that women have historically been underrepresented or even excluded from the ranks of sociologists, particularly from its higher reaches. The conclusion that virtually all feminists draw is that to counter this historic imbalance, the discipline should lower (discriminatory) barriers to women and indeed encourage a greater influx of women into the field. Justice and equity should demand no less than equal opportunity for women.

Many feminists have gone further to raise more radical claims: that secondly, the exclusion or relative absence of women from sociology has led to systematic (masculine) bias in the contents of social knowledge; or thirdly, that exclusion of women has deprived sociology of the fruits of women's distinctive ways of knowing. Feminists differ widely in their reaction to these more radical claims. The great majority would argue that the category "gender" has been unjustly and inappropriately neglected. While in the past gender was often confused with sex or effectively treated as an individual attribute of women (like their age), feminist scholarship has now brought gender relations to the foreground of the social sciences. The central contribution of feminist theory has undoubtedly been to problematize the ways we think about gender and gender relations. Far from being a "simple, natural fact," gender is now widely regarded as a contingent social construction (and often exaggeration) of differences between women and men. Moreover, such socially constructed distinctions evidently serve to legitimate and perpetuate unequal power relations between men and women; their exposure and analysis is one of the critical tasks that many feminists would accept.

The more radical claims feminists make on sociology take two forms: first, feminists should correct the male bias of existing sociology (based on the preponderance of men over women) perhaps by fostering a counter-discipline as women-centered as traditional (male-biased) sociology has been centered on male's activities; and second, feminism should draw directly on women's life experiences and thereby exploit women's distinctive way of knowing the world. The latter may be the most radical position of all, since it attributes to women (based on their historical subordination as a category) a special insight into the nature of social oppression and a stake in developing knowledge that will undermine the subordination of women and likewise related patterns of oppression based on class, race, or sexual orientation.

GENDER STRATIFICATION

Because gender involves placing people in separate categories and using this as the basis for different treatment, some degree of inequality is inevitable; one category will be considered superior to the other. When members of the higher ranked category lay claim to a greater share of societal resources -- power, prestige, and property - a system of **social stratification** is created that becomes self-perpetuating as the higher stratum also has the capacity to define what constitutes superiority and inferiority. In addition, when gender intersects with other divisions in the society -- age, race, ethnicity, or social class -- power, and privilege may be distributed in a variety of patterns. For example, although gender works to the advantage of all men, racial/ethnic minority men are disadvantaged vis-à-vis white women, and junior men in most groups tend to be less powerful than their seniors. In other words, not all men are mini-masters of the universe and not all women are helpless pawns, but within each age/race/ethnic/class category, men will enjoy greater power over their own life and those of others than will women. The ideology and practice of male dominance in both the private sphere of the household and the public arenas of work, governance, and worship is called **patriarchy** (Chow and Berheide 1994).

If patriarchy is not a product of our genes or hormones, how does it arise and become so universal? One possible answer lies in our ancestral past and is ultimately biological in the sense that only women can become pregnant and produce the milk necessary for infant survival. Because women are limited in how long and how far from the campsite they could roam, the most logical division of labor in the earliest human groups may have been to allot home-based tasks to women and those that involved danger and risk and travel to men. Along with danger, however, came many advantages--the weapons, skills, knowledge, and fruits of exploration that support claims to power. Thus, what men do comes to be considered of greater societal value than that which women do, and gendered stratification becomes a feature of the society.

Yet male dominance is not a constant; the degree to which men are privileged over women has varied greatly over time and place. In gathering bands, power differences between men and women are minimal **(egalitarianism)** because the division of labor is minimal--both men and women gather food and care for children. But when hunting becomes a specialty, the labor of the group is divided on the basis of sex; men hunt, women gather; and men's power and prestige rises. The more complex or rigid the division of tasks, the greater the power differential between women and men, reaching its highest point in agricultural societies where men are sole owners of land and cattle. Under these circumstances, particularly if a bride must leave her ancestral village and live among her husband's kinfolk, women are formally powerless, although some may be able to exercise some degree of self-direction **(autonomy)** through interpersonal bargaining (Kandiyoti 1988). In many of these societies, male honor requires absolute control over women, who are restricted in their movements and dress--hidden in the home and veiled outside it. Even today, among the Taliban ruling sect in Afghanistan, girls are forbidden to go to school and their mothers forbidden to enter the labor force.

Even without a Women's Movement to speed the process, the degree of gender inequality slowly erodes under conditions of modern industrialism for a number of reasons: (1) Elders lose control over the resources needed for their children's well-being, thus freeing young people to make their own way in the world, including their own choice of partner in a marriage increasingly based on intimacy rather than duty; (2) An ideology of political equality eventually makes it impossible to deny elementary civil rights to women, although it was not until mid-20th century that women's suffrage (the right to vote) became universal in the West; (3) Control over fertility and consequently smaller families, within which it becomes difficult to deny daughters the advantages given to sons, especially with regard to education; (4) Growth of jobs that provide women with independent incomes and a broader range of experiences outside the home. In Emma Anthony's case, she shows respect to her parents as a matter of choice, not obligation; she worked to pay for her college education; and she selected a husband on the basis of romantic love rather than an arrangement between parents. She and her husband will decide when and how many children to have and will probably treat them similarly; until then, she has a job, her own apartment, goes to movies and concerts, and takes vacations. Yet, only a few generations ago, even in the United States, a young woman would have very little of the freedom Emma currently enjoys.

For all these reasons, the power differentials between men and women decline in industrial societies - but only to a point. Not even the two most self-conscious contemporary attempts to create egalitarian social systems - the Israeli Kibbutz and the Swedish Welfare State - have succeeded in eliminating gender inequality. In the Israeli case, a gender-based division of labor emerged in which tasks that women were willing and encouraged to perform, such as food preparation and child care, were devalued relative to men's work in agricultural and industrial production, a pattern that translated into greater decision-making power for the men (Agassi 1989). In Sweden, also, despite high labor force participation and a strong commitment to equality of all citizens, women are clustered in low-status, sex-segregated occupations, receiving lower wages than comparably skilled men, in addition to assuming major responsibility for household tasks (Acker 1994). These examples suggest both the limits of reform and the essential requirements for full gender equality.

CONDITIONS FOR REDUCING GENDER INEQUALITY

There are three master conditions that enhance the status of women: economic independence, education, and control over reproduction. If you want to gauge the degree of male dominance in any society, examine the data on women's labor force participation, educational attainment, and fertility. If the first two measures are up and the third down, patriarchy is on the decline. If women are excluded from paid employment and from education beyond grammar school, and if the society's birth rate exceeds 3.0, it is very likely that women's power in the household and society is severely limited. In addition, the society must embrace an ideological framework that favors, if not full equality, at least a minimizing of overt discrimination. Finally, even if all other conditions favored gender equality, women would still be unable to take full advantage of these opportunities if they cannot share childcare. Let us examine these trends in greater detail, especially for the United States.

EMPLOYMENT

It is not enough that women work for pay; they must be able to maintain control over their earnings. In less developed nations, for example, where interventions by international economic organizations have upset the local markets that allowed women some degree of independence, the goals of "development" and "modernization" have in fact eroded the position of women within the community and the household (Blumberg 1984). Although the *maquiladoras* of Latin America and the sweatshops of Southeast Asia provide employment to women, many workers must turn over their earnings to fathers and husbands. If the women are able to retain control over their income, they have more power. In the United States and elsewhere in the industrialized world, the expansion of white-collar jobs throughout the century opened up vast areas of employment for women - in shops, offices, schools, and health care facilities. Although girls and young unmarried women had been a primary source of factory labor in the early part of the century, changes in the law and the public temper, as well as the growing power of male-dominated unions, forced them out in favor of men earning the "family wage" that enabled them to support a non-employed wife and children. Nonetheless, many women remained in the blue-collar labor force, a number that swelled during World War II, and which, contrary to the general perception, did not altogether abandon the factory for domestic bliss in the 1950s. From 1950-on, the number of American women in paid employment increased steadily until today, over 60% of American women age 16-64 are in the labor force, composing close to half of all workers. In other words, if you were asked to describe "an American worker," you would be wrong almost as many times as right if you pictured a man in a hard hat and overalls (or three-piece suit).

Employment provides more than an independent income. The workplace is a source of friends, of contact with a variety of people and situations, and of opportunities to master skills. These are the very same sources of power that provided such advantages to men in the earliest human societies. Not that the pay is inconsequential, especially for unmarried workers and single parents; it is, however, smaller than that earned by men. In general today as in the 1960s, women's wages remain between 60-70% that of men, even among those in similar employment and who work full-time, year-round. This **gender gap in wages** is narrowest for younger workers, those in public employment, and union members. But men, particularly white men, start with a pay advantage that tends to widen over time (Marini and Fan 1997); they are hired for positions of greater responsibility; promoted more often and quickly; and at the very top of the occupational status ladder, occupy all but a handful of slots. At the very top, the percentage of women corporate officers in Fortune 500 companies rose from 10% in 1996 to 10.6% in 1997, but only 3% of executive vice-presidents and higher, and 2.5% of the top earners are women (Bryant 1997).

In large part, the wage gap among full-time workers reflects the fact that most occupations remain largely **sex-segregated,** with wage scales to match. Yet even when sex segregation declines, the wage gap remains largely unchanged because both the distribution of occupations and of workers are based on rules established by those already favored in the labor market (Reskin 1988). Thus, efforts to move women into male-dominated occupations will fail to narrow the gap, either because there will never be more than a token number or because the men will move out. If the essence of gender stratification is differentiation and segregation, then the entry of women into what had been considered a male occupation threatens the entire system of privilege.

In some cases, occupations are opened to women only because men have already devalued the work. For example, when the focus of veterinary medicine shifted from the strenuous work associated with ranching and racing to the more domestically oriented care of household pets, the image of the field changed from masculine to feminine, and the men moved on. A similar process has occurred in pharmacy, now that drugs are mixed by manufacturers and dispensed in supermarkets, and in optometry now that eye tests are mechanized and glasses can be prescribed and produced within minutes at a 'vision center." Once the women move in, the occupation loses whatever prestige it once enjoyed, even though the skill level remains relatively high. As Emma Anthony discovered at the Department of Energy, although she was officially listed at the same rank as other office heads, she had less respect and influence than did the men who headed offices dealing with finances, construction, and compliance with regulations - a form of sex segregation at the executive level. Furthermore, the two sets of offices had very different career trajectories: promotions were in store for those who dealt with other powerful people; personnel and public relations were dead-end. Just "letting the girls in" will not do much to narrow gender differences in wages and advancement.

Another proposal for closing the wage gap involves the principle of **pay equity** or **comparable worth,** whereby occupations are objectively rated on the basis of skills and education required, the level of responsibility, and the conditions of labor, so that people in jobs with similar degrees of difficulty receive similar wages (Berheide, Chertos, Haignere, and Steinberg 1987). This would mean, in the example of the original court case, that nurses, primarily women, working in a state hospital would no longer be paid less than members of the all-male grounds-keeping crew. Comparable worth legislation is pending or enacted in most states, but since the legislation would cover only public employment, the vast private sector remains unaffected. Another drawback of the assessment of comparable worth is that it reinforces the idea that occupational status is the prime determinant of income (Reskin 1988; Brenner 1987). As long as occupations can be differentiated from one another along any dimension, and as long as gender or race or ethnicity or sexual preference can be used to assign people to jobs, stratification hierarchies will continue to favor those who have the power to define what is comparable, what things are worth, and who is entitled to them.

Nonetheless, despite the lower pay, less pleasant working conditions, glass ceilings and sticky floors, American women remain committed to labor force participation, entering early and staying late in life, with increasingly fewer years taken out for childbearing and child rearing (Berheide 1992). For women who are the sole providers for self and/or offspring, such participation is essential. Women at the highest levels of education and occupational prestige, for whom the **opportunity cost** (in terms of lost income and promotions) of leaving the labor force is extremely high, are more likely than other women to forego marriage and motherhood, or to return to work immediately after child birth. We have seen how these considerations weigh on Emma Anthony's choices and life chances.

EDUCATION

Because it is literally true that knowledge is power, denial of women's access to education is a major factor in the reproduction of patriarchy--from the founders of major universities in the United States to the international economic development agencies that pay for training Third World men to the Islamic fundamentalists who bar girls from school. The entry of large numbers of women into institutions of higher education is a fairly recent phenomenon even in the industrial West. Only in the 1980s, did the proportion of women high school graduates entering college begin to equal that of their male counterparts, a trend that accelerated in the 1990s. Today, women compose 55% of the student body, and, in contrast to earlier years, they are staying to graduate, although they will receive lower returns for their investment in education than will their male classmates.

This influx of women challenges the very essence of higher education, a highly masculinized environment founded by men for the training of younger men to assume governance of the economic, political, and religious institutions of the society. For many women, especially before the 1980s, colleges and universities were experienced as cold and intimidating places, in contrast to the rewards of marriage and motherhood. Conversely, primary education is a highly feminized environment, much to the discomfort of boys, who tend not to do as well as girls in the early grades. By high school, a much more gender ambiguous setting, boys are able to pull themselves together, while the girls' academic performance drops precipitously. Clearly, boys do not suddenly become more intelligent or girls less so, but the values, peer expectations, and other structural constraints of high school, combined with the biological changes of puberty, have an impact on the students. Thus, sex, gender, culture, and social structure all interact in creating a different set of pressures on girls and boys (Thorne 1993).

Although American families tend to devote slightly more resources to educating sons than daughters (Powell and Steadman 1989), the middle-class ideology of gender equality plus the smaller size of families in general, typically means that daughters will be afforded a college education, although perhaps at a less prestigious institution than their brothers. In contrast to men, women are more likely to attend community colleges and public four-year schools, and to have delayed their entry into higher education (Chronicle of Higher Education 1997). Once there, however, the women's grades are comparable to those of their male counterparts.

At the graduate level, however, men outnumber women, in part because of self-selection processes whereby only women at the top of their class decide to prolong their education in contrast to men who will enter graduate school with only moderately high grades. The opportunity costs also vary by sex: men are adding to their human capital, women are also doing so, but at the cost of delaying and possibly foregoing marriage and childbearing. Nonetheless, the proportion of women in graduate schools has grown steadily until they now compose over 40% of entering students in medical and law schools. In the fields devalued and depopulated by men, pharmacy, optometry, and veterinary medicine, women compose the great majority of recent degree recipients (Chronicle of Higher Education 1997). In business management, the proportion of Masters Degrees awarded to women the year that Emma Anthony graduated was over 30% compared to only 4% in 1970.

Sex segregation in higher education is also reflected in the low proportions of women in engineering and science programs, compared to their high numbers in the humanities and social sciences. One major study of women in science careers (Sonnert and Holden 1995) found that both differential treatment by professors and the women's own ways of dealing with information had a negative effect on career advancement, but that in scientific areas with a critical mass of women already in place, such as biology, the women did as well as the men. They did much less well where there were few other women, as in mathematics and engineering. In general, the researchers found that small gender differences at the beginning of a scientific career accumulated at every subsequent step, leading to the ultimately large differences in the sex composition of occupations in the physical sciences.

Education is power in the sense that the more you know the less you are influenced by the opinions of others. Having an independent source of information frees girls and women from dependence on a male-defined view of the world and their place in it. The higher the educational attainment of both women and men, the more likely they are to recognize gender inequality, though not necessarily to endorse group-based policies to reduce inequality (Kane 1995).

FERTILITY

Keeping women "barefoot and pregnant" is a cliché that contains more than a grain of truth. Not only do children absorb the time and energy of women and limit their involvement in the world outside the household, but control over their reproductive choices is in itself an exercise of power. Throughout history, control over one's wife and children has been central to patriarchy (the very word means both head of family and chief of tribe). To relinquish this type of power is to diminish a man's standing among his peers, which may explain why it is only in a very few fully modernized societies and only in the past few decades that women's rights in this area have been legally recognized, rights that can always be limited and revoked by politicians. One problem is that whenever and wherever women have gained the power to decide on the number and spacing of their children, they have chosen to have fewer than that desired by their husbands or the political leaders who measure a nation's greatness by the size of its population. When procreation is literally made sacred by invoking religious authority, women will be faced with a powerful array of pressures in favor of large families, at whatever risk to their own health and quality of life. No society leaves fertility decisions totally to chance or to the whim of women. In societies attempting to control population growth, such as the People's Republic of China, young women are carefully monitored to ensure that they are not pregnant and are pressured to terminate the pregnancy if there is already one other child in the family. Conversely, in societies suffering steep population declines, such as Romania in the 1960s, family planning services were terminated and women were carefully monitored to find out why they were not pregnant. In these extreme cases, we can see the degree to which fertility is political and an important component of gender inequality.

This is why the abortion issue carries such symbolic weight. For many feminists, reproductive rights are central to the struggle for equality. For others, (not all of whom are on the side of patriarchy) voluntary termination of a pregnancy signifies individualism gone wild, the triumph of selfishness over the values of family and community. The fierceness of the battle reflects the very high stakes. At this writing, the anti-abortion forces appear to have gained momentum in state legislatures, where a variety of statutes have effectively overturned women's entitlement to abortion services. This has especially affected the very young, poor, and those living in the Midwest and mountain states.

Nonetheless, the fertility rate in the United States since the mid-1970s has remained somewhat stable at 1.8-2.1 children for women of childbearing age. This is the result of several factors: (1) later age at first marriage (by at least 5 years since 1950); (2) the high risk of divorce; (3) availability of inexpensive, effective contraception; (4) the emotional investments of modern childrearing; (5) the expansion of life choices for women. Thus, while many women remain ambivalent about abortion rights, they appear to have taken for granted their ability to plan family size and to combine motherhood with other satisfying roles. Having smaller families means not only that women will have time for other things, but also that daughters and sons will have similar claims on parental resources.

On all three indices of behavior - labor force participation, education, fertility - it appears that the Women's Movement has had a powerful and probably irreversible impact on American women. But what of attitudes?

DOING GENDER

Individuals are classified female or male on the basis of certain biological characteristics. Because the genital area is typically covered, we must make further assignments on the basis of how people look and act; that is, on the basis of gender performances. In this perspective, gender is not a personal trait but, rather, emerges from social interaction - people "do gender" in their daily encounters with one another (West and Zimmerman 1987). Performances tend to follow scripts already internalized through socialization and the expectations built into situations and gendered organizations. As long as people are categorized on the basis of sex, they cannot avoid doing gender, and in doing gender, they maintain and legitimate the basis of the original distinction and all that follows from it. What typically follows, as we have seen, is that in doing gender, men display dominance, and women submissiveness, so that the gender hierarchy is reinforced.

Moreover, the gender hierarchy remains largely intact despite all the major changes in our society over this century - in the economy, the political system, education, and family life - that have supported egalitarian strivings. Jobs are still gender-typed even though occupations have undergone great change; women's work remains devalued; and the wage gap has only slightly narrowed. As one sociologist asks: "What accounts for the chameleon-like ability of gender hierarchy to reassert itself in new forms when its old structural forms erode?" (Ridgeway 1997:218). Part of the answer to preserving male privilege at the macrolevel, Ridgeway suggests, are the microlevel processes that reproduce gender and influence how people think about themselves.

These processes begin where this chapter did, with the need to categorize on the basis of sex, which then triggers gender performances, the expectations and stereotypes that determine who gets hired for what job at what salary, who changes diapers and mops the floor, who is promoted, and so forth. As you can see, the study of gender inequality combines all the levels of sociological analysis - from the most abstract structural variables such as "the economic system," to the organizations that dominate daily life such as family, school, or workplace, to face-to-face interaction such as an employment interview, exchanging jokes with classmates, or deciding who takes out the garbage. At each level, certain assumptions about men and women have created patterns that lead to inequality in power, prestige, and property. These patterns are very difficult to change because they involve privilege and few give it up readily, and also because they ultimately affect how we see ourselves.

At the same time, face-to-face encounters are a primary arena for resistance to gendered expectations. The interaction process is never totally predictable; there are unexpected, "emergent" qualities in personal relationships; role performances are negotiable. The **patriarchal bargain** refers to the overall conditions within which individual women or groups can manipulate, cajole, and otherwise attempt to improve their position and power vis-à-vis men who control their destiny (Kandiyoti 1988).

In modern industrial societies, where couples are no longer under control of family elders and where they are bound together by the need for intimacy and personal fulfillment, male dominance coexists with dyadic dependency, creating a space in which women can claim a degree of power (Fiske and Glick 1997). In the school and workplace, also, the women who enter these institutions with increased skills and self-confidence may be able to affect changes that will ultimately benefit others. In a very real sense, then, the reduction of gender inequality depends as much on interpersonal bargaining as on changes in the laws or other interventions at the societal level.

INTERVENTIONS

In a situation where everything would have to change, it is difficult to point to any one place to begin. Identities, statuses, role performances, attitudes, social structures, and ideologies are all bound up with one another; home and workplace overlap. The *"glass ceiling"* keeps even the most select group of women from the top positions in the public, private, and not-for-profit sectors, while more than half of employed women in the U.S. continue to work on the *"sticky floor"* of low-paying, low-mobility jobs.

Contrary to the claims of critics of affirmative action and other efforts to achieve equity, gender inequality is still a significant problem in the United States today. Occupational segregation by sex and by race, for example, has proved extremely resistant to change despite the considerable efforts that employers have directed toward eradicating it since passage of the Civil Rights Act in 1964. It is very resilient, responding to efforts to eliminate it by reconstructing itself in new ways. Approaches taken in the past 30 years or so to end gender inequality are disregarding first and foremost the women's movement itself.

SOCIAL MOVEMENT ACTIVISM

At this moment, mass-based feminist organizations are often more ridiculed than respected by the media. Yet we cannot overlook the enormous success of organized feminism over the past 30 years: the changes in laws, politics, the labor force, schools, families, religious institutions and practices, and the cultural climate as a whole. Major social change has occurred with widespread public acceptance of movement goals.

Not all of the social changes related to the women's movement can be quantified. Rape, childcare, sexual harassment, and legalized abortion have emerged as national issues during the career of the movement. The statement " I'm not a feminist, but..." is familiar. The goals of the women's movement have become a part of the fabric of the United States. Although the women's movement has achieved legislative victories with regard to equality in employment, credit, insurance, and other areas, the laws are often not enforced. Many organizations are forced into minimal compliance through lawsuits. Ironically, though, these legislative successes may have lulled people into believing that the battle has been won - how often have you heard the expression "post feminist?"

Indeed, so much has changed that an inevitable backlash erupted. Women and men whose comfortable worlds have been shaken by the new feminism are now mounting a powerful counter attack, aided by political and religious leaders whose authority has been threatened. At the moment antifeminist politicians dominate the U.S. Congress and most state legislatures, where they have been very successful in limiting reproductive rights, ending affirmative action programs, and dismantling the parts of the welfare state that benefit women and their children. They have been less successful in bringing women back into the home through appeals to "family values" and claims of the harm done to children by employed mothers. Feminists are taken to task for portraying women as victims and for taking the fun out of life by expanding the definition of sexual harassment to cover presumably innocent by-play.

Under these circumstances, the organized movement has assumed a defensive stance to fend off attacks (Ferree and Hess 1994). Where feminism remains strongest is among smaller, locally organized groups of women who share some special interest--surviving rape, operating battered women's shelters, practicing innovative religious forms, dealing with workplace problems, and so forth--and who often forge coalitions with like-minded though not necessarily feminist groups. Another possibility for a resurgent Feminist Movement lies in the inevitability of disillusion among today's young women who will find out how little has changed when they personally experience harassment and discrimination on the job as Emma Anthony has and violence or inequality at home.

EQUAL EMPLOYMENT LEGISLATION

A number of federal laws now protect women against discrimination in the workplace. The first major piece of legislation restricting sex discrimination was the **Equal Pay Act of 1963**, which required equal pay in situations where men and women did substantially equal work. This law was followed a year later by the **Civil Rights Act of 1964,** which protects women against employment discrimination by private employers, state and local government employers, employment agencies, and labor unions. The **Pregnancy Discrimination Act of 1978** expanded workplace protections for women to include a prohibition against discrimination against women on the basis of pregnancy, childbirth, or related medical conditions (Wisendale 1997). Most recently, the **Family and Medical Leave Act of 1993,** after having been vetoed twice by President Bush, was the first law President Clinton signed after taking office. The FMLA provides employees with the opportunity to take unpaid leave for medical reasons, for the birth or adoption of a child, and for the care of a child, spouse, or parent who has a serious health condition without risk to their jobs (Elison 1997; Marks 1997).

Affirmative action programs grew out of the federal government's attempts to counter both the formal and informal practices that lead to the exclusion of women and people of color in schools and in workplaces. As women and people of color have made gains in education and employment, some white men have responded by attacking the **Equal Employment Opportunity** (EEO) programs, claiming that sex and race inequality have been eliminated and that men are now the victims of "reverse discrimination." Though qualified according to universalistic standards, women and people of color continue to meet resistance to their entrance into higher-paying positions, including race and gender biased assumptions about their presumed qualifications (or lack thereof). For example, Segura (1989) found that Chicano and Mexican immigrant women clerical workers faced a high level of antagonism and lengthy periods of social ostracism from their coworkers and supervisors because of their racial or class background and because they had entered their jobs through affirmative action.

In response to such cross pressures, organizations differ in their commitment to EEO, affirmative action, and diversity. Some organizations marginalize EEO programs as not central to the company's interests, fail to hold managers accountable for developing and promoting women and minorities, or limit implementation of EEO, affirmative action, and diversity programs only to highly visible, and perhaps less central, positions.

WOMEN'S CENTERS

Many women's centers have been established throughout the United States. Some handle only one specific problem, such as abortion, birth control, rape, or battered wives, while others tackle any problem a woman faces. These centers have not only provided alternatives for women seeking specific services; they have also pressured traditional organizations, such as hospitals and courts, to change the way they deal with women's needs. Hospitals now provide birthing rooms, for example, and district attorneys offices and police departments now have special units trained to handle rape and domestic violence cases.

SUPPORT FROM MEN

Without strong support from men, basic change is impossible. There is evidence that younger men are more egalitarian in their attitudes and behavior than are older men (Panayotova and Brayfield 1997). A number of academics have formed a Men's Movement, applying feminist analyses to their own lives, but they are far outnumbered by both the Promise Keepers, who gather in sports stadiums to celebrate their desire once more to become head of the family and to help their wife in her household tasks, and by the men's groups devoted to camping out and getting in touch with their "inner maleness" (Messner 1997).

The most powerful influences on changing men's attitudes and behavior, however, are, very simply, one's wife and daughters. It is when their wife is refused a promotion or when their daughter is harassed in school, that many men become instant feminists. Men's support helped women win the fight to vote at the first part of the previous century and it will help women with their struggles against gender inequality in the first part of this century.

SUMMARY

1. To understand gender as a social problem, we must shift our focus from individuals to the social structure, the patterning of interactions and role performances in society. When we do so, the most important fact is that men dominate.

2. Until women realize that the troubles they have are not personal problems but are features of gendered organizational life that remain obscured by idealized images and abstract concepts of a bodiless worker in a desexualized workplace, little will or can be done to change their situation. Inequality must be perceived as unfair before it is transformed into a social problem.

3. In the case of American Women, the turning point was the mid-1960s, when a new Feminist Movement emerged from the turmoil generated by the Civil Rights and Anti-War Movements.

4. Gender is not a problem but gender inequality is. Women and men are not equals anywhere in the world.

5. Gender is not biologically based; however, it is socially constructed.

6. Cultural values placed on sex-typed behaviors tend to reflect the actual distribution of power in the society, so that the most valued traits are typically those associated with maleness.

7. When carefully measured, the distribution of presumably sex-linked traits such as intelligence, assertiveness, sensitivity, etc., is not highly gender differentiated. The range of differences is greater within all-male or all-female groups than between the group averages for males and females.

8. Most sociologists conceptualize gender as a set of social relationships (an institution) that establishes patterns of expectations for individuals, orders the social processes of everyday life, is built into the major social organizations of society, and is also an entity in and of itself.

9. Maleness and femaleness are not dichotomous; many people have characteristics of both sexes and the newly minted category transgendered suggests the range of variation.

10. When gender intersects with other divisions in the society-age, race, ethnicity, or social class-power and prestige may be distributed in a variety of patterns.

11. The ideology and practice of male dominance in both the private sphere of the household and the public arenas of work, governance, and worship is called patriarchy.

12. Gender inequality slowly erodes under conditions of modem industrialism.

13. Three master conditions enhance the status of women: economic independence, education, and control over reproduction.

14. Results from a variety of recent national surveys show considerable ambiguity alongside strong support for feminist goals. To some extent, this reflects a generalized ideology of equality that characterizes modem democracies.

15. As women enter the labor force and become educated, the reasons for excluding them from public life become increasingly difficult to justify.
16. People "do gender" in their daily encounters with one another. Performances tend to follow scripts already internalized through socialization and the expectations built into situations and gendered organizations.
17. The gender hierarchy remains largely intact despite all the major changes in our society over the past century-in the economy, the political system, education, and family life-that have supported egalitarian strivings.
18. The *glass ceiling* keeps even the most select group of women from the top positions in the public, private, and not-for-profit sectors, while more than half of employed women in the U.S. continue to work on the *sticky floor* of low-paying, low-mobility jobs.
19. Responses or interventions to the gender issue include social movement activism, equal employment legislation such as the Equal Pay Act of 1963, women's centers, and support from men.

REFERENCES

Acker, Joan 1990. "Hierarchies, Jobs, Bodies: A Theory of Gendered Organizations." *Gender & Society.* 4:139-158.
_____.1994. "Women, Families and Public Policy in Sweden." Pp.33-50. in Esther Ngan-Ling Chow and Catherine White Berheide, eds. *Women, the Family and Policy.* Albany, NY: State University of New York Press.
Agassi, Judith Buber 1989. "Theories of Gender Equality: Lessons from the Israeli Kibbutz." *Gender & Society.* 3:160-186.
Berheide, Catherine White 1984. "Women's Work 'in the Home: Seems Like Old Times." *Marriage and Family Review.* 7:37-55.
_____.1987. Cynthia Chertos, Lois Haignere, and Ronnie Steinberg. "A Pay Equity Analysis of Female-Dominated and Disproportionately Minority New York State Job Titles." *Humanity and Society.* 11:465-485.
_____.1992. "Women Still 'Stuck' in Low-Level Jobs." *Women in Public Service.* 3(Fall): 1-4.
Blumberg, Rae Lesser 1984. "Women's Work, Wealth, and Family Survival Strategy." Pp. 117-141 in Esther Ngan-Ling Chow and Catherine White Berheide, eds. *Women, the Family, and Policy.* Albany, NY: State University of New York Press.
Boxer, Sarah 1997, December 14. "Ideas and Trends: One Casualty of the Women's Movement: Feminism." *New York Times.* 4:3(1).
Brenner, Johanna 1987. "Feminization of Poverty and Comparable Worth: Radical and Liberal Approaches." *Gender & Society.* 1:447-465.
Bryant, Adam 1997, December 16. "Women Gain at the Top, But Slightly." *New York Times.*
Chow, Esther Ngan-Ling and Catherine White Berheide 1994. "Studying Women, Families, and Policies Globally." Pp. 1-29 in Esther Ngan-Ling Chow and Catherine White Berheide, eds. *Women, the Family and Policy.* Albany, NY: State University of New York Press.
Chronicle of Higher Education Almanac. 1997 August 29:18-25.
Dallek, Robert 1998. *Flawed Giant: Lyndon Johnson and His Times, 1961-1973.* New York: Oxford University Press.
Elison, Sonja Klueck 1997. "Policy Innovation in a Cold Climate: The Family and Medical Leave Act of 1993." *Journal of Family Issues.* 18:30-54.
Ferree, Myra Marx and Beth B. Hess 1994. Controversy and Coalition: The New Feminist Movement Across Three Decades of Change. New York: Twayne.
Fiske, Susan T. and Peter Glick 1997. "Hostile and Benevolent Sexism: Measuring Ambivalent Sexist Attitudes Toward Women." *Psychology of Women Quarterly.* 21:119-26.
Kandiyoti, Deniz 1988. "Bargaining with Patriarchy." *Gender & Society.* 2:274-290.
Kane, Emily W. 1995. "Education and Beliefs About Gender Inequality." *Social Problems.* 42:74-90.
Lewin, Tamar 1998, April 15. "Men Assuming Bigger Share at Home, New Survey Shows." *New York Times.*
Lipetz, Marcia J. and Catherine White Berheide 1980. "Women's Social Movements." Pp. 5-52 in Mary Ann Baker, Catherine White Berheide, Fay Ross Greckel, Linda Carstarphen Gugin, Marcia J. Lipetz and Marcia Texler Segal. *Women Today.* Monterey, CA: Brooks/Cole.
Lorber, Judith 1994. *Paradoxes of Gender.* New Haven, CT: Yale University Press.

Marini, Margaret Mooney and Pi-Ling Fan 1997. "The Gender Gap in Earnings at Career Entry." *American Sociological Review.* 62:588-604.

Marks, Michelle Rose 1997. "Party Politics and Family Policy: The Case of the Family and Medical Leave Act." *Journal of Family Issues.* 18:55-70.

Messner, Michael 1997. *Politics of Masculinities: Men in Movements.* Thousand Oaks, CA: Sage Publications.

Mills, C. Wright 1959. *The Sociological Imagination.* New York: Oxford University Press.

Panayotova, Evelina and April Brayfield 1997. "National Context and Gender Ideology: Attitudes Toward Women's Employment in Hungary and the United States." *Gender & Society.* 11:627-655.

Powell, Brian and Lala Carr Steadman 1989. "The Liability of Having Brothers." *Sociology of Education.* 62:134-147.

Quadagno, Jill and Catherine Forbes 1995. "The Welfare State and the Cultural Reproduction of Gender: Making Good Girls and Boys in the Job Corps." *Social Problems* 4:171-190.

Reskin, Barbara 1988. "Bringing the Men Back In: Sex Differentiation and the Devaluation of Women's Work." *Gender & Society.* 2:58-81.

Ridgeway, Cecilia L. 1997. "Interaction and the Conservation of Gender Inequality: Considering Employment." *American Sociological Review.* 62:218-235.

Robinson, John P.1997. *Time for Life: The Surprising Ways Americans Use Their Time.* University Park, PA: Pennsylvania State University Press.

Rubin, Gayle 1975. "The Traffic in Women." Pp. 157-210 in Rayna Reiter ed., *Toward an Anthropology of Women.* New York: Monthly Review Press.

Segura, Denise A. 1989. "Chicano and Mexican Immigrant Women at Work: The Impact of Class, Race, and Gender on Occupational Mobility." *Gender & Society.* 3:37-52.

Sonnert, Gerhard, and Gerald Holton 1995. *Gender Differences in Science Careers: The Project Access Study.* New Brunswick, NJ: Rutgers University Press.

Thorne, Barrie 1993. Gender Play: Girls and Boys in School. New Brunswick, NJ: Rutgers University Press.

U.S. Bureau of the Census 1994. "Who's Minding the Kids'?" *Current Population Reports.* Pp. 70-134. Washington, D.C.

U.S. Bureau of the Census 1997, September. "My Daddy Takes Care of Me! Fathers as Care Providers." *Current Population Reports.* Pp. 70-159. Washington, D.C.

Waldfogel, Jane 1997. "The Effect of Children on Women's Wages." *American Sociological Review.* 62:209-217.

West, Candace and Don Zimmerman 1987. "Doing Gender." *Gender & Society.* 1:125-151.

Wisendale, Steven K. 1997. "The White House and Congress on Childcare and Family Leave Policy: From Carter to Clinton." *Policy Studies Journal.* 25:75-87.

CHAPTER 7: FAMILY
CASE STUDY: AN UNEXPECTED DIVORCE

Sandy and Tom were childhood sweethearts. They'd known each other since grade school, and both knew that someday they'd be married to each other. Tom was four years older than Sandy. He finished college the same time that she finished high school, and they were married that summer. Within a year they had the first of their three children. The year was 1970.

Although Sandy was one of the top students in her high school class, she never considered going to college. She loved raising the children, and by 1975 they had three young ones in the household, ranging from an infant son to a young daughter who was getting ready to start school. Sandy was always happy and energetic, and thrived on the tasks of entertaining for Tom's business associates, keeping the house a showplace, and making clothes for the growing children.

But this happy picture of perfection all came tumbling down when Tom came home from a business trip the week of Thanksgiving in 1975 and announced that he was moving out. He'd fallen in love with a woman who worked in sales, and felt he'd "moved beyond" Sandy and her world of domestic bliss. He felt stifled. Sandy couldn't understand what she'd done wrong. Certainly this was a passing thing, and within a few weeks Tom would come to his senses and come home. Within that time period, however, Tom had removed all of his clothes as well as some of the furniture, and had moved in with his new girlfriend. When his lawyer called about arranging the divorce, Sandy realized that this was not a phase, and her marriage was over.

The next year was a living hell for Sandy. She hated the way that the divorce process turned her and Tom into enemies. She didn't want to fight about things; she just wanted everything to be the way it used to be. She found it difficult to get out of bed in the mornings and face the challenges of the day. When a friend suggested that she might be suffering from depression, she tried therapy. Once the divorce was final, however, Tom's insurance coverage stopped and she couldn't afford to continue the sessions. The children, who had always been angels, started to misbehave.

Money from the divorce settlement disappeared quickly. While Sandy had gotten the house in the settlement, it was far from paid off, and within a few months she had to put it up for sale. She moved into a two-bedroom apartment with the three children. Tom's child support and alimony payments were not nearly enough to cover expenses. Unfortunately, they seldom were on time, which forced Sandy to pay her bills late. It was difficult to adjust to the downward mobility. She couldn't buy the kinds of food she had in the past;-it was a challenge just to keep any food on the table. Finally, Sandy realized she would have to get a job.

Getting a job was easier in theory than it was in practice. Since Sandy had only a high school education and no work experience, few options were available to her. Luckily she had taken shorthand and typing in high school and had been very good at both. She polished her skills and began reading the want ads for possibilities. She was able to get a number of job offers in the first several weeks, but none of them provided childcare. Her mother lived nearby and could care for the children after school, but she could not handle the infant full-time. Finally she was lucky enough to find a secretarial position at a local university which not only had an on-site daycare center for employees, but also had a nursery school attached to the Department of Educational Psychology. Sandy was able to work full-time and have her infant in the daycare center and her younger daughter at the nursery school

For the next several years Sandy thrived in her job. She developed a new self-confidence and a pride in her ability to pull her life back together after it was shattered by her divorce. She was always exhausted at the end of the long days-essentially working two jobs, one at the office and another when she got home at night to a house which needed cleaning, and three children who needed to be cared for and fed. Nonetheless, her old, cheery self began to return.

After five years, Sandy started to date again, at first cautiously. It was difficult, however. Often she met men who were married themselves, but interested in dating her nonetheless. That was not for her. The children often seemed to resent her dates, and tension was evident whenever she had someone over for dinner.

And then she met Bill. Unlike most of the guys she'd dated, he not only didn't mind the kids; he loved playing with them. He built a huge treehouse for Tommy (the youngest) and built a life-size dollhouse for the two girls. There was one problem, Bill was nearly ten years younger than Sandy,-but they were incredibly happy together. When he asked her to marry him she didn't have to think more than ten seconds. Almost as if in a fairytale, they were wed, have had a child of their own, and the happy family of six is thriving. Bill and Sandy will celebrate their 16th anniversary this year.

SOCIAL PROBLEMS AND FAMILIES

This chapter focuses upon social problems and families. For most people in the United States, if you mention the topic of family problems, divorce is often the first thing. A family splitting up because of divorce, as illustrated by the case study, is a relatively common occurrence in contemporary life. This chapter argues that the analysis of family problems such as divorce is complex. Rather than focusing upon one particular family problem, the chapter outlines a series of issues that will illustrate the analysis of family problems using a sociological lens.

The chapter is divided into four sections. The first section briefly discusses some issues in defining families, and talks about several major theoretical perspectives for understanding family life. The second section outlines a set of basic rules, which provide some important guidance for analyzing social problems and families. The next section reviews data on how families in the United States have been changing over time. Finally, the last section returns to the case study and examines it using the perspective, which has been developed throughout the chapter, of placing family problems within the context of family change.

THE IMPORTANCE OF THEORETICAL PERSPECTIVES AND DEFINITIONS

FAMILY VARIETY AND FAMILY DEFINITION

Critical to contemporary debates about the health of the family is the definition of family. While it might seem that defining the family would be an easy task, this is far from the case. Sociologists and anthropologists typically distinguish between nuclear and extended households. **Nuclear households** include parents and their children. **Extended households** typically have more than just two generations. A third possibility is a **joint household**, in which siblings live together with their spouses and children (Historically, this third form was common in parts of India). Note that I use the term **household**, rather than family. The United States Census Bureau collects information on households (people who reside together), not on families. As a result, most of the data, which we have, are about households rather than families.

Another distinction which is often made is between a person's **family of orientation** (the family into which you are born-you, your siblings, and your parents) and a **family of procreation** (the family in which you have children of your own).

Family definitions reflect the assumptions made by a particular culture. Most definitions reflect an assumption that there will be two (and only two) parents who are of different genders. It becomes more complex when we talk about families where divorce, desertion, separation, or remarriage occurs. American conceptions of "family" do not typically include the possibility of multiple spouses. This is in marked contrast to many cultures where a man may have multiple wives (**polygamy**) or a woman may have multiple husbands (**polyandry**). The former is the most common ideal form of marriage in the anthropological literature. The latter is the least common form found in anthropological research. Similarly, these traditional conceptualizations of "family" do not typically include households with same-sex adults living together or single parents. How one defines the family shapes what is viewed as a social problem.

THEORETICAL TRADITIONS IN THE STUDY OF FAMILIES

Three major theoretical traditions have dominated the sociology of the family in the past half-century. Each views families in slightly different ways, and each has its own way of defining the family. A structural-functional approach defines the family in terms of the functions it serves for society. It is an institution responsible for procreation, socialization of the next generation, regulation of sexual behavior, protection of members, personality development, and placement of members within the society's stratification system. In contrast, a conflict perspective views the family as an oppressive institution, which maintains the status quo of unequal power relations between men and women and between different age groups. The third major paradigm, symbolic interactionism, defines families at a more micro level. A classic definition of family from this perspective is Ernest Burgess' conceptualization of the family as a "unity of interacting personalities."

THEORY BOX by Michael J. Donnelly Chapter 7 Family/Neo-evolutionary Theory

The earliest humans were small bands of hunters and gatherers who lived at or near subsistence level. The population of the world at the end of the twentieth century stands at more than 5 billion people. The single most important factor which explains this astonishing success of the human species is the development of technology—tools and other extensions and modifications of humanity's basic organic equipment, which have multiplied our capacities to produce and to control nature. Students of socioculture evolution (who tend to call themselves neo-evolutionists to distinguish themselves from the cruder, now discredited evolutionists of the late nineteenth century) argue that technology has been the driving force in human history. They typically distinguish four major epochs in human development: 1) hunting and gathering (based on simple tools used by small-scale nomadic bands); 2) horticulture and pastoralism (based on hand tools used by small-scale nomadic bands); 3) agriculture (based on large-scale cultivation using plows drawn by animals); and 4) industrialization (based on the sophisticated machinery driven not by human and animal muscle but by advanced sources of energy).

Technology is not only the driving force of history, it also provides the material basis for social organization; societies tend to be organized quite differently, to have quite different ways of living, depending on their basic technology. Think for instance of the changes in the family, which have accompanied the shift from agrarian to industrial society. In the simplest societies most of social life happened within the family, indeed kin groups functioned in many respects as all-purpose organizations-the basic building blocks out of which larger social units were formed. Even in more advanced agrarian societies; the family was still typically the basic unit of economic production. In industrial societies, however, such extended kin ties have become far weaker. Extended families tend to live in separate households, often scattered at considered distances. The nuclear family is no longer the unit of production: home and work have become different spheres. Schools, moreover, have assumed many of the family's former responsibilities for training and supervising the young. In an agrarian society parents and their children (and often-other older relatives) would tend to pass long hours together in the daily routine: at work, at meals, sharing the household. In industrial society, children, parents, and other kin spend far less time together day by day; and yet the modern nuclear family seems to have taken on new responsibilities for the private and personal lives of its members. Having lost certain broader social roles, the family is now more than before focused on the personality development of both parents and children.

Each of these theoretical traditions would think of family problems in a different way. A structural-functionalist would view something as a social problem if it interfered with the list of traditional functions served by the family institution. As a result, high rates of non-marital pregnancy would be viewed as problematic because they would indicate that the family is not adequately regulating sexual behavior. Further, if non-marital pregnancies result in single-parent families, a functionalist would see it as a major social problem since the function of socialization may not be adequately fulfilled.

In contrast, a social-conflict theorist would focus upon inequalities and conflict within the family institution. He or she would look at differential poverty rates between racial/ethnic groups, and the gender inequality within families. Finally, a symbolic interactionist would be much more likely to focus upon the micro-level of analysis. Issues of communication within the family would be important, as would be each person's definition of the situation.

Returning to the case study, we can see how analysts from each of these theoretical traditions would see different family problems in the situation of Sandy, her ex-husband, her children, and her new spouse. A structural functionalist would note that the socialization function was not being completed adequately. Evidence of this would be found in behavior problems in the children after the divorce. Similarly, the economic and protective functions of the family were also not being fulfilled, as Sandy was unable to make the payments on the house and found it difficult to pay the bills for her and her children.

In contrast, a social conflict theorist would see a different set of social problems in this case study. He or she would point to the fact that the husband fared considerably better after the divorce. The gender inequality in our society means that he was better off financially as well as emotionally after the breakup of the family.

Finally, a symbolic interactionist would focus upon problems at a micro-level. Sandy's depression after the divorce and the children's adjustment problems would be central to this type of analysis. A symbolic interactionist would point out that Sandy and Tom had very different definitions of the situation. She had fulfilled the traditional role of stay-at-home wife and mother, and couldn't understand why Tom wanted a divorce. He felt stifled and wanted to move on, seeing the family situation as holding him back from his own personal fulfillment.

A LIFE COURSE PERSPECTIVE

A variety of other theoretical perspectives can be useful in analyzing family problems[1]. In this chapter I argue for the adoption of a fourth approach for analyzing social problems in families. A **life course perspective** places family problems within a broader social and historical context. Typically this approach compares the family experience of different cohorts (a concept to be explored later in the chapter) and gives a more complete understanding of social problems in family life (see, for example, Elder 1991, Bengtson, and Allen 1993). Such an approach builds an appreciation for the interconnections between the individual, the family, and social change. It also points to the complexity of relationships between a variety of variables, making it impossible to think of a social problem like divorce in isolation from other changes. Sociologists in all three major traditions have used a life course approach to inform their research. This approach is not incompatible with symbolic interaction functional and conflict analyses.

SOME KEYS TO ANALYZING SOCIAL PROBLEMS AND FAMILIES

A FEW CAUTIONS

The family researcher Bert Adams (1995) has three cautions for anyone studying family problems. First, he suggests that "the same set of circumstances or conditions may be a problem but also a solution to another problem simultaneously." Second, he argues that "the objective solution to one person's problem may cause that person, or someone else, another problem." In the case study, the divorce was a solution to Tom's unhappiness and lack of fulfillment in the marriage. It created, however, a series of problems for Sandy and her children. Finally, Adams cautions that "whether a phenomenon is viewed as a problem or a solution may not be an objective reality at all, but may be determined by the observer's values."

This last point is central to the arguments in this chapter. While one chapter cannot carefully review all of the problems facing families today, we can try to establish a perspective for more thoroughly understanding family problems.

THE IMPORTANCE OF A HISTORICAL PERSPECTIVE

When studying families and social problems, it is critical to place contemporary social problems within a broader historical perspective. Failure to do so can result in misleading conclusions. For over a century, American society has been changing at a very rapid rate. Many people have interpreted the changes in families as negative. Some (see Popenoe 1988 and 1993, for example) have even argued that the patterns we see reflect the demise of the family as an institution. I disagree with those who argue that the family is in a state of decline. In fact, I would argue that in many ways, families are stronger than they were in the past. There are, indeed, many social problems related to families, but we can only understand those problems if we place them within historical context.

There are at least seven key issues to keep in mind when evaluating social problems and families:

It Is Important to Use Data. Often we have misconceptions about family life, and simply looking at the data can change our understanding of social problems related to families. A perfect example of this is the so-called "epidemic" of teenage births. A common assumption is that teenage births have been increasing rapidly in the last half of this century. Table 7.1 Illustrates that far from there being an epidemic of teen motherhood, recent decades have actually seen a significant decline in teenage birth rates. The birth rates for U.S. teenagers in 1980 and 1990 are considerably lower than those in 1950, 1960, or 1970.

TABLE 7.1: BIRTH RATES, BY AGE, IN THE UNITED STATES: 1940 1990
(Birth rate=live births per 1,000 women in specified age group)

Age of Mother	1940	1950	1960	1970	1980	1990
10-14	.7	1.0	.8	1.2	1.1	1.4
15-19	54.1	81.6	89.1	68.3	53.0	59.9
20-24	135.6	196.6	258.1	167.8	115.1	116.5
25-29	122.8	166.1	197.4	145.1	112.9	120.2
30-34	83.4	103.8	112.7	73.3	61.9	80.8
35-39	46.3	52.9	56.2	31.7	19.8	31.7
40-44	15.6	15.1	15.5	8.1	3.9	5.5
45-49	1.9	1.2	.9	.5	.2	.2

Source: 1940 through 1970 data are from Series B 11-19, p. 50, U. S. Bureau of the Census, Historical Statistics of the United States: Colonial Times to 1970. Washington, D.C.: 1975. 1980 and 1990 data are from Table 92, p. 75, U. S. Bureau of the Census, Statistical Abstract of the United States: 1996 (116th ed.) Washington, D.C.: 1992

Use Historical Data. The contrast between popular misconceptions about family problems and the reality of the data can be found in many areas beyond the teen birth rate. One recent article on family problems, for example, talks about a troubling trend in infant mortality in this country, implying that rates of infant death have been increasing (Tiesel and Olson 1992). When historical data are examined however, it becomes clear that infant mortality has been steadily declining over the past century. Similarly, many people assume that divorce rates have gone up steadily throughout this century. In reality divorce rates have fluctuated. They rose dramatically right after World War II, reaching a peak which was not matched until the 1970s. In the early 1980's divorce rates reached an all time high, and they have declined slightly and remained relatively constant since then (Kain 1990).

Use Long-term Data Rather than Just a Few Decades. One trend, which has often been cited as evidence that families are in decline, is the rise in singlehood (or the decline in marriage rates). Popenoe, for example, points out that the population remaining single has increased dramatically since 1960. Focusing only upon the last four decades can be very misleading, however. The 1950's had the highest marriage rate in the history of our country. In many ways, singlehood could only go up, rather than down, after the post-war marriage and baby boom. As Table 7.2 clearly illustrates, the long-term historical trend is curvilinear—rates of singlehood decreased relatively steadily from 1890 through 1960, then increased relatively steadily since then.

Place Patterns and Trends in Cross-cultural/Cross-national Perspective. Unfortunately, even social scientists tend to be ethnocentric. They do research in one country and then generalize to other nations and cultures. Our theories about family problems often do not hold up to empirical tests particularly when cross-national data are used. A good illustration of this principle is found in work by Houseknecht and Sastry (1996). A central argument in David Popenoe's work (1993) is that families have declined precipitously in recent decades. The decline has a particularly deleterious effect upon

TABLE 7.2: PERCENTAGE OF U. S. POPULATION NEVER-MARRIED: 1890-1990

YEAR	AGE 20-24		Age 25-29		Age 30-34	
	% Men	% Women	% Men	% Women	% Men	% Women
1890	81	52	46	25	27	15
1900	78	52	46	28	28	17
1910	75	48	43	25	26	16
1920	71	46	39	23	24	15
1930	71	46	37	22	21	13
1940	72	47	36	23	21	15
1950	59	32	24	13	13	9
1960	53	28	21	11	12	7
1970	55	36	19	11	9	76
1980	69	50	33	21	16	10
1990	79	63	45	31	27	16

Source: 1890 through 1970 data are from Series 160-171, p. 20 and 21, U. S. Bureau of the Census, Historical Statistics of the United States: Colonial Time to 1970. Washington, D.C.: 1970. 1980 and 1990 data are from Table 51, p. 45, U. S. Bureau of the Census, Statistical Abstract of the United States: 1992 (112th ed.) Washington, D.C.: 1992

children. Houseknecht and Sastry attempted to test this using data from four countries: Sweden, the U S, former West Germany, and Italy. Following Popenoe's definition, these researchers used a combination of eight items (including such things as divorce rate, singlehood, and non-marital birth rate) to measure "family decline." They found that on some variables, the relationship was the opposite of that predicted by Popenoe. Sweden, which ranked the highest on family decline, had the best student proficiency in reading for 14-year-olds. Italy, which ranked the lowest on family decline, had the worst reading proficiency. Some variables, in contrast, did reflect

Popenoe's theory-juvenile delinquency rates, for example, increased, as family decline was greater. Finally, some variables, such as juvenile drug offense rates, were inconclusive. Sweden had a much lower rate than the U. S. but still had a higher rate than Italy.

Acknowledge and Explore Problems with the Data. The previous illustration leads directly to the next caveat about studying families and social problems. It is critical to understand difficulties with the data, which we use to analyze family issues. The ideal situation would be to have both cross-national <u>and</u> historical data on a variety of indicators of family life to draw conclusions about the impact of family change upon other variables such as juvenile delinquency, school performance, and drug use. Unfortunately, we often do not have the quality of data, which we need, and must settle for less-than-perfect-tests of our theories.

Examine Interrelationships Between Different Variables. One of the most important things to keep in mind is that family problems cannot be understood in isolation. Changes in women's roles such as increasing labor force participation cannot be understood in isolation from declines in birth rates, shifting economic patterns, and changes in the life style expectations of families. A perfect example of this is provided in the work of historical demographer Peter Uhlenberg. In his article "Death and the Family" (1980) he suggests that we have underestimated the impact of mortality declines upon family life in the last century. For example, even though divorce rates are much higher today than they were fifty years ago, because of declines in mortality, single-parenthood is not particularly more common than it was a century ago. Uhlenberg illustrates that a typical couple today is more likely to experience a long first marriage (celebrating their 30th anniversary in their first marriage) than ever before in history! While divorce has gone up, it has not matched the decline in death. Certainly it was different to experience marital breakup as a result of the death of a spouse, but the fact remains that stable first marriages are more common today than in the past-a point which surprises most people.

Similarly, Uhlenberg's research (1974) illustrates that birth cohorts in the late nineteenth century were **less** likely to experience a "normative" pattern of marriage (Live to adulthood, get married, have children, and survive to age 50 with the marriage intact) than those born in the early 1930's (the very group which would have been in early and middle adulthood during the peak of high divorce rates in the 60's and 70's). In some ways, the "traditional" family is more common today than it was in the past.

Integrate Issues of Race/Class/Gender/Culture into All Analyses. Finally, a central principle to keep in mind is the idea that much of our understanding of families is based upon flawed research-studies which focus upon white middle-class families, research which does not seriously consider the impact of social class upon family life, and analyses of family life which do not consider the importance of variation by race or gender.

Two different studies can illustrate the importance of this final principle. An important change in families over the past three decades has been a rapid increase in the number and proportion of single-parent families. Single-parenthood has been linked to a number of family problems, including drug use, delinquency, poor school performance, and a cycle of poverty and teen parenthood. Using a national sample, Entwisle and Alexander (1996) show that when a set of variables, such as parent's education and family's economic status (two standard measures of social class), is included in the equation, children in single-parent families score no differently on standardized achievement tests than those from dual-parent families. It is the impact of social class which causes the differences.

When looking at the relationship between single-parent families and delinquency, drug-use, and heavy drinking, Thomas, Farrell and Barnes (1996) discover that the relationships between these variables vary by both race and gender. Among white males, for example, the rates of all three behaviors are significantly higher in single-mother families with no father involved than they are in two-biological-parent families. Among black males, however, there is no significant difference in the rates of delinquency, drug use, and heavy drinking between those two groups. In fact, the rate of heavy drinking among black males is slightly <u>lower</u> for those raised in a single-mother family than for those raised in a two-biological-parent family!

All of these illustrations point to the importance of keeping a set of basic principles in mind when thinking about families and social problems. Because of this it is important to review some of the basic changes which have occurred in families over the past century. While we may have many perceptions about family life in the past and present, what the data tell us about what <u>really</u> has been happening to families in the United States?

HOW HAVE FAMILIES ACTUALLY BEEN CHANGING IN THE UNITED STATES?

Often when we think about family problems we think about our own families. I'd like you to think about your own family and ask how it has changed over time. First, ask yourself how the experience of your same-sex parent was different or the same as your experience. What was their level of education? Where were they born? Did they get married? How old were they at the time? How many children did they have? How many siblings did they have? Did any of those siblings die before they reached the age of 15? Did their parents die while they were still children? Do both of your parents work? Do they define their jobs as career? Now move back one generation. Ask the same set of questions about one of your same-sex grandparents...a grandmother if you are female, a grandfather if you are a male. How did their experience compare to that of your same-sex parent? Now, if you know about them, ask the same questions about a same-sex great-grandparent. This exercise should illustrate the rapid rate of change in families. It uses the concept of a generation to compare the experience of different members of the same family.

COHORTS RATHER THAN GENERATIONS

While this exercise is an excellent way to think about change in your own family, the use of generations can be problematic in sociological research. A major difficulty is the length of a generation. If you are an only child, your generation is very narrow. A person with ten brothers and sisters has a wide generation. Imagine that a woman has her first child at age 18 and has ten children, not completing her family until she is 43. One of her oldest children could quite easily have children who are older than her youngest child. Thus there would be overlap between the generations. As a result, it is more useful to employ **birth cohorts** (everyone born in the same year) to study family problems and family change. A number of the studies which have been cited thus far employ this technique-comparing the family experience of one birth cohort to that of another. Using cohorts, let's explore some changes in family life over the past century.

SOME CHANGES IN FAMILY LIFE[2]

More Urban Households. One major change in modern industrial societies over the past century has been the growth of urban areas. In 1850 nearly 85% of the U. S. was rural. By 1980 this had dropped to about a quarter of the population. Nearly half of the population was employed in agriculture in 1850. By the 1990s the proportion had dropped to less than 3%. Rural and urban families are very different. Rural families tend to be larger. Rural residents are more likely to get married, they tend to marry earlier, they are less likely to divorce, and they are less likely to believe that women should work while they have small children. Many of the changes we see in families in this country can be linked to the movement from a rural agrarian society to an urban industrial society.

Decline in Household Size. Closely linked to the growth of an urban industrial society is the decline in household size. When the first U. S. census was taken in 1790, the most common household in the country had seven or more people. This was still true in 1900, when one in five households was that size. By 1930, however, the most common household size was two! By the 1990's well over half of all households contain only one or two people. This was true of only about one in ten households in that first census. This decline is the result of several things-a decline in non-family members in the household, such as boarders and lodgers and household workers; a decline in non-nuclear family members living in the household, such as aunts, uncles, cousins, and grandparents, and a decline in the number of children.

Decline in Fertility. Perhaps the most obvious cause of the decline in household size is the rapid decline in fertility. In 1800 the average white woman had seven children.[3] By the 1990s this has declined to less than two children in the United States. The decline in fertility and smaller households has serious implications for family life and interaction at an individual level. Think about how different it would be to have a family with ten children living in a typical one-room house of the Colonial era, compared to a family with one or two children in a suburban four bedroom home in the 1990s.

Impacts of Mortality Shift. As noted earlier, declines in mortality may be even more important in shaping family problems and family change. Orphanhood was common in the past. Children often spent part of their childhood in single-parent families in destitute poverty, since life insurance did not exist, and a single parent often could not adequately care for a family. Marriages often did not survive to the time that children had reached adulthood. In 1900 the chances were better than 50/50 that a white child would lose a member of his/her nuclear family to death before reaching the age of fifteen. For black children the chances were closer to 75% (Kain 1993). Clearly family life in the past was not without problems.

Increasing Women's Labor Force Participation. A central change of the past century has involved the continuing transformation of men and women's roles both inside and outside the home. Key to this transformation has been the increase in women's labor force participation. A common misconception is that the increase in women's work has been recent. Data from the last century indicate that the change has been continuous, however. In 1890 18.9% of women were in the labor force. In 1900 about 1 in 5 women were in the labor force (20.6%). This increased decade by decade to 29% in 1950. At that point the rate of change increased-up to 34.5% in 1960, 41.6% in 1970, and passing 1 in 2 women (51.1%) by 1980. By 1990 more than 2 out of 3 women worked in the paid labor force. (U. S. Bureau of Census 12:4). While women have entered the paid labor force, men's work in the home has not increased at nearly the same rate. Thus, most married women have two jobs-one in the paid labor force, and another when they return home to work a "second shift" (Hochschild and Machung 1989).

Mothers Working while They Have Small Children. Perhaps more important in the minds of many people than the overall rate of women's labor force participation has been a change in the proportion of women working while they have small children in the home. In 1950 only about 1 in 10 married women (with husband present) worked while their children were under the age of 6. This jumped to nearly 1 in 5 by 1960, 3 in 10 by 1970, over 2 out of 5 by 1980, and over 1 out of 2 by 1985, (U. S. Bureau of the Census 1979-1996). By 1990 the percentage had increased to 58.9%, and by 1995 63.5% of married women with children under the age of 6 worked in the paid labor force.

In the context of social problems and families, many people are concerned that children are not properly socialized when mothers work. This concern reflects a clear assumption that it is women's role, rather than men's, to raise children. Since industrialization most men have spent their day away from the home and family, yet researchers did not ask questions about the impact of those absent fathers upon children. It is only when women work that we seem to be concerned about the impact of parental absence upon children.

Age at Marriage. Another change in families about which there is some misconception has been the age at marriage. When looking at long-term data one finds a curvilinear pattern. The median age at marriage a century ago (1890) was 22 for women and 26.1 for men. It went steadily downward until it reached 20.3 for women and 22.8 for men in 1950, where it stayed through 1960. At that point it began to increase again, but more for women than men. This difference can likely be attributed to the rising proportion of women attending college. Level of education is one of the strongest predictors of age at marriage. As number of years of education increases, the average age at first marriage increases. Since 1960 there has also been a significant increase in the number of cohabiting couples-a pattern which could have a significant impact on the average age at first marriage (Bumpass and Sweet 1989). By 1990 the median age at marriage was 24 for women and 25.9 for men. This long-term historical pattern results in an average decline in the age difference between husband and wife. In 1890 there was a 4.1-year difference in the median age at first marriage. By 1990 this had declined to only 1.9 years (U. S. Bureau of the Census 1976, 1996).

Aging Families. The average life expectation in the United States has increased dramatically over the past century. As men and women are living longer, children are more and more likely to know not only their grandparents, but their great-grandparents as well. At the same time, as noted above, the fertility rate has been declining. One result of the combination of these two trends is a decrease in the numbers of cousins, aunts, and uncles. Families are growing vertically, in terms of the number of living generations, and shrinking horizontally, in terms of the number in any one generation. Some researchers refer to this as the "beanpole" family (Bengtson, Rosenthal, and Burton 1995). This change has important implications for a number of family problems, some of which will be noted below.

Increasing Proportion of Out-of-Wedlock Births. In the first section of this chapter one illustration of a myth about family change was that there are fewer teenage births in recent decades than in the 1950's, 60's, and 70's. A useful way to conclude this section is to explore one reason this misconception may exist. The data in Table 7.1 clearly show that birth rates, in general, have been declining for all ages. What these data don't illustrate, however, is that birth rates to unmarried women of all ages have been **increasing** every decade since 1940. While the increases have been most dramatic for women in their 20's and 30's, they have also increased for teenagers. The combination of overall fertility decline with an increase in births to unmarried women means that the proportion of all births, which occur outside of marriage has skyrocketed. In 1940 only 3.5% of all births were to unmarried women. The percentage remained low up through 1960, when it was still only 5.3%. It doubled in the next decade, to 10.7%. It nearly tripled over the next two decades, increasing to 18.4% in 1980 and 28% in 1990 (U. S. Bureau of the Census 1976, 1996).

It is important to remember that not all children born outside of marriage are raised by a single parent. Often members of the mother's (or father's) extended family play a significant role in child rearing. In addition, while the birth itself occurred while they were single, some of these women will eventually marry. At the same time, it should be kept in mind that a major cause of the increase in non-marital births has been a change in marital behavior since the 1950's. At mid-century, over half of single pregnant women married before the child was born. By the end of the 1980's this was true for only about 1 in 5 (Parnell 1994). Again we see the importance of a life course approach. The relative timing of events in the life course has changed, with profound implications for children in families.

Some Concluding Comments About Patterns of Change in Families. This set of changes clearly does not cover the entire range of issues related to families. It does, nonetheless, give a clear foundation for analyzing social problems and families within a broader context. It is important to keep in mind that these general patterns vary by social class, race/ethnicity, and culture. Families in all groups, for example, have experienced average declines in fertility. African Americans and Hispanic Americans, on average, continue to have higher completed family size than White Americans. Similarly, the labor force participation of women in all groups has increased. At the turn of the century, however, African American married women were much more likely to work outside of the home than White married women. Increases in labor force participation among both groups have been accompanied by a decline in the difference between the two groups.

The same type of variation can be seen when examining social problems in families such as out-of-wedlock births, single-parenthood, or poverty. As noted above, the proportion of babies born outside of marriage has gone up dramatically since 1970. This is true for both African Americans and Whites, but in all years, the rate for African Americans is consistently higher. Similarly, African American children are more likely to grow up in single-parent families, and are more likely to have families living in poverty (O'Hare, Pollard, Mann, and Kent 1995). These types of variation must always be kept in mind when examining data on problems and family change.

SOME OF THE IMPLICATIONS OF THESE CHANGES

Now that we have reviewed some principles for looking at family problems, and outlined some of the major changes in families, we can return to the case study at the beginning of this chapter and place it within a broader context. In addition, we can make some predictions about important family problems over the next several decades in the United States.

THE CASE STUDY IN HISTORICAL PERPECTIVE

Placing the case study within a broader historical and social context gives us a deeper understanding of the family crisis faced by Sandy, Tom, and their children. Remember that Sandy married just out of high school, while Tom had finished college. Returning to the historical data on age at marriage, both Sandy and Tom were a bit younger than average (the median age at marriage in 1970 was 20.8 for women and 23.2 for men), but Tom was closer to the norm. In addition, their age difference was slightly larger than the average in the U. S. at that time. Sociological research indicates that a strong predictor of divorce is early age at marriage.

Sandy and Tom's marriage occurred during a period of dramatic social change in gender roles. The proportion of women going on to college was increasing rapidly. Sandy however had not gone beyond high school. Like the majority of women in the U. S., she did not work outside of the home. Her transition to single parenthood, however, put Sandy in the labor market around 1980, the point at which the scales tipped to more than half of women in the U. S. being in the paid labor force. She worked while she had small children-also reflecting (and contributing to) national trends. Remember from data reviewed in the previous section that only 3 in 10 married mothers with small children worked outside the home in 1970 (the year Sandy and Tom were married). By 1980 it had jumped to 4 in 10, and by 1985 to 5 in 10.

As role definitions for men and women changed, it may be that Tom and Sandy were caught with two different sets of expectations. Sandy accepted a very traditional definition of the role of wife and mother. Tom's sense of being trapped and "moving beyond" Sandy may have been related to a different definition of what he wanted out of marriage and the role of a wife. It is difficult for us to know how Sandy and Tom defined the situation. The data presented in this chapter make it clear, however, that they were negotiating their personal lives during a time of rapid change in family patterns.

Many of the experiences of Sandy and her children are typical. Recall, for example, that she had many financial difficulties after the divorce. A great deal of research finds that men's economic circumstances often improve after divorce, while women and children find themselves living at a substantially lower level than before the end of the marriage (see, for example, Arendell 1986 and Smock 1994). Because of this, a number of states have been re-examining policies which guide the structuring of child support orders (Cancian and Meyer 1996).

Sandy remarried within a few years, and because of increased life expectancies, can look forward to many decades of married life ahead. While she and her children did, indeed, experience great personal and emotional pain as well as financial problems after the divorce, she will most likely have more years of married life than women in previous generations who did not divorce, simply because they or their spouses did not live as long.

This chapter has argued that it is useful to employ a life course perspective for analyzing social problems and families. Such a perspective employs historical data for different cohorts and places the experiences of individuals and families within a broader historical and social context. It gives better understanding of the individual experiences described in the case study which opened this chapter. Using this perspective also helps us make several predictions about future problems which will face families in the United States over the next several decades.

SOCIAL PROBLEMS AND FAMILIES IN THE FUTURE[4]

Examining long term patterns of social change and families provides an excellent avenue for predicting future social problems related to family life. Given the data which have been reviewed in this chapter, several specific predictions can he made.

First, the rate of divorce in the United States is likely to stay relatively high over the next several decades. It is not likely to increase significantly, nor is it likely to decrease dramatically. Many of the long-term changes, which may have contributed, to increasing rates of divorce have stabilized. The divorce rate has been relatively constant for nearly two decades now, and it is unlikely that the situation will change in the near future.

Second, a key family problem, which will receive increasing attention over the next decade, is elder abuse. As the "beanpole" family becomes more common, increasing numbers of individuals will experience extended periods of time in which they are the only people in their generation that is available to take responsibility for elderly parents. Women have typically been the caregivers in families. As more and more women are working, there is less time for the care-giving role in the middle-adulthood years. This combination of factors means that the potential for elder abuse increases and our awareness of this social problem will increase as we enter the next millennium.

Third, the increasing proportion of children born into single-parent families, combined with the increasing gap between rich and poor families in the United States means that we can expect continued and escalating problems of juvenile delinquency and violence in our society (see, for example, Wisensale 1992). One study of historical and cross-national variation in homicide, for example, found that the two greatest predictors of homicide were the level of income inequality in a society, and the divorce rate, both of which were positively related to murder. As inequality increases, the murder rate increases. The same is true for the relationship between divorce and murder. These were followed in importance by the level of welfare spending, which was negatively related to homicide rates-as welfare spending increased, homicide decreased (Gartner 1990). The dismantling of many welfare programs over the past several years may have some unintended negative consequences upon the level of violence in families.

Fourth, it is likely that the proportion of women (and men) who work in the paid labor force while they have small children will remain high, and will most likely continue to increase. Because the United States is the only industrial country in the world which does not have some form of nationally subsidized child care, the social problem of juggling work and home, and caring for the next generation will continue to be an issue. (See Kamerman 1991, for a discussion of some programs and policies in European countries).

SUMMARY

1. The United States Census Bureau collects information on households (people who reside together), not families.
2. Definitions of family reflect assumptions made by a particular culture. Most definitions assume two parents who are of different genders so it becomes complex when we talk about families where divorce, desertion, separation, or remarriage occurs.
3. A Life Course Perspective is chosen for this chapter and compares the family experience of different cohorts. Such an approach holds an appreciation for the interconnections between individuals, the family, and social change.
4. A few cautions - 1) a set of conditions may not only be a problem but also a solution; 2) the objective solution to one's problem may cause someone else a problem; 3) whether something is a solution or problem may be related to an individual's value orientation
5. Families are stronger than they were in the past. Although there are many social problems related to families, we can only understand them if we place them in an historical context.
6. Seven key issues to keep in mind when evaluating social problems and families are: 1) it is important to use data; 2) use historical data; 3) use long-term data rather than just a few decades; 4) place patterns and trends in cross-cultural and/or cross-national perspective; 5) acknowledge and explore problems with the data; 6) examine interrelationships between different variables; 7) integrate issues of race, class, gender, and culture into all analyses.
7. Generations are often difficult to conceptualize but birth cohorts (everyone born in the same year) may be more useful to study family problems and family change.
8. There are more urban households. In 1850 nearly 85% of U. S. households were rural. By 1990 less than 3% of households were rural.
9. Average household size has declined from 7 or more people in 1790 to well over half of all households in 1990 containing only 2 people.
10. A rapid decline in fertility has occurred. In 1800 the average white women had 7 children and by 1990 this had declined to less than 2

11. Orphanhood was common in the past but mortality has dropped making this much less common.
12. Women have moved into the labor force. In 1900 20.6% of women worked outside the home compared to 66% in 1990. By 1995 63.5% of married women with children under the age of 6 worked in the paid labor force.
13. An average decline has occurred in the age difference between husband and wife. In 1890 there was a 4.1 difference in the median age at first marriage. By 1990 this had declined to only 1.9 years.
14. Out-of–wedlock births have skyrocketed, nearly tripling between 1970 and 1990.
15. Men's economic circumstances often improve after divorce, while women and children find themselves living at a substantially lower level than before the end of the marriage.
16. The rate of divorce in the United States is likely to stay high.
17. Elder abuse will receive more attention.
18. The increasing proportion of children born into single-parent families, combined with the increasing gap between rich and poor families means that we might expect continued and escalating problems of juvenile delinquency and crime in our society.
19. The proportion of women with young children in the labor force will remain high and will most likely increase.

ENDNOTES

[1] One recent summary of the literature on family theories (Boss 1993) reviews some fifteen different major theoretical approaches for studying families. The interested reader should refer to this source for more complete discussions of the three major paradigms as they study families, as well as the chapters on using a life course approach for examining family life,

[2] For a more complete discussion of family change, see The *Myth of Family*, Kain, 1990.

[3] Data are presented here for white women, as systematic data for other groups are not available for most of the nineteenth century.

[4] For a more complete discussion of predictions for the future, see Edward L. Kain, *The Myth of Family Decline*, Chapter 9, Lexington Books, 1990.

REFERENCES

Adams, Bert N. 1995. "The Family: Problems and Solutions." Pp. 362-369 in Mark Robert Rank and Edward L. Kain, eds. *Diversity and Change in Families: Problems, Prospects, and Policies.* Englewood Cliffs, NJ: Prentice-Hall

Arendell, Terry 1996. *Mothers and Divorce: Legal, Economic, and Social Dilemmas.* Berkeley: University of California Press

Bengtson, Vern, and Katherine R. Allen 1993. "The Life Course Perspective Applied to Families Over Time." Pp. 469-499 in Pauline Boss, William J. Doherty, Ralph LaRossa, Walter R. Schumm, and Suzanne K. Steinmetz, eds. *Sourcebook of Family Theories and Methods.* New York: Plenus

Bengtson, Vern, Carolyn Rosenthal, and Linda Burton 1995. "Families and Aging: Diversity and Heterogeneity." Pp. 345-361 in Mark Robert Rank and Edward L. Kain, eds. *Diversity and Change in Families: Problems, Prospects, and Policies.* Englewood Cliffs, NJ: Prentice-Hall

Boss, Pauline G., William J. Doherty, Ralph LaRoss, Walter R. Schumm, and Suzanne K. Steinmetz, eds. 1993. *Sourcebook of Family Theories and Methods: A Contextual Approach.* New York: Plenum

Bumpass, Larry L. and James A. Sweet 1989. "National Estimates of Cohabitation." *Demography.* 26: 615-625

Cancian, Maria and Daniel R. Meyer 1996. "Changing Policy, Changing Practice: Mothers' Incomes and Child Support Orders." *Journal of Marriage and Family.* 58 (August): 618-627.

Elder, Glen H., Jr. 1991. "Life Course" Pp. 281-311 in E. F. Borgatta and M. L. Borgatta, eds. *The Encyclopedia of Sociology.* New York: MacMillan.

Entwisle, Doris R. and Karl L. Alexander 1996. "Family Type and Children's Growth in Reading and Math Over the Primary Grades." *Journal of Marriage and the Family.* 58 (May): 341-355.

Gartner, Rosemary 1990. "The Victims of Homicide: A Temporal and Cross-National Comparison." *American Sociological Review.* 55: 92-106, 1990.

Hochschild, Arlie with Anne Machung 1989. *The Second Shift.* New York: Viking Penguin.

Houseknecht, Sharon K. and Jaya Sastry 1996. "Family 'Decline' and Child Well-Being: A Comparative Assessment. " *Journal of Marriage and Family*. 58 (August): 726-739.

Kain, Edward L. 1990. *The Myth of Family Decline: Understanding Families in a World of Rapid Social Change*. NY: Lexington.

Kain, Edward L. 1993. "Family Change and the Life Course." Pp.499-504 in Pauline Boss, William J. Doherty, Ralph LaRossa, Walter R. Schumm, and Suzanne K. Steinmetz; eds. *Sourcebook of Family Theories and Methods*. New York: Plenum.

Kamerman, Sheila B. 1991. "Starting Right: What We Owe to Children Under Three. " *The American Prospect*. Winter.

O'Hare, William P., Kelvin M. Pollard, Taynia L. Mann, and Mary M. Kent 1995. African-Americans in the 1990s," *Population Bulletin*. 46(1).

Parnell, Allan M. 1994. Gray Swicegood, and Gillian Stevens. "Non-marital pregnancies and marriage in the United States." *Social Forces*. 73(1): 263:287 1994.

Popenoe, David 1993. "American Family Decline, 1960-1990: A Review and Appraisal." *Journal of Marriage and the Family*. 55 (August): 527-555.

Smock, Pamela J. 1994. "Gender and the short-run economic consequences of marital disruption." *Social Forces*. 73(1): 243-264.

Thomas, George, Michael P. Farrell, and Grace M. Barnes 1996. "The Effects of Single-Mother Families and Nonresident Fathers on Delinquency and Substance Abuse in Black and White Adolescents." *Journal of Marriage and the Family*. 58 (November): 884-894.

Tiesel, Judy Watson, and David H. Olson 1992. "Preventing Family Problems: Troubling Trends and Promising Opportunities." *Family Relations*. 41: 398-408.

Uhlenberg, Peter 1974. "Cohort variations in Family Life Cycle Experience of U.S. Females." *Journal of Marriage and the Family*. 36 (May): 284-291.

_____.1980. "Death and the Family." *Journal of Family History*. 5(Fal, 1980): 313-320

United States Bureau of the Census 1976. *Historical Statistics of the United States, Colonial Times to 1970*. Washington, D. C.: U. S. Government Printing Office.

_____.1979. *The Statistical Abstract of the United States: 1980*. Washington, D.C.

_____. 1996. *The Statistical Abstract of the United States: 1996*. (116th ed.) Washington, D.C.

Wisensale, Steven K. 1992. "Toward the 21st Century: Family Change and Public Policy." *Family Relations*. 41 (4): 417-422.

CHAPTER 8: AGING
CASE STUDY: COPING WITH WIDOWHOOD

Betty Miller, age 67, was widowed four months ago. Her husband Richard died of a massive stroke. Since he had been paralyzed from a previous stroke 23 months before, Betty had been struggling to care for him at home, so she felt both loss and relief when he died.

Now Betty is beginning to rebuild her life as a widow. She is just realizing that it is going to be more difficult than she had imagined. During Richard's illness and death, she had anticipated her emotional response. She also received much support from her family and friends. But she had not expected that her entire lifestyle would be threatened by her new financial situation. She just learned that her monthly income will be about $1900. With a mortgage on her condominium and other expenses, she is spending more than $3000 a month. How did this happen to her? And how can she cope?

It was a second marriage for both of them. Betty's first marriage ended in divorce when she was 33. As a single mother with two young sons, she found work as a receptionist in a small electronics company. She eventually completed an associate degree in business at a community college and advanced to a position as office manager. When she was 42, a friend from church introduced her to Richard, a recently divorced supervisor working for the county agency, who was eleven years her senior. His daughter and son were in college. When Betty and Richard married a year later, she felt lucky to have found a companion who was also generous to her sons. Richard had a good pension and decided to retire at age 60. Betty, only 49, was hesitant to leave her job. But Richard assured her that he would "take care of her financially" and wanted Betty to retire, too. Her sons were now independent, so she agreed. They sold their home in the San Francisco Bay area, moved to a community for "active adults" in Arizona, and traveled extensively.

As their children began their own families and Richard developed diabetes and hypertension, Betty convinced him to move back to the Bay area. Five years ago, they bought a comfortable condominium in a suburban community south of San Francisco near the families of Richard's daughter and Betty's younger son. They joined a church, became active in a local senior center, and enjoyed visits with their grandchildren.

Nearly three years later, Richard had a major stroke that paralyzed his right side and severely impaired his speech. After spending six days in a hospital, he was moved to a transitional care unit for rehabilitation. Then he was discharged with support from a home health agency. After five months of therapy, his speech was much better, but he was still wheelchair-bound.

Since he was no longer improving, Medicare would not continue to pay for the home health services. At first, Betty tried to manage his care alone, but she injured her back trying to lift him. She needed to pay privately for a home health aide 5 hours a day to help dress, bathe, and transfer him. Her son and Richard's son-in-law helped on weekends. The aide cost more than $1600 a month, but Betty felt that she had no choice.

Richard had handled the couple's finances until his first stroke. Then, with some help from her younger son, Betty took over. She focused on paying the bills with income from Richard's pension, Social Security, and their savings, but did not want to worry about their long-range financial status. Richard had used some of their savings to help his children with down payments to purchase homes. Betty assumed that they were loans, but discovered after Richard's death that no formal papers had been signed and that his children viewed the money as their inheritance. She also learned that her survivor's benefits for the pension were reduced by half and Social Security benefits were reduced by a third. With about $40,000 in savings, $80,000 in $150,000 mortgage, and expenses exceeding income, she now understands that she needs to make major changes.

She is in good health, except for some arthritis that causes pain in her hands and knees and a slight hearing loss. Her genetic background suggests the potential for long life, since her father survived to age 88 and her 90-year-old mother is still living with limited assistance in a senior retirement apartment. Betty realizes that she may live another 25 or 30 years. Although she is close to her younger son's family and on good terms with her other son and stepchildren, she does not feel that she can or should count on them to help her financially.

With some anxiety, Betty has asked the senior center to refer her to an employment service for older workers. Her income is too high to qualify for several job-training programs, but the service offered her skills assessment, job-hunting workshops, and some leads. Betty never used a computer when she was employed, so the counselor suggested that Betty learn to use word processing and spreadsheet programs through classes at the senior center in order to return to office work.

At first Betty resisted taking the classes. It was almost 40 years since she completed her degree and she was not confident about her ability to learn new skills. Also, she worried that her arthritis would interfere. But after three unsuccessful job interviews, she is ready to try the classes. If she can find an office position with a company that offers pension benefits and work as long as her health is good, maybe she can manage to stay in the condominium near her family and friends. She is also thinking of joining a support group for widowed persons to help her prepare for the next stage of her life.

DEMOGRAPHIC PROFILE

INTRODUCTION

Betty is part of the fastest growing segment of the population; those over age 65. Increasing longevity and the growth in the size of the older population have led to major changes in individual lives, family relationships, and the structure of our society. For the first time in history, most people can expect to survive to old age. This is a "social success" more than a "social problem!" However, the aging of society also means new challenges, including the need to develop new social structures and new attitudes to respond to population changes.

THE DEMOGRAPHIC REVOLUTION

During the 20th century, Americans have witnessed a dramatic rise in the number and proportion of persons age 65 and over. The 3.1 million older Americans in 1900 comprised about 4% of the population. By 1994, there

---

THEORY BOX   by Michael J. Donnelly   Chapter 8   Aging Functionalism

The human body is a good example of an organic system, whose survival depends upon the functioning of its interconnected parts. Damage to or loss of the heart, or the lungs, or the brain, for example, results in the organism's death; moreover impaired functioning of one part (say, the lungs) will likely cause adverse consequences for other subsystems of the body, leading eventually to a general collapse. Sociologists have long tried to think of society as a bounded social system of interrelated parts, rather like an organism or a cybernetic system. To analyze society as a functioning whole involves looking at the parts that make it up, and examining what a given part (an institution or a set of social roles) contributes to maintaining the whole. What essential role and function does each part perform? What does society need to survive and maintain itself? Whenever we can answer that question by saying society does need X (or a, b, c, d, etc.), we are describing necessary tasks that society must one way or another accomplish. These are its functional requisites for survival.

The functionalist point of view is an interesting way to examine aging. In pre-industrial societies kinship functioned in many respects as the basic building block of social organizations. Craft workshops and small farms were in many ways family affairs: families comprising several generations tended not only to live together, but also to work together; and much of the training of the young happened informally in the routine course of family life. In such a kin-based social organization, older adults and the elderly often controlled land and other economic resources; along with their power, they enjoyed also the prestige accorded traditionally to the wisdom of experience.

In industrial societies, by contrast, the family functions rather differently. Work and other economic transactions take place outside the home, and the family has ceded to formal school much of its former diffuse role in raising and training the young. These developments have in many ways diminished the social standing and prestige of the elderly. The elderly typically live in different households from their grown children, who have independent jobs and careers. Moreover, technological and social change have rendered obsolete much of what older people know, at least from the standpoint of the young. Old people often experience a sense that they have outlived their usefulness. The functionalist would make the point in more neutral terms, suggesting that after their generative and productive years older adults have exhausted much of their usefulness, given the way that the essential roles in industrial society are allocated.

---

were 33.2 million older Americans, making up almost 13% of the population (U. S. Bureau of the Census 1995). The relative growth of the "oldest old" segment of the population - those over age 85, like Betty's mother - has been even greater. It increased from 123,000 in 1900 (about .2% of the population) to an estimated 3,620.000 in 1995 (about 1.3% of the population) (U. S. Bureau of the Census 1994).

The main reasons for this "demographic revolution" have been a sharp rise in average life expectancy and an overall drop in birth rates (despite relatively high birth rates during the "baby boom" years of 1946 to 1964). Life expectancy at birth was about 47 years in 1900 (46 for men and 48 for women). By 1991, it jumped to 76 years (72 for men and 79 for women).

In the first half of the 21st century, the older population will continue to grow substantially, especially beginning 2011, when the oldest members of the "baby boom" generation reach age 65. By 2050, it is projected that the number of persons age 65+ will more than double to 68 million (almost 23% of Americans). Those age 85+ will exceed 15,000,000 (about 5% of the population) (U. S. Senate Special Committee on Aging 1991). These projections, which represent the "middle" estimates of the U. S. Bureau of the Census, may be modified by changes in mortality (death rates), fertility (birth rates), and migration. However, they are likely to be reasonably accurate: everyone who will be 65 or older by 2050 has been born!

GENDER

Because women now live about seven years longer than men, on the average, the ratio of older women to older men becomes greater with age. Among those age 65+, there are about three women for every two men; among those age 85+, there are about five women for every two men. As a consequence, older men are almost twice as likely as older women to be married (75% vs. 41%) and older women are about three times more likely as men to be widowed (48% vs. 14%) (U. S. Bureau of the Census, 1995). Coping with widowhood is an experience that most married women, like Betty and her mother, will face.

RACE AND ETHNICITY

The older population in the U.S. is becoming more diverse in its racial and ethnic composition. The U.S. Bureau of the Census (1995) estimates that 1 in 10 elderly persons were a race other than White in 1990; that proportion is projected to double by 2050. Similarly, the proportion of older adults who are Hispanic is expected to grow from 4% to 16% (Hispanics may be of any race). Due to high rates of immigration among Asians and Hispanics and high fertility rates among most minority populations, they have a smaller proportion of older members than Whites (Angel and Hogan, 1994). For example, about 8% of Blacks, 7% of other races (Asian, Native American, Eskimo, and Aleut), and 6% of Hispanics were age 65+ in 1990. However, these proportions are projected to reach 13% for Blacks, 16% for other races, and 13% for Hispanics by 2030.

CLASS

The economic status of older adults is more varied than that of any other age group; relying on age group averages in income can be very misleading. Older adults are about as likely as other adult groups to have incomes below the poverty line. In 1989, 11.4% of persons age 65+ were below the poverty line, compared with 10.2% of those ages 18 to 64. Another 15% of older adults had incomes just slightly above the poverty line (between 100% and 150% of poverty). However, many older people are financially comfortable. Including assets such as homes, savings, and investments, people over age 65 are likely to have higher net worth than younger adults. There are many subgroups of elders who are at high risk of poverty, including women, minority group members, the very old, and those who live alone (U. S. Senate Special Committee on Aging 1991). The cost of extended long term nursing home or home health care can also impoverish persons with considerable assets, since most older people have no insurance coverage for chronic health care.

GROWING OLD BIOLOGICALLY

AGING AS A BIOLOGICAL PROCESS

Most people think of aging as a biological process that inevitably leads to physical decline. Researchers in the field of **gerontology** (the study of aging) are discovering that many changes that were believed to be inevitable consequences of aging are actually due to disuse or disease (Williams 1992; National Institute on Aging 1993). According to Strehler (1977) true or **intrinsic aging** involves a universal, progressive, deleterious change in functioning that is basic to the organism. All body systems decline or lose reserve capacity due to intrinsic aging, but the rate of change is highly variable, even across systems within the same individual. Slowed reaction speed, reduced immunity to disease, and changes in muscle and bone content are examples of intrinsic aging. **Extrinsic aging** involves changes due to environmental factors, lifestyle, and disease, such as exposure to sunlight and pollutants, diet, exercise, and stress-induced illnesses.

From a social perspective, it is important to understand how aging affects a person's ability to function in his or her roles. For most individuals, intrinsic aging does not have a major impact on role functioning until the eighth or ninth decade of life. Social systems can help support or limit the opportunities available to those with both intrinsic and extrinsic age-related changes. Social intervention may also modify the conditions that lead to extrinsic aging.

THE SENSES

Age-related changes in the senses of vision, hearing, taste, smell, and touch begin in one's twenties and thirties. Vision changes include decreased ability to focus on very near objects and a decrease in the amount of light that enters the eye. Thus, by age 60, most need glasses at least for reading, and the eye admits only about one-third as much light as the eye of the average 20-year old (Atchley 1997). Visual acuity also declines with age. Nevertheless it is possible to compensate for many age-related vision changes with glasses and good lighting. On a less positive note, conditions that reduce vision, including cataracts, glaucoma, macular degeneration, and vision problems due to diabetes, become more common with age.

By age 65, most people have reduced ability to hear higher frequencies and also find it more difficult to hear with distracting background noises. Betty Miller is among the almost 30% of older adults who report hearing impairments significant enough to affect daily functioning (U. S. Senate Special Committee on Aging 1991). Because age-related hearing loss is primarily due to changes in the inner ear, assistive devices like hearing aids are usually not sufficient to fully compensate. Hearing impairment can interfere with social interaction. Some elders with hearing problems withdraw from contact with others; a few may become distrustful or even paranoid. They may also be labeled as confused or uncooperative. According to a research review by Whitbourne and Dannefer (1985/1986), poor hearing has been linked to greater risk of psychological problems.

The senses of taste, smell, and touch also tend to decline with age. These changes usually do not directly cause major problems with functioning, but may place the person at higher risk of malnutrition and injury.

PHYSICAL ACTIVITY

Physical activity and exercise tend to decline with age. Over two-thirds of adults age 65+ report having no regular exercise routine and about half are sedentary, according to the 1985 National Health Interview Survey (Caspersen, Christenson, and Pollard 1986; Kovar, Fitti, and Chyba 1992). Research has linked physical inactivity with higher risk of death and disease.

As the Institute of Medicine (1990) notes, loss of functioning due to low levels of physical fitness can diminish a person's quality of life at any age, but "the physically unfit elderly may lose the capacity for independent living (p. 230)".

Most older people report no major limitations in their ability to perform routine **activities of daily living (ADL),** such as bathing, eating, or transferring from bed to chair, or in home management tasks (often called **instrumental activities of daily living, IADL**) such as laundry, cleaning, shopping, or managing finances. However, almost 20% of adults age 65+ who live in the community report at least one ADL or IADL difficulty; more than half of those age 85+ have at least one difficulty. Women and Blacks are significantly more likely than men and Whites to report difficulties (U.S. Senate Select Committee on Aging 1991).

One physical activity that is not often associated with older adults is sexual interaction. Many people assume that both interest in, and capacity for, sexual relations decline with age. While research on sexual activity in later life is limited, longitudinal studies indicate that levels of sexual activity tend to remain stable over middle and later life (Palmore 1981). Some experts suggest that lesbian relationships (or polygamy) may make sense for older women because of the sex imbalance, but few people change sexual orientation values in later life. Unless Betty Miller happens to meet an unmarried man, she is unlikely to have another sexual partner.

It is estimated that up to 10 % of older adults may be gay or lesbian (Kimmel 1992). The common belief that older gays and lesbians are lonely and maladjusted is not supported research. Although studies of this group of elders are limited, they suggest that aging homosexuals tend to have good support systems and high life satisfaction (Deevey 1990; Kimmel 1992; Quam and Whitford 1992).

HEALTH

Most older people view their health positively. The National Health Interview Survey conducted by the National Center for Health Statistics found that nearly 71% of elderly living in the community assessed their health as excellent, very good, or good. Nevertheless, more than 80% of those over age 65 report at least one chronic condition. The most common chronic conditions include arthritis (48%), hypertension (38%), hearing impairment (29%), and heart disease (28%) (National Center for Health Statistics 1990).

One negative consequence of longevity has been an increased likelihood of becoming dependent on others due to poor health and/or disability (Verbrugge 1984). Advances in medicine and improvements in sanitation and health practices have enabled more people to prevent, delay, or minimize the risks of life-threatening illnesses. While these changes mean that more people enjoy good health for longer periods, they are also more likely to survive long enough to develop chronic, disabling conditions that may require rehabilitation and/or long term care.

There is controversy about whether it may be feasible to delay the onset of age-related diseases to "compress" illness into the last few months or years of life. This **"compression of morbidity" theory** is based on the assumption that the human life span is fixed and that people would die quickly as they approached that fixed limit (Fries and Crapo 1981). If this theory is correct, it suggests that health care should focus on prevention of chronic diseases but should not emphasize life-extending interventions for people who are near that limit. Daniel Callahan, a bio-ethicist, has argued that we should not use expensive health technologies to prolong the lives of those over age 80 or 85 (1987). Some researchers question whether the human life span is fixed (Schneider and Brody 1983). Many writers have challenged Callahan's proposal to limit health care on the basis of old age (Homer and Holstein 1990).

GROWING OLD SOCIALLY

AGEISM

Robert Butler, a geriatrician who was the first Director of the National Institute on Aging, coined the term **ageism** in 1969 to refer to systematic stereotyping and discrimination against people because they are old (Butler 1987). Ageism has real negative consequences because it affects the expectations and behaviors of older adults and others.

The general public tends to believe that the situation of old people is much worse than elders themselves report. A recent national survey (Speas and Obenshain 1995) found that a majority of adults aged 18 to 64 believed that fear of crime, inadequate income, loneliness, insufficient medical care, not feeling needed, and poor health were problems faced by "most people over 65." In contrast, only 37% of respondents 65 and older actually said they experienced fear of crime and 15% or less reported the other problems.

One example of ageism is the common stereotype that older people become senile-forgetful, confused, and unable to learn. Research demonstrates that most individuals experience only minor changes in their cognitive skills in later life. Stability is more typical than decline, and some individuals may improve skills that are based on experience, like vocabulary, inductive reasoning, and wisdom (Baltes 1993). Only about 10-15% of those over 65 develop **dementia**, permanent cognitive deficits due to damage to the brain caused by diseases such as Alzheimer's disease or atherosclerosis. Some older adults may show cognitive problems due to reversible causes like malnutrition, depression, infections, or side effects of medication. However, the false belief that cognitive decline is normal in later life can lead to employment discrimination, social devaluation, or failure to seek help for treatable causes of cognitive symptoms. Older adults who share the common stereotype may become anxious with minor gaps in their memory or, like Betty Miller, may be hesitant to learn new skills.

Negative stereotypes about aging can also lead to a desire to provide older adults with special help in response to their (presumed) poverty, frailty, or social isolation. Robert Binstock (1983) argues that public programs for older adults like Social Security and Medicare have been based on "compassionate stereotypes" that are ageist. Although such programs have improved the status of older peoples' lives, they have also led to resentment about their cost.

As Erdman Palmore (1990) notes, positive stereotypes can also have dangerous results. Recent popular images present older adults as more advantaged financially, physically, and socially than may actually be the case. These positive stereotypes may impose unrealistic expectations on elders and may encourage policies and practices that ignore the real needs of older adults. Ageism, whether positive or negative, undermines our ability to perceive older people accurately and to respond appropriately to genuine problems.

FAMILY

Misconceptions also abound in popular views of relationships between elders and their family members. Despite popular images that families "abandon" their older members, most older adults have regular and positive contact with family members. One major trend has been toward increasingly long-lasting family bonds. Despite high divorce rates, the number of marriages that reach their 50th, 60th, or even 75th anniversary is growing. Sibling ties of eight or nine decades are common. Approximately 10% of adults over age 65 still have a living parent. Four-generation families are becoming the norm. For the first time in history, most parents survive for an extended "post-parental" period when their children are adults. In fact, women are likely to spend, on average, more years with parents over 65 than with children under 18 (Cantor 1991; Hagestad 1988).

Those with children tend to live within an hour's drive of at least one child. Elders in reasonably good health tend to provide as much or more help to younger generations than they receive, although there is much variability in the range of services exchanged between older parents and their children (Eggebeen 1992). When elders do need care, as when Richard Miller had his first stroke, family members usually provide most assistance. In fact, it is estimated that family members usually provide about 80% of services used by older adults with disabilities. The primary caregivers are likely to be daughters (29%), wives (23%), other female relatives like daughters-in-law and sisters (20%), and husbands (13%) (Stone, Cafferata, and Sangl 1987). Influences such as the increase in smaller families with fewer children, increasing number of women in the labor force, and increasing incidence of divorce, step families and single-parent families may reduce the ability of families to caregiver for impaired members (Cantor 1991; Allen and Pifer 1993).

Many ethnic differences have been found in the family relationships of older adults. In particular, older members of most minority ethnic groups are more likely to live in multi-generational households and are more likely to express norms of family obligation to elders. It is not clear whether such differences are due to culture, socio-economic status, and/or other factors (Rosenthal 1986). However, researchers caution against generalizing that ethnic families "take care of their own," since many ethnic elders do not have adequate family supports (Gratton and Wilson 1988).

Class may be a better predictor of patterns of actual assistance to elder family members with disabilities. Research indicates that families from lower socio-economic levels are more likely to provide instrumental help, while those from higher levels are more likely to provide emotional help (Cantor 1979; Weihl 1983).

Considerable attention has been given to research on the effects of being a caregiver, particularly on **caregiver burden** or **stress**. Studies demonstrate that caregivers are likely to have poorer physical and mental health than age peers who are not caregivers (George and Gwyther 1986). Caregivers are also more likely to experience financial strains due to related cost of health care for the dependent person and reduced employment opportunities. The negative impact of caregiving is not uniform: most evidence indicates that women are at greater risk than men for stress and economic problems (Hooyman and Gonyea 1995; Allen and Pifer 1993; Montgomery and Datwyler 1990). Also, caregivers for persons with behavioral problems usually report higher burden than other caregivers. While objective measures of physical and economic impact of caregiving show that those in poor socio-economic and educational status suffer more, subjective measures suggest that more affluent and better-educated individuals report more stress.

Emily Abel (1991) has criticized caregiving research for its emphasis on burden and stress, rather than a more complex, full understanding of the experience. Recent research that both burden and satisfaction with caregiving can coexist and may be distinct factors (Skaff and Pearlin 1992; Stull, Kosloski, and Kercher 1994).

Betty Miller's situation in caring for her husband was typical in most respects. Men are usually cared for by their wives at home, sometimes with assistance from adult children. Betty Miller experienced both stress and satisfaction. Her use of paid help to supplement family care giving was less typical: only 11% of elders with ADL limitations receive paid care (U. S. Senate Special Committee on Aging 1991).

Although most older adults report positive relationships with family members, abuse and neglect by family members is a problem for some. A large random sample survey of older people in Boston found that 3.2% of respondents reported that they had been victims of physical violence, verbal aggression or neglect (Pillemer and Finkelhor 1988). Spouses accounted for 58% of abuse, children 24% and others, 18%. Contrary to popular belief, children who abused their parents were more likely to be dependent on the parent rather than the other way around.

Grandparenting is a highly varied role in current American society. Cherlin and Furstenberg (1986) identified five different types of relationships: 1) detached; 2) passive; 3) supportive; 4) authoritative; and 5) influential. Divorce and remarriage tend to weaken grandparent-grandchild relationships on the non-custodial side of the family, but strengthen those on the custodial side (Matthews and Sprey 1984). An emerging trend is that increasing numbers of grandparents are becoming surrogate parents for their grandchildren due to divorce, substance abuse, incarceration, AIDS, and other problems in the parental generation. More than 3 million grandchildren live with their grandparents; in about 1/3 of those households, the parents are not present (Chalfie 1994; Giarrusso, Silverstein, and Bengtson 1996). According to Minkler and Roe (1996), these grandparents are likely to face health problems, economic difficulties, lack of government support, and social isolation.

FRIENDS AND NEIGHBORS

Research on relationships between older adults and their friends and neighbors is limited. Most older adults report having friends. For example, a study of older women found that 93% had friends (Armstrong and Goldsteen 1990). In a study of elders over age 85, Johnson and Troll (1994) found that 3/4 of their respondents were in contact with a friend at least weekly. Older people tend to rely mainly on relatives for personal assistance, but friends provide companionship and emotional support (Antonucci 1990).

WORK, RETIREMENT, AND FINANCES

In previous centuries, most people continued to work as long as they were physically able to do so. Retirement supported by age-based pensions was created for military and government workers in late 19th century Europe and slowly expanded to cover more workers. In the U.S., Social Security was passed in 1935 and now covers more than 90% of older Americans. Private pensions expanded primarily after World War II. Retirement became common in industrialized countries in the second half of the 20th century partly as a result of the availability of retirement income and social norms, but also due to age discrimination in employment. It is estimated that 2/3 of men over age 65 in 1900 were in the labor force; unemployment or health problems kept most of the remainder from working. In 1989, only 17% of men and 8% of women aged 65+ were employed (U S. Senate Special Committee on Aging 1991).

Is retirement a problem or a success for individuals and for society? Evidence is mixed on both levels. For individuals, the answer is probably "it depends." Many people now choose to retire as soon as they can afford to do so and look forward to a variety of leisure and volunteer roles. These retirees typically adapt well to retirement. However, other retirees, those who often don't fare as well, lack choice over their retirement because they become unemployed, have conflicting caregiving responsibilities, or have major health problems. Research suggests that African and Latino Americans are particularly likely to experience involuntary retirement due to unemployment or disability; Rose Gibson (1993) terms this group the **unretired retired.**

At the societal level, many experts point to our collective ability to support a period of leisure for older adults as progress. Yet retirement has social costs: the productive potential of experienced older individuals is not used and the financial burden of providing retirement income for increasing numbers of old - but often physically capable - people may tax our economic system (Moody 1994).

Retirement income is highly variable. According to the philosophy of the Social Security Administration, retirement income ideally rests on a "three-legged stool" including Social Security retirement benefits, private pensions, and income from savings and other assets. Many individuals, however, rely on only one or two of those "legs." More than 9 out of 10 older Americans receive Social Security retirement benefits based on their own or their spouse's employment history. However, the average monthly benefit for individuals was approximately $740 in 1995 - barely above the Federal poverty line of $609 for individuals (Administration on Aging 1996, Social Security Administration 1996). Very low-income elders may also qualify for Supplemental Security Income (SSI), which guarantees a minimum of about $440 a month. About 70% of older Americans receive at least some income from assets like savings and investments, while about 41% receive income from private pensions.

Betty Miller's financial status is better than average for most unmarried older women. Her income is 3 times higher than the poverty line and her assets are also above average. However, she does not feel financially comfortable for several reasons: her expenses exceed her income; any significant reductions in expenses would require a major change in her lifestyle; and adequacy of her income and assets for a possibly long future is in doubt. Finding appropriate work may be difficult because of Betty's physical health, outdated work skills, and lack of confidence. Age discrimination by employers can only compound these difficulties

HOUSING

More than 90% of older adults live in independent housing, which includes single family homes and mobile homes, condominiums, and apartments. Most live in age-integrated communities and most "age in place" in homes that they have lived in for many years. Age-segregated settings, from retirement communities for "active adults" to nursing homes, are highly visible but house only a small proportion of elders.

The majority of older adults have adequate housing, but problems are common for low-income people who must rent, inner city and rural elders who may have dilapidated housing, and those whose health or disability interferes with home maintenance. In most communities, there are long waiting lists for publicly subsidized rental housing and an inadequate supply of affordable housing in the private sector.

Multi-generational households are more common than widely believed. Based on 1980 census records, Coward and Cutler (1991) estimated that 19.8% of older Americans lived in two or 3-generation households. In some cases, the elders are caregiving for grandchildren; in others, the elders are dependent on an adult child. But qualitative studies of co-residence suggest that many multigenerational families live together as a result of lifelong living patterns or a crisis in the adult child's life (Atchley 1997:197-201).

HEALTHCARE

Because health problems and disabling conditions increase with age, older adults use more health care services than younger people. For example, in 1987 people age 65+ represented about 12% of the population but accounted for 37% of hospital stays and 36% of health care expenditures. In 1994, they averaged 11 contacts with doctors compared with five contacts with doctors for younger persons (Administration on Aging 1996).

Most older Americans have insurance for acute care through the Medicare program, but there are at least three major gaps in the adequacy of health care services. The first gap is that Medicare pays only a portion of costs for acute care. For "covered" services like hospital care, physician services, and home health services, beneficiaries must pay premiums, deductibles, and co-payments. About two-thirds of those over 65+ purchase private supplemental insurance to help with these costs. But prescription drugs, routine care for vision, hearing, and teeth, and **custodial care** (long term care for chronic conditions) are not covered at all. Most people must pay "out of pocket" for those services.

The second gap is that the long-term care system has serious flaws in financing, quality, and accessibility (Binstock, Cluff, and Von Mering 1996; Estes, Swan, and Associates 1993). Long term care involves services for persons with chronic conditions, including medical care, rehabilitative care, and personal assistance. Though many people associate long term care with nursing homes, it also includes home and community-based services. The largest problem with long term care financing is that most people have no insurance to cover its cost. Medicaid may pay for long term care for those who are very poor and for those who exhaust their assets while paying for that care.

And the third gap in the adequacy of health services is that few health care professionals specialize in care for older adults. Ageism among health care professionals tends to mirror broader societal views.

In our case study, Betty Miller's husband Richard had excellent medical care and insurance coverage for his hospital stay and rehabilitation in the transitional care unit and for his first several months of home health care. Medicare covered most expenses; his supplemental insurance covered copayments and deductibles. However, like most people, he had no insurance to cover the costs of personal care to cope with his permanent disabilities. Richard and Betty Miller were not prepared for the physical, emotional, or financial costs of his long-term care.

INTERVENTIONS

OVERVIEW

There is a wide range of programs and services available to deal with the financial, health, housing, and social problems of older adults. The general public is aware of social insurance programs like Social Security and Medicare and of some kinds of services like nursing homes and senior centers. Yet many older adults and their families are unfamiliar with other programs and services until a crisis arises. Access services such as information and referral, community outreach, and case management often provide key links to services for those who know about them.

Some programs and services are important for seniors regardless of health status. Education, employment, financial, legal, and social are types of services which provide opportunities for meaningful activity and assistance with general needs.

Older adults with disabilities may need many different types of assistance to function in the home and community. DeJong, Batavia, and McKnew (1992) identify three main approaches to do so.

The first is the **medical model** and involves health professionals like physicians, nurses, and social workers who make key care decisions. Health insurance typically pays for short-term intervention and rehabilitation given this approach. The social and psychological needs of patients are not emphasized in this approach. A second approach is the **informal model** and involves services provided by family members and friends, usually without payment and usually managed by the primary care provider. A third approach is the **independent living model** which is based on the premise of consumer direction, with the person with disabilities hiring and supervising a personal assistant. Payment is typically private, although low-income persons may qualify for receiving some benefits through social service programs. The Millers, in our case study, used a combination of medical and informal approaches to meet Richard's service needs.

HOME AND COMMUNITY-BASED SERVICES

As noted earlier, most older adults live in their own homes in age-integrated communities. They are generally eligible to receive services from community organizations that serve all age groups, such as leisure activities through park districts or YMCAs; classes through colleges, universities, and adult education programs; and social services through public and private welfare agencies. Some of these organizations may offer special programs designed for older adults, though not all older participants may choose to take advantage of age-segregated programs.

In addition to generic programs for all age groups, older adults may benefit from "categorical" programs specifically geared toward older adults. Many home and community based services are part of the **aging network**, a loose web of federal, state, and local programs to help elders that grew out of the Older Americans Act of 1965. The structure of the aging-network varies across communities.

In many communities, multipurpose senior centers provide a "focal point" for a spectrum of aging network services. A study of senior centers in Maryland identified six "core" activities: crafts, exercise, information and assistance, socialization, transportation and meals (Gelfand, Bechill, and Chester 1991). They may offer additional programs; for example, Betty Miller's center has computer classes and senior employment services. Philip Taietz (1976) identified two models of senior centers: the **voluntary organization model** that relies heavily on participant involvement and the **social agency model** that emphasizes services organized by staff members. The voluntary organization model tends to reach younger, more active elders; the social agency center tends to serve older individuals with limited resources. Betty's center fits the voluntary organization type.

Older adults who are too disabled physically and/or mentally to participate in age-integrated or senior center programs may attend an adult day center. These are often used by individuals who live with or near a family caregiver; they serve dual purposes of meeting participants' needs and offering respite for the caregiver. Health model day centers offer medical and rehabilitation service, while social model day centers offer activities similar to those in senior centers adapted to the participants' abilities.

Home services may include health care, personal care, homemaker services, and home-delivered meals for persons with disabilities. In many cases, such services may serve as an alternative to institutional care. Home health services that are "medically necessary" may be covered by Medicare, but routine personal care and homemaker services must usually be paid for "out of pocket," as the Millers discovered. The cost of home services is a major barrier to their use. A review of 32 studies of community-based home care programs by Weissert and Hedrick (1994) found that they were not necessarily less expensive or more effective than institutional care, but consumers strongly preferred home care.

RESIDENTIAL SERVICES

Though the public is most familiar with nursing homes, there are many other types of residential settings that offer assistance to older adults. Nursing homes are primarily appropriate for those who need skilled medical care and/or constant supervision. Approximately 5% of older adults live in nursing homes at a point in time, though it is estimated that about 1 in 3 men and 1 in 2 women will spend at least some time in a nursing home (Kemper and Murtaugh 1991). Popular views of nursing homes are generally negative, though many provide high-quality care. Even the best facilities, however, tend to limit the privacy and autonomy of residents.

For older adults with less intensive needs for medical care or supervision, a variety of congregate housing options are available. Congregate housing combines housing (usually age-segregated) with supportive services such as cleaning, meals, recreation and/or transportation. It may be provided in single-room occupancy retirement hotels, public housing apartment, board and care homes, or retirement communities designed in budget ranges from modest to luxurious. In many cases, congregate housing can help maintain individuals with disabilities in a semi-independent setting.

A fast-growing segment of congregate housing is "assisted living." Rosalie Kane and Keren Brown Wilson define it as "any group residential program that is not licensed as a nursing home, that provides personal care to persons with need for assistance in the activities of daily living (ADL), and that can respond to unscheduled needs for assistance that might arise" (1993: XI).

SOCIETAL INTERVENTIONS

Our public policies support special programs and services for older adults. In the U.S., the first national policy for older adults was the Social Security Act, passed in 1935. This program set a precedent that dominated policies for older adults for more than fifty years: old people (defined as those age 65 or older) became "entitled" to government assistance to address the special problems of aging (Achenbaum 1983; Torres-Gil 1992).

The decade from 1965 to 1974 saw major expansion of Federal legislation in response to the growing numbers of older Americans. Among the key laws were the following: (1) **Medicare** (1965), a universal health insurance program for elderly and disabled persons (2) **Older Americans Act** (OAA) (1965), establishing the Administration on Aging (AOA) and an aging network of services (3) **Age Discrimination in Employment Act** (1967, with major amendments in 1978 and 1986), to outlaw age discrimination and, in 1986, abolish mandatory retirement (4) **Supplemental Security Income** (SSI) (1974), a welfare program to assure a minimum income floor to aged, blind, and disabled persons and (5) **Employees Retirement Income Security Act** (ERISA) (1974), protecting private pension programs.

More recent decades have seen mainly modification of earlier programs. Changes in the Social Security Act in 1983 increased taxes and raised the age of retirement with full benefits from 65 to 67 by the year 2027. The Medicare program has attempted to constrain health care costs by limiting payments for hospital care and by encouraging older Americans to join health maintenance organizations. The age-based public policies established in the U. S between the 1930s and the 1970s became highly controversial in the 1990s as their costs increased with the growing older population. Now there are serious proposals to "privatize" Social Security and to cut back Medicare order to reduce government financial responsibility for these entitlement programs.

Ironically, our laws and social policies have become more age-based during a period when the utility of age distinctions may be decreasing. Sociologists Matilda and John Riley (1994) attribute this to "structural lag," meaning that social roles and institutions have not changed quickly enough to keep up with new social realities. They argue that more age integration and a more flexible life course that allows for cyclical periods of education, work, and leisure make greater sense than linear stages, given increasing numbers of robust long-lived people who need meaningful, productive roles.

Social welfare expert Fernando Torres-Gil, Assistant Secretary on Aging in Clinton's first administration, believes that those policies need to be revised in response to changing longevity, diversity, and generational interest before the "baby boom" generation reaches retirement age (1992). Like the Rileys, he proposes more age-integration, with most benefits contingent on need. He would postpone eligibility for age-based programs until 70 and strengthen needs-based programs. The American with Disabilities Act of 1990 may be the prototype of new policies that are age-neutral in principle but of great relevance to older adults. Whether or not politicians agree with Torres-Gil's views, there is broad consensus that meeting the needs of an older population will be a major challenge in the 21st century.

SUMMARY

1. Elderly persons are the fastest growing segment of the population increasing from 4% of the population in 1900 to 13% today.
2. The ratio of older women to older men becomes greater with age.
3. The likelihood of living in a family setting declines with age for both sexes.
4. The older population in the U. S. is becoming more diverse in its racial and ethnic composition.
5. Older adults are about as likely as other adult age groups to have incomes below the poverty line.
6. There are many subgroups of elders who are at high risk of poverty, including women, minority group members, the very old, and those who live alone
7. Many changes that were believed to be inevitable consequences of aging are actually due to disuse and disease.
8. Vision, hearing, taste, smell, and touch begin to decline in one's 20's and 30's.

9. Loss of functioning due to low levels of physical fitness can diminish a person's quality of life at any age, but the physically unfit elderly may lose the capacity for independent living.

10. Longitudinal studies indicate that levels of sexual activity tend to remain stable over middle and later life.

11. 80% of those over age 65 report at least one chronic condition

12. Ageism is the systematic stereotyping and discrimination against people because they are old.

13. Most individuals experience only minor changes in their cognitive skills in later life.

14. Some recent popular images present older adults as more advantaged financially, physically, and socially than may actually be the case.

15. Most older adults have regular and positive contact with family members.

16. Elders with children tend to live within an hour's drive of at least one child and when in good health tend to provide as much or more help to younger generations than they receive.

17. Older members of most minority ethnic groups are more likely to live in multi generational households and are more likely to express norms of family obligation to elders.

18. Caregivers are likely to have poorer physical and mental health than age peers who are not caregivers and also are more likely to experience financial strain and reduced employment opportunities.

19. Only 11% of elders with ADL limitations receive paid care.

20. Grand parenting is a highly varied role in current American society.

21. Older people tend to rely mainly on relatives for personal assistance but friends are likely to provide companionship and emotional support.

22. Retirement became common in industrialized countries in the second half of the 20th century partly as a result of the availability of retirement income and social norms.

23. Many people now choose to retire as soon as they can afford to do so and look forward to a variety of leisure and volunteer roles. However, African and Latino Americans are particularly likely to experience involuntary retirement due to employment and disability.

24. Retirement income rests on a "three legged stool," including social security benefits, private pensions, and income from savings and other assets.

25. More than 90% of older adults live in independent housing, which includes single family homes and mobile homes, condominiums and apartments.

26. Older adults use more health care services than younger people.

27. The three major gaps in elderly health care coverage are 1) uncovered acute care cost such as prescription drugs, vision care, and dental care; 2) long-term care; and 3) lack of health care professionals specializing in elderly care.

28. Social insurance programs like Medicare and Social Security are available to deal with problems of older adults. Some programs provide services such as educational, employment, financial and legal assistance to persons regardless of age.

29. Older adults may benefit from many home and community-based services which are part of the aging network, a loose web of federal, state, and local programs to help elders that grew out of the Older Americans Act of 1965.

30. Senior centers often provide a focal point for aging citizens. Those too disabled physically and/or mentally may attend adult day centers. There are also home services including health care, personal care, homemaker services, and home-delivered meals:

31. 5% of the elderly live in nursing homes. Congregate housing combines housing with supportive services such as cleaning, meals, and medication. The fastest growing segment of congregate housing is assisted living.

32. Key legislation interventions are the following: (1) Medicare, (2) older Americans Act, (3) Age Discrimination in Employment Act, (4) Supplemental Security Income,(5) Employees Retirement Income Security Act.

33. Lives of older Americans are likely to change dramatically in the decades ahead. Cyclic life course may be more common with most people experiencing multiple careers, lifelong learning, social marriages, and more opportunities for leisure activities. Clearly issues of aging will become more important.

REFERENCES

Abel, Emily K. 1991. *Who Cares for the Elderly? Public Policy and the Experience of Adult Daughters.* Philadelphia: Temple University Press.

Achenbaum, W. Andrew 1983. *Shades of Gray: Old Age, American Values, and Federal Policies Since 1920.* Boston: Little, Brown and Company.

Administration on Aging. 1996. *A Profile of Older Americans 1996.* Washington, D. C.: Author.

Allen, Jessie, and Allan Pifer, eds. 1993. *Women on the Front Lines: Meeting the Challenge of an Aging America.* Washington, D. C.: The Urban Institute Press.

Angel, Jacqueline Lowe, and Dennis P. Hogan. 1994. "Demography of Minority Aging Populations." Pp. 9-21 in *Minority Elders: Five Goals Toward Building a Public Policy.* Second ed. Washington, DC: The Gerontological Society of America.

Antonucci, Toni C. 1990. "Social Supports and Social Relationship." Pp.205-226 in Robert H. Binstock and Linda K. George, eds. *Handbook of Aging and the Social Sciences.* Third ed. New York: Academic Press.

Atchley, Robert C. 1997. *Social Forces and Aging: An Introduction to Social Gerontology.* Eighth ed. Belmont, CA: Wadsworth Publishing Company.

Baltes, Paul B. 1993. "The Aging Mind: Potential and Limits." *The Gerontologist.* 33(5): 580-594.

Berman, Jules, and Donald B. Gelfand 1993. "Illness, Medical Care, and Income Maintenance." Pp. 48-65 in Donald E. Gelfand, eds. *The Aging Network: Programs and Services.* Fourth ed. New York: Springer Publishing Company.

Binstock, Robert H. 1983. "The Aged as Scapegoats." *The Gerontologist.* 23:136-143.

Binstock, Robert H., Leighton E. Cluff, and Otto Von Mering 1996. "Issues Affecting the Future of Long-term Care." Pp.3-18 in Robert H. Binstock, Leighton E. Cluff, and Otto Von Mering, eds. *The Future of Long-Term Care: Social and Policy Issues.* Baltimore: Johns Hopkins University Press.

Brody, Elaine. 1985. "Parent Care as a Normative Family Stress." *The Gerontologist.* 25:19-30.

Butler, Robert N. 1987. "Future Trends." Pp.265-267 in George L. Maddox, ed., *The Encyclopedia of Aging.* New York: Springer Publishing Company.

Callahan, Daniel 1987. *Setting Limits: Medical Goals in an Aging Society.* New York: Simon and Schuster.

Cantor, Marjorie H. 1991. "Family and Community: Changing Roles in an Aging Society." *The Gerontologist.* 31:337-346.

Caspersen, Carl J., Kenneth E. Powell, and Robert K. Merritt 1994. "Measurement of Health Status and Well-being." Pp. 180-202 in Claude Bouchard, Roy S. Shephard, and Thomas Stephens, eds. *Physical Activity. Fitness and Health: International Proceedings and Consensus Statement.* Champaign, IL: Human Kinetics.

Chalfie, Deborah 1994. *Going It Alone: A Closer Look at Grandparents Parenting Grandchildren.* Washington, D. C.: American Association of Retired Persons Women's Initiative.

Cherlin, Andrew, and Frank F. Furstenberg, Jr. 1986. *The New American Grandparent: A Place in the Family.* New York: Basic Books.

Coward, Raymond T., and Stephen J. Cutler 1991. "The Composition of Multigenerational Households That Include Elders." *Research on Aging.* 13(1): 55-73.

Deevey, Sharon 1990. "Older Lesbian Women: an Invisible Minority." *Journal of Gerontological Nursing.* 16(5): 35-37.

DeJong, G., Batavia, A. I., and McKnew, L. B 1992. "The Independent Living Model of Personal Assistance in National Long-term Care Policy." *Generations.* 16(1): 89-95.

Eggebeen, David J. 1992. "From Generation unto Generation: Parent-child Support in Aging American Families." *Generations.* 17(3): 45-50.

Estes, Carroll L., James H. Swan, and Associates 1993. *The Long Term Care Crisis: Elders Trapped in the No-Care Zone.* Newbury Park, CA: Sage Publications.

Fries, James F., and Lawrence Crapo 1981. *Vitality and Aging: Implication of the Rectangular Curve.* New York: W. H. Freeman.

Gelfand, Donald E., W. Bechill and R. S. Chester 1991. "Core Programs and Services at Senior Centers." *Journal of Gerontological Social Work.* 17(1-2): 145-161.

170

George, Linda K., and Lisa P. Gwyther 1986. "Caregiver Well-being: a Multidimensional Examination of Family Caregivers of Demented Older Adults." *The Gerontologist.* 26:253-259.

Giarrusso, Roseann, Merrill Silverstein, and Vern L. Bengtson 1996. " Family Complexity and the Grandparent Role." *Generations.* 20(l): 17-23.

Gratton, Brian and Vanessa Wilson 1988. "Family Support Systems and the Minority Elderly: a Cautionary Note." *Journal of Gerontological Social Work.* 13(1/2): 81-93

Hagestad, Gunhild O. 1988. "Demographic Change and the Life Course: Some Emerging Trends in Family Realm." *Family Relations.* 37: 405-410.

Homer, Paul, and Holstein, Martha, eds. 1990. *A Good Old Age? The Paradox of Setting Limits.* New York: Simon and Schuster.

Hooper, Celia R. 1994. "Sensory and Sensory Integrative Development." Pp.93-106 in B. R. Bonder and M. B. Wagner, eds. *Functional Performance in Older Adults.* Philadelphia: F. A. Davis.

Hooyman, Nancy R., and Judith Gonyea 1995. *Feminist Perspectives on Family Care: Policies for Gender Justice.* Thousand Oaks, CA: Sage Publications.

Institute of Medicine 1986. *Improving the Quality of Nursing Home Care.* Washington, DC: National Academy Press.

Institute of Medicine 1990. *The Second Fifty Years: Promoting Health and Preventing Disability.* Washington, D.C.: National Academy Press.

Johnson, Colleen Leahy, and Lillian E. Troll 1994. "Constrains and Facilitators to Friendships in Late Life." *The Gerontologist.* 34(1): 79-87.

Kane, Rosalie A. and Karen Brown Wilson 1993. *Assisted Living in the United States: A New Paradigm for Residential Care for Frail Older Persons?* Washington, DC: Public Policy Institute of the American Association of Retired Persons.

Kemper, Peter and C. M. Murtaugh 1991. Lifetime Use of Nursing Care, New England *Journal of Medicine.* 324(9): 595

Kimmel, Douglas C. 1992. "The Families of Older Gay Men and Lesbians." *Generations.* 17(3): 37-38.

Kovar, Mary Grace, Joseph E. Fitti, and Michele M. Chyba 1992. *The Longitudinal Study of Aging: 1984-1990* (DHHS Publication 92-1304). Hyattsville, MD: National Center for Health Statistics.

Matthews, Sarah H., and Jetse Sprey 1984. "The Impact of Divorce on Grandparenthood: an Exploratory Study." *The Gerontologist.* 24(1): 41-47.

Minkler, Meredith and Kathleen M. Roe 1996. "Grandparents as Surrogate Parents." *Generations.* 20(1): 34-38.

Moody, Harry R. 1994. *Aging: Concepts and Controversies.* Thousand Oaks, CA: Pine Forge Press.

Montgomery, R. J. V., and M.M. Datwyler 1990. "Women & Men in the Caregiving Role." *Generations.* 14(3): 34-38.

National Center for Health Statistics 1990. Current estimates from the National Health Interview Survey, 1989. *Vital and Health Statistics,* Series 10, No.176.

National Institute on Aging 1993. *With the Passage of Time: The Baltimore Longitudinal Study of Aging.* Washington, D. C.: Department of Health and Human Services.

Palmore, Erdman B. 1981. *Social Patterns in Normal Aging: Findings from the Duke Longitudinal Study.* Durham, NC: Duke University Press.

Palmore, Erdman B. 1990. *Ageism: Negative and Positive.* New York: Springer Publishing Company.

Pillemer, Karl, and David Finkelhor 1988. "The Prevalence of Elder Abuse: a Random Survey." *The Gerontologist.* 28(1): 51-57.

Quam, Jean K., and Gary S. Whitford 1992. "Adaptation and Age related Expectations of Older Gay and Lesbian Adults." *The Gerontologist.* 32(3): 367-374.

Riley, Matilda White, and John W. Riley, Jr. 1994. "Age Integration and the Lives of Older People." *The Gerontologist.* 34: 110-115.

Robert Wood Johnson Foundation 1996. *Chronic Care in America: A 21st Century Challenge.* Princeton, NJ: Author

Rosenthal, Carolyn J. 1986. "Family Supports in Later Life: Does Ethnicity Make a Difference?" *The Gerontologist* 26:19-24.

Schneider, E. L., J. A. Brody 1983. "Aging, Natural Death, and the Compression of Morbidity: Another View. *New England Journal of Medicine.* Oct 6: 309(14): 854-856

Skaff, Marilyn McKean, and Leonard I, Pearlin 1992. "Caregiving: Role Engulfment and the Loss of Self." *The Gerontologist* 32: 656-664.

Social Security Administration 1996. *Social Security: Basic Facts.* Washington, DC: Author.

Speas, Kathy, and Beth Obenshain 1995. *Images of Aging in America; Final Report to AARP.* Chapel Hill, NC: FGL Integrated Marketing.

Starr, Bernard D., and M. B. Weiner 1981. *The Starr-Weiner Report on Sex and Sexuality in the Mature Years.* San Francisco: McGraw-Hill.

Stone, Robyn, Gail Lee Cafferata, and Judith Sangl 1987. "Caregivers of the Frail Elderly: a National Profile." *The Gerontologist.* 27(5): 616-626.

Strehler, Bernard L. 1977. *Time, Cells, and Aging.* Second ed. New York: Academic Press.

Stull, Donald E., K. Kercher, and K. Kercher 1994. "Caregiver Burden and Generic Well-being: Opposite Sides of the Same Coin?" *The Gerontologist.* 34(1): 88-94.

Taietz, Philip 1976. Two Conceptual Models of the Senior Center. *Journal of Gerontology.* 31(1): 22-29.

Torres-Gil, Fernando M. 1992. *The New Aging: Politics and Change in America.* New York: Auburn House.

U.S. Bureau of the Census 1995. *Sixty-five Plus in the United States* (Statistical Brief SB/95-8). Washington, DC: U.S. Bureau of the Census

U.S. Bureau of the Census 1994. *United States Population Estimates, by Age, Sex, Race, and Hispanic Origin, 1990 to 1994,* release PPL-21. Washington, DC: U.S. Bureau of the Census, Population Division.

U.S. Senate Special Committee on Aging 1991. *Aging America: Trends and Projections* (1991 ed.). (DHHS Publication No. FCOA 91.28001). Washington, DC: U.S. Department of Health and Human Services.

Verbrugge, Lois M. 1984. "Longer Life but Worsening Health? Trends in Health and Morality of Middle-aged Older Persons." *Milbank Memorial Fund Quarterly.* 62: 475-519

Vladeck, Bruce C., and Marvin Feuerberg 1995-96. "Unloving Care Revisited" *Generations.* 19(4): 9-13.

Weihl, Hannah 1983. "Three Issues From the Israeli Scene." *The Gerontologist.* Vol. 23 Dec: 576-578

Weissert, William G. and Susan C. Hedrick (1994). "Lessons Learned from Research on Effects of Community-based Long-term Care." *Journal of the American Geriatrics Society.* 42(3): 348-353.

Whitbourne, Susan-Krauss and W. Dale Dannefer 1985/1986. "The "Life Drawing" as a Measure of Time Perspective in Adulthood." *International Journal of Aging and Human Development.* Vol. 22 No. 2 1985/1986:147-155

Williams, T. Franklin (1992). "Aging Versus Disease." *Generations.* 16(4): 21-25.

Wykle, May, and Beth Kaskel (1994). "Increasing the Longevity of Minority Older Adults Through Improved Health Status." Pp. 32-39 in *Minority Elders: Five Goals Toward Building a Public Policy Base.* Second ed. Washington, DC: The Gerontological Society of America.

CHAPTER 9: MINORITIES
CASE STUDY: FIVE VIGNETTES ON RACE IN AMERICA

Twenty years ago, the eminent sociologist William Julius Wilson (1978) offered the controversial thesis that race was declining in significance in American society. What he meant was that knowing the race of an individual no longer told much about that person's economic status, life chances, and experiences with blatant racism. Social class had become more important in explaining most of the outcomes for individuals. In short, America had left the era of the "color caste" which so well described it from the end of the Civil War through the Civil Rights Movement of the 1950s and 1960s.

Race, however, has **not** lost its significance in American society. Its significance has instead become more complex. While race by itself no longer explains the sharp inequalities in the average economic and social standing of different groups, the combination of race and social class together powerfully affect an individual's opportunities and the way in which he or she will be treated.

As the way that race is meaningful in American society has become more complicated, opinions about how to recognize and respond to racial differences and racial inequality have become more controversial. Some people argue that America should be blind to differences of race and ethnicity. Others believe that this is impractical. People respond to racial differences in a variety of different ways. The way they do so is not always conscious. The variety of reactions taken together is what makes race meaningful and controversial today. Consider the following true stories, drawn from the authors' research and teaching about race relations.

(1) In Texas, public school students take an annual achievement test known as the Texas Assessment of Academic Skills (TAAS). This test is used to hold teachers and school administrators accountable for student learning. Students who fail the tenth grade TAAS must retake the exam until they pass it, or else they cannot graduate from high school.

Teachers in Bayouview Elementary School in a suburban school district believe two things: that low-income African American children are incapable of learning to read by third grade and that the experience of failure in tests is the most painful experience a child can have. As Ms. Thompson, an experienced white teacher explained it; "We at Bayouview don't want to lower the self-esteem of our children. We don't stress learning to read because in that way they won't keep experiencing daily failure and have low self-esteem. It is better for them just to fail once a year during TAAS than to fail every reading test. The children are happier that way and feel better about themselves."

(2) Across the bayou in an Hispanic school, Maria Torres was slapped on her knuckles by Ms. Whittington, her first-grade teacher, for speaking Spanish on the playgrounds during recess. Ms. Whittington explained to the principal that speaking Spanish will hurt the children's chances of learning English and doing well on the TAAS. She hit Maria to save her from academic failure.

(3) During a discussion of race relations and inequality in America in a sociology class, Fred Gomez, whose parents left Puerto Rico in the 1960s, pointed out that neither he nor his parents have ever encountered any prejudice or discrimination directed at them, despite the fact that they are Hispanic. Fred said that he could achieve anything he wants as long as he works hard enough to get it. He said that his father and mother worked two jobs a day in order to permit him to finish high school and that he now works an eight-hour night job, while attending the university during the day. When the instructor asked some of the white students whether they and their parents had the same experiences, none of the white students reported having made such efforts to stay in school. Fred maintained that it was not that minorities have to work harder, it is just that some people are luckier than others.

(4) Thirty years ago the second author conducted a study of school desegregation for the U.S. Civil Rights Commission. One interviewee, known to the author, was a man of Latino heritage who had made the personal decision to change his social identity to that of an Anglo. He changed his name from Carlos Hernandez to Charles Henderson, and his religion from Roman Catholic to Methodist. He was asked why he decided to pass as an Anglo. His reply was that if he were Chinese American and were going to speak to his girlfriend's father to ask for his permission to marry her, the father would ask what kind of job he had. He would say that he was an aeronautical engineer and the father would reply, "Welcome to the family!" He said that if he were Jewish and were to approach his prospective father-in-law, the man would ask what kind of job the young man had. Charles (Carlos) would reply that he was a doctor or a lawyer and the father would reply, "Welcome to the family!" However, Charles (Carlos) noted, as a Mexican American, if I approached my prospective father-in-law and he asked me what I did, I would have to reply that I have some unskilled job. The father would say, "Welcome to the Family." Charles (Carlos) observed, "Our leaders tell us to be proud of our Mexican American heritage, but such heritage now (in 1968) means poverty and unemployment. That is why I became an Anglo. I was light complexioned enough and I did it. Thirty years later, Charles no longer encounters the blatant discrimination he had met with a generation ago. He is an older professional now and also is a grandfather. Most recently, he noted that his only regret is that his grandchildren speak no Spanish and cannot understand the value of their ethnic heritage. "My children are fully Anglos."

(5) A local university research team has been studying inner-city schools to determine what factors account for academic success and failure among minority children. Repeatedly, principals and teachers blamed low achievement on the lack of desire among the children and their parents to want to learn. Teachers pointed out that the parents don't care about their children's education and the children don't want to learn because doing well in school will make their friends think that they are "acting white." The same findings have been reported in studies around the country (Fordham and Ogbu 1986).

When asked to account for the academic success of low income minority children on some other campuses, teachers explained that those schools either had a better type of low income children or the schools cheated on the tests.

Finally, when asked if teachers had lower expectations for low income minority children one replied, "Oh, no. That would be discrimination and that's illegal."

These true stories show some of the complexity about how minority group membership works in American society today, and how people respond to it. Several points should be noted.

First, there is very little discussion of overt racism. Fred Gomez in the third vignette said he experienced little prejudice. Carlos Hernandez/Charles Henderson says that the amount of prejudice has gone down in his lifetime. The school personnel in the fourth vignette deny that they discriminate. Ms. Thompson and other teachers at Bayouville Elementary School in the first vignette certainly don't think that they discriminate against minority children. Prejudice and discrimination are still one part of the reality of race relations in American society, but not as overtly, as was once the case.

Second, even people who don't think of themselves as prejudiced or as engaging in discrimination do notice inter-group differences, and respond to them. Their responses vary both among members of the majority, and members of minority groups. For example, Whittington, the Anglo teacher who rapped Maria Torres' knuckles for speaking Spanish, notices that her Latino students are different from her Anglo and Black students. She responds by trying to make Maria learn to speak English like an Anglo. Is she discriminating? She certainly doesn't think so. She believes that a good knowledge of English is essential to success in the United States, and that by making her Latino students use English at all times, she was helping them meet a high standard of success.

Before dismissing her attitude, notice that Carlos Hernandez agreed with her enough that he did not pass on his own Latino identity and culture to his children. He didn't do this to avoid discrimination, but because he saw Latino culture as something that held people back from success. His actions may seem extreme, but many other minority group members in the same situation make the same decision, just as many minority group parents agree with Ms. Whittington, that it is important to teach children to operate in the language and culture of the majority group, because that is what leads to economic success.

The teachers at Bayouview elementary present the opposite reaction to the same situation. They too notice differences between racial groups among their students. They certainly do not see that they are either prejudiced or discriminating. They try to respect the needs and rights of their minority students by setting low standards of academic achievement for them. They believe that by doing this they are helping their students prepare for success by building self-esteem.

Fred Gomez in the fourth vignette would certainly disagree with the teachers at Bayouview. He is a member of a minority group, and one that is disadvantaged on objective measures. He is not ashamed of his background, and does not see any need to hide his identity. Neither is he concerned about discrimination, which he doesn't think is very important any more in American society. He believes that the solution to any inequality is simply high personal standards. With enough hard work, anyone can get ahead, as long as they are lucky. Luck, according to Fred, is color blind, and he thinks that people should be too. He certainly sees no justification for affirmative action today, and in fact thinks that such policies hold back some members of minority groups, because it teaches them to look to government programs rather than their own hard work for economic success. For Fred, losing or keeping your culture, or overcoming discrimination, are beside the point. What matters is how much you work.

A final point is made by the last vignette. Among the most difficult and important ways that race seems to matter in American society now is in its effect on the different opportunities available to children who start out in different places. Minority children from economically disadvantaged homes and neighborhoods are not necessarily predestined to failure, but they do face a difficult task if they are going to become productive adults. Good schools might offer a ray of hope, but often the schools fail to serve precisely these students. Solving this may be the most important key to the challenging problem of eliminating inequality based on race and ethnicity, so that America can realize fulfillment of the aspirations of all citizens, not just those from privileged groups.

THEORY BOX by Michael J. Donnelly Chapter 9 Minorities/Conflict Theory

Think of the "goods" in society as a pie, which must be cut up and distributed among its members. The goods which society has to offer-wealth, prestige, power, education, etc. – are finite; those competing to put forward their claims are many, and they inevitably collide with each other in pursuit of goods they desire. One of the general tasks sociologist undertake is to explain how in a given society such distribution occurs. What is the pattern by which goods are differentially distributed? How do different categories and groups of individuals in society (social classes, races, ethnic groups, men and women, children, youth, and the elderly) make out?

Conflict theorists' in particular look at how the distribution of goods benefits some people and groups at the expense of others. They want to explain why this happens, and what is the likelihood that the potential conflict of interest involved in-group competition may break out into real and active struggles between groups.

There are many potential applications of conflict theory to the experience of minority groups in the U.S. For historical reasons different ethnic groups entered the competitive struggle over the distribution of the American pie from different starting points-with differing amounts of resources like money, work skills, educational credentials, prestige, etc.

Traditionally, for instance, individuals of English ancestry held the most power and wealth; and to a considerable extent their descendants still enjoy some relative privileges. Hispanic individuals by contrast, have by and large been, and remained relatively disadvantaged. If different groups begin the race, so to say, from different starting points, and if each group has a vested interest in not falling behind, but rather in preserving or improving its advantages or position vis-à-vis other groups, then historically advantaged groups are likely (other things being equal) to discriminate against less advantaged groups.

What happens over time in the competition and conflict between different groups, however, depends on many factors. How identifiable the minority group is, is one significant factor. It is easier, for instance in a majority white society to target for discrimination dark skinned and Asian ethnic than white ethnic groups. The threat, real and imagined, that the competing groups appear to pose is a further factor. The perceived threat may be greater, for instance; when the prejudicial beliefs about how threatening it seems: a large easily identifiable group is likely to be more threatening than a smaller one in so far as it threatens to "swamp" the local labor market, to take over neighborhoods to dominate local political organizations. It is large enough; however, the existing power holders may be forced to accommodate to its needs.

CONCEPTS OF MINORITY STATUS AND RACISM

WHO IS A MINORITY?

Before we proceed further, we should pause to define the term minority, which we have used several times. The term is commonly used in the United States to describe members of non-white racial groups. However, the term can be given a more precise definition. Early in the century the concept of minority was used somewhat vaguely along with such terms as race, heritage, and nationality (see Park and Miller 1921, one of the first race relations texts). A more precise definition was advanced by the sociologist Louis Wirth (1945:347). He defined a minority group as a group with a set of physical and cultural traits that set them apart, causing them to receive unequal treatment and to see themselves as "objects of collective discrimination." Wagley and Harris (1958) elaborated this definition. Minority groups, they said, have five characteristics: (1) subordination within a complex society; (2) physical and cultural traits that are held in low esteem by the dominant society; (3) collective awareness of their distinct status based upon their devalued traits; (4) transmission of membership status from generation to generation; and (5) a tendency for intermarriage. Both of these definitions of minority groups are "trait definitions." This kind of definition has been criticized because it does not include groups that do not possess distinctive cultural physical traits, but are nonetheless subject to discrimination. Further, as R. Dworkin (1982) observed, women can be viewed as minorities and yet there is no norm of endogamy accompanying this group. In response to the concerns about trait definitions, Dworkin and Dworkin (1976, 1982, and 1999) have offered a more general definition of minority groups, one that we adopt for the present chapter.

Dworkin and Dworkin define a minority group as a group characterized by four qualities: identifiability, differential power, differential and pejorative treatment, and group awareness. Identifiability means that the group can be distinguished from dominant societal members by any number of factors, including physical traits or cultural practices, ranging from language, mode of dress, and habits, to espoused values and beliefs, customs, etc. Differential power means that on average the minority group members (in comparison with members of the dominant or majority group) have less power, fewer resources, and are less able to mobilize the resources to get their way in the presence of opposition. Differential and pejorative treatment refers to the behaviors of the dominant group in their dealing with the minority. Specifically, the term refers to discriminations in which fewer rewards or resources are provided for the minority, in which the rewards that are provided are of lesser value, lowering the standard of living, social position, and physical well-being of minority group members. Finally, minority group members tend to have a sense of group awareness; they are often reminded of their lower status and have developed an identity based upon the treatment they have received in common. Group awareness often has led to a sense of pride in the struggles engaged in by members of their group as they have combated generations of discriminatory treatment.

Dworkin and Dworkin (1999) suggest that minority status is best thought of as a process, rather than a distribution of attributes. Identifiability, together with differential power, means that minority members will be generally recognizable as distinct from the majority and, given less power, will be unable to prevent the majority from further disadvantaging the minority in terms of valued resources. The scarcity of such resources, together with the tendency for people to secure advantages for themselves, their children, and their group, leads to the unequal distribution of rewards, statuses, and power in the first place. Historically less able to compete because of the possession of fewer resources, minorities become subjected to further discrimination. Because members of minority groups often have more interactions within rather than across group boundaries, minority group members individually come to be aware of their common experiences and to believe that it is the actions of the majority that are a cause of their plight. The individual group members band together, recognize their common identity and destiny, and become a fully aware minority.

In order for individuals to come to recognize their minority group status it is necessary that they experience racism, prejudice, and discrimination, or that their experiences are interpreted for them in terms of racism, prejudice, and discrimination. That is, the reality of minority group status arises out of day-to-day events and the definition and interpretation of those events. In the absence of experiences and interpretations, it can be hard to recognize minority group status.

The ideology that places some racial and/or ethnic groups above others, that speaks of racial superiority and inferiority, is termed **racism.** Generally speaking, racism shows itself in two forms: prejudice and **discrimination.** Prejudice refers to attitudes that lead people to think and feel about other groups in a negative way. It is literally a prejudgment, not based upon facts. One way that prejudice shows itself is in feelings of social distance or a feeling that the members of the target minority group are figuratively apart from one's sense of membership in the human community. Another form of prejudice is stereotyping, which is the application of negatively defined traits and characteristics to a whole group. A stereotype is an "exaggerated belief associated with a category. Its function is to justify (rationalize) our conduct toward that category" (Allport 1954:191).

Racism and prejudice often lead to discrimination. Discrimination is behavioral. It implies not just negative beliefs about members of a minority group, but also pejorative and differential treatment. Prejudice can occur without discrimination, as in cases where individuals are prejudiced toward group members but are afraid of the consequences of violating the civil rights of those members. But discrimination can also occur without prejudice. This occurs, for example, where individuals hold no sense of social distance or endorse no stereotypes, but fear retaliation from others of their own group for associating with members of another group. Thus, the nature of attitudes and behaviors toward minority groups is highly complex.

> **THEORY BOX by Michael J. Donnelly Chapter 9 Minorities/Subculture Theory**
> The term subculture refers roughly to shared sets of beliefs, values, and norms which set apart some groups of people from the larger society or culture amidst which they live New Englanders, the beat generation, Hell's Angels, Korean Americans, all form or formed subcultures. The social bases of subcultures can be quite varied: ethnicity and language; social subcultures tend to develop some stable stylistic expressions to mark its differences from the mainstream or dominant culture. This is akin, for instance, to the way that fans of pop music dress; it is easy to pick out from their different looks the audiences for heavy metal, for punk, for folk, for country-and-western, and for a variety of other musical styles.
> There are also a variety of ways that subcultures relate to, or define themselves against, the mainstream or dominant culture; and accordingly, a variety of functions that the subcultures perform for their members. Criminal subcultures, for instance, may constitute an alternative micro society for members whose illegal activities remove them from the possibility of safe or casual interaction with legitimate society. The self-styles counterculture of radical youth is an oppositions culture which dramatically reverses or inverts the normative bases of the dominant culture. Working-class subcultures probably grow in importance and salience in proportion as the group suffers discrimination or needs to mobilize otherwise meager resources to promote its collective interest. In a more bountiful environment ethnic subcultures may evolve into little more than vehicles for folkloric memories.

WHICH GROUPS ARE MINORITY GROUPS IN AMERICAN SOCIETY?

The definition of minority groups that we use can include a diverse array of groups. These include women, a group defined by gender, and gays, a group defined by lifestyle. People who share a physical challenge such as deafness may also fit the definition of a minority group. Other chapters in this volume deal with issues concerning these groups. Our attention in this chapter is restricted to minority groups defined by race (physical appearance) or ethnicity (shared culture). It is very common to distinguish four racial groups: Whites, Blacks or African Americans, Native Americans, and Asian and Pacific Islanders, along with one ethnic or cultural group, Hispanics or Latinos. Among these groups, Whites are recognized as the majority group, and all of the others as minorities. This list of groups is familiar because it is the official list of groups designated by Statistical Directive #15 of the United States government's Office of Management and Budget (OMB). This directive has governed the collection and report of information about racial and ethnic groups in the United States since the 1970s. The need for such a list emerged in the wake of the passage of the Civil Rights Act of 1964, which gives legal protection against discriminatory treatment to members of groups who had historically experienced discrimination. This list has some value as a way to summarize information about the American population, and we will use it in this chapter for that purpose. However, the list has several limitations.

One is that it ignores sharp differences within each of the recognized categories. For example, Latinos share a common language heritage, but not necessarily much else. The differences in physical appearance, culture, and experiences in the United States among Latinos from different places of origin, from different social classes and in different parts of the United States are as great as those between Latinos and members of other groups. The Asian and Pacific Islander category likewise includes very diverse groups. Japanese Americans, for example, have higher household incomes on average than do whites, While the Hmong and Cambodians, who arrived in large numbers as refugees from the Vietnam War, are among the most disadvantaged of any ethnic population in the United States. Native Americans are members of more than 500 distinct tribal groups, each with its own cultural heritage. African Americans now are very diverse in social class, and recent immigration from Africa and the Caribbean has introduced new cultural diversity as well.

A second difficulty with any list of ethnic groups is that it is not always clear who is in what group, because of mixture between them. While group identities are often very important in American society, it is also important to remember that they are not always divisive, and that people from different groups often share households and common kinship. A Native American is now more likely to marry a White than to marry another Native American (Eschbach 1995). About one-third of married Asian Americans and Latino Americans have a spouse from a different group. Among the OMB defined minority racial and ethnic categories, only African Americans continue to experience very low rates of intermarriage--fewer than 5 % of all marriages by an African American in 1990 was to a member of another racial group.

THE HISTORICAL LEGACY OF INEQUALITY

FROM CASTE TO ETHCLASS

The second half of the 20th century has been a time of tremendous change in intergroup relations in the United States. It is difficult to understand current relations between majority and minority without understanding the legacy of the past. This is true in two respects. First, it is important to understand how much intergroup inequality has changed since the end of World War II. Second, it is important to understand how the past has shaped the present.

During the first half of the 20th century the condition of African Americans in the United States had caste-like characteristics (see Warner 1936, Dollard 1949, and Davis, Gardner and Gardner 1941). The situation of Mexican Americans in many parts of the southwest was similar (Montejano 1987). Native Americans were among the poorest of all Americans, living in underdeveloped and isolated reservation communities in the rural West. Asian American populations were small, in part because of U. S. Immigration law and laws which denied citizenship to non-White immigrants.

To say that Black-White racial differences were caste distinctions means that roles, statuses, and opportunities were rigidly defined and overwhelmingly unequal. Intergroup interactions resembled what van den Berghe (1967) described as paternalistic relations, involving master-servant relationships. Membership in the caste was transmitted from generation to generation and there was almost no mobility across caste lines. As such, no matter how badly the most disadvantaged whites fared economically or in terms of most life chances, they knew that the majority of minority group members fared even worse.

A series of U.S. Supreme Court rulings culminating in the Brown I and II decisions of 1954 and 1955, the Civil Rights Movement of the later 1950s and 1960s, and a number of civil rights acts and desegregation decisions in the 1960s and 1970s erased the caste-like nature of race relations in America.

However, what has emerged in place of the caste distinctions of the past is not a situation of full equality of racial groups, but rather a setting in which the interplay of racial, ethnic, and social class differences perpetuates new kinds of inequality.

Milton Gordon (1964, 1978) coined the term ethclass to described this new kind of inequality that emerged with the end of caste inequality. Ethclass refers to the cross-classification of ethnicity or race and class. The suggestion is that racial differences are much less salient to members of the minority group who are of high economic status. Well-off members of minority groups are often very conscious of their minority identity. Others frequently respond to them in terms of stereotypes based on identity. However, it is for the poorer and less educated members of a minority group that minority group identity most strongly influences life opportunities.

Several of the vignettes at the start of the chapter illustrate this point: children who are both poor and members of minority groups are often treated very differently from students who are poor but members of the majority, or who are members of minority groups but not poor. Children in these latter two groups are often pushed to success, while teachers often make excuses and set low standards for disadvantaged minorities.

Recently, Farley (1995) has moved beyond the race relations model developed by van den Berghe (1967) and Wilson (1973, 1978) to characterize Black-White relations in particular at the end of the 20th century as "fluid competitive race relations" (1995:89). In such relations, there is a residual of the older caste system that results in sometimes-subtle disadvantages for the minority group members. While both the majority and the minority are competitors for the same scarce resources (in the caste system neither competed in a common sphere) and are protected by common laws, the group members think of themselves as distinct and the minority may often have less power, prestige, and property to be converted into increased resources. There remains prejudice and discrimination, often but not always of a subtle nature.

DIVERSITY OF MINORITY EXPERIENCES

A second point to remember in analyzing patterns of inequality is the sharp differences in the experiences of different members of minority groups in American society. Frequently, sociologists and lay people will describe differences between members of the white majority and **all** members of **any** minority. However, it is important to remember the diversity of minority experiences as well. Each minority group has had a very different history in the United States, and that the current problems and concerns of different minority groups may be very different.

African Americans. Inequality between Blacks and Whites is in large part the legacy of the enslavement of African Americans by Whites. Ownership of one human being by another was outlawed at the end of the Civil War in 1865, but in many southern states, where the overwhelming majority of African Americans lived, it was replaced by a legal code known as *Jim Crow*. Jim Crow laws mandated a strict separation between Blacks and Whites. The laws disadvantaged African Americans in several ways. African Americans were denied access to most public accommodations, were restricted to segregated and inferior schools, and were effectively barred from most middle class occupations. Jim Crow laws helped to ensure that the majority of African Americans would remain agricultural workers in southern states, and that they would be without political power (Myrdal 1944).

The Jim Crow system of legally sanctioned racial segregation and domination began to crumble in the 20th century, although it was not completely dismantled until the 1960s. Many sociologists and historians attribute the decline of Jim Crow to changes in the American economy from an agricultural to an industrial base. This shift removed much of the economic rationale for Jim Crow. It also led to large-scale migration of African Americans from the rural south to the urban north. In 1900, 90% of African Americans lived in one of the former confederate states. By 1960, this proportion was down to about 50%, which remains the case today. When they moved northward, African Americans gained the right to vote and increasingly contested legally sanctioned inequality between the races. Another reason for the end of Jim Crow was the growing recognition that a system of legally sanctioned racial inequality was an embarrassment to the United States' role as the leader in the cold war conflict between Western democracies and the communist governments of the Soviet Union and China.

Jim Crow and slavery have now been ended, but their legacy has been hard to overcome. One part of this legacy is the suspicion, separation, and sometimes hostility between Blacks and Whites. The remarkably low rate of intermarriage between Whites and Blacks which we have mentioned may be one very clear sign of the sharpness of the divide between Blacks and Whites - nothing like it exists between the White majority and any other minority group in the United States. Another important legacy has been that African Americans entered the post-Jim Crow period with a tremendous economic disadvantage relative to the position of Whites. They had much less formal schooling, and much less personal wealth to invest in their schooling. Overcoming this legacy has proved difficult.

Native Americans. Inequality between Native Americans and Whites is the legacy of the expansion of White settlement across the American continent between the 1600s and the 1800s. In contrast to what was the case for African Americans, competition between European Americans and American Indians was about the control of **land**, not labor. In the 19th century, many Native groups agreed under threat of military force to exchange their land for the right to live peaceably on designated reservations and promises of economic assistance. Native tribes were also politically recognized as "nations within nations." They have a special relationship to the federal government, and have limited rights of self-government.

The conflict between Natives and newcomers had tragic consequences for Native Americans. Native populations were decimated by the diseases introduced by the foreign interlopers, by warfare, and by the loss of their traditional economic base as their lands were taken away. Many tribes lacked a food supply after they were settled on reservation lands because these lands were frequently arid and unproductive. Promised assistance from the United States government was often meager or non-existent. Partly as a result, health conditions and mortality rates among Indians were extremely high early in the 20th century.

The period after World War II has seen enormous changes in the status of American Indians and their relationship to the United States government. A large number of Indians moved to cities in the post-war period, so that by 1990 only about one American Indian in three lives on a reservation. The Red Power movement in the 1960s and 1970s helped to raise consciousness and pride in American Indian identity among both urban and reservation Indians. Tribes are increasingly asserting their rights of self-government, and some are developing strong reservation-based economies. Still, the majority of Indian reservations face daunting problems of underdevelopment, and experience high rates of unemployment and material poverty. Native Americans remain the most economically disadvantaged of the principal minority groups in the United States on average.

Latinos. The presence of a large number of Latinos in the United States goes back to the 19th century. The Mexican presence in the southwest preceded the arrival of citizens of the United States in these areas. This area became part of the United States after the Treaty of Guadalupe Hidalgo was signed to end the war between the United States and Mexico in 1848. A large number of Mexicans have migrated to the United States throughout the 20th century. A majority came as laborers. From the 1940s to the 1960s, many of these workers were admitted to the United States under the **bracero** program, which allowed seasonal agriculture workers to sojourn in the United States. More recent immigration continues to be dominated by unskilled workers, and is now frequently directed to metropolitan areas as well as farming areas (Bean and Tienda 1987). Mexicans are the largest Latino group in the United States, numbering 13 million in 1990.

The island of Puerto Rico became a United States territory at the conclusion of the United States' war with Spain in 1898. Puerto Ricans are United States citizens, and have the same right of free mobility to and throughout the United States as other Americans. Beginning in the 1940s, a large number of Puerto Ricans have migrated to the U.S. mainland. More than 3 million Puerto Ricans live in the United States mainland, with the largest concentration—more than a million--in New York City. Puerto Rican migrants to the mainland include some persons with a high level of professional training, but on average both the schooling and incomes of Puerto Ricans are relatively low (Rivera-Batiz and Santiago 1996).

The third largest Latino group (more than 1 million in 1990) in the United States are Cubans. A large number of Cubans entered the United States as refugees after the communist revolution in Cuba that was led by Castro. This immigration from Cuba included many persons with a high level of education and some wealth. As a result, Cubans have tended to fare much better economically in the United States compared to other Latino groups. More recent refugees from Cuba, particularly during the Mariel boatlift of 1980, have not had the same advantages (Bean and Tienda 1987).

Smaller groups of immigrants and refugees have come to the United States from Spanish speaking countries of the Caribbean, Central America, and South

America. These immigrants have been very diverse in their cultures, in their physical appearance, and in their levels of education and degree of personal wealth. Many, but not all, Latino immigrants to the United States have low levels of education and are primarily unskilled workers. Incomes for these workers tend to be very low. This is the case partly because they do not possess skills that are valued by American employers, and in part because of discrimination (Bean and Tienda 1987).

One question that many sociologists asked about these immigrants is whether the United States' economy has the capacity to absorb the volume of migration from Latin America that it continues to experience. The most common assumption about immigrants to the United States is that over time they will assimilate into the American melting pot. The immigrant group may not speak English very well, and may not share the values of the majority of Americans. The first generation may be restricted to the poorest jobs, both because they do not have the skills that American employers value, but also because of discrimination. However, the **assimilation** model assumes that the children and grandchildren of the immigrants will come to be very much like other Americans in terms of their basic values, their language skills, and the levels of a education, and their economic standing. This is the vision of the United States as a melting pot of cultures.

Some Latinos do follow the path of the assimilation model. Carlos Hernandez (Charles Henderson) from the fourth vignette at the start of the chapter is an excellent example of assimilation. One may question whether it is necessary or desirable to assimilate as much as Mr. Henderson did, losing contact with his own heritage, and not passing it on to his children. But another question is whether it will be possible for Latinos to assimilate, even if they wanted to. In the 1980s alone, immigration added 5.5 million new Latinos to the United States population. If they had all tried to follow Charles Henderson's lead, could they have succeeded? Would they have found that the American majority was not willing to accept 5.5 million Charles Hendersons into the melting pot, and was not in possession of 5.5 million new good jobs to spare for Hispanic immigrants?

Some sociologists think that the major problem facing Latinos is that the United States doesn't have enough jobs to provide all those who are now migrating to this country the same opportunity for economic advancement that was offered to immigrants in the past. Thus one possibility is that many new Hispanic immigrants will, like inner city African Americans, find themselves trapped in poor jobs with little opportunity for economic advancement for either themselves or their children. This view of what will happen to many Hispanic immigrants is the **segmented assimilation model**. This suggests that immigrants will assimilate, but they will follow different paths. Some like Fred Gomez and Carlos Hemandez will adjust well to life with members of the majority just as the assimilation model predicts. But others will assimilate into a minority identity, more like that of disadvantaged African Americans who live in inner city neighborhoods.

Asian Americans. Asian Americans are the newest and the fastest growing minority in the United States. In 1900, there were just 250,000 Asian

Americans in the United States, and Asian Americans were just 0.2% of the population of the United States. By 1998, the Asian origin population grew to more than 10.2 million, and Asian Americans are now 4% of the American population. The most rapid growth of the Asian population in the United States began in the 1970s. The delayed growth of the Asian population in the United States occurred because U.S. law severely restricted the immigration of most Asians from the 1880s until a major reform of immigration law in 1965 (Edmonston and Passel 1994). On average, Asian Americans have been the most economically successful of any minority group. Asian American household incomes are generally higher than those of White households.

Asian American family structures have remained more intact than have those of other minority groups. The Asian income advantage over Whites reflects several factors. One of these is the generally high education of Asian immigrants to the United States. In 1990, nearly 40% of adult Asian immigrants to the United States were college graduates, compared to a quarter of Whites, and about 1 in 10 Blacks and U.S. native Hispanics (Mare 1995). Another reason that Asian households have higher incomes is that Asian households are more likely to pool income from several workers.

When families of the same size are compared, the Asian income advantage goes away. Asian American income per person is only 85% of that of Whites (U.S. Bureau of the Census 1993). Asian Americans have lower earnings than Whites, given equal levels of skill and education. Thus it appears that Asian Americans do face some discrimination in the United States in spite of having the common reputation of being a "model minority." In one survey, 15% of Asian Americans report that they have personally experienced discrimination while looking for a house, and 30% report discrimination while looking for work.

As is true for Hispanics, the future prospects of Asian populations in the United States are uncertain. The high degree of economic success of many Asian Americans raises questions about whether Asian Americans will, in the long run, meet all criteria (especially differential power) that are part of the definition of minority group status. About one-quarter of Asian Americans who are born in the United States and who are married have a White spouse; indicating that the social distance between Whites and Asians is not as great as for some other groups. Some Asian Americans have also been reluctant to embrace programs such as affirmative action that are meant to assist members of minority groups, because they believe that the effect of such programs is often to reduce rather than increase opportunities for Asians. This is the case because Asian Americans, with their strong educational backgrounds, are often over-represented rather than under-represented in selective colleges and desirable occupations. However, problems of differential and pejorative treatment do persist for members of the group. In addition, some Asian groups-particularly refugees from Southeast Asia-did not arrive with the same educational advantages of other groups, and their experiences in the United States have been more like those of other minorities than like those of recent Korean, Chinese and Japanese immigrants.

LEGAL EQUALITY AND ECONOMIC INEQUALITY

As these brief sketches have all mentioned, the post-World War II period has seen major changes for each of the four minority categories. The legal framework that maintained caste-like distinctions between the majority and minorities was dismantled. Protections against discrimination were implemented. Affirmative action programs created opportunities for members of minority groups where none had existed before. Nonetheless, there continue to be large inequalities in the average economic standing of members of different racial and ethnic groups.

Non-Hispanic White Americans had the highest income per capita of any of the principal racial categories in the United States in 1990 ($15,700), followed by Asian Americans at ($13,700). Income for Blacks ($8,900), Hispanics ($8,400), and American Indians ($8,300) were much lower. Ten percent of non-Hispanic whites had incomes under the poverty line, compared to 14% of Asians, 25% of Hispanics, 30% of Blacks, and 31% of Native Americans. These differences in income mirror a wide variety of other differences in standard of living between members of minority groups and the white majority, such as personal wealth and quality of housing. There are also minority disadvantages in health and longevity.

Explaining the persistence of inter-group differences after discrimination has been made illegal, is one of the important tasks for sociologists who study the problems of minority group members. Scholars have come to realize that the explanation of current intergroup inequality requires putting together several factors. One set of explanations focuses on the effect of minority group status given the changing structure of the United States and world economy in the past several decades. A second set of explanations looks at **differences in the neighborhood**, and school environments of children from different groups. A third set of explanations looks at **intergroup differences in marriage, divorce, and out-of-wedlock childbearing**. Let us examine in turn how each of these factors works.

ECONOMIC CHANGES

In 1940, 92% of African Americans lived in households that had income below the federal poverty line. (The poverty line is an income threshold set by the federal government that indicates that a family will have difficulty meeting its basic needs). By the early 1970s, the Back poverty rate had fallen to 31% - still about 4 times higher than the poverty rate for Whites, but much lower than it had been 30 years before. In 1940 the average black male worker earned about 43% of the wage of average white male worker. By 1980, this figure had improved to 73%. Thus there was a substantial movement towards equality in this period, but a large gap still remains.

Why did the gap close quickly in this period? The most important reason is the rapid growth in the American economy during and after the Second World War. This growth benefited almost all Americans. For example, the average income of American families nearly doubled between 1950 and 1980, after taking into account inflation (Danziger and Gottschalk 1993). This growth created possibilities for **structural mobility.** Structural mobility occurs when economic expansion increases the number of good, middle class jobs available. The expansion of employment opportunities creates a good environment for increased racial equality because the increase in the number of good jobs means that one group can gain without taking jobs from another group.

Unfortunately, contrary to hopes for full racial equality, the era of rapid structural mobility came to an end in the middle of the 1970s. Changes in the American and world economy have increased the competition for good jobs. These changes include increasing global economic competition, movement of certain kinds of labor intensive manufacturing to countries with inexpensive labor costs, and increasing substitution of technology for labor in production jobs. These changes have had two results. First, a high level of education is necessary in order to earn a good wage in the United States. Second, demand for unskilled workers has decreased.

These changes have slowed the movement towards economic equality between Blacks and Whites. The economic changes create greater disadvantages for members of minority groups because of past disadvantages. As competition for good jobs became stiff, there is a premium for having an advantaged social and economic position to start with.

The way that this works is clear if one thinks in terms of competition between different kinds of families to give their children a chance to land a good job. This competition is stacked in favor of families where the parents are college educated and have a good job and a high income. Children in these families learn good verbal skills at home. The family can send them to a private school, or buy a home in a school district with an excellent college preparatory curriculum. The child may be conditioned from a young age to expect a successful professional career, and may even get an early start on a career through a job arranged through a family friend. By contrast, a child starting in a single-parent family in an inner city neighborhood may enjoy none of these advantages. She may experience considerable pressure from neighborhood peers to give little attention to schoolwork. She may attend a school like Bayouview Elementary where the teachers do not set high standards. Even if she enjoys success at school, her family's financial situation may make college attendance an unrealistic dream.

What Wilson (1978) and others have suggested is that the end of structural mobility has created a difficult context in which to overcome the legacy of the American racial caste system. While blatant racism is now a less common, differential distribution of social and economic class statuses among different racial and ethnic groups continues to perpetuate their inequality.

This situation has several implications. First, minority group members on average face a competitive economic situation with fewer resources to compete. Majority group members on average do pass their inherited advantages to their children. Second, many people are aware that race and class are correlated. As a result, some people tend to stereotype members of minority groups with attributes of the least advantaged members of the group. Some majority group members may assume, for example, that a minority group member who appears unexpectedly in their neighborhood is probably poor and therefore untrustworthy, and phone the police to report their suspicions. Another result is that awareness of intergroup differences leads some members of minority groups to see race and ethnicity as the primary determinant of opportunity. At the same time, many members of the majority may be less sensitive to differences in opportunities between different groups, and interpret differences in average outcomes for different groups as the result only of hard work or random luck. This divergence of perception can lead to resentment and conflict.

SEGREGATION BY RACE AND CLASS

Another aspect of majority-minority relations has been the persistence of residential segregation of different groups. Integration of residential communities was a chief goal of reformers who sought to implement civil rights legislation in the 1960s. Dominant social theories taught that integration was the best way to promote harmonious intergroup relations (Gordon 1964). Residential segregation also imposed unfair disadvantages on minority group members. By limiting members of minority groups to particular neighborhoods, the price of housing for minorities was increased, and the quality of housing that was available was frequently deficient.

The post-war period saw major changes in laws and attitudes about racial segregation. In 1948 the United States Supreme Court ruled that restrictive covenants that prohibited the sale of some houses to members of a minority group were illegal and could not be enforced. The Fair Housing Act of 1968 made it illegal to discriminate in the rental and sale of a house to someone on the basis of race. Attitudes about racial segregation softened as well. For example, in 1963, 60% of white Americans agreed with the statement that "white people have the right to keep blacks out of their neighborhoods, and blacks should respect that right." By 1982, opinion had dropped to 31% (Schuman, Steeh, and Bobo 1985:74-75).

Despite these changes in law and attitudes, the last several decades have seen only small decreases in the amount of racial segregation, particularly between Blacks and Whites. Sociologists use a measure called the **index of dissimilarity** to describe the amount of segregation between members of two different racial groups. This index reports the percentage of members of a group that would have to move in order to achieve pure integration of neighborhoods. It takes the value 0 in the case of pure integration, and 100 in the case of pure segregation. In 1980 the index of dissimilarity between Blacks and Whites was about 80 for Northern cities and about 70 in Southern cities, and has since declined little (Massey and Denton 1993) Whites and Blacks still live in separate neighborhoods. There is less segregation between other minority groups and the White majority.

In some ways, the problem of residential segregation has been getting worse rather than better since the l950s. What has been happening is that our metropolitan areas are spreading out. The car has become increasingly central to the organization of American cities, and to the lifestyles of Americans. The 1950s saw the introduction of the interstate Highway system which allowed fast and easy access to the outer fringes of metropolitan areas, and the emergence of the middle class suburban housing development (Jackson 1985).

The growth of the suburbs set in motion one of the most difficult and troubling of all contemporary social problems: the decline of the central city, along with the concentration of minorities in these cities. Most American metropolitan areas are organized into political units consisting of a large central city surrounded by politically independent suburban township and cities. Frequently, each suburb will take steps to regulate the amount and quality of housing available within its boundaries, prohibiting the high-density housing type that is typically occupied by disadvantaged populations. The effect of such **exclusionary zoning** policies is to limit the most needy of residents of a metropolitan area to one or two municipalities in the area, typically the central city.

The concentration of disadvantaged populations in the central city can trigger a spiral of decline. As disadvantaged populations settle in central cities, tax rates can rise because of the need for municipal spending to support the social service needs of this troubled population. Crime rates rise because of the concentration of poor and jobless people who may turn to crime, or who may (due to their defenselessness) become victims of crime. The quality of schools also deteriorates. More and more middle class families living in the impacted city see the diminished quality of life in their community and the increasing taxes, and decide that it is time to move to a more attractive suburban community that has exclusionary zoning in place. As businesses watch their most skilled employees move to the suburbs, they may choose to relocate their plant to a suburban industrial park. This out-migration leads to a further loss of tax base to the city, which is forced either to raise taxes or to decrease the quality of the services it provides. Investment in basic infrastructure such as the maintenance of streets may decline. The spiral can continue until affected cities become so burdened by the combination of declining tax base and rising demands for services to needy populations that they become unable to fill their basic functions.

The new segregation of metropolitan areas that has emerged over the past several decades is in many respects more about economic class than it is about race. There are many minority suburbanites. However, it has most often been members of minority groups who have been unable to escape concentrated urban poverty areas. In 1990, more than 4 million African Americans lived in city neighborhoods where more than 40% of the people had incomes below the federal poverty line. This means that about 1 out of every 6 urban African Americans lived in such a high poverty neighborhood, as did 1 in 10 Hispanics. By contrast, only 1 in 70 Whites lived in a high poverty neighborhood (Jargowsky 1996).

Why does this segregation matter so much? Sociologists in the 1990s put much less emphasis than they once did on the importance of integration to help reduce prejudice. Indeed, it is not clear that intimate contact between members of different groups always does reduce prejudice and conflict. But the new kind of segregation that has developed does impose costs. The most important problem is the emergence of what William Julius Wilson (1996) has called jobless ghettos. As some inner city neighborhoods have become abandoned by nearly everyone who has the opportunity to do so, the people who remain behind live in areas of concentrated poverty. A relatively small percentage of adult men have jobs that provide for their families. Children and teenagers see few legitimate adult role models that can demonstrate the rewards of working in a job in the mainstream economy. Crime seems more glamorous and rewarding, and the streets become unsafe. Government employees such as police officers and teachers who work in these troubled communities start to see their role as one of containment and control rather than help and service. Retail stores leave the area because they find that they cannot make a profit. Houses are not kept up, and many are abandoned. Such communities are very difficult environments in which to raise children to be productive adult members of society.

The set of issues raised by current patterns of segregation are among the most difficult problems facing American society. The political scientist Paul Peterson (1981) describes a conflict between two deeply held American values: freedom and equality. Issues of segregation put that conflict in sharp relief. It is a basic American freedom to be able to live in the neighborhood that one wants to, and to live, work, go to school, and associate with the people that one chooses. Yet if people with the choices and opportunities that come with high levels of income and wealth use that freedom to set themselves off from others, and to abandon their support of services like schools and law enforcement for all members of the community, then it is hard for American society to offer equal opportunity to all.

SCHOOLING

Schooling links issues of neighborhood residential segregation and occupational opportunity. The quality of the schooling that one gets depends in part on the resources that one's community can devote to training the young. Effective schools are essential to the molding of children into productive adult workers who can support themselves and provide for their own children. The desire for good schools-together with the belief that schools with a large proportion of poor and minority students are bad schools-is one of the most important reasons that middle class people of all races flee cities for suburbs.

Complex societies face the continual task of controlling access to scarce resources commodities including power, prestige, and property. The education system is the principal vehicle for sorting individuals into categories of privilege and disadvantage. Generally speaking the greater amount of education individuals have, the greater their life chances, that is, the greater is their chance to get good jobs, and to convey wealth and privilege to their children.

The changes in the economy that we have discussed have greatly increased the importance of education to economic attainment. At the beginning of the 20th century, the economy was labor intensive. There was an abundance of jobs that could provide some means of familial survival even for individuals who had not completed their education through high school. In fact, in 1900 just one in sixteen young people finished high school; by the start of World War II this figure had increased to just under 1 in 2. Today more than 3 out of 4 Americans graduate from high school (Mare 1995).

Our current competitive labor markets require substantial levels of skill in order to get and keep a quality job. American society emphasizes the attainment of credentials to signal the possession of such skill. The sociologist Randall Collins says that the United States has become a "credential society" (1979). What he means by this is that it is not simply good enough to know how to do a job; it is necessary also to have a diploma or college degree to prove it. Employers sometimes require a degree that reflects a level of education that is higher than necessary for the performance of a job. As education has become more important to getting a good job, differences in the quality and quantity of education that an individual receives have become increasingly important to economic success.

The experiences of minorities in education have reflected their disadvantaged status. Until the Supreme Court's 1954 decision in Brown Brothers v. Board of Education of Topeka, Kansas, racial distinctions were explicitly used to sort minorities into their own schools. In many cases the fiction that schools for minority students were "separate but equal" clashed with the reality that schools for minority students had vastly inferior resources. For example, in the 1930s, Southern states spent on average 3 times as much for the education of each white pupil than for each black pupil. The average school term in schools for African Americans was 13% shorter than in schools for white children. The per pupil value of school property in schools for African Americans was one-fifth that in schools for whites. "Separate but equal" really meant separate and unequal (Myrdal 1944).

A series of Supreme Court rulings between 1954 and 1974 gradually broke down these formal barriers to the equality of educational opportunity. However, minorities, particularly poor minorities, remain disadvantaged in the education that they receive. For example, minority students are less likely to have access to computers and other technological resources in their schools than are majority group members. Inner-city schools may sometimes have higher per pupil allocation of public funds because of the federal support (especially Title X economically disadvantaged schools), but this difference is more than compensated for in wealthier communities by private contributions from Parent-Teachers Associations and family resources.

Part of the minority disadvantage is that low-income minority children often come to school less prepared to learn because their parents have fewer educational resources in the home than do majority group children. The Office of Educational Research and Improvement of U.S. Department of Education (1995) reported that minority children in inner-city schools tend: a) to come from homes where their parent(s) have been less able to help the child become academically ready for schooling and less able to assist them in their homework; b) to more often arrive for the first time at school unable to identify colors, recognize all letters, count to fifty, or write their first name than do majority children; and c) to be more likely to have tantrums, fear speaking to strangers (including teachers), fidget in class, and have shorter attention spans than majority group children. School teachers and administrators, like those in the fifth vignette, are not wrong that many disadvantaged minority students can be difficult to teach.

The disadvantages caused by an unsupportive home continue to affect the school performance of these minority children throughout their years in the school system. Researchers have found, for example, that many low-income minority students experience a "summer setback." That is, they return to school in the fall with poorer math and reading skills than they had when they left school the previous spring. By contrast, middle class and majority group children actually improve these skills throughout the summer at about the same pace that they do during the school year. Investigation showed that what is happening is that children in middle class households are likely to include learning activities like reading among the things that they do in the summer, while students in low-income and minority households do not (Heyn 1978).

These disadvantages are compounded when school systems and teachers-like those at Bayouville Elementary-label minority students unteachable and therefore provide them with a poorer quality education than that which is offered to more privileged students. Inner-city school children are more likely to be taught mathematics and English by teachers who are not certified to teach in those areas and who did not have an academic major or minor in those subjects. Advanced courses that enhance the prospects for later college success are not offered in many inner-city schools, because these schools do not have teachers qualified to teach them or enough students with the prerequisites or motivation to take them.

Inner-city schools are plagued by high rates of student dropout, in part because many students believe that nobody in the school cares about them or whether they do well in school (LeCompte and Dworkin 1991). Alienation of both teachers and students in the inner city is often rampant (Dworkin 1987, 1997). The National Center for Educational Statistics reported that the dropout rate for students in 1993 was 7.9% of individuals between the ages of 16 and 24. The dropout rates for minority students were higher: 13.6% for African Americans and 27.5% for Hispanics. While numerous dropouts-especially if they are white-will eventually get their GED (high school equivalency diploma) those who drop out from school are significantly more likely to experience unemployment or underemployment. LeCompte and Dworkin (1991) report that high school dropouts are twice as likely to remain unemployed than high school graduates. Higher rates of minority dropout lead to smaller percentages of minorities entering college, and graduate and professional careers. It lowers as well the number who eventually enter the teaching profession, lowering the number of role models for the next generation of minority children in the inner city.

Good schools for minority children are vital if American society is to overcome persistent inequality between members of different racial groups. All available evidence suggests that if people do not emerge from their late teens with good work skills, it is hard to teach them later in life. For example, government job training programs for adult welfare recipients with very low levels of education and no vocational skills are costly and tend to be ineffective (Heckman 1994). The costs to society of school systems that fail minority children are high.

CHANGES IN FAMILY STRUCTURE

The American family has experienced enormous changes in the past four decades. We are marrying at later ages than we once did. More of us never get married. If we do get married, we are more likely to divorce. These changes have had important implications for the living arrangements of American children, who are now much more likely to spend at least part of their childhood years living in a non-traditional household. All racial groups in the United States have experienced these changes to some degree, but their impact has been felt the greatest by minority populations, especially African Americans.

The scope of these changes has been dramatic. In 1960, just 5% of American children were born to an unwed mother. In 1990, this figure had climbed to 28% (Blank 1997:35). Because of the increase in the proportion of children who were born to single mothers and the increase in divorce, children are increasingly likely to be raised by a single parent. In 1990, only about one African American child in three was living with both a mother and a father. About one-half of American Indian children, and two-thirds of Latino children were living in such a traditional-two parent family. By contrast, four out of every five White and Asian American children were living with both of their parents.

The causes of the changes in family structure are complicated. There is disagreement about whether these changes are good or bad for the parents. Almost everyone agrees that the rise of single parent families has been very bad for children, and especially for minority children. One problem is that single-parent (usually single-mother) families are very likely to be poor. In fact, single parents and their children are the poorest group in American society today. More than half of all African American, American Indian and Latino families headed by a single mother have an income below the poverty line. More than one-quarter of all African American children live in a poor family with a single mother.

Research has shown that children raised in single parent families are more likely than other children to be disadvantaged throughout their lives. As children, they tend to be short and thin for their age. Their academic skills tend to be poor. They face greater problems in cognitive and physical development, and have a higher risk than other children of dropping out of school and becoming single parents themselves (Blank 1997).

Minority children who face the quadruple burden of living in poor, single-parent households, attending poor schools, and living in high poverty neighborhoods have the deck stacked against them from birth. It is certainly possible for a child to emerge from such an environment as a successful and productive member of society, but it is not easy. The condition of such children is the most acute problem of minority group status today.

DISCRIMINATION

Under civil rights laws passed in the 1960s, it is illegal to discriminate by race in hiring, promotion, the setting of wages, and in renting or selling a home. Does discrimination against minorities occur nonetheless? Research confirms that it does. Discrimination is more subtle and occurs less frequently than it once did, but it is still practiced.

Sociologists commonly make a distinction between two kinds of discrimination: **taste discrimination** and **statistical discrimination**. Taste discrimination refers to differential treatment of a member of another group because of a personal dislike for, or desire not to associate with persons from that group. Statistical discrimination does not necessarily involve a negative evaluation of the minority, and the underlying belief is not necessarily wrong. For example, a bank officer might decide not to make a business loan to a creditworthy minority loan applicant because of a belief that the proposed business will have difficulties because of the racism of a segment of the customer base. A personnel officer may choose not to admit a minority applicant into a desirable training program because analysis of company records shows that minority graduates of the program have in the past been twice as likely as majority group members to quit the firm for a better job. In either case, the person making the judgment may be right more often than not, so that it seems to be simply a rational business decision. To use racial identity in this way, however, restricts opportunities by race. Statistical and taste discrimination are both illegal.

Some of the clearest evidence that discrimination is practiced in hiring and in rental and sale of housing comes from audit studies. The methodology of audit studies is that two applicants, one White and one a member of a minority group, apply for the same job or approach the same real estate agent about renting or buying a home. The researcher makes sure that the two applicants are nearly identical in all respects but one: height, weight, manner of dress and style of speech, educational attainment, job experience are the same. The only variable is race.

One audit study of hiring that was conducted in 1990 found that White job applicants experienced favorable treatment in 20 % more cases than did Black applicants (Urban Institute 1991). A study of housing discrimination showed that 59 % of Black homebuyers and 56 % of Hispanic homebuyers received less favorable treatment than did non-Hispanic whites. The minority homebuyers were refused service, were shown fewer homes, or were shown homes of poorer quality or in less desirable neighborhoods. Minority renters faced similar barriers (Urban Institute 1992).

Another way that sociologists study discrimination is by comparing the earnings of minority and majority workers with the same productive attributes. In making these comparisons, the researcher uses statistical controls for factors such as previous work experience, schooling, and performance on IQ tests. One study comparing the earnings of young Black men compared to young White men during the years 1988 to 1992 found that Blacks earned on average about 4 to 5% less than did whites who had the same credentials and skills and who worked the same job in the same part of the country (Ferguson 1995). A study comparing wages of Whites and Hispanics found no differences in earnings between Hispanics and Whites with a college degree, and small earnings disadvantages for Hispanics with lower levels of education (Stolzenberg 1990).

In considering the effects of discrimination on earnings, it is important to distinguish between discrimination by the employer and discrimination before employment that affects both the opportunity to get a job and performance on the job. Frequently it is the behavior of employers in hiring, promoting, and setting wages that comes under closest scrutiny. However, findings from statistical studies of racial differences in wages imply that the biggest, portion of the wage gap between members of majority and minority groups occurs because of differences in skills and credentials rather than in returns to skills and credentials. Thus, as Ferguson (1995:67) concludes, "the most important disparities in opportunity may occur before young people even enter the labor market: in the provision of schooling and other resources that influence skill building and socialization of youths. These include not only current disparities in the quality of schooling and recreation and discouraging messages from society at large, but also racial inequities in past generations of institutions that prepared parents and grandparents for their roles as teachers and care givers."

There are other forms of discriminatory treatment sometimes accorded to minorities that are not directly tied to economic well-being, but may be among the "discouraging messages from society at large" to which Ferguson alludes. Feagin and Sikes (1994) conclude, for example, that even middle class African Americans contend with what they call "everyday discrimination." This means, for example, routine slights and snubs in casual interactions with co-workers and strangers, together with occasional overly racist treatment, and blatant discrimination. Even if most majority group members do not engage in this kind of behavior, members of minority groups may experience it with regularity. This is the case simply because members of minority groups are out-numbered by members of the majority. In the United States today there are 6 whites for every Black, 6.5 whites for each Hispanic, 20 whites for each Asian or Pacific Islander, and 97 whites for each Native American. Thus, on average, racial and ethnic minorities in the United States interact far more frequently with members of the white majority than whites do with members of minority groups. Dealing with "everyday discrimination" in a world in where one's race leads to insulting treatment can create considerable stress, and requires the development of psychological coping strategies in order to navigate everyday life with a measure of ease.

Another form of discriminatory treatment of minority group members involves the use of racial identity by police and other authorities, such as security guards and store "loss prevention" officers, as an indicator of criminal disposition. Police officers will sometimes regard the presence of an African American in a predominantly White neighborhood as sufficiently suspicious to justify questioning the African American in order to discover criminal intent. The courts discourage police use of race as an indicator of criminality, but do nor forbid it and do not subject the police to a high standard to justify race-consciousness in their actions. A large majority of African American males, including those with professional credentials, report at least one encounter with police where their race appeared to be a factor leading to the encounter (Kennedy 1997).

Contemporary forms of discrimination are much harder to identify and document than was the case when racial distinctions were caste distinctions. For example, in an older era when restaurants put signs on their doors saying things like "No Dogs or Indians Allowed," it was clear where matters stood between the races. Now, debates and judgments about the extent of discrimination take place in contexts where it is uncertain what is happening. For example, when an employer must choose 1 out of 10 equally qualified applicants for a job, how can a minority applicant judge whether her own application was denied because of her race or simply by random luck? It often takes statistical information to make such a judgment--statistical information that may be hard to interpret. In this situation, there is often sharp disagreement about both the fact and extent of contemporary discrimination. The legal regulation of discrimination is similarly difficult₁ because it can be difficult to meet legal standards of proof.

AFFIRMATIVE ACTION

Beginning in the 1960s, the federal government adopted racially conscious social policies as one response to the evident inequality of racial groups. These policies included the designation of specific minority groups as protected classes who had standing to pursue formal complaints of discrimination. This legislation was passed primarily in response to Jim Crow discrimination against African Americans, but the protection of the legislation was extended to other racial minorities, including Hispanics, Asians and Pacific Islanders, and Native Americans. Women were also designated as a protected category in initial legislation. Age (being over 40), disability status and sexual preference have subsequently been added as protected categories.

Though the intent of much early civil rights legislation was to make society "color-blind" except to protect against discrimination, policies emerged in the 1960s to promote **affirmative** action to correct racial inequality. Affirmative action programs typically involve setting targets for minority representation in awarding of contracts, hiring or in admission to a selective university or apprenticeship program.

Affirmative action programs were begun in part because of difficulties with the enforcement of anti-discrimination law on a case-by-case basis in response to complaints. Such proceedings are costly for all concerned: the complainant who has to prove a difficult case, the company which has to defend itself; the government agency that has to investigate complaints, and the court that rules on their merits. In the early years of anti-discrimination enforcement, it became clear that it is easier to prove a case of discrimination concerning promotion and treatment of a minority worker than one concerning hiring. This is the case because workers have a lot of information about how non-minority co-workers with similar qualifications are treated by their company, but rejected job applicants have little information about fellow applicants. This creates unexpected and undesirable consequences: it is the company that hires the most minority workers that is the target of the most discrimination complaints.

Affirmative action programs that judge compliance with anti-discrimination law using a statistical standard of representation seem to have advantages over a judicial model of anti-discrimination enforcement for all concerned. From the point of view of proponents of minority hiring, statistical targets are an effective way to get minorities into jobs. From the point of view of companies, targets set clear standards for performance. Compliance with statistical standards of equal hiring is a strong defense against individual complaints of unfair treatment. It is also easier for government bureaucracies to monitor a firm's compliance with a target than to investigate every questionable hire and personnel decision. Because of these advantages, affirmative action programs quickly became a focus of anti-discrimination policy.

Affirmative action programs have proven controversial. In order to meet targets, it is sometimes necessary to give a job, a contract, or a place in college to a minority group applicant who seems less qualified than a majority group applicant for the same opportunity. To many Americans, this policy seems unfair to individuals even if it is meant to be fair to groups. One criticism is that the person who is denied a job because of a racial target did not necessarily gain any personal benefit from past discrimination, and is thus asked by society to pay the full price for a benefit enjoyed by someone else. Another criticism is that affirmative action offers most help to the middle class and highly educated members of minority groups, while it does little for the poor and low-skill people of all races who most need assistance.

Critics also suggest that costs of affirmative action programs to minorities out-weigh their benefits. One criticism is that while wages for minority workers have increased in the era of affirmative action, rates of employment have gone down, particularly for African American men. One hypothesis about why this has happened is that American manufacturing companies have moved their factories overseas since the passage of civil rights legislation in order to avoid the regulatory control of their personnel policies by the federal Equal Employment Opportunity Commission. Another hypothesis is that some U.S. companies continue to resist hiring minority workers in order to avoid the risk of civil rights lawsuits by unhappy workers (Jencks 1992). A second criticism of affirmative action is that it devalues the achievements of minority students and workers, by creating a widespread belief that these accomplishments are not earned but are granted through affirmative action programs.

Defenders of affirmative action point to evidence of continuing discrimination against minority workers as reason to continue these programs. Under this hypothesis, it will be necessary for the government to continue to make sure that minority group members get their fair share of opportunities, because the informal processes through which opportunities are awarded continue to be racially conscious, even if the operation of this racial consciousness is subtle. These defenders say that we need to take affirmative action to counter the growing movement towards the bifurcation of opportunities between rich and poor, majority and minority, that seems to be occurring in American society. These defenders say that we can ill afford to become a nation divided between a predominantly White suburban professional class that passes the advantages of class on to their children and grandchildren, while African Americans and new immigrants are locked in multi-generational poverty in jobless ghettos in the cities. Thus they see affirmative action as one of the tools that will help to break down the correlation between race and class.

Alan Wolfe (1998) reports that despite the sharp disagreement about affirmative action, defenders and critics of it share a common sense that merit should be the primary criteria for granting access to scarce and valuable resources such as jobs, college admissions, and government contracts. Where disagreement lies is in whether affirmative action accomplishes or interferes with that end. Critics of affirmative action think that abolishing it will mean that judgments will be colorblind. Advocates of affirmative action think that without affirmative action, rewards will be distributed through a process that is subtly color conscious. The evidence reviewed in this chapter suggests that minorities continue to experience some discrimination. Critics say that this doesn't necessarily justify affirmative action, because two wrongs don't make a right.

Whatever the merits of arguments for and against affirmative action, it is clear that race and ethnicity will continue to be an important public policy problem as the United States enters the 21st century. In some respects, the shape of the current controversy marks how far the nation has come along the road to racial equality. Minority status is no longer a synonym for exclusion from the mainstream of American social and economic life, as it was just 50 years ago. But full equality has not been achieved, and techniques for attaining it remain elusive and controversial.

SUMMARY

1. A minority group is defined as a group characterized by the four qualities of identifiability, differential power, differential and pejorative treatment, and group awareness.
2. Minority status is best thought of as a process
3. The reality of minority group status rises out of day-to-day events and the definitions and interpretations of those events.
4. The ideology that places some racial and/or ethnic groups above others, that speaks of racial superiority and inferiority, is termed racism, and shows itself as prejudice and discrimination.
5. Statistical directive #15 of the United States Government's Office of Management and Budget recognizes these groups: Whites, Blacks or African Americans, Native Americans, and Asian and Pacific Islanders, along with one ethnic or cultural group, Hispanics or Latinos. Whites are the majority and the others minorities.
6. During the first half of the 20th century the condition of many minorities had caste-like characteristics. This changed with the Civil Rights Movement of the 1960s and ethclasses emerged. In the late 20th century, Farley (1995) characterizes Black-White relations in particular as "fluid competitive race relations."
7. There is a diversity of minority experiences, individually as persons and collectively as a group. For example, the inequality between Blacks and Whites is largely the legacy of enslavement of African Americans by Whites and the emergence of a legal code known as Jim Crow after the Civil War in 1865. For Native Americans, the legacy of inequality can be traced to the expansion of White settlements westward across America between the 1600s and the 1800.
8. Changes in the American and world economy have increased competition for good jobs and have created greater disadvantages for members of minority groups because of the legacy of past disadvantages.
9. There have been only small decreases in the amount of racial residential segregation as measured by the *Index of Dissimilarity*

10. Schooling links issues of neighborhood residential segregation and occupational opportunity.
11. Minority children who face the quadruple burden of living in poor, single-parent households, attending poor schools, and living in high poverty neighborhoods have the deck stacked against them from birth.
12. Although illegal, discrimination does exist it is subtler and occurs less frequently than it once did. Its legal regulation is difficult because of legal standards of proof.
13. Whatever the arguments for and against affirmative action, it is clear that race and ethnicity will continue to be an important public policy issue as the United States enters the 21st century.
14. Full equality has not been achieved and techniques for attaining it remain elusive and controversial.

REFERENCES

Allport, Gordon W. 1954. *The Nature of Prejudice.* Cambridge, MA: Addison Wesley.

Apple, Michael 1998. *Education and Power.* Boston: Routledge and Kegan Paul.

Bean, Frank and Marta Tienda 1987. *The Hispanic Population of the United States.* New York: Russell Sage Foundation.

Blank, Rebecca 1997. *It Takes a Nation. A New Agenda for Fighting Poverty.* New York and Princeton: Russell Sage Foundation and Princeton University Press.

Collins, Randall 1979. *The Credential Society.* New York: Academic Press.

Danziger, Sheldon and Peter Gottschalk 1993. *Uneven Tides. Rising Inequality in America.* New York: Russell Sage Foundation.

Davis, W. A., Gardner, B. B., and Gardner, M. R. 1941. *Deep South: A Social Anthropological Study.* Chicago: U. of Chicago Press.

Dollard, John 1949. *Caste and Class in a Southern Town.* New York: Harper.

Dworkin, Anthony Gary 1987. *Teacher Burnout in the Public Schools: Structural Causes and Consequences for Children.* Albany, NY: SUNY Press.

Dworkin, Anthony Gary and Rosalind J. Dworkin 1976. *The Minority Report: An Introduction to Racial, Ethnic, and Gender Relations.* New York: Praeger.

_____.1982. Second Edition. New York: Holt, Rinehart, and Winston.

_____.1999. Third Edition. New York: Harcourt Brace.

Edmonston, Barry and Jeffrey S. Passel, eds. 1994. *Immigration and Ethnicity. The Intergration of America's Newest Arrivals.* Washington D.C.: Urban Institute Press.

Eschbach, Karl 1995. "The Enduring and Vanishing American Indian: America Indian Population Growth and Intermarriage in 1990." *Ethnic and Racial Studies.* 18:89-109.

Farley, John E. 1995. *Majority-Minority Relations.* Saddle River, N. J: Prentice-Hall.

Feagin, Joe R. and Melvin P. Sikes 1994. *Living with Racism. The Black Middle-Class Experience.* Boston: Beacon Press.

Ferguson, Ronald F. 1995. "Shifting challenges: fifty years of economic change toward black - white earnings equality. An American Dilemma Revisited." *Daedalus.* 124(1): 37-68.

Fordham, S. and J. Ogbu 1986. "Black Students" School Success: Coping with the Burden of "Acting White" *Urban Review.* 18:176-206.

Gordon, Milton Myron 1964. *Assimilation in American Life; the Role of Race, Religion and National Origins.* New York: Oxford University Press.

_____.1978. *Human Nature, Class, and Ethnicity.* New York: Oxford University Press.

Harrison, Roderick J. and Claudette E. Bennett 1995. "Racial and Ethnic Diversity." In Reynolds Farley, ed. *State of the Union. America in the 1990s. Vol. 2. Social Trends.* New York: Russell Sage Foundation.

Heckman, James 1994. "Is Job Training Oversold?" *The Public Interest* #115.

Heyn, Barbara 1978. *Summer Learning and the Effects of Schooling.* New York: Academic Press.

Jackson, Kenneth 1985. *Crabgrass Frontier: The Suburbanization of the United States.* New York: Oxford University Press.

Jargowsky, Paul A. 1996. *Poverty and Place. Ghettos, Barrios and the American City.* New York: Russell Sage Foundation.

Jencks, Christopher 1992. *Rethinking Social Policy. Race, Poverty and the Underclass.* Cambridge, MA: Harvard University Press.

Kennedy, Randall 1997. *Race, Crime, and the Law.* New York: Pantheon Books.

LeCompte, Margaret D. and Anthony Gary Dworkin 1991. *Giving Up on School: Student Dropouts and Teacher Burnouts.* Newbury Park, CA: Corwin/Sage Publishers.

Mare, Robert 1995. "Changes in Educational Attainment and School Enrollment." In Reynolds Farley, ed. *State of the Union. America in the 1990s. Vol. 1.* Economic Trends. New York: Russell Sage Foundation.

Massey, Douglas S. and Nancy A. Denton 1993. *American Apartheid. Segregation and Making of the Underclass.* Cambridge, MA: Harvard University Press

Montejano, David 1987. *Anglos and Mexicans in the Making of Texas, 1836-1986.* Austin: University of Texas Press.

Myrdal, Gunnar 1944. *An American Dilemma. Vol 1. The Negro Problem and Modern Democracy.* New York: Harper and Row.

National Center for Education Statistics. 1995. *The Condition of Education 1995.* Washington, D.C., U.S. Department of Education, Office of Educational Research and Improvement. NCES #95-273.

Park, Robert E. arid Herbert A. Miller 1921. *Old World Traits Transplanted.* New York: Harper and Brothers.

Peterson, Paul 1981. *City Limits.* Chicago: University of Chicago Press.

Rivera-Batiz, Francisco and Carlos Santiago 1996. *Island Paradox. Puerto Rico in the 1990s.* New York: Russell Sage Foundation.

Schuman, Howard, Charlotte Steeh, and Lawrence Bobo 1985. *Racial Attitudes in America. Trends and Interpretations.* Cambridge: Harvard University Press.

Stolzenberg, Ross. 1990. "Ethnicity, Geography and Occupational Achievement of Hispanic Men in the United States." *American Sociological Review.* 55:143-154.

Urban Institute 1991. "Hiring Discrimination Against Young Black Men." *Policy and Research Report.* Summer 1991.

_____.1992. "New Evidence of Urban Housing Discrimination." *Policy and Research Report.* Winter 1992

United States Bureau of the Census 1993. 1990 Census of Population and Housing. Summary Tape File 3C. Machine Readable File. Washington D.C.: U.S. Bureau of the Census.

Van den Berghe, Pierre 1967. *Race and Racism: A Comparative Perspective.* New York: Wiley.

Wagley, Charles and Marvin Harris 1958. *Minorities in the New World.* New York: Columbia University Press.

Warner, W. Lloyd 1936. "American caste and class." *American Journal of Sociology.* 42:234-37.

Wilson, William J. 1973. *Power, Racism, and Privilege.* New York: The Free Press.

_____.1978. *The Declining Significance of Race: Blacks and Changing American Institutions.* Chicago: University of Chicago Press.

_____.1996. *When Work Disappears. The World of the New Urban Poor.* New York: Alfred A. Knopf.

Wirth, Louis 1945. "The problem of minority groups." In Ralph Linton ed. *The Science of Man in the World Crisis.* New York: Columbia University Press.

Wolfe, Alan 1998. *One Nation, After All.* New York: Viking Books.

CHAPTER 10: HEALTH CARE
CASE STUDY: ILLNESS IN THE UNITED STATES

Thanksgiving was one time of the year when all three generations of the Ludwig family were together, and this year was no different. As the years went by, they realized they shared less and less: they lived in different geographic areas, they belonged to different churches, their life styles were quite dissimilar, and they often disagreed with each other. But on Thanksgiving it was the custom to gather at the home of the Ludwig family elders, Ella and Harry. John, their son, his wife Donna, and their 35-year-old daughter, Margaux, had arrived laden with all that was needed for this festive occasion.

Of course they were prepared for Ella's protests she could have made dinner for them all. Donna said it was time Ella let others do more. "Besides," she said, "you're no doubt exhausted with taking Dad to the hospital every day for treatments." Harry, who had diabetes since he was in his thirties, nearly forty years, now was on dialysis. Ella had to take him to the hospital since his sight was too poor for him to drive. Ella remarked it wouldn't be so bad if the city hadn't closed the hospital that used to be near them in the inner-city area where they lived. "They said they couldn't afford to keep it open but I think it was because those rich doctors with their fancy cars wanted to have a new place close to where they live in the suburbs. Now all of us have to drive to where they are; they don't care about us or how far we have to go to get their help." "It's a good thing we have Medicare," Harry said. "Don't know how we'd pay for my care without it. Those bills are out of this world."

"Dad," John said, "You know Donna and I told you, if you need any help, we're well able to step in with what you need." "That's not what I mean," his father growled, "they just don't care what they charge, not the doctors, the druggists, or the insurance companies." Donna stepped in hoping to stop an argument. "But just think of all the wonderful things they can do for you today." "A few years ago they didn't have the equipment they have today. You wouldn't be alive today, Harry, if it wasn't for someone inventing that dialysis machine. And don't forget that I am going to have my heart repaired in a few months and if doctors hadn't cared I wouldn't be able to have my faulty mitral valve repaired so I can be good as new. My mother had the same problem as I have, but she died because no one had developed the heart-lung machine or the skills to go right inside the heart to repair it." "Well," Harry replied, "that may sound great to you, but I still say it costs too much and I'm not sure all these newfangled gadgets are so great. They aren't making me feel any better and I think sometimes the old ways were better." "God," Margaux said, "can't we talk about anything else but our ailments?"

At that her grandmother came over and hugged her. "What's the matter, honey" she said, "Every time you're here lately you are so pale and so irritable?" And to everyone's surprise Margaux burst into tears. With her grandmother hugging her ever tighter, Margaux's tears subsided "Grandma, I'm sick. As a matter of fact, I'm very sick." John and Donna turned to their daughter, just as she made the most difficult confession of her life. "I have AIDS." Her grandmother pulled back from her as Margaux continued on, "While I was working in Seattle, you see, I was dating this guy in a band, and I knew he had used drugs before I met him, but he was clean. I know he was. But we had, you know, sex and we didn't use any protection. Oh, God, I can't believe this is happening to me."

Both John and Donna were stunned by this news. "Margaux," said her father, "with all your schooling, all your smarts, and all that's written about this disease, how could you be so irresponsible?" "John, John," said Donna plaintively, "let's leave the whys for later. Let's worry about what Margaux is going to do now. She has no insurance and we want her to have the best of care." "But Mom, it's not just the insurance, they know about it at my new job, too, and I'm afraid they might let me go. Most of the other women there refuse to go into the john after I've been there and the guy I was dating hasn't called in weeks. Oh, I was the one who wanted us to stop talking about our troubles. Look at us now!" It took some time for all the tension of the moment to dissipate, but eventually all the family members agreed that Margaux's dilemma, as well as the rest of the family's problems weren't going to be easily solved. This was a Thanksgiving they would not soon forget.

The health issues discussed by the Ludwig family may sound as though they are unusual, perhaps even problems that would not occur within a single family. In a time when people are living longer lives, when exposure to disease is often more likely because of the ease of moving about in many different social groups, and when medical technology has created new ways to repair the body and sustain it, it is more common than it was only a few decades ago, to find these health concerns impacting family life. This chapter will consider these health situations by focusing on changes occurring in the types of illnesses prevalent in our society, changes in the people who use our health care system, changes in the costs of health care, the providers of health care, and the interventions being recommended to improve our health care system. At the same time, this chapter will suggest there are some critical questions that need to be addressed by each of us as we consider health issues in the future.

THE CHANGING WORLD OF HEALTH AND HEALTH CARE

To understand our health care system today, it is useful to take a brief look at the development of medicine as illnesses change, at who cares for the ill, where illnesses are treated, and who pays for health care. As a starting point it may be useful to compare disease and other forms of illnesses today with what existed in the past.

HISTORY OF SOCIAL ILLNESS

The diseases and illnesses that concern most of us today are the ones we read about frequently: cancers of all sorts, heart disease, AIDS or other diseases that destroy our immune systems, and, of lesser concern, colds, flu, or tooth decay. But were these the same diseases or medical difficulties that existed when man first roamed earth? It might surprise you to find that many of the same diseases and illnesses we encounter in the world today existed hundreds of thousands of years ago. Most of us would expect that the bacteria or virus from millions of years ago could not have survived to today. And probably most of us would expect, even if they did exist today, medical science would have found a way by now to eradicate those "old" causes for diseases and the illnesses they produce. Surely most of us would anticipate the way we live today would protect us from the accidents our early ancestors could not prevent. Surprisingly, these expectations have not been completely realized.

Theory Box by Michael J. Donnelly Chapter 10 Health Care

In a modern market society most people live from their labor, earning wages or salaries out of which they acquire in the marketplace the goods and services they need or desire. Health care is one of the key services modern consumers' demand. In the contemporary United States, for instance, total expenditures on health care amount to well over 10% of the gross domestic product. But health care is not a commodity like other goods and services. Most of us would agree that access to health care should be based on need, and not primarily on ability to pay. Luxury cars may effectively be within the reach only of the wealthy, but we would find it offensive if access to expensive life-saving medical procedures were similarly restricted only to the wealthy. In principle, our society recognizes that health care is a special need which ought to be satisfied; in other terms, society at large acknowledges a stake in the health of its citizens, and society is unlikely to function effectively if it neglects provisions for maintaining the health of its members. Hence the assumption underlying social policy on health care: society should provide basic health care on the basis of need; everyone in need of health care should receive the (basic) care they need, no less and not necessarily any more than they need.

In practice, this assumption is modified and compromised for a variety of reasons. One set of issues involves what constitutes "adequate" care. From the point of view of consumers, adequate or basic care may seem like second-class care. When we think of our own health or that of our loved ones, we are likely to want the best care available and we would be unlikely to resign ourselves to lower-level basic care. Similarly health care providers (physicians and hospitals) may have various incentives to "try everything" (including perhaps unnecessary or unjustified treatments) when health and life itself are at stake. From both the demand and the supply sides there may in other words be pressures to raise the bar, to judge what is adequate care by the standard of the best that is medically available. Technological advances have also dramatically extended the possibilities for medical interventions, and have raised the costs of health care accordingly. Health planners face difficult trade-offs; how, for instance, can they balance the good of providing kidney dialysis to sustain the lives of a needy few against the good of a mass vaccination campaign which would benefit many? Both courses of action would be good, but given finite resources, decisions may need to be made -ultimately about who lives.

How can we know the same diseases and medical problems we see today existed before? It is the anthropologists and paleontologists, students of early human existence, who have deciphered medical information that dates from hundreds of thousands of years ago. The clues are in the materials that remain and are found when places where man once lived are uncovered (Ackerknecht 1982). To find out about the beginnings of disease, scientists search for this evidence in preserved fragments of early ancestors, such as their teeth and bones, or in mummies, and in prehistoric works of art like cave drawings. Their findings suggest there has never been a time when those inhabiting the earth, even animals, were free from injuries and disease. Their evidence in fossil and skeletal remains give clues that early inhabitants of earth suffered from fractures, from scurvy, arthritis, dental diseases, tuberculosis, bone tumors, and even leprosy. These diseases can be found today in many parts of the world including the United States. Perhaps it is not surprising our prehistoric ancestors broke bones when they fell as they chased after their catch for that evening's meal, or perhaps when their evening meal chased them. Or maybe it is not too difficult to imagine these ancestors lived long enough to be arthritic, or that their way of life did not offer them the proper nutrition to avoid diseases like scurvy or rotting teeth. What is surprising though is we have yet to eradicate many of those medical problems that existed millennia ago.

DISEASE AND ILLNESS TODAY

While the studies of early human groups can tell us what diseases existed centuries ago and enlighten us about the fact that many of the same diseases exist today, what this research cannot reveal with certainty is the causes of death in that early time, or how many people died from these different causes. These facts are known as mortality statistics. This type of information could be known only after written records were available for study. Today most developed countries keep consistent records of health statistics so it is possible to trace over time what illnesses are most common in a given year, what illnesses or accidents cause the death of people, and many, many more facts about health in the United States and other countries around the world.[1]

Knowledge based on changing health patterns is important for many reasons. For example, when there is an increase in an illness such as has occurred world-wide with AIDS, this knowledge encourages health researchers and, hopefully, governments and foundations who support health research to focus attention on this disease in hopes of reducing its power to kill. To understand how data can be important, think of yourself as the head of a foundation that could invest millions of dollars into health research. Suppose you were given the following table of information (Table 10.1) about the changes in leading causes of death in the United States from the beginning of this century, 1900, and ninety plus years later. What decisions would you make about where to invest your foundation's dollars in health research?

The information in Table 10.1 indicates the changes in the ten major reasons for death in the United States at the beginning of this century and in the year, 1992. In 1900 the top three leading killers were acute infectious diseases including influenza and pneumonia, tuberculosis, and gastroenteritis. Other causes of death at the beginning of this century also have as their explanation infections from micro-organisms. These include chronic nephritis, diseases of infancy like measles, mumps and hepatitis, and diphtheria, which affects both children and adults. By 1992, tuberculosis and gastroenteritis lost their place among the top ten killers, possibly because of antibiotics that could diminish the deadly effect of these infections. The development of antibiotics and vaccines to immunize people from certain diseases, and other types of drugs undoubtedly reduced the numbers of persons dying of chronic nephritis, an inflammation of the kidney. Death from diphtheria, a childhood disease, is known to be completely preventable if children are vaccinated. Strict health regulations regarding immunization using vaccines have almost completely wiped out diphtheria in the United States even though it still exists in other parts of the world (Lee 1996).

If you are the head of this prosperous research foundation, what new information would this table give you? Certainly you would realize by inspecting this table that heart disease, cancer, influenza and pneumonia, and accidents remain, even after ninety plus years, on the list of leading causes of death in the United States. That fact suggests a need for more research as to why these health problems are still leading causes of death, and in fact have, except for influenza and pneumonia, risen to the top of the 1992 list. That influenza and pneumonia deaths still are among the top ten is surprising since a vaccine for both has been developed that can greatly reduce the chances of these infections and their seriousness. According to the Centers for Disease Control and Prevention (1994) over 31,000 deaths from influenza and pneumonia could be prevented each year if people followed the recommendations for immunization. Lee (1996) suggests that physicians are twice as likely to use antibiotics rather than immunization despite the known success of these vaccines. Part of the difficulty may rest with people reluctant to go to the doctor for preventive care or to spend the money to get immunized; another part is possibly that it is the rare doctor who takes the time to persuade patients of the need to be immunized.

While Table 10.1 reports leading causes of death, this information is more exact when we know how many persons died in each of the 10 categories. In 1992, 33%, or 717,000 people, of all individuals who died did so as the result of heart disease while 24% of all deaths, or 520,578 persons, succumbed to cancer. Stroke, the next leading cause, affected 7%, or 143,769 of those who died. Each of the other seven causes listed killed 4% or less of those who died, while any of the other causes of death not listed in the top 10 account for only 18% of those who died. In other words 18% of those who died in 1992 died from some cause not among the ten listed above in Table 10.1; in contrast, 82% died from one of the causes specified in the 10 categories of the table.

The major killers, heart disease, and cancer together, took the lives of 57% of those who died in the United States, more than half the number of persons who died in 1992. These two diseases are often considered chronic diseases rather than infectious diseases since many heart disorders are the result of heart defects that may have existed at birth. Many heart defects may be the result of infections that occurred earlier, such as rheumatic fever, but any infection creates in some people a possibility of developing heart defects at a later time. Cancer, too, is considered a chronic disease even though its cause is not clearly defined as yet. Cancer is considered to result when cell growth goes "wild" in the sense of developing abnormal cells that crowd out healthy cells. It is clear that chemicals or other physical irritants in the environment can result in abnormal cell growth but, at the same time, heredity can influence this growth of malignant cells. In any event, knowing how difficult it has been to reduce the hazards of these illnesses in this country during this century perhaps your decision as head of this foundation would be to invest monies in research of cancer and heart disease.

Yet there are other health problems replacing the six causes listed in 1900 that could attract your attention and dollars. These 6 new leading causes of death include stroke, lung disease, diabetes, AIDS, suicide, and homicide. Possibly you would chose to concentrate your efforts on AIDS. Perhaps you, like many people, are frightened by the rapid increase in AIDS throughout the world, an infectious disease caused by the human immunodeficiency virus (HIV), and the fact no cure has yet to be found. Perhaps, like the Ludwig family, you have children who are exposed to the hazards leading to AIDS and would like to see some vaccine developed that would not only protect them but would end this dreaded disease.

This HIV virus damages the immune system permitting infections, which could normally be kept in control, to overwhelm the body and eventually cause death. How many individuals in the United States are afflicted with AIDS? In the data from the table for 1992 deaths, it is the 8th leading cause of death, killing 33,566 Americans in 1992. Two years later, in 1994, it was the leading cause of death for adults 25 to 44 years of age, killing more in that age group than heart disease, cancer, or accidents (National Center for Health Statistics 1997). It is estimated there are about 14 million cases of AIDS throughout the world with about one million of these children. In the United States, according to The Centers for Disease Control data, there were about one million and a half cases of HIV in 1993 and about a half million plus cases of full-blown AIDS (Centers for Disease Control 1994).

In an article in USA Today, (May 1992:72) Larry Kramer reports there is one new case of HIV infection every 54 seconds, one death from AIDS every 9 minutes, and 267 new AIDS cases reported each day. Among college students, Mr. Kramer reports 1 college student in every 1000 is infected with AIDS. One of the difficulties with the HIV infection is people who have contracted the virus can remain without symptoms and therefore knowledge that they are infected for up to 10 years or longer. That is undoubtedly what happened with Margaux Ludwig whose friend had stopped using drugs. Possibly he was carrying the virus from a contaminated needle exchange and had yet to have any symptoms, such as chronic fevers, night sweats, mysterious weight loss, or constant diarrhea, symptoms that would lead to blood tests that identify the existence of the virus. So, if you as the controller of dollars for research found the eradication of AIDS as the most compelling reason to invest in AIDS research, your decision might be based on the mortality figures of Table 10.1 and your concern with this world-wide infection.

Many of the major causes of death in the 1990s are considered preventable or less likely to lead to death if appropriate health measures are taken. For example, cancer, stroke, or diabetes have early warning signs that help people to detect the existence of these diseases before it is too late to either cure them or keep them in remission or under control. Yet many people ignore the tests that can detect cancers or fail to follow a healthy life style that might reduce the chances of the disease occurring. Certainly this is true for AIDS, a newcomer to the list of killers. If prevention is likely when care and informed sexual behavior and drug use is practiced, the question becomes why are prevention measures not taken? Moreover the question of who should be responsible for the prevention of disease or illness deserves to be evaluated. Should the United States do as many other developed countries do by increasing regulations that require immunization, health examinations, and stricter control of substances and health behaviors known to be unhealthy? Or do we, as a society, value individual freedom so greatly we allow each person to determine what they will do about their health and health care even though their decisions may leave others with the necessity of paying for expensive care for some who chose not to take precautions to prevent illnesses?

Table 10.1 Comparison of Leading Causes of Death in the United States in 1900 and 1992

Ten Leading Causes of Death 1900	Ten Leading Causes of Death 1992
1. Influenza and Pneumonia	1. Heart Disease
2. Tuberculosis	2. Cancer
3. Gastroenteritis	3. Stroke
4. Heart Disease	4. Lung Disease
5. Cerebral Hemorrhage	5. Accidents
6. Chronic Nephritis	6. Influenza and Pneumonia
7. Accidents	7. Diabetes
8. Cancer	8. AIDS
9. Diseases of Infancy	9. Suicide
10. Diphtheria	10. Homicide

Source: National Center for Health Statistics 1993. *Vital Statistics of the United States. USGPO 1993 and U. S. Department of Health and Human Services 1995. Monthly Vital Statistics Report.* March

A recent article in the New York Times by Barry Meier (1997) portrays the issues raised above regarding responsibility for prevention. Meier reports that over the past year, Florida, Idaho, Minnesota, North Carolina and Texas have passed laws that could result in stiff penalties for minors who try to buy or possess cigarettes or chewing tobacco. It is known these are risky health behaviors leading to cancers of the mouth, throat, and lungs or other illnesses. Some cities, the article reports, are using undercover police to catch minors who smoke, while some schools that test students for substances like marijuana also screen for nicotine. Violations of these laws or regulations that led to convictions result in students losing their driver's license, fines of up to $1000, loss of participation in athletics, even imprisonment for as long as 6 months.

Why would there be a need to resort to such drastic measures, measures that some see as an unwanted intrusion on the freedom of individuals to choose their own behavior? The justification for this encroachment is found first in information from the Centers for Disease Control and Prevention that 35% of high school students are cigarette smokers and second, in the knowledge that health education programs have failed to halt the growth in the number of minors who use cigarettes. Many people recognize the addictive quality of tobacco use and the likelihood of its use leading to cancer, heart disorders, or lung diseases; many know the cost of caring for persons with these illnesses. Yet it is difficult to persuade people to change habits they enjoy. The question is, should deterrents such as those discussed in the Meier article be put in place as preventive measures similar to the requirement of vaccinations for children to immunize them against various devastating diseases? When should such health regulations be used?

Are there countries where such requirements to prevent diseases or accidents are strictly enforced by governments? Examples exist. A case in point would be in Russia where for many years; health records of all workers have been kept by state health employees (Haug 1976). These include, among other medical records, when women have had a Papanicolaou smear test, a simple, painless, test used most commonly to detect cancer of the uterus and cervix. The Pap test as it is commonly called, can reveal uterine or cervical cancer at a stage when these cancers produce no visible symptoms, have done no damage, and usually can be completely cured. If the state health worker finds that a woman has not gone for her annual Pap test, the worker will be notified and followed until the test is done. Is this intruding on a person's freedom when the government makes decisions about cancer prevention and requires testing, or is this a government that cares about workers' health and is zealous in averting illnesses that can be prevented? Is our country showing concern for its citizens by allowing them to forego medical tests that will prevent cancer and improve many people's quality of life? Or is our country respecting individuals' right to make their own health decisions?

Possibly you feel that this regulating of health tests as is done in Russia could only happen in a country where state authority has always been a dominant force. Another example is found in Sweden, a country that few would find authoritarian. But Sweden is a country with health problems related to excessive use of alcohol. There, government has enacted laws permitting a police officer to stop people without cause to administer a breath analysis test to assess if the level of alcohol in the person's system is beyond a "safe" level. It is a country with laws that hold a person hosting a party where alcohol is served as responsible for the guests at the event. The host can be arrested and serve a jail sentence if a guest is allowed to leave the party to drive home in an intoxicated state. Again the question is who would you say should be responsible for the health of the public when illnesses and accidents can be prevented --- the individual or the government?

Finally, looking again at Table 10.1, the inclusion in 1992 of suicide and homicide among the top ten killers suggests it is more important than ever to consider those conditions in our society today that result in these seemingly non-infectious, non-degenerative causes of death, such as accidents. In 1995, 6% of all persons who died did so of injuries, which includes accidents, homicides, and self-inflicted injuries leading to death, more specifically, suicides. More males died of injuries than females, particularly in the age group from 20 - 24 years. Among the injury deaths, unintentional injuries like car accidents, falls, an accidental gun wound, accounted for 61% of the deaths, suicides for 21%, and homicides for 15% deaths. It is no longer surprising that suicides are highest among the elderly and homicides highest among those individuals 20 - 24 years of age. In this 20 - 24 age group, men are five times as likely to die of injuries as women. Moreover, injury deaths are two to three times higher in metropolitan areas than in other more rural cities. Facts like these point out there are differences in death rates by age, by gender, or degree of urbanization. They bring to our attention the knowledge there are differences in who becomes ill and who dies. Explanations are needed as to why these differences exist, and what influences they have on the health of people.

INFLUENCES ON HEATH STATUS

HISTORY OF SOCIAL EPIDEMIOLOGY

It is common today to find agreement that there are connections between who gets ill, injured, or who dies depending on such characteristics as race, age, gender, or even where people live or work. The study of the connections between health status, that is, peoples' health or illnesses, and social factors, such as age, gender, place of residence, or occupation, is called **social epidemiology**. This field of study examines the association between causes of diseases or physical impairments and where these occur, and how these illnesses are distributed within a population. The hope is by finding where diseases exist there is a possibility to find patterns that help to identify causes of various illnesses.

EPIDEMIOLOGY TODAY

There were many incidents that occurred during the last several years where unusually large numbers of people became ill or died, and explanations as to why were not immediately apparent. The number of service men who participated in the Persian Gulf War and suffered from serious illnesses after they returned to the United States became the concern of epidemiologists and others. Massive amounts of information were gathered to gain an understanding of the illnesses reported: the areas in which these soldiers were located in the Gulf, where their units fought, what jobs they held, how many other persons in their units reported similar symptoms or no symptoms, past illnesses, and the like. First it was determined more soldiers were reporting similar physical difficulties than would have been expected. Then an analysis of data resulted in an initial determination there was no physical explanation for these illnesses, apparently leaving only emotional causes as an explanation. For many people such a decision was difficult to accept because it allowed many to believe that somehow the illness was the fault of the soldiers, that in some way they had a weakness not acceptable for a soldier. More often than not, there is a stigma or disgrace attached to illnesses defined as having an emotional rather than a physical cause.

Fortunately for the men from the Persian Gulf War further data concluded there was a connection between where these soldiers had been located and exposure to noxious chemicals. It took the detective work of social epidemiologists to solve this medical mystery. It does not mean these soldiers were cured, only that there is now an understanding of the cause of the illnesses they have, and hopes for means to help them.

Epidemiology accepts not only that certain germs thrive best under certain environmental conditions to cause serious illnesses, but that certain characteristics of people do as well. Qualities such as gender or certain physical characteristics, qualities acquired as people grow older such as their social class, lifestyle behaviors, and aspects of physical and social environment, all affect health and therefore how long people live. For example, we North Americans can expect that, if we were born in 1995, our life expectancy would be to live to the age of 75.8 years of age. Not bad if you consider that world wide today, according to the World Health Organization, life expectancy is 66 years (Newsweek 1998). What matters most in determining how long you can expect to live? In the United States, it is known that differences in gender and race as well as where you live, the work you do, the kind of health care you have available, and many other considerations can affect your life expectancy. What is not as clear is what are the most critical influences affecting life expectancy. **Life expectancy**, is the number of years a person born in a given year can expect to live. This figure is developed by looking at past information about people from year to year and using prediction statistics to estimate how likely someone born in a particular year can expect to live. The accuracy of these estimates depends on how much is known about what influences health and illnesses. This type of prediction is similar to the one you might make whether to take an umbrella with you to work, or class, or wherever. Your prediction depends on what knowledge you have accumulated about whether it will rain such as the grayness of the clouds in the sky, the weather report, or the ache in your knees. The more understanding we have of what contributes to longer lives, the better our predictions of life expectancy.

We know that today men on average die younger than do women and that often differences in longevity exist between racial and ethnic groups in our society (National Center for Health Statistics 1997). These data indicate white females can expect to live to the age of 79.6, white males to the age of 73.4, or about six fewer years. Black females can expect to live to the age of 73.9, black males to the age of 65.2, or nearly nine fewer years. So females, white or black, born in the United States will live longer than white males as well as black males. White females live longer than black females; black males live fewer years than white males. But females have a higher life expectancy than their male counterparts If living long is your goal, then as these data suggest, it is best to be born female. These kinds of differences in life expectancy have existed in the United States since the early part of this century.

There are several alternative explanations for the differences in life expectancy for men and women. Research on the topic points out that in the early part of the 1900s there was little difference between how long men and women lived. Gradually the difference widened. In an effort to explain why it was that the life expectancy in the early part of this century was similar for men and women, it is necessary to examine when these persons with similar life spans were born and what their lives were like. This means examining where they lived, what they did, their family size, and whatever else was believed affected their health. Researchers concluded after studying this group of people that these men and women worked on farms primarily. Their work life and the environment they lived in across the country for men and women was much the same. Their values, expectations, and what was available to them were similar for both groups. Given this likeness in their lives, researchers find the existence of similar ages for death between these men and women not unusual. As our country became more industrialized and as life styles and expectations for men and women changed these same researchers reason life expectancy could be expected to change. The emphasis in this explanation places the influence on length of life as mostly dependent on what we do, how we live, what we value. It leads us to believe that social, environmental, and occupational differences best explain life expectancy.

What other social or cultural influences would contribute to a longer life for women in the United States? Medical researchers have reported for many years that men are more likely to die of heart disease than are women. Research findings indicate this difference may in large part be due to the fact men indulge in health behaviors that lead to heart disease: Men smoke more than do women and are more likely to work in stressful situations. Interestingly, in the last few years, women in larger numbers are beginning to smoke earlier and more than they did previously. At the same time men are smoking less. Moreover, more women are now participating in the work force and working in jobs formerly not available to them that demand competitive and assertive behavior. Further, our culture still expects women, even those working at full time positions outside the home, to be the major caregiver and homemaker, most often itself a second full time position. It is not surprising, if we accept the explanation that work stress and smoking are critical causes of heart disease, that recent evidence indicates deaths from heart disease among women are increasing. It is expected that this will decrease the gender differential of life expectancy between men and women. The change in smoking habits has affected the rate of cancer deaths for men and women as well. Lung cancer among women is increasing as it declines among men. This is true of some of the other cancers caused by exposure to dangerous cancer-causing environments in some work places, places in which few women previously held jobs.

Our society and its culture still accepts it is "natural" for men to be aggressive, to use alcohol as well as guns, and to indulge in risky behaviors or be employed in hazardous occupations. As women increasing participate in similar activities we can expect their life expectancy to parallel that of men.

Some researchers find an alternative theory is needed to explain the differences in life expectancies, They suggest that women have always had certain biological and genetic characteristics that protect them while men have not inherited these defenses. They agree some of the difference may be explained by such matters as environment, work, health care, and the like, but insist inherited characteristics matter as well. For example, during the first 28 days in the life of a newborn when infants are more likely to die as a consequence of genetic problems or difficulties during the birth process, it is male infants who are more at risk. Further, there are some advantages to hormonal differences that appear to affect women positively during their lifetime. Certainly recent research involving gene studies presents evidence that changing some inherited gene structure can affect length of life and health. This suggests that our genetic inheritance affects our lives. Even so, while some research finds biological or genetic factors can affect length of life, often more weight is accorded to the influence of social, environmental, and occupational differences.

Data have established that in earlier times the differences between how long men live compared to women was far less than it is at present, a fact that again suggests that what people do, how they live, and what is important to them affects health perhaps more than the characteristics they inherit at birth. Or is it that there is something unique about our society in the United States? Some of the information needed to answer this question can be found in Table 10.2 below. This information reports the life expectancy for people born in 1993 in fifteen different countries in the world, all with a population of five million plus persons. China and Russia, countries with populations over five million, are not included because the health data for them are not available for this time period to the World Health Organization or other agencies that collect this international information.

If we wish to answer whether life expectancy in the United States is different from that of other countries, the data of Table 10.2 are helpful. How long people born in 1993 are expected to live is reported for each of 15 countries along with their rank order. The ranking is from highest to lowest life expectancy. For example, Japanese men have the longest life expectancy compared to men from all other countries listed in this table, so they are ranked number 1. This is true for Japanese women as well. French men are ranked 8th highest among the 15 countries; French women are 2nd highest in life expectancy. What we know from this table is that life expectancy for those born in the United States is lower then that of most all of the other countries. In fact, the United States ranks 14th of these 15 countries for both men and women, next to the lowest number of years for men and lowest for women. To repeat a line used earlier in this chapter, if you want to live longer it is best to be born as a native in Japan or nearly any of the other 14 countries listed in this table. You will note there is only about 4 ½ years difference in life expectancy for men between those living in Japan and the United States, about 4 years for women, and wonder what all the fuss is about. But for most people adding that many years to our lives will seem important particularly as we grow older.

A second piece of information reported in Table 10.2 is that in every country women live longer than men. In most countries the difference in life expectancy is similar to the United States, about six and a half years. France has the greatest disparity between men and women, eight and a half years. That these differences between life expectancy of men and women exist everywhere suggests there may be reality to the assumption that women have some biological and genetic differences that add to their longevity. At the same time, the information that there are differences among the various countries suggests there may be reality to the assumption that different social and cultural values, differences in environment and occupations continue to impact longevity among men and among women. It is apparent that both assumptions are plausible. It is probably best at this time to accept both ideas as viable ones. It is not possible to say longevity is completely a function of biology (nature) nor is it completely a function of what happens to us after our biological/genetic self is determined (nurture). Rather it would appear both must be considered. We are still obligated to continue research to determine what factors are most critical to a long life.

Table 10.2: Life Expectancy Between Men and women Born in 1993 in Selected Countries: Population Five Million Plus

Country	Population in Millions	Life Expectancy Men	Rank	Life Expectancy Women	Rank
Japan	125	76.5	1	83.1	1
Sweden	9	75.5	2	80.8	5.5
Switzerland	7	75.0	3	81.7	3
Canada	28	74.9	4	81.4	11.5
Australia	18	74.7	5	80.8	5.5
Netherlands	15	74.3	6	80.5	8.5
United Kingdom	58	73.9	7	79.5	11.5
France	58	73.8	8	82.3	2
Italy	57	73.7	9	80.5	8.5
Spain	40	73.4	10	80.7	7
Austria	8	72.9	11	79.5	11.5
Germany	81	72.8	12	79.3	13
Denmark[1]	5	72.7	13	---	---
United States	258	72.2	14	78.8	14
Finland	5	72.1	15	79.6	10

Sources: World Health Organization: *World Health Statistics Annuals.* Vols. 1990-1994. Geneva; *United Nations: Demographic Yearbook 1994.* New York; Centers for Disease Control and Prevention, National Center for Health Statistics, *Vital Statistics of the United States* 1994. Vol. II, Mortality, Part A. Washington. The United Nations is the author of the original material.

Does it really matter whether it is nature or nurture that is most important? It does if you recognize that it is almost impossible to change what we are born with, or our nature. But it is feasible, though often difficult, to change most social and cultural values, that is, to improve the environment, to educate about stressful situations so as to change their impact, even to change risky health behaviors. Change in smoking behavior is an example that this can happen even if it takes time and extensive education. Since it is possible to bring about changes in attitudes and behavior as well as reduce some of the environmental and occupational hazards, it appears more reasonable to focus on changes in these areas rather than on those biological and genetic difficulties that affect health.

A look at infant deaths among different countries gives additional support to the idea that different behaviors and values in a society affect health. Data from 1995 (National Center for Health Statistics 1997) indicate that **infant mortality**, which is defined as the number of deaths of infants under one year old for every 1,000 babies born, was at a record low in the United States. In 1995 there were 7.9 infant deaths per 1,000 births. The same data disclose that among Blacks, nearly two and a half times more infants died in 1995. American Indians and Hispanic Americans also have higher infant mortality rates than those of whites; Asiatic Americans are the one group in the United States whose infant death rate is lower than that of white Americans. This information clarifies that among different racial and ethnic groups there are differences in infant mortality. Some would say a person cannot change race or ethnic heritage, so accept these differences as a fact of life. But is it possible to be assured that the differences among these groups and the rate of infant mortality is due to racial or ethnic heritage? It may be there are other factors that affect these groups and their health status more critical than race or ethnicity. Most research does find that there are other significant considerations that can influence these infant mortality rates

While the rate of poverty in the United States decreased to 14% of all Americans by 1995, the poverty rate for children less than 18 years old was at 20%. Children are 30% of all Americans but closer to 40% of those persons defined as poor (National Center for Health Statistics 1997). The rate of poverty differs for children in different ethnic/racial groups. 39% of Hispanic American children are included in the poverty category, 42% of African Americans, 53% of Puerto Ricans, and 16% of White Americans. The vast majority of those impoverished live in inner cities. As the elderly Ella Ludwig complained about having to go some distance to get her husband to his physician and the hospital for dialysis treatment, doctors, other health professionals, and hospitals have in many cases left the city centers, moving to more suburban areas (Duke 1996). One of the results can be that health care is less accessible and readily available to the less advantaged in America. It is not difficult then to suspect that the health care available may be a factor in infant mortality. One way to examine this is to begin to compare our health care system to that of other countries.

Most of us would assume that the United States has one of the lowest, if not the lowest, infant mortality rate in the world. After all, most of us would reason, we are an economically developed country with one of the finest health systems in the world, and some of the best medical professionals and technology. Therefore we should be able to prevent many of these infant deaths. For example, if the kind or amount of health care in a given country is a deciding factor in keeping infant mortality rates low, then we would anticipate that even though other circumstances might also cause infant deaths, the level of health care could make a difference.

One measure of the level of health care in a country is to examine how much a country spends per person on health care, known as per capita spending, and also to look at the percent of a country's Gross Domestic Product (GDP) spent on health. **Gross domestic product** is the total amount of goods and services produced by a country. It is the sum of what is spent by individuals and nonprofit organizations for goods and services, plus the business investment in equipment, inventories, and new construction, plus Federal, State, and local government purchases of goods and services, plus the sale of goods and services abroad minus purchases from abroad. A certain percent of this total dollars from goods and services will be spent by a country on whatever services they value. These services could include health care, military expenses, social services, education, the arts, and the like. By looking at how much a country spends on these different items you can make a judgement about which are seen as most valued. Will a country spend more on health care than on education, or on running the government, or military expenses? By looking across countries, you can judge if one country uses a greater percent on, say, health care than some other country, and once again make a judgement as to how much value is placed on health care versus other items.

Table 10.3 includes information on the infant mortality rate in 1993 for the same set of countries as in Table 10 2^2. The table also reports health care expenditures for each person as well as the percent of the Gross Domestic Product (GDP) spent on health care. In addition these items are ranked according to which country spends the most (1) to the least (15) and which has the highest (15) to lowest (1) infant mortality rate.

The country with the lowest infant mortality rate is ranked a 1 (the best) while the country with the highest is ranked a 15 (the most unfavorable). With regard to the two categories of spending, per capita spent on health care and the percent of the Gross Domestic Product spent on health care, a rank of a 1 is the country spending the most and a rank of 15 is the country spending the least.

Looking at the infant mortality rates of 1993, the country with the fewest infants dying within their first year of life is Japan (4.35 babies per 1000 births). The country with the most newborns dying of these fifteen countries is the United States (8.37), nearly twice the number as in Japan. If we look at how much is spent per person on health care, the United States is number one ($3465), spending the most, a third again more for each person in the United States than the country that is the next highest spender per capita, Switzerland ($2294). In addition, the United States spends a far greater percent of their Gross Domestic Product for health care (13.5%) compared to any of the other countries.

Table 10.3: Infant Mortality Rates and Rankings for Selected Countries,
Per Capita Health Care Spending and Percent of Gross Domestic Product for Health Care 1993

Country	Infant Mortality Rate	Infant Mortality Rank	Per Capita Health Spending	Rank Per Capita Spending	% GDP for Health	% GDP Rank
Japan	4.35	1	$1473	10	6.9	13.5
Finland	4.40	2	$1357	12	8.3	9.5
Sweden	4.84	3	$1348	13	7.9	11
Denmark	5.40	4	$1362	11	6.6	15
Switzerland	5.55	5	$2294	2	9.6	5
Germany	5.84	6	$1869	5	9.5	6
Australia	6.11	7	$1606	8	8.5	8
United Kingdom	6.24	8	$1211	14	6.9	13.5
Netherlands	6.27	9	$1614	7	8.8	7
Canada	6.30	10	$2010	3	9.8	2
Austria	6.49	11	$1965	4	9.7	3.5
France	6.82	12	$1866	6	9.7	3.5
Italy	7.16	13	$1561	9	8.3	9.5
Spain	7.19	14	$1005	15	7.3	12
United States	8.37	15	$3465	1	13.5	1

Sources: World Health Organization: *World Health Statistics Annuals*. Vols. 1990-1994. Geneva; United Nations: *Demographic Yearbook* 1994. Washington; National Center for Health Statistics. *Health, United States, 1996-1997 and Chartbook* 1997. The United Nations is the author of the original material

Is there evidence that spending affects infant mortality? The four countries with the lowest death rates among newborns are Japan, Finland, Sweden, and Denmark. They are also the countries spending among the least for health per person, ranking respectively 10,12,13, and 11 of the 15 countries. They are also among those spending less of their Gross Domestic Product on health. Spain is an interesting contrast to the United States in that Spain spends little per person on health care and a small percent of their Gross Domestic Product but has, like the United States, a high infant mortality rate. What common sense would suggest before looking at this table is if too little is spent on health care, mortality will be high, which is the situation in Spain. The data about the United States contradict this with high spending and high rates of infant death. For the most part, the data of this table fly in the face of what we might expect: an expectation the more a country spends on health care, the fewer the number of newborns will die. If you look back at life expectancy information in Table 10.2 and combine it with the information on health spending in the table above, once again the United States, the big spender, is the country with the fewest years of life expectancy of these 15 countries.

How can some of these contradictions be explained? What these tables can not tell us is whether the money being spent goes to support things that do not greatly affect mortality or longevity. For example, the monies may go to medical research or building construction or technology that do not necessarily have an immediate effect on infant mortality. Adequate monies may not be spent on public health programs to educate people how to take care of themselves when they are pregnant, or spent to provide pregnancy and nutrition clinics to protect expectant mothers or newborns. Programs such as these might be beneficial in decreasing infant death. Sufficient funds may not be spent to support medical schools to educate more obstetricians, family physicians, or pediatricians and offer pay to these kinds of physicians sufficient to make these specialties as attractive as others. Or it may be the attitude and willingness of some people to indulge in hazardous health behaviors putting themselves and their newborns at risk. If this last is true, any efforts of the health care system to protect such individuals is wasted. Perhaps we are back to the dilemma of who should be responsible for health, government or individuals? Should government continue to spend dollars on health care if individual citizens do not participate in protecting their own health? In any event, more knowledge of how the health care system in the United States is structured may help in understanding health status in this country.

HEALTH CARE SYSTEMS

HEALTH CARE IN AN EARLIER TIME

During Colonial times there were a few physicians, trained primarily in England, who came to this country. Anyone, if he were male, wishing to be a physician could seek an apprenticeship to these few men. How long a time and what these apprentices learned was different depending on the skills, interests, and patience of the physician with whom they worked. It was common for anyone to call themselves a physician if they had an interest in medicine and the ability to convince others of their power to heal. Most often these were people educated in some other field, like the ministry or law. Some medical care was provided by women, usually in the role of midwives or, since many were shopkeepers, in mixing remedies they believed helpful as cures for the illnesses they diagnosed for their customers (Starr 1982). Would you be willing to turn for your health care to people with little or no training in medicine or take advice from people lacking in scientific training as was the situation in this earlier time? Or do you think it best if health care is delivered only by persons who have the training and a license for this job? To understand these questions it is helpful to know how education for health care developed in this country.

It was not until 1775 that the first medical school was established at what is now the University of Pennsylvania, then the College of Philadelphia. This school, like the others founded shortly after that time, excluded women. It was in the 1840s the first women could receive medical training, this at the New England Medical College in Boston, the first medical school exclusively for women in the world (Walsh 1978). While several of the early medical schools followed the teaching methods and curriculum used in the reputable schools of Europe, many of those founded in the United States in the early 1800s were of limited value to the development of rigorous medical training. Rather schools sprang up because they were profitable. The only requirement to enter was the ability to pay the fees. Licenses, distributed often with less than a year's training, were more often meaningless certification because the schools had no well-defined course of study or tests to confirm that what was taught and what was learned covered topics agreed to be necessary to the field of medicine. It was not until the early 1900s that a concerted effort by the American Medical Association, the medical society founded in 1846 to represent the most qualified physicians of that time, pointed out the hazards of having schools for profit. Their argument was that the focus of these schools was on making money not on educating. The American Medical Association successfully supported the closing of these medical schools. The 126 medical schools existing today were accredited before they were granted permission to educate for a degree in medicine. They are based in universities, are nonprofit, and all require the same basic curriculum and testing for competency and licensing.

Were these requirements and protections needed earlier and still needed today? Some people would say that it is not so much medical practices and who provides care that is so important to good health but rather improvements in the nonmedical factors noted earlier, such as sanitation and public health. Yet a look at life expectancy and infant mortality even as late as the beginning of this century indicates what a hazardous health period this was and suggests the importance to longevity of medical procedures and scientific knowledge. For example, men born in 1900 could expect to live to only 46.3 years of age while women to the age of 48.3. In that same year, the infant mortality rate per 1000 children born in the United States was nearly 80 infant deaths for white infants and more than 130 for non-whites (U.S. Bureau of the Census 1975). Comparing this to the information of Tables 10.2 and 10.3 it is easy to see how improved our health is today. Yet many who look at this earlier time period do not focus on the early deaths and short life span but consider that health care was delivered by people who cared, people you could trust, people you could pay with food from your farm or gardens, or often not pay at all if you could not afford to do so (Thomas 1983). An important question is whether we would, in fact, trade the health care system of that time for what we have today.

HEALTH CARE TODAY

Anytime present day health care in the United States is discussed it is not unusual to hear that health care is too expensive, too hard to find, too unequal in its distribution, and too often provided by people who do not really care about you. Harry Ludwig, for example, faults doctors who he believes care more about money and their own conveniences than about their patients. Many people complain they cannot understand how the system works or what it can do for them. This is understandable because the delivery of health care is much more complicated than it was even 50 years ago. Further, the delivery of health care continues to change rapidly. To understand what is happening it is useful to look at the changes that have occurred as to who delivers care and how it is financed.

Today if you were to become ill enough to seek medical care, it would be provided, at least for most people, by a physician whose license is that of M.D. a medical doctor, or possibly an O.D., an osteopathic doctor. These are the two groups of physicians accepted today as members of **traditional medicine** in the United States. Others delivering health care are considered a part of an **alternative medical system**. As noted earlier in this chapter, medical schools in this country are now required to follow strict standards in educating physicians, and in the process there is a particular accepted way to define what makes someone ill and how they can be cured. The inclusion today of osteopathic physicians as part of accepted mainstream medicine is an example of how those with an alternative belief about causes of illness become absorbed into the nearly closed profession of medicine. **Osteopathy** was based originally on the belief illness was caused by dislocation of bones in the spinal column with the cure manipulation of the spine and other muscular and skeletal structures of the body. To the traditional physician this was no more than quackery. But today, osteopathic doctors practice in the same fields as medical doctors and are accepted by the AMA as a specialty area of training. Interestingly the history of this change indicates that it was not due to traditional medical doctors accepting the ideas of osteopathy. Rather, that practitioners of osteopathy are educated and trained more and more like medical doctors even though they still give some credence to the importance of the muscular-skeletal system for good health. It was not until doctors of osteopathy brought their beliefs more in line with the traditional medical education that they were accepted. This tells us how difficult it is in this country to find acceptance for alternative types of medical treatment.

Among those licensed as M.D. or O.D. there are a vast variety of specialties. Some are primary care doctors who specialize in family practice, general medicine, or internal medicine. Sometimes pediatricians or obstetrics/gynecologists are included in this group. **Primary care physicians** are usually considered the logical persons to go to first when entering the health care system. There are over 100 other specialty areas intended to prepare physicians to care for more acute and complex medical problems. Doctors with training in surgery, orthopedics, cardiology, infectious diseases, or genetic counseling are just a few of these specialty-area physicians. Primary physicians would ordinarily refer patients to these specialists when a health problem requires the specialist's advice about a single disease, like leukemia, AIDS, heart disease, or when high-technology diagnostic tests or therapeutic interventions, such as by-pass surgery or radiation therapy, are required. Originally medical schools in this country trained most physicians to be primary caregivers. Today this is not true. As recently as 1980, nearly 40% of medical school graduates planned to have primary care practices; this decreased to 15% in early 1990s. This is in contrast to other industrialized countries where nearer to 60% of physicians are in primary care practice.

Does this shortage of primary doctors matter? It does when patients must go to specialists for problems that are not acute. Not only is specialty care more expensive but often specialists are not interested in the general health of the patient, thus overlooking health problems not in their particular area of expertise. For example, if Harry Lugwig goes to a endocrinologist, a physician trained in care of diabetes, and has no family doctor, problems such as the flu, sinus infections, heart abnormalities, or simple aches and pains probably are not cared for by this physician. Without a primary care physician, Harry will have to see other specialists at a greater cost. Perhaps more important than cost is the fact that no one physician has Harry's complete medical record, or follows his health "career".

Why are there not more primary care doctors if their care would be useful for the ordinary health problems most patients bring to the doctor? A number of reasons are proposed. One is that faculty in medical schools do not encourage students to select primary care, which they believe is of less value. Moreover, students' experiences in medical school do not expose them to primary care since most patients they care for during training are in a hospital setting, quite ill with acute problems. Most medical students see very few of the minor, every-day illnesses more common today. In addition, many primary care doctors complain that referrals of patients to specialists result often in the patient not returning to them since one specialist refers the patient to other specialists. In any event, doctors in practice or teachers in medical schools know being a specialist provides more prestige, less frantic work schedules, more opportunities to work in prestigious hospitals with an abundance of high technology, colleagues to support them, and better incomes.

How real is the income difference? In 1994, all specialties averaged together earned 64% more income than did primary care doctors (see The American Medical Association 1994, and Simon and Burn 1996). Most people given these facts would not choose primary care if income were a critical factor in the choice no matter how much primary care doctors are needed. Fortunately there are physicians who enjoy taking total care of patients, and often their families, with their diverse health problems. But there are obviously too few of these practitioners available today in the United States.

It is possible that in some geographical areas where there is a scarcity of all kinds of physicians, like inner cities or rural areas, medical care might be provided by nonphysicians or **mid-level practitioners** such as a nurse practitioner, nurse clinician, or a physician assistant. These are people who do some of the tasks ordinarily performed by primary care physicians and have received some advanced or special technical training. Many physicians have tried to limit medical care by these mid-level practitioners arguing that they do not have sufficient training to take care of patients independently. The number of these health care workers is increasing, in part because of physician shortages in some areas, but also because these mid-level practitioners charge less than most doctors, a situation appealing not only to patients but to others, such as insurers who pay for health care. An important question to be raised is whether the training physicians have really is better than that of these other mid-level practitioners. If licensed physician care is better, then are patients who must use alternative caregivers receiving less than the best quality of care because physicians are not available to them or their health care plans will not pay for physician care? Research has focused on how satisfied patients are with care by nonphysicians, and most patients are satisfied. Differences in quality of care are less studied, so research to date does not answer clearly the question of quality. Research is needed to answer whether the care between physicians and alternative practitioners is really a difference in quality or only a bias not to trust anyone but a medical doctor.

The use of alternative ways of obtaining health care is not new. Remember the clergy, shopkeepers, medicine men, and the like used in the early days when our country was settled. Today alternative caregivers are more sophisticated and knowledgeable but are considered by many as outside the mainstream of medicine. Nurses or physician assistants are not the only groups fighting to be accepted as legitimate. Acupuncturists, chiropractors, faith healers, and other practitioners who have an entirely different explanation for the causes of illness and its cure, are often considered to offer care not useful or even dangerous to patients particularly if this keeps them from making use of traditional care.

Our society appears to be more accepting of some changes in health care. What appears more difficult is agreement by whom as well as how and where health care should be delivered. If you become ill you would most likely see a health care provider either at the physician's office or hospital. In some cases you might see a physician at an emergency center, a name for the "doc in a box" operations scattered about neighborhoods where you can go for care for emergencies such as a minor sports injury or a sore throat and fever. You might see your doctor at an ambulatory surgical center for minor, low risk outpatient surgical procedures. While home health care is more usual today, it is rarely the physician who comes to your home. Families continue to be the major caregivers when a person needs care at home. But that care today is quite different than it was at an earlier time. First of all, many people find they are taking care of elderly parents or other family members for a long period of time. They know they cannot afford the high cost of long-term care or professional help but nonetheless desire to protect and shelter their loved ones.

Families are performing an unprecedented level of medical care in their homes. This is sometimes because it is often less costly to do so at home, or that insurers will not pay for long or more frequent hospital stays. Medical techniques have become so advanced they can be handled by lay people with little training. It is not unusual to find families who give intravenous feedings or chemotherapy at home, or those who operate dialysis machines there as well. There is, of course, a downside to this. Such care is well beyond simply giving comfort, and often results in caregiver exhaustion that is physical, emotional and financial as well. The question is, should this be expected of families as a part of their duty to family? Or should our health care system find other means to meet a growing need within our population? This again returns to the question of who should take responsibility for health care.

Another difficulty with home care today is that relocating in order to have work has ended a time when most members of a family lived in the same community. This means family care is not always or easily available. Communities now must develop health care providers to substitute for family care. Once again, if these agencies or providers do not exist to offer home care or if the cost of this care is high, many ill people face inequality in their access to health care.

Despite some of these problems, it is doubtful that many would forego the advances in medical care. As Donna pointed out the medical developments made within the last fifty years are amazing. Technology and medical know-how has permitted physicians to repair or even replace the human heart and other organs. It is commonplace to keep alive babies so immature that they are smaller than an adult hand. It is possible to immunize people against most dreaded diseases, to use drugs and other therapies to cure people of illnesses they could never have survived even 20 years ago. Contrary to an earlier time, the changes that have occurred in medicine have increased the likelihood for survival.

One of the changes, as Harry Ludwig found, is that care is not always easy to find. His health problems are exacerbated by the closing of an inner city hospital. These closings happen in rural areas as well. This requires people to travel long distances, often creating a situation where patients in need but with no readily available means to get to more distant hospitals must forego treatment until they are quite ill. When hospitals were first built in the 1700s through the 1800s most were built to provide care for people without family or the means to pay for care. The staff of hospitals were primarily volunteer and their responsibilities were to keep patients comfortable and ease their dying. Well-to-do patients could afford doctors and nurses in their home and had families or paid staff to care for them.

Gradually the purpose of hospitals changed. As medicine became more scientific, very technical surgical procedures were heavily used to cure many diseases. Hospitals, where these surgical procedures and after care could occur, grew both in number and prestige. Curing of patients rather than helping in their dying became the focus of hospitals. Skilled nursing was needed as well as technicians to help physicians with diagnoses and surgeons in their work.

By the 1900s federal, state, local governments, and private funds supported the growth of hospitals, as they became the centers for all health care. By the middle of the 1900s, there were about 6500 hospitals with about one and a half million hospital beds available to care for the rich and the poor. But more recently medical procedures and care have once again changed hospital use. Use has declined as low risk surgeries or non-invasive procedures requiring minimal after care are performed often as outpatient procedures (heart catheterizations, cataract, or hernia surgery, for example). Costs to operate hospitals increase as equipment, technical staff, and professionals are needed for more difficult and involved procedures such as transplanting of organs, various therapies for cancer, or preservation of life for premature babies or for the aged person. At a time when hospitals are performing many new and sophisticated functions, many are closing. The number of hospitals and hospital beds has not changed dramatically from early 1900s to now with 6,374 hospitals and 1,228,000 beds in 1994 even though the population has grown. What has changed is their accessibility. New hospitals are not, for the most part, built in rural, low population areas or areas where poorer people live. Further, many hospitals today employ more physicians than ever before. This has meant doctors close their private practices to work where the hospitals are, further reducing their availability most often to those who can least manage to follow them.

Often the closing of hospitals happens because they are old and out-of-date facilities. But just as often this happens because of developments in how illnesses are treated and paid for. For example, advances in knowledge and new technical equipment capable of diagnosing illnesses or saving and extending lives now cost so much that no individual doctor could afford them; rather hospitals become the source for this technology. Hospital expenses have gone up so fast insurers will pay less for care in a hospital setting, forcing doctors to send patients home sooner than in the past and patients to find other means to care for themselves at home. As more hospitals are run by for-profit groups the organization and management of hospitals has changed. Only about half of hospitals today are **nonprofit hospitals**. Nonprofit means any surplus monies existing at the end of the year's operation is reinvested back in the hospital. In contrast, proprietary or **for profit hospitals** use surplus monies to pay dividends or bonuses to investors. In addition to these categories of hospitals, there are **government hospitals**. Federal ones are primarily for veterans and their families; state funded hospitals mostly care for the mentally ill, while locally funded ones are those that serve predominately the poor, charity cases, those without any means to pay for medical care. Today many hospitals have become more like other business operations. They are bought up by hospital chains and these chains are merging into a few strong for-profit organizations worth billions of dollars. It is clear that medical care delivered to make a profit has an entirely different purpose than care given primarily to provide ease and comfort to the dying or to give the best quality of care no matter the length of time involved in this care or the cost. Why is cost now an issue?

The health care system in the United States follows the economic pattern of other sectors of this country: it is highly decentralized with limited central planning, and a multitude of different programs to provide health services. Profit is an important motive for the providers of health care, but also the institutions, insurers, and those who develop and produce the technical materials needed. This fosters many groups with different interests, such as doctors, drug companies, hospitals, insurance companies, all competing in a free-market endeavor. This has led to a complex and expensive health care system. Recently there has been pressure to change the way this system operates as its costs increase dramatically.

Most plans call for some variation of health systems such as exist in every other industrialized country of the world except the United States and South Africa; some form of a national health care system where everyone is insured by a third party such as the government or possibly a union. A distinguishing mark for the different systems is the degree of centering control within the government. The least extreme form of control is similar to the Canadian system where all citizens are insured but with minimal centralization as each province has significant authority to regulate providers and health institutions. At the next level of control is a health system like that in Sweden where most health facilities are owned by the state, which also sets wages and pays workers out of state monies assuring all citizens of some level of health care. The most extreme is a system that employs all health care workers, pays them, and owns and manages all health institutions, once again insuring health care for all. Russia is an example of this system. The United States has never accepted a national health plan partially because there is fear that changing the system with more government and central control may mean less adequate care and partially because those who compete in the system fear it will take control from them giving it to the government. But the U.S. is not a totally private system.

For every dollar spent on health care, 47 cents comes from public monies and 70% of this 47 cents is from Medicare and Medicaid programs. Medicare is nationwide health insurance protection for people 65 years of age and over or those receiving social security disability payments, and people with end-stage kidney disease. It does not matter how rich or poor you are, you are eligible for this public funding. The program began in July, 1966, funded through the Social Security Act. When a person qualifies for Medicare, hospital insurance coverage is automatically provided. Supplemental medical insurance to cover certain other health care services, like doctor visits or medical examinations but not drugs, is another part of Medicare coverage if an individual opts to pay a very reasonable premium for this coverage. The funding for Medicare is raised primarily from a tax on what people earn.

Medicaid is another government health program put in place in 1967. It is jointly funded by the federal government and the states. Each state is responsible for administering this program. It provides medical benefits for certain low-income persons in need of medical care as well as some elderly residents of nursing homes. Every state is required to provide health benefits, but it is left to each state to determine which benefits will be covered, the rates of payment to providers, and who is eligible. For this reason, Medicaid programs vary greatly from state to state as to who is covered and what is covered.

For every health care dollar spent, the largest part is for hospital care, 35 cents of each dollar or 35% of all money spent on health care. The next largest amount (26%) is spent on other personal care which covers dental, other professional services, home health care, drugs and other non-durable goods, vision products, and other miscellaneous health services. Nineteen cents of every health care dollar pays for physician services, while 8 cents is for nursing home care. Other spending of 12 cents is for the administering of programs, government public health, and research and construction. (Health Care Financing Administration 1997).

The Health Care Finance Administration (1997) indicates that there has been an enormous increase in what it costs to pay for health care in the United States. In 1960, the total cost was $26,800,000,000. By 1996, this amount increased to nearly 40 times the 1960 figure. For the first time the nation's spending for health care broke the one trillion dollar mark, an average spending of $3, 759 for each of the 275 million people living in the U.S. Compare this to the $141 per person spent just 36 years before in 1960. Most see the increase as the result of the cost of Medicare and Medicaid. Both Medicare and Medicaid have grown 126% since 1970. Today these two public programs use more than one-third of the nation's total health care money and they are responsible for almost three-quarters of all public spending on health care. In 1996, 36.1 million people received care through Medicaid and 38.1 million through Medicare.

There are changes in who pays for health care. In 1960, 75% of the total monies available for health care came from the private sector. The proportion of private funding has decreased radically over the years to 53% in 1996. In any event, there is no question health care, both private and public, is costly in the United States. Its increasing cost means other areas in need of funding such as education, environment, or defense may not receive the share of dollars needed. The dilemma is the dollars for health care, while producing a high quality, sophisticated health care system, have not afforded longer lives or fewer infant deaths as exists in other industrialized countries. Nor has the system afforded the same quality of care everywhere in the United States for all of its citizens.

As in the earlier part of this century there is a two-tiered system of health care. Today those who can afford excellent insurance coverage are a tier or class of people who have access to more and possibly better quality of care then those without, who comprise a second tier. The U.S. Census Bureau reports (U.S. Census Bureau 1997) the number of persons in the U.S. without any insurance continues to increase: in 1996, 15.6% of the total population, or nearly 42 million persons were not covered by health insurance. Of these not covered, 10.6 million, or 14.8%, were children under the age of 18 years. About 29% of those 18 to 24 years of age were not covered either. More than half of the uninsured are a part of families with a full-time worker and another 30% are in families with a part-time worker. Eighteen million of these uninsured people worked full time and another 5 million held part-time jobs. That many of these without insurance are working persons is counter to the stereotype that the uninsured are the unemployed. Not surprisingly, those without coverage who worked during 1996 were employed in smaller firms, many of which did not have health benefits for employees. In addition to the numbers without any insurance coverage, there are millions more who are underinsured, people with insurance policies that do not cover important health services or require hefty out-of-pocket payments. A recent estimate (Short and Banthin 1995) suggests between 70 and 75 million Americans were inadequately insured in 1994. Certainly the size of these two groups, the uninsured and underinsured, explain in part why cost for health care is high. Since these are people with little choice but to use emergency rooms for care or are those who receive care from doctors, hospitals, and other health service agencies for which they cannot pay fully, the cost of their care has to be covered by others, whether it is doctors or hospitals absorbing this into their cost of doing business, or everyone paying more to help cover these uncompensated costs.

THE FUTURE

While we have not yet reached a golden age when disease no longer exists, the advances made in medical knowledge as well as the development of extraordinary medical techniques and equipment have moved us far from an earlier time. What is apparent is the need to share the benefits of this knowledge and technology with more people not only within the United States but also around the world. At the same time, it is equally important to recognize there is much to be learned from other countries and peoples whose understanding of health and illness may be different but of value in solving some of the most difficult medical questions. A fascination with new health technology and the sophisticated procedures that are a part of medical care in the United States can blind many to alternative ways to look at illness and its cure and curers. Recognizing what others have done might help this nation find ways to distribute medical care and health services more equitably.

This chapter stresses the importance of recognizing that no matter how good a nation's health care system is there is a need for the citizens of that nation to realize the importance of taking individual responsibility for health care. It is probably only when we make the effort to understand both our own bodies and what keeps us healthy that we can understand in what ways we can have a healthier nation. This chapter emphasizes the importance of understanding there is an important connection between our personal health and the world in which we live and work. By knowing this, it is possible to consider how changes in nutrition, water pollution, work stress, sanitation, or risky health behaviors could create an even healthier nation than the effort to find further costly medical technologies How to resolve the cost of health care and keep improving health remains unresolved. This chapter can only bring to your attention some of the issues to be understood in hopes that further study will help you to make wise and beneficial choices about health care in the future.

SUMMARY

1. Many of the same diseases or medical difficulties that we encounter today existed hundreds of thousands of years ago.

2. In 1900 the top three leading causes of death in the United States were infectious diseases including influenza and pneumonia, tuberculosis, and gastroenteritis. By 1992 these diseases were replaced by chronic diseases such as heart disease and cancer as well as stroke, lung disease, suicide, and homicide.

3. If appropriate measures are taken, many of the major causes of death in the 1990s are considered preventable or less likely to lead to death..

4. We frequently associate inferior health conditions with underdeveloped nations, but in our own *developed* country, decisions, or choices are regularly made that keep many from enjoying the best of health.

5. Epidemiology accepts not only that certain germs thrive best under certain environmental conditions to cause serious illnesses but that certain characteristics of people (social class and life style behaviors) do as well.

6. In the United States, it is known that differences in gender and race as well as where you live, the work you do, the kind of health care you have available, influence life expectancy..

7. Changes in behavior and values can be used to improve a society's health.

8. Most research finds that there are significant considerations that can influence infant mortality rates such as economic status, particularly as measured by poverty rates.

9. Health care is less accessible and readily available to the less advantaged in America.

10. Since countries spending the most on health care do not necessarily have the lowest infant mortality, does money spent on health care go for things that greatly affect mortality and longevity? The answer may be that it does not.

11. During colonial times, it was common for anyone to call themselves a physician if they had an interest in medicine and the ability to convince others of their power to heal.

12. It was not until the early 1900s that a concerted effort by the American Medical Association resulted in accredited medical schools based in universities which are nonprofit and require the same basic curriculum and testing for competency and licensing.

13. Certainly today death rates have come down and life expectancy increased. Yet many who presently look at health care in America focus on health care that was delivered by people in an earlier time who were concerned about you, people you could trust, that you could pay with food from your garden or farm, or often not pay at all if you could not afford to do so.

14. The delivery of health care today is complicated and rapidly changing.

15. It is difficult to find acceptance for alternative types of medical care.

16. In the early 1990s, less than 30% of American physicians were primary care physicians compared to 60% in other industrial countries. Not only are specialists more expensive but they are generally not interested in the general health of the patient.

17. Being a specialist provides more prestige, less frantic work schedules, more opportunities to work in prestigious hospitals with an abundance of technology, supportive colleagues, and better incomes.

18. In some geographical areas where there is a scarcity of all kinds of physicians, like inner cities or rural areas, medical care might be provided by nonphysicians or mid-level practitioners such as nurse practitioners, nurse clinicians, or physician assistants.

19. Our society appears more accepting of some changes in health care. What appears more difficult is agreement as to by whom as well as how and where health care should be delivered.

20. While families continue to be the major caregivers when a person needs care at home, the care is quite different than earlier times.

21. Medical techniques have become so advanced they can be handled by lay people with little training (home dialysis, intravenous feeding, etc.)

22. Sometimes home health care leads to caregiver exhaustion. Other times, it interferes with work demands when family members do not live in the same community.

23. Few people would forego the advances in medical care.

24. Care is not always easy to find. Some hospital close due to facilities being old and out-of-date but it also happens because of developments in how illnesses are treated and paid for.

25. Care delivered to make a profit has an entirely different purpose than care given to provide ease and comfort to the dying or to give the best quality care no matter length of time involved in this care or the cost, as was somewhat possible in earlier decades.
26. The health care system in the United States follows the economic pattern of other sectors in this country; it is highly decentralized with limited central planning, and a multitude of different programs to provide health services. Profit has been an important motivator for physicians, hospitals, insurers, and the developers of technology.
27. Recently there has been pressure to change to some form of national health care system where everyone is insured by a third party such as the government. This system exists in all other industrialized countries except the United States and South Africa.
28. A distinguishing mark for the different health care systems is the degree of centering control within the government. For example, the Russian government employs all health care workers and owns and manages all health care institutions.
29. The United States spent over one trillion dollars on health care in 1996 which is $3,759 for each person.
30. Increasingly the health care bill is being paid for by public dollars. The dilemma is that while producing a high quality, sophisticated health system, the dollar expenditure has not afforded longer and/or fewer infant deaths as exists in other industrialized countries.
31. There is a two-tiered system of health care-those who have excellent insurance and those who do not.
32. A part of the cost of those without insurance and underinsured is absorbed into the cost of health care providers doing business so that everyone pays more to help cover these uncompensated costs.
33. When considering how important and valuable health is to a nation, it is important to decide how much individuals should take responsibility for their health and how much responsibility they wish to give to their government.

ENDNOTES

[1] Excellent current statistical data about health comes from the U.S. Department of Health and Human Services, Public Health Services, The Centers for Disease Control, and The National Center for Health Statistics. Most information is published several times a year. Publications from The World Health Organization and The Organization for Economic Cooperation and Development are two excellent resources for international data.

[2] While information on life expectancy for Russia and China was not available for Table10.2; some data was available on infant mortality and percent of gross national product spent as well as population for these two countries. China, with a population of 1243 million people, spends 4.5% of their gross national product for health care. Their infant mortality rate is 27 infants per 1000 born. Russia, with a population of 147 million, spends 3.0% of their gross national product on health care, and has an infant mortality rate of 36 babies per 1000 born.

[3] Today men of science find value in many of the remedies scoffed at earlier. Pharmaceutical companies and others try to preserve areas of the world where herbs and other plants yield powerful new drugs. The advice of medicine men is sought for their knowledge of medical care. A book that highlights the importance of early cures and curers is "Honey, Mud, Maggots, and Other Medical Marvels" by Robert and Michele Root-Bernstein.

REFERENCES

Ackerknecht, Erwin H. 1982. *A Short History of Medicine* (Revised edition). Baltimore and London: The Johns Hopkins University Press.

American Medical Association (AMA) 1995. *Physician Market Place Statistics* (ed. M. Gonzales). Chicago: American Medical Association.

Duke, Kathryn S. 1996. "Hospitals in a Changing Health Care System." *Health Affairs.* 15(2).

Haug, Marie R. 1976. "The Erosion of Professional Authority: A Cross-Cultural Inquiry in the Case of the Physician." *Millbank Memorial Fund Quarterly/Health and Society.* Winter: 83-106. Cambridge, MA and Oxford, U.K.

Kramer, Larry 1992. "We Have Lost the War Against AIDS." *USA Today.* May, p. 72.

Lee, Jason S. 1996. "Adult Immunization Priorities in the United States." *The Millbank Memorial Fund Quarterly.* 74(2): 284-307.

McKinlay, John B., and Sonja McKinlay 1977. "The Questionable Effect of Medical Measures on the Decline of Mortality in the Twentieth Century." *Millbank Memorial Fund Quarterly.* Vol. 55, Pp.422-423.

Major, R. H, ed. 1945. *Classic Descriptions of Disease.* Springfield, Illinois.

Meier, Barry 1997. "States and Cities Impose New Laws on Young Smokers." *New York Times.* December 7, Section 1, p. 1.

National Center for Health Statistics 1997. "Health United States, 1997." United States Department of Health and Human Services. Maryland: Hyattsville.

National Center for Health Statistics 1997. "Health, United States, 1996-1997 and Injury Chartbook" Maryland: Hyattsville.

Newsweek 1998. "The WHO Has Seen the Future, and It's Full of Good Health." June 1,1998, p. 10.

Root-Bernstein, Robert S. and Michele Root-Bernstein 1997. *Money, Mud Maggots, and other Medical Marvels.* Boston and New York: Houghton-Mifflin.

Short, P.F., and J.S. Banthin 1995. "New Estimates of the Underinsured Younger Than 65 Years." *Journal of the American Medical Association.* 274:1302-6. Chicago, Illinois.

Sigerist, Harry B. 1951. *A History of Medicine.* New York.

_____.1960. *On the History of Medicine.* New York.

Simon, Carol J., and Patricia H. Born 1996. "Physician Earnings in a Changing Managed Care Environment." *Health Affairs.* 15(3).

Starr, Paul 1982. *The Social Transformation of American Medicine.* New York: Basic Books.

Thomas, Lewis 1983. *The Youngest Science: Notes of a Medicine- Watcher.* New York: The Viking Press.

U.S. Bureau of the Census 1975. *Historical Statistics of the United States, Colonial Times to 1970.* (Bicentennial Edition, Part 2). Washington, D.C.

_____.1997. March 1997: *Current Population Survey.* Washington, D.C.

Walsh, Mary R. 1978. *Doctors Wanted: No Women Need Apply.* New Haven, Connecticut: Yale University Press.

CHAPTER 11: ECONOMY AND WORK
CASE STUDY: MCDONALD'S INFLUENCE
ON ECONOMY AND WORK

It's likely that almost all members of your social problems class have eaten at McDonald's. You probably enjoyed at least one "fun meal" when you were a kid, and if you've been recently; you may have enjoyed a Big Mac with fries and a chocolate shake. If you were of a mind to eat in a more nutritionally sound manner, you might have ordered a McGrilled Chicken Classic (plain) for only one seventh the amount of fat in a Big Mac. Maybe you kicked back and chatted with friends, or watched kids play on the slide. In any case it's unlikely you were thinking of the significance of the establishment. However, according to a leading U.S. sociologist of work, George Ritzer, "McDonald's is one of the most influential developments in twentieth-century America." (p. 1) His book, *The McDonaldization of Society* (1996) is only one of a number of scholarly volumes--not to mention journal articles and accounts in the mass media--to consider the import of fast food (see, for example, Leidner 1993; Reiter 1991; Emerson 1990; Love 1986). Here is some background on the company known by its golden arches and some experts' comments on why McDonald's is significant beyond its own operations.

In 1937 brothers Richard and Maurice McDonald opened a small hot dog stand with a dozen stools and carhop service near Pasadena, California. Three years later they added a larger restaurant--featuring pork sandwiches and ribs-- with the stainless steel fixtures and open kitchen that became hallmarks of the company. In 1948 they revamped their operation with changes that proved crucial in the creation of a massive corporation: they developed a speedy self-service operation based on a restricted menu featuring cheap hamburgers and began a shift from the teen to the family market. Burgers cost 15 cents, fries 12 cents a bag, and shakes 20 cents, and prices were not raised for nearly 20 years (Emerson 1990).

It was Ray Kroc, a milkshake machine salesman for Multimixer of Chicago, who masterminded the refinement of the concepts and expansion of the business. In 1954 he captured the right to franchise the drive-in system nationally and with partner Harry Sonneborn began to acquire sites of new McDonald's stores and in 1955 to lease them to franchisees. Over the next decades Kroc and colleagues introduced new product lines, including the Big Mac in 1968, and various architectural changes, such as indoor seating and the familiar mansard roof decor in 1968, drive-through windows in the 1980s (following Wendy's lead), playgrounds, and, more recently, "upscale" two-story restaurants and small satellite eateries located within department stores, schools, and even hospitals. Consistently maintained, however, have been certain core corporate goals: "Q.S.C.&V" which stand for quality, service, cleanliness, and value for money.

As noted above, sociologist Ritzer (1996) has analyzed McDonald's because of its reverberations not only for the fast-food business but for American society and, indeed, the world, as well. He views the growth of this company as a paradigm of a far-reaching process he calls McDonaldization:

"the process by which the principles of the fast-food restaurant are coming to dominate more and more sectors of American society as well as of the rest of the world." (p. 1) It has been a model for numerous other fast food and restaurant franchise operations as well as similar ventures in entirely other industries, for example, the Body Shop selling ecologically sensitive cosmetics or The Limited marketing clothing. 10% of America's stores are franchises, and they account for 40% of our retail sales p 3). Ritzer suggests that the McDonald's model has proven irresistible because of four dimensions: 1) efficiency, or the optimum method for getting a job done; 2) calculability, the emphasis on the quantitative aspects of the products sold (size and cost) and service offered (the time it takes to get the product); 3) predictability, the assurance that the product and service will be the same over time in all locations; and 4) control, especially through the substitution of predictable nonhuman for human technology.

Ritzer and others have noted some positive outcomes of McDonaldization: for example, a larger proportion of people have a wider range of goods and services available, we get what we need quickly, conveniently, and in predictable quality, affordable products are available for people who cannot afford customized versions, and as consumers we (usually) are welcomed whatever our race, gender, social class, or nationality. The McDonald's corporation pays 100% of the general and administrative costs for the Ronald McDonald House Charities which support 180 Ronald McDonald Houses in 14 countries, residences that since 1974 have housed over 2 million family members whose children are in treatment at nearby hospitals. Over 18,000 volunteers have donated more than a million hours a year in meal preparation and other services to these families. The Charities has also awarded over $150 million in grants to other organizations that serve children (http://www.rmhc.com/index.html)

On the other hand, the very rationality of the McDonaldization model-with its emphasis on efficiency and control--results in irrationalities, such as adverse effects on the environment from efforts to feed cattle for beef and to grow the perfect potato for fries, a dehumanizing setting for workers and diners, the eclipsing of the richness of local cultures with globalization, and other adverse outcomes of extremes of competition. These and other issues can be seen virtually every day in media accounts such as the following, all of which appeared in the press during the writing of this chapter:

**Beleaguered McDonald's franchisees, looking to reinforce the chain's core service imperative, are undertaking a team-oriented motivational program at the grass-roots level to knock waiting time for drive-through customers down by half a minute or more. Rewarding the unit with the highest number of consecutive orders ready when a customer pulls up to a pick-up window, the initiative has spread from a Norfolk, Va., regional manager's plan throughout the mid-Atlantic coast and is expanding. A rural Pennsylvania restaurant broke the national record, which had been 4,000 consecutive orders, meeting that high-speed goal 8,044 times over 10 straight days. During the contest the average car waited 62 seconds to get a meal. The company rewarded the Pennsylvania restaurant with a trophy and $1000 and the franchisee gave each crew member who worked during the 10-day stretch a cash bonus based on the number of hours put in to win." (Stevens 1997)

**"Even as McDonald's wages war on its competitors by lowering the prices its customers pay for hamburgers, the global chain is battling to keep the price of its own labor affordable at a restaurant in this Montreal suburb. More than 90% of the employees of the McDonald's restaurant here have agreed to join the local International Brotherhood of Teamsters affiliate. [but] ......'McDonald's is fighting it to the end,' said Henri Van Meerbeeck, a Teamsters organizer leading the effort to have the McDonald's workers certified as union members. The McDonald's workers currently earn an average of C$6.90 per hour, or about U.S.$5, according to sources close to the case. The minimum wage in Quebec is C$6.70. The restaurant would be the only unionized McDonald's in North America. While situations such as [McDonald's are] largely unheard of south of the U.S.-Canada border, Canadian restaurateurs from coast to coast have grown accustomed to the unionization of their employees. Unlike their counterparts in the United States, however, Canada's workers all have medical insurance provided by the government and funded through taxes. Canadian fast-food workers usually seek union representation to obtain higher starting wages, seniority-based promotion and scheduling, and formalized grievance procedures, the union representative said (Hamstra 1997).

**"McDonald's Corp. said Friday that it is ready to launch what it called an unprecedented promotion that will slash the price of some of its most popular sandwiches to 55 cents and include a major new advertising campaign. The fast-food giant said its franchisees approved a national value-meal program that includes lowering the cost of some of its sandwiches to 55 cents when purchased with a soft drink and French fries. Jack Greenberg, chairman of McDonald's USA said, 'This initiative will be good for our customers, our franchisees and our business.' While the low-price promotion carries some risks, McDonald's and its franchisees need to do something to pull out of a year-and-a-half-long slump in sales growth" ("McDonald's Franchisees..." 1997).

**"Burger King, long the kid brother to mammoth McDonald's, is teaching its rival a lesson in marketing this month: When it comes to fast food, keep it simple. BK's new Big King, an enormous double cheeseburger launched Labor Day weekend as a rival to the Big Mac, has sold at nearly twice the rate the company expected. The secret to the American stomach, circa 1997? The Big King has 75% more beef than the Big Mac, an extra 12 grams of fat (yum!) and no soggy third bun in the center. Most important, it has cost just 99 cents. Such a simple strategy--more food for less money--contrasts with McDonald's weird pitch for the Arch Deluxe and its recent 55 cent promotion, a complicated scheme in which customers paid 55 cents for the Big Mac and certain other sandwiches, when accompanied by the purchase of any size beverage and fries except... .no, never mind." ("Mac Attack," 1997)

**"Story after story lately has reported on the fate of McDonald's Corp--and most have cataloged disaster. McDonald's marketing ploys--the Arch

Deluxe, the 55-cent burger--have been a laughfest. U.S. profits have slipped. Market-share numbers showed that archrival Burger King has gained on McDonald's last year...[Still,] McDonald's has: (1) 42% of the US burger market; Burger King, 19% happy hunting abroad, (2) (see selection below on McDonald's international expansion), (3) A lock on the hearts and tummies of American kids and exclusive rights to Disney promotions through 2006." (Solomon and McCormick, *Newsweek,* November 17,1997)

**With a 42% share of the U.S. fast-food burger market, McDonald's still easily outpaces its rivals. Nonetheless, the problems under the famous Golden Arches are far more serious than a failed Arch Deluxe here or a french-fry war there. Quite simply, McDonald's has lost some of its relevance to American culture. Since 1987, McDonald's share of fast food sales in the U.S. has slipped almost two percentage points, to 16.2%. The drop has come even as the company has increased its number of restaurants by 50%. Domestic sales have climbed only 18% since 1989, while operating profits haven't even kept pace with inflation. McDonald's is one of the nation's most insular large companies, with a management team more typical of a private company than a global powerhouse. Consumers who eat fast food at least once a month say that both Wendy's and Burger King offer better-tasting fare. Americans now spend more on prepared meals sold at delis, supermarkets, and causal dining restaurants such as Applebee's International Inc. than they do at burger chains....." (Leonhardt 1998).

**"McDonald's will soon undertake what could be McMission: Impossible. Hot food. Served faster. To order. Every time. What may be McDonald's best hope for its own fast-food salvation is hidden away in a research facility. McDonald's is frantically developing cutting-edge equipment to make better food. For the first time in decades, McDonald's is putting hotter, fresher food first. Not new products like the failed Arch Deluxe. Not new ingredients. But hot food served faster. With freshly toasted buns. Moist meat. And no pickles if you don't want them. Costs to develop, install, and market the new system could approach $500 million, analysts say. 'Made for you' will become the chain's market mantra within 18 months when all 12,000 McDonald's stores nationwide are expected to have installed the technology. The Lab's goal: to serve hot meals to all. a maximum of 3½ minutes from the time they walk in the door...... ." (Horovitz 1998)

**Too many people see McDonald's not as a global company, but as a U.S. corporation with some overseas operations,' says James Cantalupo, CEO of McDonald's International. The company is now building a stunning 85% of its new stores overseas. About half of McDonald's business already is done abroad. The 45% of McDonald's stores that are overseas yield 63% of the company's profits." McDonald's is present in 105 countries outside of the U.S. Of its total of 22,246 stores, 9,997 are overseas. In sales, $16.4 billion of its earnings were in the U.S. in the last year; $15.4 billion were in overseas operations. (Solomon and McCormick 1997)

WORK AS A SOCIAL PROBLEM

We will return to the case of McDonald's throughout this chapter, for it exemplifies some key issues surrounding work in contemporary society. Many aspects of work at McDonald's and elsewhere can be seen as social problems, yet it must be noted at the outset that the *absence* of work is a far greater problem for individuals and for society as a whole. Periods of high unemployment are marked by falling incomes, social instability, and heightened physical and psychological pathology. Data gathered in Europe show that the unemployed are much less satisfied with life than employed people; even the generous benefits provided by a welfare state are no substitute for a job (Oswald 1997:1822). In the U.S., studies indicate that unemployment is often accompanied by physical and mental deterioration. Joblessness has been associated with general threats to health like elevated blood pressure and higher cholesterol levels (Kasl, et al.)

During the Great Depression of the 1930s, one-fourth of the workforce was without work, making the era one of the most traumatic times in U.S. history. Nothing like the Great Depression has recurred, yet recession-induced unemployment has been a regular feature of the last fifty years. And even when aggregate levels of joblessness have been low, sizeable pockets of unemployment have remained. Residents of inner cities and remote rural areas are particularly prone to suffer from high levels of unemployment. Also, as we shall see in a later section, members of some minority groups are disproportionately affected by unemployment. Consequently, many of the social problems of the inner city can be directly traced to a persistent lack of job opportunities, especially for young people (Wilson 1996).

Federal and state governments have established unemployment compensation programs to mitigate some of the worst consequences of joblessness. These programs have softened the blow, but they do not completely offset the financial losses of unemployment, particularly when it is prolonged. Benefits average less than $200 per week, a below-poverty income for a family of four. Moreover, these benefits are provided for a limited time period, usually well under one year.

WORK AND THE LABOR FORCE TODAY

The second half of the 1990s were a time of low unemployment, with the official rate hovering below 5%. However, the availability of an adequate number of jobs does not insure that all is well. For many workers, even a full-time job means a low income, poor working conditions, and tyrannical supervisors. And even when times are good, many workers remain justifiably anxious about an impending recession or a corporate restructuring that might leave them out in the cold. At the same time, however, the inherent dynamism of a modern economy can create new jobs, better working conditions, and enhanced opportunities for workers. In the next few pages we will consider how the work environment has changed, along with the key forces that have produced these changes.

"Work" encompasses an immense variety of tasks; the U.S. Department of Labor's *Dictionary of Occupational Titles* lists over 20,000 separate occupations. An occupation is generally considered to be an activity that generates a paycheck, but a great amount of work is not directly remunerated. The most numerically important unpaid jobs center on housework and childcare. Because they do not involve monetary transactions, these forms of work do not show up in statistics that measure a nation's gross national product (GNP). This results in a paradoxical situation; if I wash my car and my neighbor washes hers; no work has been done as far as government statistics are concerned. Yet if I wash her car for $5 while she washes mine for the same amount, $10 gets added to the GNP.

It is also not generally appreciated how much work is done by unpaid volunteers. In 1993 an estimated 89 million Americans--nearly half the population over the age of 18--volunteered their labor. In that year, 19.5 billion hours of volunteer work were performed, an average of 4.2 hours per week for each volunteer (Hodgkinson, et al.1995). As was noted in the introductory case study, many community volunteers put in a substantial number of hours while providing services to parents and children at Ronald McDonald Houses.

Although most paid work is performed by employees who occupy a fairly permanent position, growing numbers of workers are now doing what the U.S. Bureau of Labor Statistics labels "contingent work." This consists of work that depends on (is contingent upon) an agreement or contract between the employee and employer that covers only a limited time period (U.S. Bureau of Labor Statistics 1995). Compared to regular workers, contingent workers are young (16-24) and enrolled in school. Also disproportionately female and Black, they work in service industries, and as operatives, fabricators, and laborers. However, some contingent workers occupy higher levels of the job structure, where they provide professional, service, and administrative support, to the firms that temporarily hire them (U.S. Bureau of Labor Statistics 1995). In general, however, contingent work is paid less and includes fewer benefits (such as health insurance) than the same work done on a noncontingent basis. Contingent workers are less protected by labor and employment laws, and most part-time and temporary workers would prefer to have full-time and permanent jobs (U.S. Bureau of Labor Statistics 1995; Commission on the Future of Worker-Management Relations 1994).

Increases in the use of involuntary part-time and contingent work may disguise the actual level of employment, because many workers are counted as employed even though they are not full-time workers (Walters 1996). More generally, employment and unemployment statistics may not present an accurate picture of reality because certain simplifying assumptions have to be made about the size of the labor force and the number of workers holding jobs. According to the U.S. Federal government, one segment of the officially defined labor force consists of non-institutionalized people over the age of 16 who were employed for pay or profit, or who worked 15 or more hours as unpaid workers in a family enterprise. The other segment is made up of unemployed people; these in turn are divided into people who were temporarily absent from their jobs for non-economic reasons (vacation, illness, and labor-management disputes, for example) and those who had no work when surveyed, but who had made efforts during the previous four weeks to find a job (for more information in the way that the labor force is defined, see Auster 1996). Consequently, "discouraged workers" who have given up in the search for a job are not counted either as members of the ranks of the unemployed or of the labor force in general. At the same time, unpaid houseworkers and volunteer workers also are excluded from the official labor force, as are people who earn an income in the "underground economy."

Employed members of the labor force do their work in many different settings. It is conventional for economists and others who study work to divide the world of work into three broad categories. The "primary sector" includes work in the production of raw materials. In this sector are found farmers, miners, fishermen, oilfield workers, and other workers who produce the resource commodities that are the material foundation of the economy. The "secondary sector" encompasses all forms of manufacturing; this is the sector in which workers make steel, assemble automobiles, produce electronic goods, and sew garments. Finally, according to one tongue-in-cheek definition, workers in the "tertiary sector" (or service sector) make anything that cannot be dropped on your toe. This sector encompasses services such as education, medical care, entertainment, and government. Although McDonald's workers make hamburgers and other food items, their industry is also put into the tertiary sector because the conversion of raw materials into a final product (e.g., a bun, sauce, and a frozen beef patty into a hamburger) is of less importance than direct service to the customer (taking orders, serving up the food, and keeping the place clean). As we shall see, McDonald's typifies service-sector employers in some ways, but is atypical in others.

A key trend in the historical evolution of work has been the decline in the relative number of workers employed in the first two sectors. At the beginning of the 19th century, the majority of workers were farmers, and even by the century's end, about a third of the labor force was still engaged in farming. Manufacturing took on a growing importance during the latter half of the 19th century, and by the beginning of the 20th century about 28% of workers were employed in this sector. Manufacturing employment reached its highest level in relative terms around 1950, when it provided jobs for about 36% of the workforce (for a historical tabulation of sectorial shifts in the U.S. labor force, see Hodson and Sullivan 1995: 264). Although the absolute number of manufacturing employees has not declined since then, it has not kept up with the expansion of the labor force. Manufacturing accounts for approximately 22% of the workforce today, while only 3% work in the primary sector. Everybody else works in the service sector.

TECHNOLOGY, MANAGEMENT, AND THE EVOLUTION OF WORK

One of the key forces propelling these changing patterns of employment has been technological advance. New technologies have transformed work by creating new industries; diminishing the need for physical labor, and stimulating the development of new skills while making some existing ones obsolete. Although technological change has had profound effects on work, it is important to understand that technology has not been an autonomous force. In North America, Western Europe, and Japan, technological transformation has been closely associated with the rise and development of capitalism. The essence of capitalism is the private ownership of capital, which can be simply defined as anything used for the production of goods and services--machine tools and factory buildings, offices and computers. In a capitalist economy, the development of technology will necessarily be shaped by an economic system based on private ownership and the need to make profits.

Most capitalist enterprises are characterized by a split between those who own the firm (as owners, partners, or stockholders) and those who receive a wage or salary in return for their labor. Although many one-person firms exist in a capitalist economy, the great majority of enterprises are staffed by paid employees, who by definition do not own the place where they work or the equipment they use. Some firms have profit-sharing arrangements or offer their employees shares of their stock, but most workers put in their hours in order to earn a wage or salary.

The rise of industrial capitalism has been closely associated with efforts to increase profits by improving the efficiency and productivity of employees. The realization of this quest has brought dramatic changes to the size and configuration of the workplace. In the middle of the 19th century the typical manufacturing enterprise was a workshop with a dozen or so workers; by the early 20th century a single factory could contain thousands of employees. An admittedly extreme example of a large enterprise was the Ford Motor Company in the 1920s, which employed 10,000 men at its River Rouge plant just to cast machine engine parts. Thousands of other workers were engaged in the many industrial processes necessary for the production of automobiles--everything from the production of steel to the final assembly of the cars (Hounshell 1984; 216-302).

Accompanying increased size was a growing complexity of industrial operations. Modern enterprises are characterized by an extensive division of labor, i.e., the breaking down of an operation into many small, specialized tasks. In the 18th century the Scottish economist Adam Smith described how pins were made by combining a number of simple tasks, each one the responsibility of a specialized worker (Smith 1937:3). Today, Smith could readily observe the division of labor in a local McDonald's restaurant, where one person takes orders, another cooks the fries, and another puts Big Macs together.

Changes in the size of the workforce, coupled with specialization and division of labor, created a host of organizational and managerial problems. The supervision of a single foreman was sufficient when a few workers labored with simple hand tools in a small workshop. The situation changed dramatically as huge manufacturing enterprises displaced traditional craft enterprises. Ford's response to the inherent difficulties of managing an immense and diverse labor force was the development of the assembly line. First used for large-scale meat packing, the relentlessly moving line brought precise coordination and rigid scheduling to the factory floor, while at the same time subjecting workers to an iron discipline. A similar pattern can be seen in McDonald's operations, where food is prepared, cooked, and served in a precisely planned, sequential manner within strict time limits.

Another mode of coordinating and disciplining workers was devised by Frederick W. Taylor, a metallurgical engineer turned efficiency expert. Under Taylor's system of Scientific Management, all job tasks were determined by specially trained industrial engineers. It was the worker's responsibility to do exactly what he or she was told, and to do it in the precise amount of time allotted. The resultant productivity improvements, it was asserted, would simultaneously increase the firm's profits and the employee's pay packet (Kanigel 1997). Scientific Management never really took hold, but its underlying philosophy continues to inform managerial practices. For example, work is precisely programmed at McDonald's and other fast-food establishments. Lights and buzzers signal when to turn a burger patty or take the fries out of the deep-fat fryer. Special tools like french fry scoops and ketchup dispensers dole out the precise quantity needed. Each store has a computer system that tracks inventory and sales, schedules work, and monitors sales according to product, time of day, and individual worker (Leidner 1993: 43-50).

In the decades since Taylor's death in 1917 managers have continued to seek "the one best way" of organizing work processes. Their efforts have led to significant productivity gains, but at the same time considerable harm has been done by managers who have espoused Taylor's philosophy of removing all planning, thinking, and decision-making from the men and women actually doing the work. For Scientific Management the ideal worker was little more than a flesh-and-blood robot who rigidly followed management's orders. As a result, a great deal of shop-floor wisdom was denigrated and ignored.

The deficiencies of Scientific Management were made apparent by research conducted in the 1920s and 30s. Of particular importance were the investigations of what came to be known as Human Relations School of Management. While studying work processes at the Hawthorne, Illinois plant of the Western Electric Company, the researchers found that the on-the-job behavior of workers was influenced by their membership in a social group. For example, contrary to Taylor's emphasis on economic rewards as the sole source of worker motivation, the output of Western Electric workers was strongly affected by the norms of their work groups. As a result, some workers produced below their capabilities because production in excess of group norms invited social ostracism (Roethlisberger and Dickson 1939).

Today, fast-moving, technologically sophisticated economies need workers who are the antithesis of unskilled functionaries doing routine operations over and over. Flexibility, responsibility, and "people skills" are vital attributes in many enterprises and industries; these are precisely the attributes that the assembly line and Scientific Management ignored, or even worse, tried to root out.

In many cases, the search for productivity improvements has been cruder than the ones used by Ford and Taylor. Instead of developing improved systems for boosting productivity, many firms have simply sacked a portion of their labor force, expecting the remaining employees to produce the same output. This tendency became especially pronounced in the 1980s and early 1990s, when "downsizing" became a common corporate practice. The result has been "meaner and leaner" business organizations that were able to show higher profits to their shareholders. But many of the gains were temporary. It is now apparent that a good many firms are now suffering from what has been labeled as "corporate anorexia," an inability to perform effectively due to an excess zeal in laying off workers. What management saw as a rational reduction of costs turned out to be irrational as far as long-term prospects are concerned.

EMPLOYMENT TECHNOLOGICAL CHANGE

As was noted above, employment in the industrial sector has been declining in relative importance. Although the absolute number of employees in manufacturing industries has not dropped, their share of the labor force has fallen dramatically as employers have sought higher profits through the application of labor-saving, productivity-improving technologies. In recent years substantial numbers of industrial jobs have been lost, as computer-operated machinery has displaced human labor. For example, in the late 1980s the Ford Motor Co. used only half as many production workers to make about the same number of vehicles that it did a decade earlier. Technological employment is not confined to industrial jobs; during the early 1980s the widespread use of musical synthesizers led to a 35% drop in recording jobs for acoustic musicians (Jalon 198). Even executives have felt the pinch, as large numbers of middle managers have been made redundant by the development of computer-based technologies that have taken over many tasks related to the gathering and transmission of information.

The loss of jobs due to technological advance is not a new phenomenon. People have long feared the replacement of human workers by machines; in the early 19th century a group of textile workers who came to be known as the Luddites smashed their employers' machinery in response to a perceived threat to their jobs. Technologically induced unemployment is still a legitimate concern, but the effects of technological advance on employment are more complicated than they appear at first glance. It is certainly true that technological advance can eliminate particular jobs, as many auto workers, studio musicians, and middle managers will sadly attest. But labor-saving technologies do not eliminate work as a whole.

In the first place, technological advance creates whole new industries and many new jobs; no one worked as a x-ray technician before the discovery of x-rays a hundred years ago. Second, the adoption of labor-saving technologies cannot reduce the total amount of work, as a simple economic analysis will show. In most cases, an employer replaces an employee with a machine in order to cut costs by improving productivity. When the cost of a product is cut, several outcomes are possible. First, the cost of the selling price of the product may drop. This may induce consumers to buy more of the product, which will create more job opportunities in the other segments of the product's manufacture. If consumers do not increase their purchases of the cheaper product, they have more money left in their pockets, and that money can be spent on other goods and services, which will in turn increase employment opportunities in the firms that make them. Of course, lowered production costs may not result in lower selling prices; a producer may appropriate higher profits instead. But the enhanced profits may be used to expand the enterprise, and this will bring more jobs in its train. Alternatively, the higher profits may be distributed as dividends to stockholders or as higher salaries for management. When this increased income is spent, it generates jobs in the firms that produce whatever is purchased. In short, technological change may eliminate certain jobs and alter the distribution of income, but it cannot destroy work itself.

THEORY BOX by **Michael J. Donnelly**   **Chapter 11**   **Work and Economy/Gender Stratification**

All human societies categorize individuals as male and female. Moreover, all cultures prescribe at least some activities which are restricted to (or only appropriate for) men, and other activities appropriate only to women. Some division of labor among women and men appears to be a cultural universal, although there is so much variation in where particular cultures draw the lines between men's activities and women's activities, that such "gendering" of activities seems to be more a matter of socio-cultural beliefs than of biologically-based sex differences.

The differentiation by gender amounts in most cultures also to **stratification** by gender; that is, women's positions and status in society tend to be subordinate to those of men. In the United States, for instance, if we consider the basic components of what sociologists call socio-economic status-education, occupation, income-women's subordination in American society is readily apparent. Before the mid-nineteenth century women were almost entirely excluded from higher education. Even as small and then growing numbers of women gained access to higher education, men were still more likely over many decades to complete college. In the economy there has been, and there remains, a clear split between "women's work" and "men's work." Women workers are concentrated in personal services, the retail sales, and various clerical positions (secretary, receptionist, clerk), while men predominate among corporate directors, high prestige professionals and White-collar administrators, and blue-collar supervisors. The occupations in which women predominate tend moreover to be concentrated at the lower end of the status and prestige hierarchy, and they bring lower incomes.

There are, however, signs of change in these patterns. Women are now seeking education in traditionally male fields in much larger numbers. About 40% of U.S. law students, for instance, are women; if the trends in law school enrollments continue, the legal professions will over time become less and less a male preserve. Anti-discrimination laws have also somewhat lowered barriers to women's entry into male-dominated occupations. The long-term effects of these developments are likely to change perceptions of what is "appropriate" work for men and women and perhaps an eventual blurring of the distinction between "men's work" and "women's work" (1975).

WORK IN THE GLOBAL ECONOMY

A similar story can be narrated about the globalization of the economy. There is no question that work in the industrially developed world has been affected by the widespread importation of goods produced abroad. As has happened with the technological transformation of the industrial sector, foreign competition has eliminated many jobs (while at the same time creating a fair amount of economic and social disruption in the countries to which the jobs have migrated). Low-skill manufacturing jobs have been particularly vulnerable to foreign competition. When all an employer needs and wants is cheap labor, an American worker will find it very difficult to compete with workers in Asia or Latin America who earn one-tenth the wage of their counterparts in the U.S.

The inability to compete with low-wage foreign competition has significantly diminished the number of jobs in domestic industries such as textiles and footwear. At the same time, however, the purchase of inexpensive foreign goods has left consumers with more money to spend on other things, and these purchases stimulate job creation in the firms that provide them. As with the effects of technological change, the story is complex, and the gains and losses are not equally distributed. The majority of workers and consumers benefit from foreign trade, but for workers in some industries, the consequences of foreign competition can be devastating.

SERVICE SECTOR JOBS IN A DYNAMIC ECONOMY

The loss of manufacturing jobs due to technological advance and foreign competition is often blamed for the stagnation in workers' earnings that has been evident since the mid-1970s. Offsetting these losses, the growth of the service sector has provided many new job opportunities, but it is often asserted that the typical service-industry job consists of flipping burgers at the local McDonald's. This is hardly the case. The service sector is extremely diverse, encompassing everyone from millionaire athletes and entertainers to fast-food employees making the minimum wage.

The service sector has been the main source of jobs in recent decades, and this trend will continue into the next century. According to the U.S. Bureau of Labor Statistics (1994), from 1994 to 2005, the service industries will account for 16.2 million out of an expected 16.8 million new wage and salary jobs. Health service jobs will account for one-fifth of these new jobs and educational services (primarily teaching) will account for about one-eighth. At the same time, jobs in the primary sectors will grow modestly or even decline. The largest decline is expected to be in mining (down by about 28%), but agricultural occupations will probably grow by 5%.

In the secondary sector, manufacturing jobs are expected to decline by about 5%, while construction jobs should grow by about 10%. Low-paying jobs will account for much of the expansion of service-sector employment. Even though these jobs will increase by small percentages, there are already so many of them that small percentage increases translate into large numerical increases. Topping the list of occupations expected to show the greatest numerical growth are cashiers, followed by janitors and cleaners, retail salespersons, and waiters and waitresses. The ten fastest-growing occupations in terms of percentage increases are (in rank order) personal home care aide, home health care aide, systems analyst, computer engineer, data base administrator, physical therapist, residential counselor, human services worker, medical assistant, and paralegal.

Although the number of low-skill, poorly paid jobs will continue to increase, the trend is clearly in the direction of occupations that require a considerable amount of educational preparation. Jobs requiring a bachelor's degree are expected to grow by 23%, while those requiring less than a bachelor's degree are expected to grow by only 12%. Income also has been closely tied to educational attainment, and will continue to do so. In the 1970s, high school dropouts and high school graduates saw their earnings advance by averages of 45% and 42%, respectively, while the earnings of college graduates went up by 53%. During the 1980s, however, the earnings of high school dropouts and high school graduates increased by only 14% and 20%, respectively, while college graduates enjoyed average earnings increases of 55% (Bernstein 1996: 90).

DIFFERENTIALS AND DISCRIMINATION IN LABOR FORCE EXPERIENCES

If you think of who serves you at McDonald's, you immediately realize that the employees do not represent a cross-section of the U.S. labor force. The chances are that the workers are strikingly young. Firefighters in most communities are disproportionately White and male; clerical workers are, as a rule, female; the certified nursing assistants you meet in nursing homes and hospitals are likely to be African American, Latina, or immigrant women; factory workers generally come from working class families and physicians disproportionately from upper-middle class origins. Our "chances" in the labor force are very much shaped by our race, ethnicity, gender, social class, age, disabilities, immigrant status, place of residence, and/or sexual orientation. These factors influence our occupations, earnings, likelihood of being unemployed, and opportunities for promotion and good benefits such as health care insurance (for example, see Higginbotham and Romero 1997; Robles 1997; Jacobs 1995; Tomaskovic-Devey and Risman 1993; Amott and Matthaei 1991; Croteau 1996).

One of the most striking changes in the 20th century labor force has been the increased participation of women (U.S. Bureau of the Census, 1900-1960). Throughout U.S. history women--most particularly poor women, widows, African American women, Latinas, and Asian and other immigrant women-- have worked for pay. However, in 1900 slightly less than one fifth of the labor force was female; by 1995 women were almost half of paid workers (46%). From the 1940s to mid 1960s labor force activity increased most among women past their prime childrearing years but in recent decades younger women have increased their employment rates, and now, at all educational levels, mothers of young children are the fastest growing component of the U.S. labor force (Hayghe 1997) Participation has increased among women of all race and ethnic groups, and, by 1995, 60% of Black women, 59% of White women, and 53% of Latinas were employed. In short, women's rates of labor force participation have come to closely resemble men's, as has their pattern of participation across the life cycle (Bianchi and Spain 1996).

There remain, however, significant gender gaps in occupations and earnings. These have narrowed in recent decades with women's increased educational attainment and continuity of labor force participation, as well as opportunities opened through job expansion in certain sectors and equal rights efforts stemming in part from Title VII of the 1964 Civil Rights Act. Also significant has been changing ideas about gender roles in late 20th century America (Wootton 1997; Reskin and Padavic 1994).

Data on the gender distribution by occupation yields two important themes (Wootton 1997). First, the gender distribution of workers in some occupations has shifted substantially: for example, the index of occupational segregation by gender (which indicates the percentage of women who would have to shift occupations to reflect their proportion in the overall labor force) fell from 67.6 in 1970 to 58.1 in 1985 to 53.5 in 1995 as women made inroads into selected areas, particularly management, some professions, and sales. Women gained particularly in occupations in which employment was expanding over the past two decades.

The second important theme is that men and women--and workers of different race and ethnic groups--are still disproportionately concentrated (or "segregated") in different occupations. Compared to men, women workers are concentrated in fewer of the 503 detailed occupational categories used by the census, and vast numbers still work in primarily "female" occupations, including secretary and related clerical occupations, retail sales, personal services, food preparation, school teaching, nursing, and cashiering. With the exception of "miscellaneous salaried manager," the top ten occupations employing women in 1990 (the latest census available) were the same as the top ten list for women in 1940 (Reskin and Padavic 1994). And even these measures of occupational sex segregation mask the actual extent of sex segregation in the workplace inasmuch as men and women in the same occupations often perform different jobs and have different employers. Male bakers, for instance are concentrated in unionized, high-paying establishments that mass produce baked goods while most female bakers work in retail sales for low pay (Steiger and Reskin 1990). In law, women attorneys tend to be concentrated in probate, tax, family law, and securities while litigation is a predominantly male specialty. Within firms, women attorneys are less likely than men to be in positions of power, generally make less money, encounter more difficulty in creating new business contacts, and have more difficulty dealing with sexual harassment and with balancing work and family (Pierce 1995; Rosenberg, Perlstadt, and Phillips 1997). In short, they hit the "glass ceiling" that limits women's ascent to the top of their fields.

Analyses that consider the combined effects of sex and race on occupational segregation have revealed that almost twice as much segregation is based on sex as on race: women and men from the same racial/ethnic group are more segregated from each other than are Blacks and Whites of the same sex. Nonetheless, race and ethnicity are still very important predictors of one's likely occupation. Within each sex, people of color and Hispanics regardless of color tend to work in less desirable occupations than Whites, with grave consequences for their earnings.

The reasons for contemporary occupational and job segregation are complex and they deserve far more attention than can be offered here. (Readers are encouraged to see the text's chapters on gender, family, minorities, and education for relevant discussion). Our nation's history helped to shape these differentials as the residual effects of slavery, discrimination against immigrants, and patriarchal legal and social customs that restricted opportunities for people of color and women. The social class structure is a powerful force in maintaining differential "chances," partly because it is a crucial determinant of educational attainment which is, in turn, a major factor in employment opportunities. Schools serving low income neighborhoods and areas with high proportions of people of color and recent immigrants tend to be poorer in quality, and children in these schools are less likely to pursue higher education than are children from more privileged families and residential areas. Also not to be discounted in explaining occupational segregation is employer discrimination of various types. Despite laws against doing so, employers show preferences in hiring-- channeling women and men, Blacks, Latinos, Asian Americans and Whites, into different positions, in offering on-the-job training, and in promoting workers, among other ways (Reskin and Padavic 1994; Jacobs 1995; Dunn 1997; Weber and Higginbotham 1997)

Together these factors that shape occupational segregation--what employees bring to the workplace and what opportunities they are offered-- result in significant differentials in pay and risk of unemployment. Fortunately, the gender gap in annual earnings has narrowed since 1973 when women earned only 57% of what men did. Now--as women have invested in more education and labor force experience and widened occupational choices, and employers have lowered barriers-- full-time, year-round women workers earn slightly over 70% of what their male counterparts do. Still, this pay differential is significant in the lives of women, particularly single mothers, and contributes to women's greater risk of poverty (see text chapter on poverty).

Since 1975 women in all groups have been slowly closing the pay gap with White men but the same cannot be said for African-American and Hispanic men (Reskin and Padavic 1994). The data portrays the persistent differences in income among racial and ethnic groups in our nation.

Race and ethnic differences are very striking with regard to unemployment as well. For example, in 1996 the percent of Whites who experienced unemployment at the same time during the year was 10.8%; among Blacks the figure was 18.0% and among labor force participants who were of Hispanic origin it was 16.6 (U.S. Bureau of Labor Statistics 1997b). These differences constitute a long-standing problem, and the passage of time does not necessarily bring progress. Indeed, employment ratios reveal that nonWhites have lost ground over the past 30 years, (Eaton and Kisor 1996). Whereas Black men and women were more likely than Whites to be employed in 1940, they were less likely to have jobs by the 1980s when, for example, one of five Black men aged 16-64--twice the rate for White men--was not in the labor force. The reasons for this differential in unemployment are complex but certainly include factors discussed earlier in the chapter. The geographic restructuring of the economy has disproportionately eliminated jobs held by inner-city Blacks, globalization that has reduced the demand for low-skilled labor, and discriminating practices by employers have continued to disadvantage people of color.

CONFLICTS BETWEEN WORK AND FAMILY

Another of the most commonly discussed work-related problems for many American workers is the difficulty of finding a healthy balance between their responsibilities at home and on the job. Bookstores offer a steady supply of popular books that ask how we can love our children, do well by our boss, and not sacrifice ourselves (see, for example, McKenna 1997; Peters 1997 as recent examples). Almost daily talk shows, news magazines, and newspaper articles contribute to our ongoing, often heartfelt and heated public discussions about problematic aspects of combining work and family. It is important to note, however, that having multiple roles is not necessarily a bad thing. Depression rates are higher in people with only one life role, for example, and women with families and jobs enjoy better mental and physical health than those with a single role (Crosby 1991; Kritz-Silverstein, Wingard, and Barrett-Connor 1992, Chafetz 1997). The social problem is how to mold institutions to allow us to do reasonably well the several roles we value and need.

Most Americans have multiple roles throughout life; two of those most commonly held simultaneously are employment and family. A young worker at the beginning of a career may have few family responsibilities and feel that she can invest heavily in work without "cheating" herself or loved ones. But, for single parents, dual-earner married couples with children at home, or workers who are primary caretakers for elderly or disabled family members, multiple demands can be overwhelming. Sociologists use the term role overload to refer to the tension resulting from having too much to do because of the demands of several roles (e.g., spouse, parent, employee, volunteer, community activist). Particularly stressful is role conflict, when two or more roles pose contradictory demands that should be met at the same time. For example, what's the single mother who barely survives on her meager earnings at McDonald's to do: miss work, lose her earnings, and irritate her supervisor, to pick up her chronically ill child immediately when the school calls, or stay at work and neglect her child's needs?

A number of factors contribute to family-work role overload and conflict. As have seen, women's labor force participation patterns have changed dramatically over the century, and now most mothers (not to mention fathers) are employed. Divorce rates have risen and, as most children remain with their mothers, these now-single mothers have little choice about working.

With recent legislation, single mothers who formerly could stay at home with young children with the help of Aid to Families with Dependent Children are now required to enter training programs and find employment. Workers and families are being affected by another trend as well: the steady move towards a 24-hours-a-day, seven-days-a-week economy. Less than one-third of all employed Americans 18 and older in 1991 regularly worked a standard workweek, i.e., daytime employment 35 to 40 hours a week, Monday through Friday (Presser and Cox 1997). One-fourth of dual-earner couples work different shifts--for example, one during the day, the other at night; among couples with preschoolers a third of couples do so. This arrangement may take a toll on marital stability, but many couples have no options: one half of those working nonstandard hours do so because of job requirements. As discussed earlier, the demand for workers in these jobs--many of them in the service sector (clerks, nursing and nurses aides and food service workers)--is growing and the occupants are disproportionately women.

One pressing need is for more childcare of high quality. Already more than half of mothers who have children under one year of age are employed outside the home. Two-thirds of women with three to 5 year olds and three fourths of women with 6 to 13 years olds are employed (Presser and Cox 1997). Some Americans have mixed feelings about the appropriateness of sending children off to daycare, but the fact is that most parents work outside the home. Perhaps those who worry can gain some perspective in considering that in many cultures around the world the care of young children is shared among many kinspeople, including older siblings, and children grow up to responsibly assume adult roles. Further, in our own society, a historical perspective reveals that when White middle-class women stayed home to care for children, many women of color and working class woman left their children in the care of others when they went out to work, sometimes as domestic workers who helped wealthier women by caring for their own children (Romero 1992; Glenn 1992). Further, studies have shown that high quality childcare outside the home does not negatively affect children's development (Barnet and Barnet 1997).

Parents and experts are concerned about both the availability and quality of childcare. At present, of our 21 million children under 5, 40% are cared for by one parent during the workday, 21% by relatives, 31% by employees of childcare centers, 14% in family childcare homes, and 4% by sitters in the children's own home. (The total exceeds 100% because some children have more than one form of care). Many parents cannot find spaces they want in childcare centers or licensed childcare homes, especially for infants, and they worry about standards of care as well. In light of recent findings that the earliest years are critical for children's developing the brain structure to process information, develop language skills, and express emotions normally, any parent would fret about one evaluation: that perhaps only 15% of children under 5 are in truly high quality programs while another 15 are in settings of such poor quality that the children's health and development is threatened (Barnet and Barnet 1997).

As our population ages, those now worried about finding dependable childcare will shift their concern to care for their elderly relatives. According to one study, at least 16% of the U.S. workforce now assumes responsibility for care of older family members; by 2020 this figure will double, to at least 33%. Few workers and employers are prepared for addressing the needs of aging relatives who often experience periodic crises and a decline stretching over many years. Eldercare may be more stressful than child-rearing in ways, occurring as the children-workers are themselves aging and perhaps raising more mixed feelings of sadness, anger, guilt, and fear of loss ("Eldercare. " 1995).

Employed women disproportionately bear the brunt of combining family and employment responsibilities. Sociologist Arlie Hochschild (1989) popularized the concept of the "second shift," using it to describe a very real pattern documented by many other researchers as well: full-time working women come home to do another "job." In dual-earner couples, women do most of the housework, childcare, and elder care. Husbands of employed women, for example, spend about one-third as much time on housework as their spouses, and as a result have more leisure time. While fathers in the U.S. have increased their contributions to childcare over recent decades, mothers still put many more hours into childcare, coordinate the out-of-home care, and are seen by their children's schools or other social institutions as having primary responsibility (Dunn 1997; Chafetz 1997). Likewise, women assume much more responsibility for care of elderly relatives--on both sides of the family--than do their husbands (Abel and Nelson 1990). Many sociologists agree that, as a group, men have resisted change in family roles, and concur that such change is essential if women are to gain equality both at home and in the workplace.

Unpaid family work is a special burden for single custodial parents. In the U.S., 25% of families with children in the home are headed by single parents, the vast majority of these by mothers. As Dunn (1997) has noted, these single parents must perform for both parents--supporting the family with their jobs, doing housework and childcare completely unaided. Mother-only families are disproportionately poor, Black, and Latino, and if they live in neighborhoods with inadequate institutional supports, they may also be involved in the "third shift" or unpaid community work (Dickson 1997). In some poor and working-class communities, activism and unpaid community labor must compensate for inadequate public services. Mary Pardo's (1997) work on Madres del Este de Los Angeles, Santa Isabel, and Lynda Dickson's (1997) analysis of turn-of-the-century Black women's clubs show the ways in which unpaid community labor is essential for a community's maintenance and for poor families' access to goods and services that higher- class families pay for (as, for example, when parents exchange labor for children's school fees). Such work may be distinguished from "volunteerism": for the poor, the third shift may be **required** for children's and families' safety, education, and basic food and shelter requirements (Romero 1997a).

Of course, role overload and conflict result not only from responsibilities to family and community, but--perhaps more importantly--from too few family-friendly policies on the part of employers and government. Many of today's work settings evolved at a time when the vast majority of employees were men, most of whom had wives to do all the domestic labor. The place of work was fixed; work days and hours were inflexible; children weren't allowed (Chafetz 1997). The professions, such as medicine and law, came to require an extended training program that goes into the typical years of family formation. New recruits into the professional and managerial careers were-and are expected to give their all, to work long hours, travel, entertain, relocate, and more. While other occupations have different sets of expectations, many make it difficult to combine family and work. Like the single mother employed at McDonald's, workers who are paid by the hour will lose income if they take time off to attend to a sick child or elderly parent. Jobs which require rotating shifts--day and night--make it extremely difficult for parents who need childcare. Many firms have not welcomed mothers of infants who want to breast feed, a practice highly recommended for the health of the mother and child alike ("Pioneering Firms..." 1997). The intervention section of this chapter addresses some policies that employers and government have adopted to help to ease the burdens that workers experience as they try to fulfill their goals of being good family members and good workers.

WORKERS' EXPERIENCES: SATISFACTION AND ALIENATION

In our society paid work has great personal and social significance: We rely on our jobs for income to buy the necessities of life; our work shapes the patterns and social ties of our daily lives; it influences the social status we have; it is a often a factor in our self-esteem and identity. Social observers have long been interested in how workers experience this activity--work—which is so significant in our lives. In particular, social scientists have been interested in the alienation or self-actualization that people experience as a result of their jobs, and in worker's job satisfaction, a summary evaluation that people make of their work.

Our experiences of work and our attitudes and behaviors on the job are often complex, however. Indeed, people can be satisfied and dissatisfied with their jobs at the same time. Overall, survey research shows that most people try to make the best of their situation at work and report being moderately satisfied with it. Even in the most tedious jobs many people have a capacity to gain at least some satisfaction, for example, from workplace rituals they enjoy, friendships, a sense of community, and pride in doing their tasks well. At the same time, they may express deep-seated dissatisfactions that stem from many sources, such as low pay, feelings of powerlessness and isolation, a rapid pace of work set by a machine, close supervision, or poor human relationships ("Pioneering Firms..." 1997)

Further, our ability to study workers' experience of their jobs is imperfect. Social scientists often use survey research with close-ended questions to query workers' satisfaction with their jobs. The answer they obtain depends on how a question is posed. Regarding job satisfaction, for example, the phrasing "How satisfied are you with your job as a whole?" results in high levels of reported satisfaction, with three quarters of workers responding that they are "fairly" or "very" satisfied. A question that allows respondents to consider alternatives--for instance, "If you had it to do over again, would you go into the same line of work?"--results in lower levels of satisfaction, with only 40% of workers responding affirmatively (Hodson and Sullivan 1995). Studies that use qualitative research methods, in which investigators themselves work as employees alongside the workers they study or engage in extensive interviews with workers, perhaps over a long period of time, are able to present much more nuanced findings on workers' complex experiences of work (see, for example, Diamond 1992; Lamphere and Zavella 1997; Hondagneu-Sotelo 1997; Milkman 1997).

While recognizing the limits of our ability to adequately describe a complex matter, social scientists have nonetheless been able to shed considerable light on some of the major causes and consequences of workers' alienation or self-actualization. Alienation occurs when work does not adequately provide for the human need for identity and meaning; such work provides extrinsic rewards, such as pay (and often too little of that), but not intrinsic rewards, such as pride in workmanship. This concept is derived from Karl Marx's critique of early capitalism. He noted that workers were alienated from the products of their labor and the process of work; their work did not allow them to be engaged in creative activities, and, working in isolation, they are alienated from others. Today we often think of these ideas as they have been translated into the subjective experiences of powerlessness, self-estrangement, meaninglessness, isolation, and normlessness (Seeman 1959).

Self-actualization occurs when work contributes to the fullfillment not only of material needs but to broader human needs as well. This notion draws on the work of Abraham Maslow who posited a hierarchy of needs--physiological needs, for example, for food and sex; safety needs, for a secure physical and emotional environment; belongingness needs, for acceptance and friendship; esteem needs, for recognition and attention; and self-actualization needs, for development of our potential. We are concerned about the higher level needs only after the lower level needs are met. According to this theory, the most alienating jobs are those that do not provide minimum physiological and safety needs. The "best" jobs go beyond meeting our physiological needs; ideally, they allow us to develop to our highest potential (Hodson and Sullivan 1995).

Social scientists have found that alienation and self-actualization are influenced by many factors, including the nature of one's job and the technology it utilizes. Jobs that allow workers autonomy and that engage them with complexity and change are more self-actualizing than repetitious work that lacks in variety and must be done at a predetermined pace. Workers at the rural Pennsylvania McDonald's restaurant that is trying to break the record for speedy service, cited in the case study, are likely to be more alienated than their friends whose jobs allow them more control and variety. Technology can cut both ways: it can increase self-actualization, opening us to new worlds (through the internet perhaps) or making our jobs more creative, but in many sectors it is often deployed in ways that heighten alienation by increasing external control over the pace and flow or monitoring workers' "productivity." The structures of work organizations and their policies regarding pay, benefits, and opportunity ladders for promotion also influence the experience of work. For example, satisfaction is generally higher in smaller firms, or small units within large entities, than in larger work settings.

Whether we are relatively self-actualizing or alienated in our jobs has consequences for our job attitudes, our commitment to our employer, and our behaviors at work. Regarding behavior, researchers have noted that all workers--those who are happy and those who are dissatisfied--make behavioral adjustments at work to maximize their benefits and minimize the costs to themselves. Whereas satisfied employees tend to work hard and even initiate changes that benefit their employer, disgruntled workers express their dissatisfaction through high absenteeism, quitting, sabotaging the outcome of tasks, stealing, or in other ways resisting oppressive working conditions. History is full of workers' efforts to make their work "work" for them. Sometimes workers unite in unions to maximize their benefits; sometimes they work in more informal ways. For example, Romero (1997b) has shown how Chicanas doing domestic service in private homes are "modernizing" this work to make it higher paying, more autonomous, and less dehumanizing than other low-status low-skilled occupations available to them.

Gender, race, and age are, as we have seen, important influences on one's "chances" in the labor force, and you might guess--correctly--that workers of different groups vary in their satisfaction with work. These differences reflect the general finding that higher status workers with "good" jobs enjoy more satisfaction than those with less desirable ones. Younger workers are generally less satisfied with their jobs than older workers. They may have more education and expect more than they can find in entry-level positions; older workers, on the other hand, may have had the time to secure jobs that meet their needs or they may lower their expectations with time (Kanter 1977). Workers from racial and ethnic minority groups, and women workers are, as we have seen, over represented in jobs that entail lower pay and poorer benefits, more repetitive and less creative work, and fewer chances for training and promotion. Data are consistent regarding the higher levels of dissatisfaction with work expressed by minority groups, with the strongest contrast being between Black and White workers (Hodson and Sullivan 1995). Recent data on White, Black, and Latino women workers confirm that racial/ethnic discrimination compounds gender gaps in these workers' assessments of their jobs (U.S. Department of Labor, Women's Bureau 1994).

This 1994 national survey of working women, based on a scientific national random sample, illustrates several points we have made about people's experience of work as well as documenting contemporary women's attitudes about work. These results show, for example, how complex workers' feelings towards their employment are, and how their reactions to their work are shaped by their status (e.g., pay and occupations) in the labor force. The findings also reveal how workers who report high levels of satisfaction with work in response to a broad survey question can still have plenty of serious concerns. Overall, the majority women reported satisfaction with their employment: fully 79% of respondents claimed to "love' or "like" their jobs overall. Choosing three responses from a list of eleven possibilities of what they like best about their jobs, participants ranked enjoying co-workers, having flexible hours, liking what they do, getting paid well, and having good benefits as attractive features of their jobs, in that order. However, there were significant differences by income and occupation: women earning less and women in lower status occupations are more likely to emphasize satisfaction with co-workers whereas those in more lucrative and prestigious occupations link their satisfactions to pay, benefits, and liking what they do.

The study found a powerful consensus among working women about what is wrong with their jobs--a consensus that crossed all occupations, incomes, generations, races, and regions of the country. The top problems identified fell into three general categories: pay and benefits do not provide adequate economic security; workplace culture does not support a balance between work and family obligations; and women do not get recognition and credit for their skills nor access to training to increase their marketability. In the following section, we consider some ways in which these and other problems examined thus far in the chapter may be at least partially addressed.

INTERVENTIONS

Work, for previous generations, was seen as a stable loyal commitment between the worker, his family, and one firm or company. The company man who retired after 30 years with his gold watch could be proud of his record and contributions to the organization. This norm of full time work with one or few organizations over a lifetime in exchange for decent pay and benefits as well as social activities has been recently eroded by changes in the economy as discussed previously. The impact of women's entering the work force in substantial numbers has also affected work as there is increasingly no "wife" at home to raise children, tend to domestic matters, and support the worker in his or her career.

As a result, there are substantial pressures on federal, state and local governments, organizations, and individual workers to adapt to the changing workforce and economic imperatives. Although the social problems of work and economy are complex and not easily alleviated, many interventions have been attempted and proposed to address these problems and some of them have met with a measure of success. These three interventions will be discussed: (1) the organization of work, (2) advanced technology and (3) responses to globalization.

THE ORGANIZATION OF WORK

One response to the changing economy and work force has been reorganizing the very structure of work. Flexible and contingent work forms have increased substantially as companies find that their needs for flexibility sometimes match their employees' needs.

Flexible Work Arrangements. Flexible work simply refers to work arrangements that are freed from the typical on-site 9 AM to 5 PM work day structure and include flextime, the compressed work week, telecommuting, part-time work, and various forms of contingent work. Flextime exists when workers have some choice in the starting and ending times of their work days, for example working from 7 AM to 3 PM or 11 AM to 7 PM rather than from 9 AM to 5 PM. This results in the same 8-hour day but gives workers choice in what time they are at work, thus freeing them for getting their children to or from school or simply sleeping late. Compressed work week refers to working only 4 days in a week rather than the usual 5 days. In this arrangement, hours worked may increase to 10 or more hours per day in order to result in the usual forty hours worked per week. Telecommuting removes workers from the work site and places them in satellite offices or at home to use computers or telephones to complete their work responsibilities.

While these techniques offer both worker and organization some measure of flexibility, they also require considerable coordination between employees and the organization to ensure that those who must work together are available at the same time and with the opportunity for adequate communication. Most organizations that use these techniques only offer them to the upper level employees or are in industries that require a high degree of flexibility such as those that compete in international markets (Osterman 1994). Organizations that use flexible arrangements are increasing in number and most find that employee retention, morale, and performance are increased while conflicts between work and family are reduced (Golden 1996; Hohl 1996; Shepard et al. 1996). The balance between family and work is mediated by flexible work for both men and women yet studies show that the effect is different for each gender (Giele 1979; Staines and Pleck 1986). Men are more apt to become active parents and share in domestic work when they have highly flexible (and less demanding) jobs although other factors such as unexpected pleasure in caring for children, having joint custody or a female partner who is work committed or more successful than themselves are also important (Gerson 1994). However, women who work at home or with flexible schedules do more domestic chores than do women employed in traditional full time on-site jobs, and thus take on a heavier "second shift" (Silver and Goldscheider 1994).

These flexible arrangements may leave intact the full-time, stable employment situation of the worker. On the other hand, part-time work has increased dramatically as its benefit as a flexible strategy has recognized. With part-time work, either through job sharing (two workers sharing a single full time position) or jobs designed as part-time rather than full-time positions, employers can retain workers who might otherwise quit and workers can keep an income while going back to school or raising children. Other forms of work reorganization, often called contingent work, no longer assume full time or stable work commitments. As discussed previously, contingent work is temporary and flexible, designed to allow organizations to be responsive to economic forces and supplement yet not replace stable work. It is also a mechanism for job transitions (temporaries may become permanent), and for helping workers balance family life and work (Commission on Future of Worker-Management Relations 1994; Lenz 1996). Flexible and contingent work arrangements favor those workers such as the elderly, semi-retired, but active, who prefer a reduced workload. (Morrison 1986; Sijuwade 1996)

There are some drawbacks to the contingent work solution, however. Contingent work is paid less and includes fewer benefits than the same work done on a non-contingent basis. Contingent workers are less protected by labor and employment laws, and most part time and temporary workers are involuntary; they would prefer full time and permanent jobs (U.S. Bureau of Labor Statistics 1995; Commission on the Future of Worker-Management Relations 1994). Contingent workers are more susceptible to sexual harassment and other problems due to the temporary and unstable nature of their employment situations (Rogers and Henson 1997).

ADVANCED TECHNOLOGY: HELP OR HINDERANCE?

The deliberate and thoughtful use of technology can alleviate many work-related social problems. The growing use of team-based work groups combined with information technologies, such as email and teleconferencing, results in increased effectiveness but is a challenge for management (Mankin et al. 1997; Rathnam et al. 1995). Such communication and computer technologies also support home-based and flexible work arrangements so that the "office" is no longer only located in the building of the organization. Work can be done at any hour in any location with the use of pagers, cell and digital telephones, fax machines, and computers. This has a positive effect on productivity and increases the accountability of workers. The downside is that those same workers may never again "leave the office." Virtual networks also alter the nature of communication between co-workers to be more blunt and impersonal yet also more creative and uninhibited (Wellman et al. 1996).

Working in high technology industries can be isolating and unstable. The semi-automatic production processes currently in place isolate workers. High unemployment also characterizes work in these industries. These effects, however, can be mediated by the cooperation of unions and management in creating meaningful work environments and enhancing empowerment that can be gained from the skills that are developed in this work (Hodson 1985).

Over time, workplace safety has increased in the United States due to governmental regulation, the influence of unions, and organizational self-regulation. A nine-year study of twenty-six industries found that in some years, greater union coverage was associated with fewer serious on-the-job accidents (Taylor 1987). One study suggests that employers maintain their own safety programs regardless of governmental regulations because increased workplace safety increases worker productivity, stabilizes salaries, and lowers insurance costs (Hood 1995). However, organizations that employ innovative structures (such as cooperative organizations) and those that are employee-owned (Employee Stock Ownership Plans) are not necessarily safer than conventional firms. This is largely due to their precarious economic conditions (Grunberg et al. 1996).

ECONOMIC DIVERSIFICATION: RESOUBSES TO GLOBALIZATION

As we have seen, work is increasingly exported to developing countries that attract companies by providing an environment in which government regulations are few or nonexistent. Often organizational incentives to be profitable far outweigh ethical responsibilities. This compromises not only worker safety but environmental health and economic accountability as well. While these problems seem insurmountable, federal regulations, public exposure of organizational practices, and consumption patterns (such as consumer boycotts) may have some impact.

Treaties such as the North American Free Trade Agreement (NAFTA) contain provisions that have as their aim the creation of better working conditions for workers in low-wage countries, but the impact of these provisions has not yet been fully assessed. Some corporations in the U.S. are using flexible work, rather than exporting work, as a response to economic globalization (Borgers 1996). Consumers also have choice over the firms that receive their business, and their purchases can significantly impact the way business is done (Ritzer1996). Patronizing small business or businesses that embrace socially and ecologically responsible practices is an intervention that, if enough consumers participate, can be effective. Ben & Jerry's, for example, is a business that was founded with a commitment to socially responsible practices such as using local products in the manufacture of their ice cream and donating a percentage of their earnings to community service projects (Lager 1994). Their market share has increased dramatically as consumers embrace their commitment to quality products and ethical behavior. However, their success and subsequent growth has resulted in increasing pressures to abandon their innovative practices. Such firms often price their products at a higher rate to reflect the higher-quality production processes as well as the risks of being relatively new businesses in highly competitive markets.

Thus, consumers from upper income levels are those with the resources to patronize such businesses. Those in lower economic income levels are less able to support such businesses on a discretionary basis. Supporting local businesses however can also be done by participating in local community activities, such as farmers' markets, which have been experiencing resurgence across the country. The market for organic produce has risen dramatically in the past few years partly due to its availability at farmers' markets, the increasing numbers of natural food stores, and growing public awareness about food products (Sugarman 1977).

CONCLUSIONS

Interventions for social problems of work and the economy exist at the governmental level with regulations and enforcement, in business practices, and in consumer and work group behaviors. Although these interventions may address only portions of the social problems at work and may themselves present other problems, it is clear that many viable solutions are actively sought by different constituencies in society. At the same time, however, no set of interventions can permanently resolve all of the conflicts inherent in our working lives. A worker, no matter if she is taking orders at the local McDonald's or arguing a case before the U.S. Supreme Court, will be beset by the multiple demands of her employer, family, work colleagues, and customers and clients. Meanwhile, mergers, technological advances, and globalization will continue to bring fundamental alterations to the workplace. Our challenge will be to create interventions that allow increases in efficiency and productivity while fostering a work environment that allows workers to earn a decent living and to develop their individual capabilities to the fullest.

SUMMARY

1. While aspects of work may be seen as problematic, the absence of work is a far greater problem for individuals and society. Unemployed persons may experience physical and mental deterioration while at the societal level unemployment may lead to political instability.
2. Unemployment in the second half of the 1990s has been low with the official rate hovering around 5%; however, employment in a full-time job can still mean a low income, poor working conditions, and tyrannical supervisors.
3. Increases in the use of involuntary part-time and contingent work may inflate the actual level of employment because many workers are counted as employed even though they are not full-time workers.
4. As primary sector jobs (production of raw materials)and secondary sector jobs (manufacturing) have decreased, service sector jobs have increased in the USA.
5. Technological advances, such as the invention of the automobile and development of the factory to produce it have been a key force propelling changing patterns in employment.
6. Assembly lines and Taylor's Scientific Management were responses to changes in the size of the enterprises, specialization and increased division of labor, but they created many new problems at the same time.
7. The loss of jobs due to technological advance has long been feared. In reality technological change may eliminate certain jobs and alter the distribution of income, but it can not destroy work itself.
8. The majority of workers and consumers benefit from foreign trade, but for workers in particular industries may suffer job losses or lower wages.
9. While the shift to service sector jobs is often blamed for stagnation of workers' earnings, the service sector is extremely diverse, and many service-sector workers receive wages and salaries that are well above average.
10. Although many workers will continue to hold low-skill, poorly paid jobs, the trend is clearly in the direction of occupations that require a considerable amount of educational preparation.
11. "Chances" in the labor force are heavily influenced by our race, ethnicity, gender, social class, age, disabilities, immigrant status, place of residence, and/or sexual orientation.
12. Workers often have a difficult time finding a healthy balance between responsibilities at home and at work.

13. People can be satisfied and dissatisfied with their job at the same time. Social scientists have also found that alienation and self-actualization are influenced by many factors including the nature of one's job and the technology it uses.
14. One response to the changing economy and work force has been reorganizing the structure of work such as establishing flexible work arrangements.
15. The content of jobs can also be designed to meet the needs of labor and management. Empowering workers may make them even more effective, and more satisfied at the same time.

REFERENCES

Abel, Emily K. and Margaret K. Nelson, eds. 1990. *Circles of Care. Work and Identity in Women's Lives.* Albany: State University of New York.

Amott, Teresa L. and Julie A. Matthaei 1991. *Race, Gender and Work: A Multicultural Economic History of Women in the United States.* Boston: South End Press.

Auster, Carol J. 1996. *The Sociology of Work: Concepts and Cases.* Thousand Oaks, California: Pine Forge Press.

Barnet, Richard and Ann Barnet 1997. "Childcare Brain Drain?" *The Nation.* 264(18):May 12, Pp.6-8.

Bernstein, Aaron 1996 "Is America Becoming More of a Class Society?" Business Week, February 26:90.

Bianchi, Suzanne M. and Daphne Spain 1996. "*Women, Work, and Family in America.*" *Population Bulletin.* 51(3):47. Washington, DC: Population Reference Bureau.

Borgers, Frank 1996. "The Challenges of Economic Globalization for U.S. Labor." Critical Sociology. 22, 2:67-88.

Chafetz, Janet Saltzman (1997) "'1 Need a (Traditional) Wife!': Employment-Family Conflicts." Pp. 116-124 in Dana Dunn, eds. *Workplace/Women's Place. An Anthology.* Los Angeles: Roxbury Publishing Company.

Commission on the Future of Worker-Management Relations 1994 "Report and Recommendations: Executive Summary" Commission on Future of Worker-Management Relations: Final Report.(http://www.ilr.cornell.edu/library/e_archive/Dunlop/summary.html)

Crosby, Faye 1991. *Juggling: The Unexpected Advantages of Balancing Career and Home for Women and Their Families.* New York: The Free Press.

Croteau, James M. 1996. "Research on the Work Experiences of Lesbian, Gay, and Bisexual People: An Integrative Review of Methodology and Findings." *Journal of Vocational Behavior.* 48:195-209.

Diamond, Timothy 1992. *Making Gray Gold: Narratives of Nursing Home Care.* Chicago: University of Chicago Press.

Dickson, Lynda F. 1997. "The Third Shift: Black Women's Club Activities in Denver, 1900-1925." Pp.216-234 in Elizabeth Higginbotham and Mary Romero, eds. *Women and Work: Exploring Race, Ethnicity, and Class.* Women and Work. Vol. 6. Thousand Oaks, CA Sage Publications.

Dunn, Dana 1997. *Workplace/Women's Place, An Anthology.* Los Angeles: Roxbury Publishing Company.

Eaton, James and Manown Kisor, Jr. 1996. "Secular and Cyclical Patterns in White and Nonwhite Employment." *Monthly Labor Review.* 119(5):May 30-36.

"Eldercare Replacing Childcare as Workplace Concern." 1995 *Secretary.* 55:(February)6.

Emerson, Robert L. 1990. *The New Economics of Fast Food.* New York: Van Nostrand Reinhold.

Gerson, Kathleen 1994. "A Few Good Men: Overcoming the Barriers to Involved Fatherhood." *American Prospect.* 16(Winter):78-90.

Giele, Janet Zollinger 1979. "Changing Sex Roles and Family Structure." *Social Policy.* 9(4)32-43.

Glenn, Evelyn Nakano 1992. "From Servitude to Service Work: Historical Continuities in the Racial Division of Paid Reproductive Labor." *Signs: Journal of Women in Culture and Society.* 18(1):1-43.

Golden, Lonnie.1996. "The Economics of Worktime Length, Adjustment, and Flexibility: A Synthesis of Contributions from Competing Models of the Labor Market." *Review of Social Economy.* 54(1):1-45.

Grunberg, Leon, Sarah Moore, and Edward Greenberg 1996. "The Relationship of Employee Ownership and Participation to Workplace Safety." *Economic and Industrial Democracy.* 17(2):221-241.

Hamstra, Mark 1997. "McDonald's, Starbucks Wrangle with Canadian Organized Labor." *Nation's Restaurant News.* 31(20):2 (http://gilligan.prod.oclc.org:3055/FETCH...next=html/fs_fulltext.htm%22/fstx9.htm)

Hayghe, Howard V. 1997. "Developments in Women's Labor Force Participation." *A Monthly Labor Review.* (120) 9: 41-46.

Higginbotham, Elizabeth and Mary Romero 1997. *Women and Work: Exploring Race,. Ethnicity and Class.* Women and Work, Vol. 6. Thousand Oaks, CA: Sage Publications.

Hochschild, Arlie 1989. *The Second Shift.* New York: Viking Press.

Hodgkinson, Virginia, Heather Gorski, Stephen Hoga, and E. B. Knauft 1995. *Giving and Volunteering in the United States. Vol. II Trends in Giving and Volunteering by Type of Charity.* Washington, DC: Independent Sector.

Hodson, Randy 1985. "Working in 'High-Tech': Research Issues and Opportunities for the Industrial Sociologist." *Sociological Quarterly.* 26(3):351-364.

Hodson, Randy and Teresa A. Sullivan. 1995. *The Social Organization of Work.* Second ed. Belmont, CA: Wadsworth Publishing Company.

Hohl, Karen 1996. "The Effects of Flexible Work Arrangements." *Nonprofit Management and Leadership.* 7(1):69-86.

Hood, John 1995. "OSHA's Trivial Pursuit: In Workplace Safety, Business Outperforms the Regulators." *Policy Review.* 73:59-64.

Hondagneu-Sotelo, Pierrette 1997. "Working Without Papers in the United States: Toward the Integration of Legal Status in Frameworks of Race, Class, and Gender." Pp. 101-125 in Elizabeth Higginbotham and Mary Romero, eds. *Women and Work: Exploring Race. Ethnicity, and Class.* Women and Work. Vol. 6. Thousand Oaks, CA: Sage Publications.

Horovitz, Bruce (February 20, 1998). "Reinventing McDonald's." *USA Today,* Pp. 1 B-2B.

Hounshell, David A. 1984. *From the American System to Mass Production, 1800-1932.* Baltimore: Johns Hopkins University Press. Pp.216-302.

Jacobs, Jerry, ed. 1995. *Gender Inequality at Work.* Thousand Oaks, CA: Sage Publications.

Jalon, Allan (December 6, 1985). "Synthesizers: Sour Sound to Musicians" *Los Angeles Times.*

Kanigel, Robert 1997. *The One Best Way. Frederick Winslow Taylor and the Enigma of Efficiency.* New York: Viking Penguin.

Kanter, Rosabeth Moss 1977. *Men and Women of the Corporation.* New York: Basic Books.

Kasl, Stanislav, Susan Gore, and Sidney Cobb 1975. "The Experience of Losing a Job: Reported Changes in Health, Symptoms, and Illness Behavior" *Psychosomatic Medicine.* (March-April).

Kritz-Silverstein, Donna, Deborah L. Wingard, and Elizabeth Barrett-Connor 1992. "Employment Status and Heart Disease Risk in Middle-Aged Women: The Rancho Bernardo Study." *American Journal of Public Health.* 82(2): Feb, 215-219.

Lager, Fred 1994. *Ben & Jerry's. The Inside Scoop.* New York: Crown Trade Paperbacks.

Lamphere, Louise and Patricia Zavella 1997. "Women's Resistance in the Sun Belt: Anglos and Hispanics Respond to Managerial Control." Pp. 76-100 in Elizabeth Higginbotham and Mary Romero, eds. *Women and Work Exploring Race. Ethnicity, and Class.* Women and Work. Vol. 6. Thousand Oaks: CA: Sage Publications.

Leidner, Robin 1993. *Fast Food, Fast Talk: Service Work and the Routinization of Everyday Lift.* Berkeley, University of California Press. Pp. 49-50.

Lenz, Edward A. 1996. "Flexible Employment: Positive Work Strategies for the 21st Century." *Journal of Labor Research.* 17(4):555-566.

Leonhardt, David March 9, 1998. "McDonald's: Can It Regain Its Golden Touch?" *Business Week.* Pp. 70-77.

Love, John F. 1986. *McDonald's: Behind the Arches.* Toronto: Bantam Books.

_____September 22, 1997 "Mac Attack." Time, p. 64.

_____March 1, 1997 "McDonald's Franchisees OK Price Cuts." Los Angeles Times. Pp. D1 & D3.

Mankin, Don, Susan Cohen, and Tora Bikson 1997. "Teams and Technology: Tensions in Participatory Design." *Organizational Dynamics.* 26 (Summer): 63-76.

McKenna, Elizabeth Perle 1997. *When Work Doesn't Work Anymore: Women, Work and Identity.* New York: Delacorte.

Milkman, Ruth 1997. *Farewell to the Factory: Auto Workers in the Late Twentieth Century.* Berkeley: University of California Press.

Morrison, Malcolm H. 1986. "Work and Retirement in an Aging Society." *Daedalus.* 115(1):269-293.

Osterman, Paul 1994. 'How Common is Workplace Transformation and Who Adopts It?" *Industrial and Labor Relations Review.* 47(2):173-~88.

Oswald, Andrew J. 1997. "Happiness and Economic Performance" *The Economic Journal.* 107(November):1822.

Pardo, Mary 1997. "Working-Class Mexican American Women and 'Volunteerism' 'We Have to Do It!'" Pp. 197-215 in Elizabeth Higginbotham and Mary Romero, eds. *Women and Work: Exploring Race, Ethnicity, and Class.* Women and Work. Vol. 6. Thousand Oaks, CA: Sage Publications.

Peters, Joan K. 1997. *When Mothers Work: Loving Our Children without Sacrificing Ourselves.* Reading, MA: Addison-Wesley.

Pierce, Jennifer 1995. *Gender Trials: Emotional Lives in Contemporary Firms.* Berkeley: University of CA Press.

"Pioneering Firms Bring Breast-feeding to Work." *USA Today.* December 8, 1997. p. 22A.

Presser, Harriet B. and Amy G. Cox 1997. "The Work Schedules of Low-Educated American Women and Welfare Reform." *Monthly Labor Review.* 120(4):25-34.

Rathnam, Sukumar, Vijay Mahajan, and Andrew Whinston 1995. "Facilitating Coordination in Customer Support Teams: A Framework and its Implications for the Design of Information Technology." *Management Science.* 41:1900-1921.

Reiter, Ester (1991) *Making Fast Food.* Montreal: McGill-Queen's University Press.

Reskin, Barbara and Irene Padavic (1994) *Women and Men at Work.* Thousand Oaks. CA: Pine Forge Press.

Ritzer, George 1996. *The McDonaldization of Society.* Rev. ed. Thousand Oaks, CA: Pine Forge Press.

Robles, Barbara 1997. "An Economic Profile of Women in the United States." in Elizabeth Higginbotham and Mary Romero, eds. "Women and Work: Exploring Race, Ethnicity, and Class." *Women and Work.* Vol. 6. Thousand Oaks, CA: Sage Publications.

Roethlisberger, F. J. and William J. Dickson 1939. *Management and the Worker.* Cambridge, MA: Harvard University Press.

Rogers, Jackie Krasas and Kevin Henson 1997. "Hey Why Don't You Wear a Shorter Skirt? Structural Vulnerability and the Organization of Sexual Harassment in Temporary Clerical Employment." *Gender and Society.* (April).

Romero, Mary 1992. *Maid in the USA.* New York: Routledge.

_____(1997a) "Epilogue." Pp.235-248 in Elizabeth Higginbotham and Mary Romero, eds. *Women and Work: Exploring Race, Ethnicity, and Class.* Women and Work. Vol. 6. Thousand Oaks, CA: Sage Publications.

_____(1997b) "Chicanas Modernize Domestic Service." Pp. 358-368 in Dana Dunn, ed., *Workplace/Women's Place, An Anthology.* Los Angeles: Roxbury Publishing Company.

Rosenberg, Janet, Harry Perlstadt, and William R. F. Phillips 1997. "'Now that Were Here': Discrimination, Disparagement, and Harassment at Work and the Experience of Women Lawyers." Pp. 116-124 in Dana Dunn, ed., *Workplace/Women's Place: An Anthology.* Los Angeles: Roxbury Publishing Company.

Seeman, Melvin 1959. "On the Meaning of Alienation." *American Sociological Review* 24(6):783-791.

Shepard, Edward M. III, Thomas J. Clifton, and Douglas Kruse 1996. "Flexible Work Hours and Productivity: Some Evidence from the Pharmaceutical Industry." *Industrial Relations.* 35(1): 123-139.

Sijuwade, Philip O. 1996. "U.S. Older Workers: Their Employment and Occupational Problems in the Labor Market." *Social Behavior and Personality.* 24(3): 235-238.

Silver, Hilary and Frances Goldscheider. 1994. Flexible Work and Housework: Work and Family Constraints on Women's Domestic Labor." *Social Forces.* 72(4):1103-1119.

Smith, Adam 1937. *The Wealth of Nations.* New York: Modern Library (Originally published in 1776) p. 3.

Solomon, Jolie and John McCormick (November17, 1997). "A Really Big Mac." *Newsweek.* Pp. 56-58.

Staines, Graham L. and Joseph H. Pleck 1986. "Work Schedule Flexibility and Family Life." *Journal of Occupational Behavior.* 7(2):147-153.

Steiger, Thomas and Barbara F. Reskin 1990. "Baking and Baking Off: Deskilling and the Changing Sex Make-up of Bakers." In Barbara F. Reskin and Patricia A. Rooss, eds. *Job Queues, Gender Queues: Explaining Women's Inroads into Male Occupations.* Philadelphia: Temple University Press.

Stevens, Shannon 1997. "McDonald's Franchisees Refocus on Putting Fast in Fast Food." *Brandweek.* 38(36):9
(http://gilligan.prod.oclc.org:3055/Fletch.next=html/fs_fulltext.htm%22:/fstx6.htm)

Sugarman, Carole December31, 1997. "Organic? Industry is Way Ahead of Government." *The Washington Post.* (http://web.lexis-nexis.com).

Taylor, G. Stephen 1987. "A Reanalysis of the Relation Between Unionization and Workplace Safety." *International Journal of Health Services.* 17(3):443-453.

Tomaskovic-Devey, Donald and Barbara Risman 1993. *Gender and Racial Inequality at Work.* Ithaca: New York State School of Industrial and Labor Relations, Cornell University.

U.S. Bureau of the Census, 1900-1960, *Historical Statistics of the United States: Colonial Times to 1970,* Bicentennial Edition, part 1, series Dl1-25; (1970~1995) U.S. Bureau of Labor Statistics, *Employment and Earnings* 43, no.1: tables 1 and 2. The source of this table is Suzanne M Bianchi and Daphne Spain, 1996, "Women, Work, and Family in America" Population Bulletin 51 (December). Reprinted by permission of the Population Reference Bureau

U.S. Bureau of Labor Statistics 1994. *The Employment Outlook:* 1994 to 2005. BLS Bulletin 2472. (http://stats.bls.gov/oco/oco2003.htm.).

U.S. Bureau of Labor Statistics August, 17, 1995. *New Data on Contingent and Alternative Employment Examined by BLS.* Washington, D.C.: U.S Department of Labor, (http://stats.bls.gov/news.release/conemp.toc.htm.)

_____ (1997a). "Occupational Pay in the United States, November 1995." U.S. Department Of Labor.

_____ (1997b). "Labor Force Statistics from the Current Population Survey. Table 4. Extent of Unemployment During the Year by Race, Hispanic Origin, and Sex, 1995-96. (http://Iwww.bls.gov/news.release/work.t04.htm)

U.S. Department of Labor, Women's Bureau 1994. *Working Women Count!* Washington DC: Government Printing Office.

Walters, William. 1996. "The Demise of Unemployment?" *Politics and Society.* 24(3):197-219.

Weber, Lynn and Elizabeth Higginbotham 1997. "Black and White Professional-Managerial Women's Perceptions of Racism and Sexism in the Workplace." Pp. 153-175 in Elizabeth Higginbotham and Mary Romero, eds. *Women and Work' Exploring Race, Ethnicity, and Class.* Women and Work. Vol. 6. Thousand Oaks, CA: Sage Publications.

Wellman, Barry, Janet Salaff, Dimitrina Dimitrova, Laura Garton, Milena Gulia, Caroline Haythornthwaite 1996. "Computer Networks as Social Networks: Collaborative Work. Telework, and Virtual Community." *Annual Review of Sociology.* 22:213-238.

Wilson, William Julius 1996. *When Work Disappears: The World of the New Urban Poor.* New York: Knopf.

Wootton, Barbara H. 1997. "Gender Differences in Occupational Employment." *Monthly Labor Review.* 120(4): 15-24.

Zieger, Robert H. 1986. *American Workers, American Unions, 1920-1985.* Baltimore: The Johns Hopkins University Press. Pp. 26-61

CHAPTER 12: POVERTY
CASE STUDY: THE HOMELESS ON HOMELESSNESS

The summer in New York City doesn't really get started until July. June, on the whole, is usually quite pleasant with only the subtlest hints of the oppressive hot and steamy weather of the dog days of an East Coast summer. For the many homeless men and women in New York who live outdoors - those who call parks, crowded street corners, bridge abutments and abandoned lots home - shifts in the weather mark the passage of time. Extremes of temperature present special challenges, but they do little to alter daily routines of survival.

I first met Brenda in a small sliver of a park sandwiched between the intersection of two bustling avenues. A thin African-American woman in her late-thirties, Brenda told me that she had been homeless for over 2 years, ever since she and her husband split up. She had 4 children who lived in Delaware, but refused to ask them for help. She relied instead on panhandling and odd jobs to earn the money she needed to live.

Like many of New York's homeless, Brenda used to live in Penn Station - one of the city's two train stations. She and those she lived with were evicted when the police "cleaned up" the Station. The park I met her in, with its broken slotted benches and weed-filled planters, seemed safe from such attempts at urban betterment and was close enough to the Station to provide the convenience of its lockers and remodeled public bathrooms. I asked Brenda why she remains outdoors, rather than going to a shelter. New York is after all one of only a few cities that guarantees homeless individuals space in public shelters. She hesitated for a moment and told me, as if it were obvious, "Shelters are inhumane, worse than the streets. I'm a person with dignity, I'm just too old to be treated badly."

As we talked, Tanya, a Puerto Rican woman in her mid-thirties came over and hugged Brenda warmly. At first, she was suspicious of me, avoiding eye contact and conversation. In time, her suspicion waned and she grew curious. She asked me a battery of questions - where I went to school, where I lived, where I was born, and whether or not I had a boyfriend. I answered her questions honestly and openly and soon Tanya and Brenda began to talk candidly about their lives.

Both women agreed that the most important aspect of survival on the streets was cooperation. Tanya explained, "We sleep together; we eat together. We have one sandwich, one pack of cigarettes and we split it. Just like before, Brenda had chicken before [I arrived] didn't eat earlier so we shared." Cooperation in obtaining and distributing food and cigarettes, they told me, occurs not only between close friends who "watch out for each other," as Tanya and Brenda do, but also takes place among the other men and women who inhabit this small park. "We share, equally, all the time," Brenda told me. "We have this group, OK. We help each other out until we can get out of this."

Companionship offers the women more than the material stuff of survival. "We see each other everyday," Tanya explained, "and if we don't (we) ask.

You're supposed to let somebody know where you are." Time spent together makes the environment safe. It ensures that there is always someone around to watch your back in case of trouble, "in case you was out there sliding." Both Tanya and Brenda boasted that "...we (residents) help each other," yet both women confessed that such solidarity was very much the product of necessity. Tanya explained, "Even though we might not be able to stand each other, we might even dislike each other, we're all in the same boat and we have to help each other."

Though their lives as homeless women who share a small park in New York have much in common, the two women disagreed sharply as to why they were homeless. Tanya blamed herself:

"I'm out here because I'm stupid right now. When I say stupid I don't mean stupid as far as ignorance. As far as schooling I went to College. I'm here because I like getting high. I'm being realistic. And this is why a lot of people are homeless right now. They got a lot of problems. Certain people are on welfare and stuff. Welfare gives you a certain amount of money"...

Before Tanya could finish her sentence, Brenda interrupted:

"And that doesn't mean anything, you can't do nothing with it. You can't do anything with the amount of money that they give you. That's the way the system is it's keeping us like this. It keeps you one step in and one step out. I'm not on welfare or anything like that. I can't even get on that shit the system is so fucked up. You know you can't blame us for being out here. You can blame the politicians. It's all types of people who live out here. I wasn't a drug addict when I came out here. I did drugs, but I wasn't addicted. I don't do crack. Now I think I'm becoming an alcoholic."

Unlike Tanya, Brenda put the responsibility for her homelessness on others, specifically on a political and economic system that had, as she saw it, given her a raw deal. Brenda and Tanya are just two of the millions of Americans who are poor. Life on a park bench, as revealed in this excerpt, illustrates many aspects of poverty that will be explored in the chapter that follows. We will return to details of their story as we attempt to answer three basic questions about poverty in America: who are the poor? Why are they poor? What can be done to help them?

DEFINITIONS OF POVERTY: HOW AND WHERE DO WE DRAW THE LINE?

Most everyone would agree that Brenda and Tanya are poor. Most everyone would agree as well that one doesn't have to be homeless to be poor. Plenty of people who have homes suffer other forms of deprivation significant enough that we would consider them to be poor as well. When we begin to think about who is poor and who isn't we inevitably ask the question, "Where do we draw the line?" How do we decide from among those who don't have a lot whom we consider to be poor?

It is customary in tackling such a question to propose a poverty threshold or, more colloquially, a **poverty line**. A poverty threshold is, quite simply, a number or a set of numbers, usually representing household income. Individuals who live in households whose income falls below the threshold for their household size are considered to be poor; those who live in households above the line are not. Where we decide to draw these lines, clearly matters. If we decide that for a family of four, the threshold should be $17,500, then a husband, wife, and their two children with an annual income of $16,000 are poor. If we set the threshold at $15,000, then they are not. Same family, same way of living. The only difference is how we classify them.

Classification is important for a number of reasons. Poverty thresholds allow us to decide what number or percentage of the population is counted as poor. These numbers, to the extent that they are accurate, reveal the extent of poverty as a social problem at any point in time. The **poverty rate,** defined as the percentage of individuals in the population who live in households whose income falls below the appropriate poverty threshold, is one measure of the overall economic well-being of our society (Ruggles 1990:1). Consistent methods of measuring the poverty threshold apply across regions, and between different groups. Those who design, implement, and evaluate poverty policies and programs rely on measurements to assess whether or not their programs are working. That is, if they are reaching those groups and individuals that they initially intended to help (Ruggles 1990: 1). Classification is a first step toward any solutions to the deprivation felt by those who live in poverty. Deciding where to draw the line is not easy however. Debates over the appropriate method for setting the poverty threshold have continued unabated for more than thirty years since the government undertook to measure who was poor.

ABSOLUTE POVERTY

Government reports and programs rely on an absolute standard for measuring poverty. The **absolute poverty** standard defines "people (as) poor if they lack access to minimally adequate levels of income or consumption" (Ruggles 1990: 7). That is, the poverty threshold is the important comparison. We can evaluate the level of poverty over time; level of income a household of a particular size requires to maintain an objectively defined "minimum decent standard of living." Households below the threshold are presumed to lack the ability to enjoy such minimum standards. In 1995, for example, the government believed that a family of four required $15,569 to live decently.

Where do such numbers come from? The absolute poverty standard emerged from a series of studies conducted by Mollie Orshansky in the 1960's. Orshansky developed "a set of poverty thresholds for different types of families that consisted of the cost of a minimum adequate diet multiplied by 3 to allow for other expenses" (Citro and Michael 1995:17). Calculating the poverty threshold in this manner requires deciding how much food a household of a particular type needs, how much this food costs, and then multiplying by 3. The minimum adequate diet, often referred to as the "thrifty food budget," is based on basic physiological needs as understood by experts (Citro and Michael 1995:31). It is concerned with the minimum of provision needed to maintain health and the capacity to work. It emphasizes the capacity to *survive* and the ability to maintain *physical efficiency* (Rein in Townsend: 1970:46 emphasis added).

Many scholars have criticized the absolute poverty standard currently used by the government. First and foremost, they have questioned the arbitrary nature of the "minimum decent standard of living?" Does it apply consistently across all people, all groups, and all regions? Is the same basic standard valid today, as it was 30 years ago? The absolute poverty standard changes with the price of goods not with their pattern of consumption. But consumption patterns have changed and, as a consequence, the poverty standard fails to reflect the circumstances in which people live today (Ruggles 1990:17). Others have argued that in assessing "the minimum decent standard of living," it is important to take into account necessities other than food. Simply assuming that shelter, medical care and clothing and other expenses should take up twice a family's food budget may be inadequate particularly when the cost of goods such as housing and medical care often rise faster than the cost of food. In urban areas, in particular, where housing costs have risen quickly, the absolute poverty standard may fail to capture the poverty that many individuals and families face.

Recent work in studying poverty thresholds has sought to move beyond calculating the appropriate multiple of the food budget, and towards identifying what poor people need and how able they are to attain it. Citro and Michael have argued that the Orshansky measure be replaced by one that takes into account actual prices of three types of goods: food, clothing and shelter adjusted not only for family size but also geographic location and time period. The critical issue, they argue, is "a family's *ability* to attain a living standard above the poverty level by means of its own resources." That is, "...what matters is someone's *actual* standard of living, regardless of how it is attained" (Citro and Michael 1995:36-37).

RELATIVE POVERTY

Other criticisms of the absolute poverty standard focus not on the method for calculating the "minimum decent standard," but rather on the appropriateness of such a standard at all. Another approach to measuring poverty identifies the poor based on their position within the society as a whole. Put simply, the poor are those who have less than others. The **relative poverty** standard defines the poor as those who fall lowest on the **income distribution** at a particular point in time. There are several different ways of measuring a relative poverty threshold. All start with the income distribution, which is a ranking of every household in America according to annual income from highest to lowest. Some argue that the standard should be based on a percentage of the median, or middle value, within this income distribution. That is, that 50 or 60 or 70% of the median income is an appropriate poverty threshold. Others argue that those in the lowest 10% or 20% are, according to a relative standard, considered poor. The poverty threshold in this instance is simply the highest income of any household within the 10% or 20% who are considered poor (Ruggles 1990: 18-19). These approaches are best illustrated by reference to an example of a hypothetical society of 10 households with an income distribution depicted in Table 12.1 below:

Using this example, to calculate a poverty threshold based on 50% of the median income, we would first calculate the median, which in this case is the midpoint between the 5th an 6th household, or $39,000 and then multiply it by .5, resulting in a poverty threshold of $19,500. To calculate a poverty threshold based on the lowest 20% of the distribution, we would look to the 9th household and say that the poverty threshold is $21,000.

Relative standards of poverty offer the advantage of locating our understanding of poverty within the context of society as a whole (Rein in Townsend 1970:46). In this respect they are more sensitive to the impact of societal norms on our understandings of a decent standard of living. Advocates of relative standards argue that what we believe is decent varies over time and is a factor of the overall level of affluence of a society and not the objective assessment of experts. Minimum standards for housing, for example, have increased dramatically over time as overall affluence has raised expectations and understandings of what constitutes decent dwellings. Relative definitions also take into account the extent to which individuals and families may feel deprivation with respect to what others have. Poverty in this respect takes into account not only physical needs but psychological well being as well.

Table 12.1: Income Distribution of a Hypothetical Society

Household #	Income ($)	Household #	Income $
1	$100,000	6	$38,000
2	$95,000	7	$29,000
3	$80,000	8	$24,000
4	$60,000	9	$21,000
5	$40,000	10	$10,000

Despite such positives, relative definitions have received little acceptance in the public policy arena. Opponents of relative measures argue that they are too much of a "moving target" to form the basis of anti-poverty policy. Changes in the distribution of income, they claim, can produce changes in the relative poverty threshold without any measurable impact on the consumption patterns or opportunities of the poor. They argue that the goal of policy is to mitigate physical suffering, the extent of which can only be measured by an absolute standard that takes into account the real costs of the goods and services the poor need in order to survive.

WHO ARE THE POOR?

Despite its problems, the Orshansky absolute poverty threshold remains the principal means by which the incidence and rate of poverty is assessed in America. In the section that follows we take a look at what government numbers based on the absolute (or Orshansky) threshold tell us about who is poor. We consider as well what is known about those who experience the most extreme form of poverty, homelessness.

THE BASIC NUMBERS

In 1995, 13.8% of the population lived in households whose incomes fell below their size-appropriate Orshansky threshold. That is to say, in 1995, 36.4 million Americans were poor because they lacked the resources to support a "minimum decent standard of living." Many of these people were extremely poor. Of the 36.4 million below the threshold, 13.9 million-- 5.3% of the total population -- lived in households whose incomes were less than half the poverty line. This figure translated to $7,784.50 for a family of four.

While even small changes in the poverty rate affect millions of Americans, the overall rate tends not to fluctuate a great deal. After a period of significant decline during the first half of the 1960's, the poverty rate has been relatively constant, varying only within 2% points of the current 13.8% figure (All figures from Poverty in the United States: 1995, (U.S. Department of Commerce: September 1996)).

Poverty is, in part, a function of economic conditions. During periods of economic downturns, for example the recessions of 1980-81 and 1990-91, the poverty rate increased. During times of economic growth, when unemployment is lower, we see fewer poor people. However, the declines in poverty rates are less steep than the increases associated with recession. That is, it takes longer for good times to have an impact on the poverty rate than bad times. What's more, the overall poverty rate has never fallen below 11% meaning that even in the best of times a large number of Americans live in poverty.

THE UNHOUSED POOR

The above numbers, which are based on a survey of households, no doubt leave out some of America's poorest people, those like Brenda and Tanya who call a park bench home. Brenda and Tanya are often referred to as the literally homeless (Rossi 1989). That is, people who live and sleep on the streets, in bus and train stations, or abandoned buildings. This definition of homelessness also includes men, women and children who live in public and private shelters, as well as welfare hotels and Single Room Occupancies (see O'Flaherty 1996:13-15 for a discussion of the problems involved in classifying shelters). It is important to enumerate the number of literally homeless Americans as a first step in designing and implementing policies to alleviate the problem. Unfortunately, the U.S. census has never been able to adequately estimate the size of the unsheltered homeless population (see O'Flaherty 1996:37). That is, the men and women who do not reside in public or private shelters, welfare hotels and single room occupancies but live, as Brenda and Tanya do, in small parks in and around the urban landscape.

Although virtually everyone agrees that the problem has grown worse since the late 1970's, there is little agreement over the magnitude of this growth. For example, in the late 1970's, when Americans began to notice more and more people sleeping in public places, advocates argued that 2 to 3 million Americans were literally homeless (Hombs and Snyder 1982; Jencks 1994:1). Politicians scrutinized these numbers and in 1984 asked the Department of Housing and Urban Development (HUD) to systematically estimate the number of homeless people in America. HUD officials arrived at a much smaller number, arguing that 250,000-300,000 Americans were homeless (Jencks 1994, HUD 1984). In an attempt to reach some numerical compromise between the advocates and politicians, researchers worked to develop strategies and techniques to systematically count the number of literally homeless in the United States (O'Flaherty 1996; Jencks 1994; Burt 1992; Hopper 1991: Rossi 1989; Freeman and Hall 1987).

To date, still no single estimate receives widespread acceptance. National estimates of numbers of homeless persons range from 250,000 to 3 million people depending, of course, on the definition of homelessness used as well as the methodology employed for counting (Shlay and Rossi 1992). The most highly touted estimate, however, suggests that approximately 300,000-400,000 Americans were literally homeless. Estimates above 500,000, according to one observer, would be harder to defend (Jencks 1994:13).

To summarize, the number of men, women and children who are poor, using an absolute definition of poverty, has fluctuated over the past 36 years. During times of economic growth, the number falls, though not nearly as much as we would like it to. Even in the best of times, a good number of Americans live in poverty. These "official" poverty estimates, however, do not take into account those Americans who lack conventional dwelling, like Brenda and Tanya, who are referred to as the literally homeless. Estimating the size of this population continues to challenge those who attempt to understand the magnitude and nature of homelessness in America. Others, however, resist national estimates, claiming that "...the extent of homelessness, especially on the national level, is essentially "unknowable" (Rossi 1989:47).

A CLOSER LOOK

Poverty affects Americans of all ages, and all ethnic and racial backgrounds. It affects men and women, those who live in cities, suburbs, and small towns in every state of the country. Contrary to stereotypes often seen on television and in the movies of poor urban Blacks, the majority of poor people are White (68.4%) and live outside of central cities (55.3%). Though poverty affects all Americans, it does not affect them equally. That is members of certain groups are more likely to be poor while members of other groups are less likely. For example, the poverty rate among senior citizens, those 65 and over, is likely to be 10.5%, which is lower than the 13.8% average. On the other hand, the rate of poverty among children under 18 years of age is 20.8%. These numbers indicate that children are just about twice as likely to live in poverty as senior citizens (All figures from Poverty in the United States: 1995 (U.S. Department of Commerce: September 1996)).

Poverty rates are highest among Blacks and Hispanics, female headed households, children, central cities and rural areas, and the South and West regions of the United States. Poverty rates are lowest among middle aged men living in suburban metropolitan locations.

Unlike the **"old homeless,"** - a homogenous group composed largely of older (beyond middle age), White, single men, -- the **"new homeless"** are more diverse, affecting Americans of all ages, races and ethnic backgrounds (Shlay and Rossi 1992; Hoch and Slayton 1989). In addition, homelessness is no longer confined to the **skid row** sections of major cities. Skid rows consisted of those areas of town occupied by cheap bars, restaurants, and lodging houses for men who drifted in and out of the cities looking for work (Allen 1993). Today, the homeless can be found throughout major and minor metropolises, in their suburbs, and in ex-urban and rural towns (McConnell 1992; Hopper 1990; Hoch and Slayton 1989).

Like poverty, homelessness affects some more than others. Although the majority of homeless are male, making up close to 75% of the homeless population, the emergence of women, such as Brenda and Tanya, and children continue to make up a significant proportion of the "new homeless" (Shlay and Rossi 1992). Approximately one third of the urban homeless are families with children (Reyes and Waxman 1987). Although the majority of homeless are non-Hispanic White, over 40% of homeless people are Black and 12% Hispanic. Like the housed poor, then, although the majority of homeless are White, homelessness disproportionately effects Blacks and non-White Hispanics. Keep in mind, there are more Whites in society than Blacks and non-White Hispanics. Although a greater number of Whites may be poor and/or homeless at any given time, they make up a smaller population of the White population. Even more, these racial and ethnic differences express themselves across regions. For example, the homeless in northern regions are more likely to be Black than in southern and western regions. Lastly, 35% of the homeless are under 30 years old and 7% over 60 years old. That is, the majority of homeless people are middle-aged, with an average age of just over 35 (Shlay and Rossi 1992). Brenda and Tanya clearly represent the "new homeless."

WHY ARE PEOPLE POOR?

Numbers and trends tell us a great deal about the diversity of men and women, adults and children who live in poverty. They tell us that poverty can affect virtually everyone. Despite television and film images that might lead us to think that poverty is a problem confined to the urban ghetto, the numbers remind us that the majority of poor Americans are White (68.4%), and live outside of central cities (55.3%). They tell us as well that some Americans, Blacks and Hispanics, residents of urban areas, those who live in female-headed households, are far more likely to live in poverty than others. A Black person is more than 3 times as likely to be poor as a White person. A disparity of this size cannot happen simply by chance. And so in asking the basic question of why people are poor, scholars typically focus on why certain people are more likely to be poor than others (All figures from <u>Poverty in the United States: 1995</u> (U.S. Department of Commerce: September 1996)).

Most contemporary work exploring poverty in America focuses on African-Americans in the inner city. According to William Julius Wilson, a leading scholar of urban poverty, this focus is justified. He writes, "By 1991, the central cities included close to half of the nation's poor. Many of the most rapid increases in concentrated poverty have occurred in African-American neighborhoods" (Wilson 1996:11). David Ellwood, former Assistant Secretary of Health and Human Services concurs. He argues although the ghetto poor do not comprise the majority of poor people in America, "...they are visible enough and troubled enough to justify special consideration" (Ellwood 1988:195). What, then, does the literature tell us about the causes of ghetto poverty?

Much of the debate centers around three proposed interpretations of the problem -biological, cultural, and structural. **Biological explanations** seek to demonstrate innate and inherited characteristics of particular individuals that predispose them to poverty. Though largely unaccepted in the scholarly community, biological explanations purport to explain Black poverty along genetic lines. **Cultural explanations**, like biological ones, also have an individualistic orientation, that is they **blame the victim** (Ryan 1976) by locating the cause or causes of poverty within poor people themselves (Dordick 1994). For culturalists, the problem is not genes, but rather behavior and values, which are distinctive from and less desirable than those held by, middle-class Americans. Cultural and biological explanations have been countered by arguments that emphasize the structural causes of poverty (Dordick 1994). Rather than *blaming the victim* for her or his poverty, **structural explanations** focus on the ways in which economic opportunities and rewards are unequally distributed in American society. Structuralists emphasize such issues as joblessness, discrimination in education, housing, and hiring, and the unequal impact of economic transformations in explaining the causes of poverty. Structural explanations transfer the blame for poverty away from the poor and toward the society as a whole.

BIOLOGICAL EXPLANATIONS

Biological explanations for poverty have been around as long as poverty itself. In the late 19th century, when with rapid industrialization, poverty emerged as a significant social problem in urban America, so too did a philosophy of **Social Darwinism**. Social Darwinists believed in the genetic inferiority of the poor and argued for a philosophy of "survival of the fittest," in which principles of natural selection would eventually eliminate the evolutionarily unfit poor. The popularity of such beliefs has ebbed and flowed in the last century. In 1994, with the publication of a book called *The Bell Curve: Intelligence and Class Structure in American Life* (1994), the late Richard Herrnstein and Charles Murray brought biological explanations of poverty back into the forefront of national debate. The book makes three claims. First, and least controversial, is that in a modern, technologically sophisticated society where information is the most important product, intelligence is more highly associated than ever before with economic success. Second, and more controversial, is that 60% of intelligence is inherited, that is it is in the genes. Third, and most controversial, is that Blacks as a race -- owing to genetic differences -- are less intelligent than Whites, and that this inherited condition is the cause of persistently higher rates of poverty. The consequences of such a position are dramatic. Because Herrnstein and Murray locate the root cause of poverty within the genetic make-up of individuals, they question "the extent to which the environment influences group social outcomes and whether intervention programs can compensate for the handicaps of genetic endowment" (Wilson 1996:xv). Quite simply, they are skeptical of any social programs, such as **Head Start,** that are developed to help raise the educational opportunities of the poor.

The publication of *The Bell Curve* provoked a firestorm of criticism from a broad spectrum of poverty experts. Numerous scholars painstakingly picked apart the design and methodology of the studies linking intelligence and race, arguing that the evidence presented in the book is either flawed or misinterpreted. Others attacked the arbitrary and difficult line drawn between genetic and environmental influences. Some asked a more basic question. Even if we accept that 60% of intelligence is inherited - as the authors hope that we will - that leaves 40% up to the environment, a significant proportion that simply can't be ignored. Despite the publicity surrounding the book's publication, acceptance of biological explanations of poverty among scholars and experts is quite low. Most of those currently involved in thinking and writing about poverty fall into one of the two schools discussed below.

CULTURAL EXPLANATIONS

Cultural explanations look to behavior and values to explain why certain people are poor. They are rooted in the basic assertion that there is a **culture of poverty,** that produces and reproduces a set of behaviors and values that create deprivation among those who adhere to and practice them. The term "culture of poverty" was originally coined by Oscar Lewis, an anthropologist who studied life in the poor villages of Mexico and Puerto Rico (Lewis 1959). Lewis argues that the poor develop a set of strategies, ways of acting and behaving, to cope with living in poverty. These strategies, which together comprise a "culture of poverty," are "both an adaptation and a reaction of the poor to their marginal position in a class stratified, highly individuated, capitalist society" (Lewis in Moynihan 1968:188).

The culture of poverty, as Lewis describes it, consists of 62 behavioral and personality "traits" that help the poor to cope with the material, psychological and emotional consequences of economic deprivation, social immobility and chronic unemployment (Gans 1995; Wilson 1987; Massey and Denton 1993; Lewis 1959). These "traits" include, for example, the inability to defer gratification, a lack of impulse control, low educational goals, and a faulty work ethic. Even though Lewis explicitly connects the emergence of these cultural "traits" and patterns to structural conditions in society, he argues that the culture of poverty perpetuates itself from one generation to the next, independent of persistent poverty. That is, the poor as a group come to value hard work, education, and the future less than those in the middle class. In a society that value education and a strong commitment to hard work, these "traits," or different values, are barriers to the upward mobility of poor Americans. That is, once the culture of poverty is internalized, it prevents young children from taking advantage of opportunities to better themselves (Gans 1995; Denton 1993; Wilson 1987). By abandoning core middle class American values of efficiency, success, hard work and self-reliance, the poor are depicted as having a distinct and dysfunctional "lower-class culture" (Thio 1996, Massey and Denton 1993, Banfield 1970). The notion that poor are different from the rest of us has, in recent years, been captured in the newest buzzword for describing a morally undeserving, as well as materially impoverished, poor -- the **"underclass"** (Gans 1990). The term, the underclass, was originally coined by the Swedish economist Gunnar Myrdal (1963) to describe the victims of a society undergoing a rapid dismantling of its industrial base (Gans 1995:28). Myrdal defined the underclass as "an unprivileged class of unemployed, unemployables and underemployed who are more and more hopelessly set apart from the nation at large and do not share in its life, its ambitions and its achievements" (Gans 1995:28). Myrdal, in defining the underclass, did not allude to particular cultural and behavioral characteristics. Rather, the underclass was an economic term that described a particular class segment's relationship to the labor market in light of a rapidly changing, **post-industrial economy** (Gans 1995).

During the 1970's, however, the focus of the term shifted away from unemployment and joblessness to describe a kind of acute and persistent poverty, involving deviant, harmful, and anti-social behaviors, associated primarily with urban Blacks and Hispanics (Gans 1990). The underclass are "poor people of color in America's inner cities...aliens in their own country, defined primarily by their deviant values" (Katz 1989:197). They are "...strangers in our midst act[ing]in ways unlike middle-class Americans" (Katz 1989:7). Specifically, accounts of life among the underclass focused on teenage motherhood, drug use and abuse, and crime. Black teen-age mothers and "dangerous" Black males dominate the images of the underclass (Katz 1989:195). The emergence of the term **behavioral underclass** depicts a harder and more overtly racial edge to the traditional culture of poverty argument. A focus on laziness, lack of motivation and lack of educational ambition has been supplanted by an emphasis on a more actively sinister way of life. Where the poor were once blamed for what they didn't do - work hard, save, study - they are now blamed for what they do - have babies, take drugs, and commit crime. Sexual promiscuity and criminal amorality have, through the language of "the underclass," come to supplement the list of traits that Lewis and others originally identified as "the culture of poverty."

Another behavior blamed by culturalists for persistent ghetto poverty is **welfare dependency** (Mead 1992, Moffitt 1992, and Murray 1984). Proponents of this explanation for poverty argue that a "liberal welfare state" encourages dependency. That is, generous welfare benefits and permissive policies and programs encourage long-term welfare use as an alternative to work. This dependency, which according to proponents of this position encourages unwed, childbearing, teen-age pregnancy, and female-headed families, promotes a way of life in which escape from poverty through work is impossible (Massey and Denton 1993; Wilson 1987). "Those who are dependent are inactive, ineffectual, and even irresponsible in the eyes of many" (Bane and Ellwood 1994:68). Welfare dependency models that blame the victim echo many of the basic premises of the culture of poverty, arguing that the growth of liberal welfare policies encourages "quasi-pathological" behavioral and cultural "traits" that result in greater and persistent poverty and exacerbate the differences between poor and non-poor (Wilson 1996; Gans 1995; Bane and Ellwood 1994).

Tanya is a culturalist. When she claims that "I'm out here because I'm stupid... because I like getting high," her words and tone evoke the above cultural understandings that blame the poor for their problems and that label and stigmatize them physically, psychologically and morally, from the rest of society (Katz 1989). In their explanations of homelessness, culturalists echo much of the more general approach to poverty, focusing on particularly exacerbated pathologies that produce this more extreme form of poverty. Put more simply, if the poor are quasi-pathological, the homeless are pathological.

In explaining homelessness culturalists focus particularly on mental illness and substance abuse as key causes (Baum and Burnes 1993; Fischer and Breakey 1991; Bassuk 1984; Bassuk et al 1984). Current research suggests, however, that only 33% of the homeless suffer from mental illness and only 27% have an alcohol addiction (Shlay and Rossi 1992:138). What's more, it is hard to determine from those who do suffer from such maladies, whether these were the cause of their homelessness or simply the consequence.

Brenda, unlike Tanya, recognizes this. She does not blame herself for her homelessness. Rather, she blames society. Specifically, she mentions the politicians and the economic system for "keeping us like this." Brenda's words and sentiments are an appropriate introduction to the structural approach to understanding poverty - a way of thinking that offers a powerful critique to the arguments addressed above. By linking the increased numbers of poor and homeless to changes in the political economy - shrinking labor markets; the destruction of low cost housing in the inner cities - structuralists seek to refute the cultural understandings of poverty and homelessness by focusing on circumstances clearly outside the control of individuals (O'Flaherty 1996; Wolch and Dear 1993; Marcuse 1990; Hopper 1990; Rossi 1989; Hoch and Slayton 1989).

STRUCTURAL EXPLANATIONS

Structural explanations are offered as a counter-argument to biological and cultural explanations that place the blame for poverty on the individual. These approaches explain poverty by examining how society in general and various social and economic institutions in particular keep certain groups of individuals economically and socially disadvantaged. Unlike biological and cultural explanations, structural interpretations focus not on how people behave or think but rather on how they are treated by forces and circumstances clearly outside their control. Members of different groups receive different treatment in America, structuralists argue, and that is why poverty is so unequally distributed in America.

In approaching the particular circumstances of inner city Blacks, structuralists fall into two camps. One camp emphasizes the importance of race in the perpetuation of Black poverty. They argue that racial discrimination is at the root of persistent ghetto poverty. Another camp argues for the importance of class - that is the relation of inner city Blacks to the labor market -in explaining the problems of the inner city. For these writers, it is the lack of jobs in the inner city and not racial discrimination that is at the root of the poverty problem. (Massey and Denton 1993; Willie 1989; and Wilson 1978, 1987, 1996). The debate over the relative importance of race over class forms the cornerstone of structural arguments against cultural theories of the poverty.

Those who emphasize the importance of race in explaining why a disproportionate number of urban Blacks live in poverty argue that Blacks are denied equal access to the resources and benefits of American society (Massey and Denton 1993; Willie 1989; Pinkney 1984; and Glasgow 1981). **Institutional racism,** that is, the systematic exclusion of particular groups from equal participation in the various institutions of society, means that

Blacks are economically and socially disadvantaged. That is, their economic opportunities are blocked due to racial discrimination in the housing market, job market, and educational system. Douglas Massey and Nancy Denton, in *American Apartheid: Segregation and the Making of the Underclass* (1993) argue that **residential segregation** is an important factor in explaining the rise of a disproportionately Black underclass residing in urban ghettos. As a consequence of racial segregation, they argue that "geographically concentrated poverty is built into the experience of urban Blacks..." (Massey and Denton 1993.118). Others argue that labor markets and schools are also segmented on the basis of race. That is, high paying jobs in business, such as executive positions, tend to go to Whites who have access to better educational opportunities. Lower paying, dead-end jobs, such as clerical and custodial positions, tend to go to Blacks who, because of racial discrimination, lack equal access to educational opportunities.

Those who emphasize class as a central cause of urban poverty do not deny the importance of racial discrimination, but focus instead on the structural transformation of the inner-city economy (Wilson 1978,1987, 1996). William Julius Wilson, in *When Work Disappears: The world of the New Urban Poor* (1996), is the principal proponent of class-based explanations. Economic and industrial restructuring, technological advances, geographic and demographic shifts in the supply and demand for labor in the inner-city, the increasing suburbanization of employment, as well as the out-migration of middle class Blacks who take their businesses and job contacts with them have contributed to what Wilson refers to as the "jobless ghetto" (Wilson 1996).

Joblessness, not racial discrimination in housing markets, labor markets, and schools is the primary cause of poverty among inner city Blacks, he argues. Wilson (1996) argues that "Inner-city joblessness is a severe problem that is often overlooked... A neighborhood in which people are poor but employed is different from a neighborhood in which people are poor and jobless" (p. xiii).

The debate over the relative importance of race and class factors in explaining Black poverty is one of emphasis. Racial discrimination clearly exacerbates the problem of inner city joblessness. Likewise, the dearth of jobs in the inner city clearly magnifies the impact of racial discrimination. That both racial discrimination and joblessness plague the inner city means, according to Massey and Denton, that we should not ask "whether race *or* class perpetuates the urban underclass, but how race *and* class interact" (Massey and Denton 1993:220). Understanding this relationship has critical consequences for the kinds of policies developed to combat highly concentrated poverty within these growing jobless **ghettos.**

Structural accounts of homelessness draw a great deal from the more general literature on poverty. Racial discrimination and joblessness clearly have a lot to do with the incidence of homelessness, particularly in American cities. Another important structural factor in understanding homelessness is the destruction of much of the low cost housing stock in the inner city and the associated increase in housing cost. Rents in major cities consistently rise faster than **inflation** and this has made housing less affordable for all city residents, but in particular for the poorest individuals and families many of whom are **precariously housed,** and, as a consequence, end up homeless. When Brenda blames the politicians, she is blaming them not only for a lack of work but also for a lack of affordable housing.

PULLING IT TOGETHER

In recent years, some researchers have begun to try to bridge the gap between structural and cultural understandings of poverty. Both Massey and Denton, and Wilson recognize that they must address the high rates of teenage motherhood and single parenting found in ghetto neighborhoods and that such circumstances reinforce economic marginality and poverty. Massey and Denton (1993), for example, argue that racial segregation provides the structural conditions for an oppositional "culture of segregation" that "devalues work, schooling, and marriage..." (p. 8). That is, high rates of unemployment, and social and economic isolation make it difficult for ghetto residents to conform to middle class ideals of work, marriage, and childbearing. In order to protect themselves against the constant assaults on their morality and self-esteem, ghetto residents adopt an oppositional **culture of segregation** that "attaches value and meaning to a way of life that the broader society would label as deviant and unworthy" (Massey and Denton 1993:167). Wilson, as well, recognizes the emergence of ghetto-related behaviors in response to blocked opportunities and economic marginality. For Wilson (1996), "...ghetto-related behaviors represent particular cultural adaptations to the systematic blockage of opportunities in the environment of the inner city and the society as a whole" (p.72). Massey and Denton see ghetto culture as drifting farther and farther away from the norms and values of mainstream American society. The important distinction here is that culture is not cause but consequence. Both authors, however, remain focused on the structural conditions that give rise to certain kinds of *situational* values, norms, and behaviors that, although they help the poor survive, often perpetuate their economic marginality (Stack 1974; Liebow 1967). They seek not to define a "culture of poverty" but rather a "more subtle kind of cultural analysis of life in poverty" (Wilson 1996:72).

A growing body of research, encouraged by the pioneering work of Carol Stack (1974), suggests that many of the behaviors and relationships engaged in by the poor are, in fact, quite functional adaptations to trying circumstances. Stack's work on female-headed families, showed that kinship among women, although different from middle class standards, is highly resilient, organized, and lifelong. Without the support of husbands, women come to depend on extended family and close friends to support their families. There are, however, consequences to such extended domestic networks. According to Stack (1974), "Attempted social mobility away from the kin network of exchanges and obligations, by means of marriage or employment, involves a precarious risk in contrast to the asylum gained through generosity and exchange" (p. 125). That is to say the types of behavior it takes to survive poverty does indeed negatively impact one's abilities to exit it.

Nowhere is this dilemma more evident than among the homeless. Recall Tanya and Brenda. They eat together, sleep together, share everything they have with one another, and protect each other. For Tanya and Brenda, as well as other homeless men and women, surviving day-to-day is a full time job that requires endless cooperation. "We share, equally, all the time," Brenda remarked, "We help each other out until we can get out of this." But this constant struggle for survival results only in enough income and protection to meet their daily needs. "None falls behind, but none gets ahead either" (Dordick 1997: 36, See Liebow 1994).

The above examples underscore the importance of poverty research that attempts to synthesize structural and cultural interpretations of the causes of poverty. "Any sensible model of behavior," writes David Ellwood, "emphasizes the role of opportunities [structure] along with values and motivation [culture]" (Ellwood 1988:197, brackets added). Culturalists, such as Lawrence Mead (1986), as well recognize that values and behavior are shaped by external social forces. Welfare, some culturalists argue, is problematic because it fosters a variety of "ghetto-related" behaviors and values, as well as encourages long-term dependency. The transition from welfare to work will be accompanied, they argue, by a change in values (Ellwood 1988). What distinguishes structural and cultural explanations, in light of attempts to synthesize, is the relative importance of social and environmental forces. Culturalists emphasize the need to change motivation and behavior whereas structuralists focus on changing the opportunities available to poor Americans. "Opportunity and incentive influence culture, which influences behavior, which influences opportunity, which influences culture, ad infinitum" (Ellwood 1988:199).

Similar attempts at synthesis occur in homeless research as well. In *The Homeless,* Christopher Jencks (1994) attempts to forge a synthesis between structural and cultural understandings of the problem. He argues, on one hand, that such factors as structural changes in the labor market and the housing market have contributed to the increases in the number of homeless. He argues as well, however, that individual failings - mental illness, substance abuse, and poor social skills - are important. While culturalists agree with the latter, blaming Tanya for "getting high" and Brenda for "becoming an alcoholic," and structuralists look to the lack of affordable housing to explain their situation, Jencks would argue that taken alone, neither of these explanations are sufficient. Rather, he argues, "we need to replace our instinctive either-or approach to blame with a both-and approach" (Jencks 1994:48).

IMPROVING THE POOR AND HOMELESS

Discussions as to the causes of poverty are important because they affect the kinds of policy national, state, and local governments adopt in response to issues of poverty and homelessness. Until recently, many of the principal policy programs run by the government had as their primary focus alleviating and lessening the hardship and deprivation of recipients.

Income supplements such as Aid to Families with Dependent Children (AFDC), in-kind benefits such as Food Stamps, medical assistance through Medicaid, and housing assistance through Public Housing were all part of a "safety net" designed to ensure a certain minimum standard of living below which individuals and families would not fall. Many of these programs had their roots in the Great Depression and as such were designed as temporary relief for people who had fallen on hard times. The presumption was that individuals would cease to need aid when the economy got better or their luck with respect to the job market improved. As such these programs were more concerned with the condition of poverty than with solving its underlying causes.

In recent years, these anti-poverty programs have been criticized as encouraging dependency and doing little to provoke people to attempt to improve their condition. Critics argue that programs designed to provide temporary relief have evolved in practice to become permanent sources of support and a "way of life." Armed with a cultural understanding of poverty, these individuals have argued that welfare programs must do more than alleviate misery, they must also help and provoke poor people to work. Based on the belief that the behavior and attitudes of the poor are at least partly responsible for their condition, these new approaches seek to change the character and outlook of program participants.

These changes are reflected most fundamentally in the Welfare Reform of 1996. This measure abolished AFDC, replacing it with a program called Temporary Assistance to Needy Families. This program replaced what had been an entitlement of cash assistance for all women and children who fell below a certain income level with a set of block grants to states to administer what are referred to as "welfare to work" programs. That is, states are expected to design and implement programs that help welfare recipients transition to work. What had been a permanent guarantee of aid was changed to a five-year period of eligibility conditional upon welfare-to-work program participation. Similar eligibility guidelines and protocols were applied to Medicaid, Food Stamps, and a number of housing assistance programs.

A similar emphasis on poverty policy that promotes changes in behavior can be seen in the implementation of what has been called a Continuum of Care strategy - phased in starting in 1994-- for dealing with homelessness. Now, policy-makers seek to offer a new kind of "affordable" housing that also offers a range of "supportive services" designed to "help individuals and families help themselves and provide them with the opportunity to better themselves"(Priority: Home! The Federal Plan to Break the Cycle of Homelessness:" 5). HUD refers to this blending of housing and services as a "continuum of care," the linchpin of which is "supportive housing." "Supportive housing" is supposed to provide its residents not only with a safe place to live but also with whatever "mental health, job training, education, substance abuse, family support, HIV, and independent living skills" services they need. These services are intended to help the homeless make the transition so that they can live "independently to the greatest extent possible" (U.S. Department of Housing and Urban Development, Office of Community Planning and Development, "Continuum of Care" April 1994:1-3). Reflected in these policies is a paradigm shift in the approach of the federal government toward social service provision. Much as recent welfare legislation represents a move away from notions of a safety net and of entitlements, so too does the new housing policy stress the responsibilities of those receiving aid to better themselves and become independent.

It is too soon to evaluate the impact of these changes. The new welfare bill went into effect in July of 1997 although many states applied for extensions because they were not ready for their welfare to work programs. Advocates of the changes point to a reduction in welfare rolls that has already been observed, while opponents argue that these reductions are the result of a sustained economic upturn rather than any government effort. What's more the stricter eligibility of all these programs may discourage many poor people from even seeking help. Welfare programs have always targeted specific populations and the number of people on welfare is not synonymous with the number of people living in poverty. Critics also warn that with the dismantling of the system of entitlements, the nation is simply not prepared in the event the economy takes a downturn.

The changes in poverty and homelessness policy clearly seek to improve poor and homeless people. They seek, put very simply, to make people like Tanya a little less "stupid." The years to come will demonstrate whether she or Brenda is right.

SUMMARY

1. The "poverty line" is a number or more accurately a set of numbers usually representing household income. Individuals who live in households whose income falls below the line are considered poor; those who live in households above the line are not.
2. Poverty thresholds allow us to decide what number or percentage of the population is poor. The "poverty rate" gives us the percentage of individuals in the population who lives in poverty.
3. Government reports and programs rely on an absolute poverty standard for measuring poverty.
4. An alternative to the absolute poverty standard is the relative poverty standard that defines the poor as those who fall lowest on the income distribution at a particular point in time.
5. Although several criticisms have been made against the absolute poverty threshold, it remains the principle means by which the incidence and rate of poverty is assessed in America.
6. In 1995, 13.8% of the population - 36.4 million Americans -- lived in households whose income fell below the poverty line. The poverty rate fluctuates during periods of economic growth and decline.
7. The above numbers do not take into account America's poorest people, the homeless. No single national estimate of the number of homeless people receives widespread acceptance.
8. Poverty rates are highest among Blacks, Hispanics, female-headed households, children, central cities and rural areas, and the South and West regions of the United States.
9. No longer a homogenous group comprised of older, White, single men confined to skid row sections of major cities, the "new homeless" include women and children, are younger, racially and ethnically diverse, and geographically dispersed. Although the majority of homeless people are White, over 40% of homeless people are Black and 12% Hispanic.
10. Although the majority of poor Americans are White and live outside of central cites, most contemporary work exploring poverty in America focuses on African-Americans who live in the inner-city neighborhoods.
11. Biological explanations seek to demonstrate innate and inherited characteristics of particular individuals that predispose them to poverty.
12. Cultural explanations are rooted in the basic assertion that the poor develop a distinct and ultimately dysfunctional set of behaviors and values that help them cope with living in poverty.
13. The newest buzzword for describing the morally undeserving, as well as materially impoverished, poor is the "underclass."
14. Culturalists also blame welfare dependency for persistent ghetto poverty.

15. Both biological and cultural explanations blame the victim by locating the cause or causes of poverty within poor people themselves.
16. In explaining homelessness, culturalists' focus particularly on mental illness and substance abuse as key causes. Tanya is a culturalist.
17. Structural accounts of homelessness draw a great deal from the more general literature on poverty. In addition to racial discrimination and joblessness, particularly in American cities, structuralists take into account the lack of affordable housing. Brenda is a structuralist.
18. What distinguishes cultural and structural explanations, in light of attempts to synthesize, is the relative importance of social and environmental forces. Culturalists emphasize the need to change motivation and behavior whereas structuralists focus on changing the opportunities available to poor Americans.
19. Similar attempts at synthesis occur in homeless research as well. This both-and approach looks to changes in the labor and housing market as well as individual failings, such as mental illness and substance abuse, as contributing to the increases in the number of homeless.
20. Recent reforms in government policies toward the poor and homeless reflect a cultural understanding of the problem. They have moved from a system of entitlements concerned with improving the conditions in which the poor live to a set of initiatives to improve the behavior, attitudes, and values of the poor themselves. It is too soon to evaluate the consequences of these policy changes.

SUGGESTED READINGS

Bane, Mary Jo, and D. T. Ellwood 1994. *Welfare Realties: From Rhetoric to Reform.* Cambridge: Harvard University Press.
Dordick, Gwendolyn A. 1997. *Something Left to Lose: Personal Relations and Survival Among New York's Homeless.* Philadelphia: Temple University Press.
Edin, Kathryn and Laura Lein 1997. Making Ends Meet: How Single Mothers Survive Welfare and Low Wage Work. New York: Russell Sage Foundation.
Gans, Herbert J. 1995. *The War Against the Poor: The Underclass and Antipoverty Policy.* New York: Basic Books.
Jencks, Christopher 1994. *The Homeless.* Cambridge: Harvard University Press.
Liebow, Elliot 1994. *Tell Them Who I Am: The Lives of Homeless Women.* New York: The Free Press.
Massey, Douglas A, and N. A. Denton 1993. *American Apartheid: Segregation and the Making of the Underclass.* Cambridge: Harvard University Press.
Mead, Lawrence 1992. *The New Politics of Poverty: The Nonworking Poor in America.* New York: Basic Books.
Rossi, Peter H. 1989. *Down and Out in America: The Origins of Homelessness.* Chicago: The University of Chicago Press.
Wilson, William J. 1996. *When Work Disappears: The World of the New Urban Poor.* New York: Alfred A. Knopf, Inc.

WEB SITES:

For information on Welfare and Welfare Reform: *www.hhs.gov*
For information on housing policy for the poor and homeless: *www.hud.gov*

REFERENCES

Allen, Irving L. 1993. The City in Slang: New York Life and Popular Speech. New York: Oxford University Press.
Bane, Mary Jo, and D. T. Ellwood 1994. Welfare Realities: From Rhetoric to Reform. Cambridge: Harvard University Press.
Banfield, Edward. 1970. *The Unheavenly City.* Second ed. Boston: Little, Brown.
Bassuk, Ellen L 1984. "The Homeless Problem." *Scientific America.* 251:40-45.
Bassuk, Ellen L, L. Rubin, and A. Laurist 1984. "Is Homelessness a Mental Health Problem?" *American Journal of Psychiatry.* 141:1546-1550.
Baum, Alice S, and D. W. Burnes 1993. *A Nation in Denial The Truth About Homelessness.* Boulder: Westview Press.
Burt, Martha R. 1992. *Over the Edge: The Growth of Homelessness in the 1980's.* New York: Russell Sage.

Citro, Constance F, and R.T. Michael, eds. 1995. *Measuring Poverty: A New Approach*. Washington, D.C: National Academy Press.

Dordick, Gwendolyn A. 1994. "Countering the Culture of Homelessness: The Importance of Personal Relations to the Study of Homelessness." Presented at the annual meeting of the American Sociological Association, August, Los Angeles, CA.

_____.1997. *Something Left to Lose: Personal Relations and Survival Among New York's Homeless*. Philadelphia: Temple University Press.

Edin, Kathryn, and L. Lein 1997. "Work, Welfare, and Single Mothers' Economic Survival Strategies." American Sociological Review. 61:253-266.

Ellwood, David T. 1988. *Poor Support: Poverty in the American Family*. New York: Basic Books.

Fischer, Pamela J, and W. R. Breakey 1991. "The Epidemiology of Alcohol, Drug, and Mental Disorders Among Homeless Persons." *American Psychologist*. 46:1232-1238.

Freeman, Richard B, and B. Hall 1987. "Permanent Homelessness in America." *Population Research and Policy Review*. 6:3-27.

Gans, Herbert J. 1968. "Culture and Class in the Study of Poverty: An Approach to Antipoverty Research" in Daniel Patrick Moynihan, ed. *On Understanding Poverty: Perspectives from the Social Sciences*. New York: Basic Books

_____.1990. "Deconstructing the Underclass: The Term's Danger as a Planning Concept." *Journal of the American Planning Association*. 56(Summer): 271-277.

_____.1995. *The War Against the Poor: The Underclass and Antipoverty Policy*. New York: Basic Books.

Glasgow, Douglas G. 1981. *The Black Underclass: Poverty, Unemployment, and Entrapment of Ghetto Youth*. New York: Vintage Books.

Hannerz, Ulf 1969. *Soulside: Inquiries into Ghetto Culture and Community*. New York: Columbia University Press.

Herrnstein, Richard J, and C. Murray 1994. *The Bell Curve: Intelligence and Class Structure in American Life*. New York: The Free Press.

Hoch, Charles, and R. A. Slayton 1989. *New Homeless and Old: Community and the Skid Row Hotel*. Philadelphia: Temple University Press.

Hombs, Mary E, and M. Snyder 1982. *Homelessness in America: A Forced Marched to Nowhere*. Washington, D. C.: Community on Creative Non-Violence.

Hopper, Kim 1991. "Assessment of S-Night 1990: Repeat Enumerations, Structured Interviews, and Brief Ethnographic Studies of the Street Census Project." Center for Survey Methods Research. Washington, D.C.: Bureau of the Census.

_____.1990. "Advocacy for the Homeless in the 1980's." Pp.160-173 in Caroll M. Caton, ed. *The Homeless in America*. New York: Oxford University Press.

Jencks, Christopher 1994. *The Homeless*. Cambridge: Harvard University Press.

Katz, Michael B. 1989. *The Undeserving Poor: From the War on Poverty to the War on Welfare*. New York: Pantheon Books.

Kornblum, William 1984. "Lumping the Poor: What *Is* the Underclass." *Dissent*. September: 295-302.

Lewis, Oscar 1959. *Five Families: Mexican Case Studies in the Culture of Poverty*. New York: Basic Books.

_____.1968. "The Culture of Poverty." Pp.197-220 in Daniel Patrick Moynihan, ed. *On Understanding Poverty: Perspectives from the Social Sciences*. New York: Basic Books.

Liebow, Elliot 1967. *Tally's Corner: A Study of Negro Streetcorner Men*. Boston: Little, Brown and Company.

_____.1994. *Tell Them Who I Am: The Lives of Homeless Women*. New York: The Free Press.

Marcuse, Peter 1990. "Homelessness and Housing Policy." Pp.138-159 in Carol M. Caton, ed. *In Homelessness in America*. New York: Oxford University Press.

Massey, Douglas A, and N. A. Denton 1993. *American Apartheid: Segregation and the Making of the Underclass*. Cambridge: Harvard University Press.

Mayer, Susan, and C. Jencks 1988. "Poverty and the Distribution of Material Hardship." *The Journal of Human Resources*. 24:88-114.

McConnell, J. 1992. "Living Out: The Social Organization of Two Suburban Homeless Communities." Presented at the annual meeting of the American Sociological Association, August, Pittsburgh, PA.

Mead, Lawrence 1992. *The New Politics of Poverty: The Nonworking Poor in America*. New York: Basic Books.

Moffitt, Robert 1992. "Incentive Effects of the U.S. Welfare System: A Review." *Journal of Economic Literature*. 30:1-61.

Murray, Charles 1984. *Losing Ground: American Social Policy 1950-1980*. New York: Basic Books.

Myrdal, Gunnar 1963. *Challenge to Affluence*. New York: Pantheon Books.

O'Flaherty, Brendan 1996. *Making Room: The Economics of Homelessness*. Cambridge: Harvard University Press.

Orshansky, Mollie 1965. "Counting the Poor: Another Look at the Poverty Profile." *Social Security Bulletin*. 28:3-29.

Pinkney, Alphonso 1984. *The Myth of Black Progress*. New York: Cambridge University Press.

Rein, Martin 1970. "Problems in the Definition and Measurement of Poverty." Pp. 46-63 in Peter Townsend, ed. *The Concept of Poverty*. London: Heinemann Educational Books, Ltd.

Reyes, Lilia M, and L. Waxman 1987. "The Continuing Growth of Hunger and Poverty in American Cities." Washington, D.C.: "United States Conference of Mayors."

Rossi, Peter H. 1989. Down and Out in America: The Origins of Homelessness. Chicago: The University of Chicago Press.

Ruggles, Patricia 1990. *Drawing the Line: Alternative Poverty Measures and Their Implications for Public Policy*. Washington, D.C.: The Urban Institute.

Ryan, William 1976. *Blaming the Victim*. New York: Vintage Books.

Shlay, Ann B, and P. H. Rossi 1992. "Social Science Research and Contemporary Studies of Homelessness. " *Annual Review of Sociology*. 18:129-160.

Stack, Carol 1974. *All Our Kin: Strategies for Survival in a Black Community*. New York: Harper & Row Publishers.

Snow, David et al. 1986. "The Myth of Pervasive Mental Illness Among the Homeless." *Social Problems*. 33:407-423.

Stone, Michael E. 1993 *Shelter Poverty: New Ideas on Housing Affordability*. Philadelphia: Temple University Press.

Thio, Alex 1996. *Sociology*. Fourth ed. New York: Harper Collins Publishers, Inc.

U.S. Bureau of the Census 1996. *Poverty in the United States*: 1995 Series P-60, no.194.

U.S. Department of Housing and Urban Development 1984. "A Report to the Secretary on the Homeless and Emergency Shelters." Washington, D. C.: Office of Policy Development and Research.

Willie, Charles V. 1989. *The Caste and Class Controversy on Race and Poverty: Round Two of the Willie/Wilson Debate*. Second ed. New York: General Hall, Inc.

Wilson, William J. 1996. *When Work Disappears: The World of the New Urban Poor*. New York: Alfred A. Knopf, Inc.

_____.1987. *The Truly Disadvantages: The Inner City, the Underclass, and Public Policy*. Chicago: The University of Chicago Press.

_____.1978. *The Declining Significance of Race.' Blacks and Changing American Institutions*. *Second* ed. Chicago: The University of Chicago Press.

Wolch, Jennifer, and M. Dear 1993. *Malign Neglect: Homelessness in an American City*. San Francisco: Josey-Bass Publisher.

CHAPTER 13: EDUCATION
CASE STUDY: TWO CONTRASTING SCHOOLS

Children who go to school in towns like Glencoe and Winnetka learn to read by 2nd or 3rd grade. By the time they get to 6th or 7th grade, many are reading at the level of the seniors in the best Chicago high schools. By the time they enter 9th grade at New Trier High, they are in a world of academic possibilities that far exceed the hopes and dreams of most schoolchildren in Chicago. "Our goal is for students to be successful," says the New Trier principal. With 93% of seniors going on to 4-year colleges-many to schools like Harvard, Princeton, Berkeley, Brown and Yale-this goal is largely realized.

New Trier's physical setting might well make the students of Du Sable High School envious. The Washington Post describes a neighborhood of "circular driveways, chirping birds and White-column houses." It is, says a student, "a maple land of beauty and civility." New Trier students have superior labs and up-to-date technology. One wing of the school, a physical education center that includes three separate gyms, also contains a fencing room, a wrestling room and studios for dance instruction. In all, the school has seven gyms as well as an Olympic pool. The youngsters, according to a profile of the school in Town and Country magazine, "make good use of the huge, well-equipped building, which is immaculately maintained by a custodial staff of 48."

"This is a school with a lot of choices," says one student at New Trier; and this hardly seems an overstatement if one studies the curriculum. Courses in music, art and drama are so varied and abundant that students can virtually major in these subjects in addition to their academic programs. The modern and classical language department offers Latin (4 years) and 6 other foreign languages. Elective courses include the literature of Nobel winners, aeronautics, criminal justice, and computer languages. In a senior literature class, students are reading Nietzsche, Darwin, Plato, Freud, and Goethe. The school also operates a television station with a broadcast license from the FCC, which broadcasts on 4 channels to 3 countries.

The ambience among the students at New Trier, of whom only 1.3% are Black, says *Town and Country*, is "wholesome and refreshing, a sort of throwback to the Fifties." It is, we are told, "a preppy kind of place." In a cheerful photo of the faculty and students, one cannot discern a single nonwhite face.

Our next visit was to P.S. 79 in New York City, an elementary school. "We work under difficult circumstances," says the principal, James Carter, who is Black. "The school was built to hold 1,000 students. We have 1,550. We are badly overcrowded. We need smaller classes but, to do this, we would need more space. I can't add 5 teachers. I would have no place to put them."

Some experts, I observe, believe that class size isn't a real issue. He dismisses this abruptly. "It doesn't take a genius to discover that you learn more in a smaller class. I have to bus some 60-kindergarten children elsewhere, since I have no space for them. When they return next year, where do I put them?

"I can't set up a computer lab. I have no room. I had to put a class into the library. I have no librarian. There are two gymnasiums upstairs but they cannot be used for sports. We hold more classes there. It's unfair to measure us against the suburbs. They have 17 to 20 children in a class. Average class size in this school is 30." The school is 20% Black, 70% Hispanic. Few of these kids get Head Start. There is no space in the district. Of 200 kindergarten children, 50 maybe get some kind of preschool."

I ask him how much difference preschool makes. "Those who get it do appreciably better. I can't overestimate its impact but, as I have said, we have no space."

The school tracks children by ability, he says. "There are 5 to 7 levels in each grade. The highest level is equivalent to 'gifted' but it's not a full-scale gifted program. We don't have the funds. We have no science room. The science teachers carry their equipment with them."

We sit and talk within the nurse's room. The window is broken. There are two holes in the ceiling. About a quarter of the ceiling has been patched and covered with a plastic garbage bag.

"Ideal class size for these kids would be 15 or 20. Will these children ever get what White kids in the suburbs take for granted? I don't think so. If you ask me why, I'd have to speak of race and social class. I don't think the powers that be in New York City understand, or want to understand, that if they do not give these children a sufficient education to lead healthy and productive lives, we will be their victims later on. We'll pay the price someday in violence, in economic costs. I despair of making this appeal to conscience in New York today. The fair-play argument won't be accepted. So you speak of violence and hope that it will scare the city into action"(Source of the case: Jonathan Kozol 1991, *Savage Inequalities: Children in America's Schools*. New York: Crown Publishers, Pp. 65-66, 88-89).

THE ISSUE OF EQUAL OPPORTUNITY

The United States, land of opportunity! Millions have flocked to its shores for new starts, for the chance of becoming rich and free. High hopes have been placed on schools, hopes that they could provide opportunity for all children, regardless of background. However, the dream is not the reality for many Americans, and our task in the following pages is to explore why. This chapter considers what equal opportunity means, why it is so elusive for many people, and what role schools and classroom teachers play in the process of equal opportunity.

EQUALITY OF EDUCATIONAL OPPORTUNITY

First, we look at the meaning of equal opportunity and the perspectives used to study it. Second, we consider specific factors related to educational opportunity: teacher expectations, testing, ability grouping, desegregation and integration, gender differences in classrooms, discipline, at risk and dropout behaviors, early childhood education programs, curriculum issues, and family environment. Third, we will discuss some of the proposed solutions such as choice, voucher systems, and magnet schools.

From African-American, Hispanic American, and Native Americans to Cambodian, Vietnamese and other refugees from Southeast Asia, hopes of parents that their children would have a chance to rise to a higher status have hinged on schools and teachers. Schools are physically accessible to most families; therefore, they are easy, visible targets for the frustrations, criticisms, and conflicts which symbolize groups struggling to get ahead. Schools are often pressured not only to prepare students to be successful, but also to adapt to the needs and demands of communities in which they are located. Pressures include training in both the native language and English, multicultural education, and sensitivity to different cultures.

Equal Opportunity exists when all people, including those without wealth, prestige or power in society, have an equal chance of achieving a high socioeconomic status in society regardless of their gender, minority status, or social class. This requires removing obstacles to individual achievement such as prejudice, discrimination, and cultural barriers.

The meaning of equality of educational opportunity has wavered between providing equal school resources-the same quality of teachers, physical facilities, textbooks and technology-to all children, to ensuring equal outcomes--comparable jobs and economic status (Coleman 1990). Conflicts arise over differential treatment of children in school and unequal outcomes of the educational process in terms of occupational opportunities, status, and resulting income and wealth.

Two conflicting sets of values pervade American society and affect the institution of education: equal access versus individual freedom. Equal access means that every individual starts out with the same opportunities; unequal opportunities are justified only if they provide advantages to the unprivileged, or if they benefit all. Affirmative Action policies stem from this view. The individual freedom argument holds that individuals are entitled to what they have justly earned, regardless of their status. This means that some will come out ahead in the competition for limited resource--education, jobs, and income--in part because of initial advantages. These conflicting values are played out in many issues affecting schools. For instance, do placement and achievement tests provide equal access to all students, or is there a bias against some students?

Among those groups most often stuck in the bottom rung of schools and societies are racial, ethnic, gender, religious, and linguistic groups whose culture and behavior patterns are different from the dominant American middle class patterns. This problem is accentuated by the dramatic shifts underway in public school enrollments; the number of White students in most states is shrinking, while minority enrollments are increasing. In 1996, minority children made up 37.5% of elementary school enrollment: African American 17.6%, Hispanic 14%, and Asian 4.4%. By 2030, Hispanic students will be the largest minority group in schools with 20% (projected) (*The Condition of Education 1989*, Vol. 1): U.S. Government Printing Office 1989).

APPROACHES TO UNDERSTANDING EQUAL OPPORTUNITY

Just as we all have individual views that help us explain how society works, social scientists have several different views of society. Three theories from the sociological tradition represent the dominant thrusts in much of the research on education: structural-functional, conflict, and interaction theories.

STRUCTURAL-FUNCTIONAL THEORY

Structural-functional theory starts with the assumption that society is made up of interdependent parts, called institutions; these include family, education, religion, politics, economics, and health. As long as these parts work together in a balanced state, the system functions smoothly. Each institution serves some necessary purpose or function in the society; that is, it contributes some necessary activity. The functions served by education are as follows: (1) Passing on to students the culture, knowledge, skills, values and behaviors necessary for society to continue; (2) Social control and personal development which helps to maintain order; (3) The selection and allocation function which helps to determine where people are placed in society; (4) The change and innovation function which refers to creating new knowledge. Structural-functionalism tends to emphasize the positive role of education in the maintenance of stability in society, and is less concerned with social problems than is conflict theory. Nonetheless, some aspects of current educational systems are dysfunctional.

CONFLICT THEORY

Conflict theory takes a very different view of society and educational systems; it assumes that tension and potential conflict exist in society between competing individuals and groups. Those with power and positions in society control wealth, material goods, privilege, and influence. Those without power struggle to compete for more of what society has to offer. Part of this drama is played out in the institution of education, for education is seen by many as the avenue for getting ahead in life.

Research from the conflict perspective tends to focus on those tensions created by power relationships that ultimately cause change in the system. Some conflict theorists see mass education as a tool of capitalist society that controls access to private elite education and entrance into higher levels of education and jobs through the selection and allocation function.

One branch of conflict theory which focuses on education argues that schools help reproduce the parents' social class in students; they do this by treating students in ways that reinforce their class backgrounds. Cultural reproduction and resistance theories argue, very generally, that those who dominate capitalistic economic systems (usually wealthy and powerful individuals) have the power to mold others to suit their own needs and purposes. Individuals are at the bottom or top of the social class hierarchy because classes are reproduced and perpetuated, in part through what students learn and the type of education they receive.

Consider the following comparison of 5 elementary schools in contrasting communities that seem similar in outward appearances. The two *working-class schools* stressed following the steps of a procedure, mechanically, by rote, with little decision making, choice, or explanation why it was done a particular way. The *middle-class school* stressed getting the right answer. There was some figuring, choice, and decision making, for instance, asking the children how they got an answer. The *affluent professional school* stressed creative activity carried out independently, with students asked to express and apply ideas and concepts, and think about the ideas. The *executive elite school* stressed developing one's analytical intellectual powers, reasoning through problems, conceptualizing rules by which elements may fit together in systems, and applying these to solving problems. Included here is successful presentation of self (Anyon 1989)

Note how the informal practices in each school served to reproduce the social classes represented by the majority of students in that school. These informal aspects of the curriculum of schools are preparing students for their future productive roles in society. The working class is being prepared for future wage labor that is mechanical and routine, the middle class for bureaucratic relations to capital such as low-level management positions; the professionals for leadership positions, and the elite for decision-making, analyzing and manipulating the system.

Another ethnographic study documents the use of time and space values and structures to transmit social class. In Head Start settings serving low-income children, time and space tended to be more rigidly structured for the children than in other centers where children had some control over decision-making about their activities. These school patterns again follow social class patterns (Lubeck 1984).

Both structural-functional and conflict theory focus on schools and educational systems in societies-the big picture. However, many researchers consider small group and individual interactions in schools and classrooms as their primary interest.

INTERACTION THEORIES

Interaction theories focus on individuals in groups, from teacher-student dyads to interactions in classrooms and schools. For instance, interaction theorists have studied teacher expectations of students and how students respond; the higher the expectations and more encouragement students receives the higher student achievement. Student attitudes, values, self-concepts, and aspirations also are correlated directly with achievement.

Labeling theory, one branch of interaction theory, focuses on how members of society label other individuals, that is how they define the behaviors of others, and how that definition affects the individual being labeled. For instance, if a child is told often enough that she or he is dumb or will amount to nothing, the child is likely to adopt that view, or label, of him or herself and acts accordingly.

Though there are many theories used to explain the dynamics of schools, these are three dominant ones; others are often variations of these three, as in the case of labeling theory.

To study schools, social scientists combine a theoretical approach with research methods appropriate for gathering needed information. The most frequently used methods are analysis of national data on schools; systematic observations of classrooms and other educational settings; surveys to ask questions of students, teachers, and others on the topic of study; and case studies to analyze one educational setting in depth. From the many research studies, social scientists have amassed valuable data about how schools work. A key topic of interest has been equal opportunity. Let us now turn to research which bears on the questions and actions related to equal opportunity in education.

CLASSROOM INTERACTIONS AFFECTING EQUAL OPPORTUNITY

Classroom interactions and practices have implications for school and system-wide decision-making. The following discussion is divided into actions that relate to classrooms, to school or system-wide structures and decisions, and to major policy issues. Though most of the actions overlap, they are grouped for convenience.

Estimates put teachers-student interactions at over 1,000 a day. That doesn't take into account the interactions between colleagues. In each interaction, messages are passed, and each message impacts on the self-image of individuals, as illustrated in the following example.

TEACHER EXPECTATIONS

Children's manners of dress, names, physical appearances, race, sex, language usage and accent, parents' occupations, and the children's responses to teachers affect teachers' attitudes toward students. Most teachers come from middle-class backgrounds, and tend to gravitate toward those who are most similar. Teachers may unintentionally let factors such as those listed above affect their behaviors toward and expectations of children.

Interaction theory helps us to understand the interactions between teachers and children, and expectations of both which affect school experiences. Children pick up the subtle or sometimes not so subtle cues from teachers' expectations. If the teacher has low expectations for Johnny, this can become a *self-fulfilling prophesy*; he takes on the belief of his teacher and perhaps his parents and peers that he is dumb, and he behaves accordingly. His achievement reflects his self-concept, developed through interactions. In the 2nd school described in the opening case study (Kozol 1991), a climate of hopelessness has come to prevail, with teachers discouraged about the children's ability to learn and children believing they cannot learn. This atmosphere pervades the school and becomes the reality, reinforcing the hopeless attitudes.

Positive teacher attitudes, approaches, encouragement, and expectations for learning are key to success. Sociologists know that some inner-city schools have turned achievement levels around through combinations of rigorous expectations, parental involvement, homework, and belief in children's abilities to achieve (Brookover 1996; Good 1981).

GENDER DIFFERENCES

The classroom provides very different experiences for girls and boys. Differences in achievement levels, academic and social interests, and discipline stem from several sources such as cultural traditions and stereotypes about the proper roles of women and men, and norms, which evolve from these beliefs. One of these beliefs is that differences in achievement and experiences of women and men are biological, or explained by *biological destiny*. Yet evidence shows that there are few if any differences in male-female learning abilities; cultural beliefs are the crucial difference. For instance, variations in learning styles, math and science achievement, and test results often thought to be gender related overlap between men and women across cultures, showing that cultural influences, not biological factors, are the main cause of gender differences. According to scientific studies, in only a few broad areas might inherited characteristics influence learning, and even there evidence is not conclusive.

In elementary school, boys tend to have more problems sitting still to learn to read and write; they tend to have more discipline problems because of their activity level, and receive more attention (sometimes negative) from the teacher. Some researchers argue that girls are stronger in verbal abilities and boys in visual-spatial abilities. Many possible explanations have been explored, including hormonal factors and gender differences in use of brain hemispheres. However, there is so much overlap between boys and girls within cultures and variations between cultures that cultural expectations rather than biological are the strongest explanations of differences (Bellisari 1989). For example, girls who receive encouragement in math and science have comparable levels of achievement to boys. Women outperform men in science and math in some societies; for instance, Asian-American women outperform many American men, in part because of family encouragement and emphasis on achievement in school (Baker and Jones 1991). In societies where women accept stereotypes of low ability in math, women may believe they cannot achieve resulting in a *self-fulfilling prophecy* (Gose 1995; Renzetti and Curren 1992). Studies such as the High School and Beyond Transcript and National Educational Longitudinal Study Transcripts (1992) conclude that there are no differences in overall intelligence between the sexes. Any differences that do exist between individuals relate to such factors as parental support, teacher expectations, study habits, and values related to women excelling in math-all cultural, not biological factors.

This research has highlighted several interesting gender differences: First, girls tend to form intimate 'chumships" while boys relate through groups organized around activities such as sports (Tavris 1990). Even conversational styles differ (Tannen 1991). These differences become significant in later life as people enter the work force. Businesses, dominated by men, are likely to be formed around group activities-negotiating, competing, compromising-skills boys learn in group activities such as sports. Second, teacher behaviors and expectations differ by gender. Groupings for activities often reflect gender differences; boys are asked to do the heavy tasks; boys play outside in groups more than girls, and are more competitive than girls. These experiences again, carry over into adult activities in the workplace. Third, girls achieve higher grades throughout their public school education, and do better in reading, writing, and literature. However, curriculum choices often put girls behind in math and science by high school, and they may not be tracked toward subjects that can lead to higher paying careers in engineering and technology. If teachers understand the dynamics of classroom interaction and placements they can act to reduce gender differences which have negative impacts on equal opportunity.

POLICIES, PRACTICES, AND TECHNIQUES
EFFECTING EQUAL OPPORTUNITY

School policies made at the local state and national levels affect the success of different groups of students. Particularly important in this are policies of ability grouping, retention of at risk students and integration of ethnic and racial minority students.

ABILITY GROUPING

One of the most hotly debated practices in school systems is ability grouping (also called tracking or streaming). It is the practice of grouping students into different levels of classes depending on their classroom ability, test results and teacher input. The practice is most common in math and reading, and sometimes occurs in science. Does it help or hinder the majority of students? The answers are not simple because many variables enter into the discussion. How are students tested and how are placements made? Does tracking take place in one subject area or all subjects? Is the system flexible, that is can students move from one track to another, or is it rigid-once placed, that is it? Are students in the same track for all subjects?

Each of the dominant theoretical approaches provides a different perspective on ability grouping. For example, functional theorist's point out that tracking allows individuals to advance based on their achievement or merits. Conflict theorists argue that not all students, regardless of merit, have an equal chance to advance due to methods used for placement and differences in quality of education between rich and poor students. Interaction theorists look at the dynamics of schools and classrooms and the expectations for students from different backgrounds, which influence teacher judgments and the placement process.

Testing is a primary method of placing students in ability groups. Yet critics argue that tests give students from certain social class backgrounds advantages in placements. Poor and minority students fall disproportionately at the bottom in testing results and therefore in placements. Placement may also reflect school needs-filling study halls, boosting classes with low enrollments, assigning students to remedial classes to keep special funding, meeting staff preferences for course assignments, and giving experienced senior teachers better students (Riehl 1992).

Ability grouping often begins in elementary school where placement correlates with children's language skills, appearance, and other socioeconomic variables (Oakes 1990). Once placed in a group, change is uncommon unless it is downward. By 8th grade, students' science groupings affect their future science curricula. Some children come from families that are more sophisticated in dealing with the schools, and can influence the placement of their children in classrooms (Schiller and Stevenson 1992). The key point is that ability grouping does not always represent students' actual ability; many factors filter into placement (Kilgore 1991).

"AT RISK" STUDENTS AND DROPOUTS

Eleven percent of students between 16 and 24 in the United States drop out of high school; 1 in 3 Native Americans and 1 in 4 Hispanic students won't graduate from high school. In school districts where ethnic diversity is greatest, retention rates are lowest. Although rates for female and male students are similar, there are differences by family income level, region, and urban-rural areas. Dropout rates for Whites and Hispanics have leveled off since 1988, and have dropped slightly for African-Americans (U. S. Department of Education 1999).

What causes students to drop out? The main reasons cited by students for dropping out, according to the National Education Longitudinal Study of 1988 and the 1990 Follow Up Survey, are that they arrive in school sick, hungry, homeless and destitute. These and other problems often make staying and succeeding in school virtually impossible. Schools such as those described in the case study are so poor and crowded that they cannot begin to offer support to students who need help. Counseling, advising, help with courses, and career planning are lacking. These children often receive no supervision outside of the school. A student can "disappear" and the absence is hardly noticed. Drugs, alcohol, bilingual language issues, and heavy work responsibilities are risk factors for potential dropouts, but probably the most serious problem is peer group influence; many children are faced with pressures to join gangs at a time when the long-term payoff from education seems remote (Garner 1991). Dropouts remain unemployed at a much higher rate than the population at large. Thus, this group costs society in lost human resources, welfare costs, and sometimes prison costs.

Discipline techniques used in schools can encourage poor students to drop out. For instance, *at risk* students are often in trouble, and suspension and expulsion reinforce their feelings that they are misfits in the school; these measures also put them farther behind in their studies.

TESTING

Are standardized tests biased? Fairness of tests has been challenged on many grounds; cultural bias in the questions, the test situations, problems of comprehension for bilingual students, and preparation which gives some students an advantage are some of the reasons. What do we know about tests and equal opportunity?

Arguments for and against the use of tests for placement in school classes or tracking, and for acceptance into institutions of higher education focus on the issues of equal opportunity. Many functionalists argue that standardized tests give everyone an equal opportunity by testing them with the same instrument. However, others (including many conflict theorists) argue that tests are biased in several ways against poor and minority test-takers.

One issue underlying the debate has to do with "what" tests are measuring. Intelligence tests (IQ), for instance, have been used to place students, but there are questions about what intelligence tests actually measure. Several scientists have challenged the notion of **one intelligence**, proposing instead that there may be multiple intelligences not measurable with our current instruments (Gardner 1987). If this is the case, placements based on intelligence tests may be invalid.

Another issue revolves around the question of cultural bias in tests. Can we really devise a culture-free aptitude or achievement test that doesn't disadvantage students from certain backgrounds? Some educators argue that the content of these tests is dictating the national curriculum by determining what should be taught in high school classrooms. Whatever our view, the arguments over the use and abuse of standardized tests as a means of placement continues to be of concern in the quest for equal opportunity. Since testing is likely to continue as a means of placement, it behooves us to be aware of the controversies and take precautions against misuse of tests in our own schools and classrooms.

Can anything be done to insure fairness? As long as tests are used, other means of corroborating test scores should be used. What are teachers' observations of the student's abilities, motivation, and interests? Do students excel in some subjects and not in others, and is this taken into consideration in placements?

DESEGREGATION AND INTEGRATION

In 1954 the U. S. Supreme Court ruled that separate is not equal, meaning that segregated schools do not provide equal educational opportunity for students. The result was court ordered desegregation. Desegregation refers to enrollment patterns in which students of different racial groups attend the same school, rather than students separated in racially isolated schools or classrooms. Integration refers to cases in which students of different racial backgrounds not only attend schools together, but also includes effective steps to overcome the disadvantages of minority students and to develop positive interracial contacts (Ornstein and Levine 1988).

Since the 1964 Civil Rights Act required school districts to take action to desegregate, courts at every level have been interpreting rulings for their districts. For example, a 1992 Supreme Court ruling (Freeman v. Pitts: Case No.89-1290) gives back to local districts some control over aspects of their operation such as assignment of students to schools; this decision had been under court jurisdiction in desegregation plans.

A group of social scientists presented a summary statement of social science research on the value of desegregation efforts over the past 20 years. The findings fall into 4 categories: (1) The desegregation of a school district can positively influence residential integration in the community, (2) Desegregation is associated with moderate academic gains for minority group students and does not harm White students, (3) Desegregation plans work best when they cover as many grades as possible, when they encompass as large a geographic area as possible, and when they stick to clearly defined goals over the long haul, (4) Effective desegregation is linked to other types of educational reform (Orfield 1992).

One method of achieving desegregation is magnet schools, a way of distributing students on the basis of subject concentration areas. Schools specializing in the arts or science and math attract students from a variety of social classes and racial groups, and in some cities have proven to be an effective way to desegregate and integrate schools. In the fall of 1992 there were approximately 5,000 magnet schools nationwide.

Several federally sponsored programs are designed to promote achievement and integration. Programs for pre-school children such as Head Start and high school students such as Upward Bound are part of government compensatory education programs; they give students from poor backgrounds extra help to prepare them for first grade and for college respectively. The most positive results are seen in the improved elementary school achievement of Head Start children.

However, one major concern is that students entering integrated schools face social and academic tracking, continuing patterns that lead to different treatment and unequal opportunity. Individual classroom teachers need to be aware of the ways in which students are grouped and group themselves in classrooms. Avoiding rigid groupings and encouraging integrated activities can improve school climate and achievement levels for minority students.

Debate surrounds bilingual educational programs in which classes are taught in two languages, like Spanish and English. Many argue that teaching children in their native languages hurts them in the competitive system, and that English facility is crucial to get ahead in American society (Levine and Levine 1996). Others argue that children are disadvantaged by being taught in a language they do not know. They wish to retain their cultural language and heritage, and they may resent being considered unacceptable the way they are. The debate continues even in minority communities. In the 1993-94 school year, 23% of 4th graders were in schools offering bilingual education, and 52% were in schools offering English as a second language. The current thinking seems to favor two-way bilingual education that gives English-speaking children and native speakers of other languages the chance to learn both languages; this policy has been implemented in some California schools (Garcia 1993).

PROPOSED SOLUTIONS

SCHOOL CHOICE AND VOUCHERS

Each new President, each new Secretary of Education, each new crisis in education brings forth proposals to solve problems in education. Most of these plans present little which has not been thought of and tried in the past, but memories are short and new plans are presented as the salvation for schools. Progressive education, back-to-back basics, alternative schools, competency-based education, magnet schools, and accountability have all been touted as the answer to our educational problems.

The education plan supported by the Bush and Clinton administrations has been **school choice**. The idea is that parents select the school with the philosophy and curriculum best suited to their children's needs. This free choice puts schools in competition for the tuition money that each child brings, and the idea is that the competition should enhance efforts of school personnel to perform and produce quality education. Ideally, parents would become more involved in their children's education, a factor social scientists know increases achievement. Related ideas are **voucher systems** and charter or community schools; children and their families would receive a voucher to pay tuition at a school of their choice, or for schools that would meet special needs of students.

On the surface, the idea sounds exciting-give parents a say in their children's education and create competition to improve schools. However, critics including many conflict theorists have several problems with the proposals. We will focus on the ones which relate to equal opportunity.

Urban public schools, already in serious trouble, would become the dumping ground for students not enrolled in other schools, and private schools which would be supported in part by public funds under choice plans, would create further divisions and inequalities in society by becoming more selective in their admissions of students. The best teachers would be siphoned off to better schools.

Some have predicted the demise of public school education and desegregated schools. One critic put it this way: "choice plans of the kind the White House has proposed threaten to compound the present fact of racial segregation with the added injury of caste discrimination, further isolating those who.....have been consigned to places nobody would choose if he had any choice at all" (Kozol 1991).

The bottom line seems to be that there is little research on school choice that supports improvement in education for low-income youth, a group communities most need to reach. Choice plans could even perpetuate or increase the gap between wealthy and poor youth because high-income youth would continue to receive better education.

NATIONAL EDUCATION GOALS PANEL

The **National Education Goals Panel** presented the following goals for U.S. Education to be accomplished by the year 2000: (1) All children in America will start school ready to learn, (2) The high school graduation rate will increase to at least 90%, (3) American students will leave grades 4, 8, and 12 having demonstrated competency in challenging subject matter, including English, mathematics, science, history, and geography; and every school in America will ensure that all students learn to use their minds well, so they may be prepared for responsible citizenship, further learning, and productive employment in our modern economy, (4) American students will be the first in the world in science and mathematics achievement, (5) Every adult American will be literate and will possess the knowledge and skills necessary to compete in a global economy and exercise the rights and responsibilities of citizenship, (6)Every school in America will be free of drugs and violence and will offer a disciplined environment conducive to learning (National Education Goals Panel 1993:3). This is a tall order, but from what social scientists have learned about the schools, some clear patterns for bringing about improvements in equal opportunity and quality of schools are emerging.

Mounting evidence supports the positive effects of parental involvement on student achievement. If parents participate in school-sponsored activities, attend school meetings, help children with their scheduling, and oversee homework, children get the message that education matters and that their parents are supportive (Epstein 1995; Epstein and Dauber 1991). Family relationships are better predictors of positive achievement and grades than all other variables, according to recent research (Dornbusch and Ritter 1992). Some schools that have sponsored programs to involve parents have had good success in raising achievement levels.

Early childhood education experiences such as Head Start have proven successful in giving children from less advantaged backgrounds a positive start in school. Some public schools are also offering early childhood classes (Mitchell 1990). For children of working parents and for those living in poverty, preschool offers a home away from home and early socialization in what, ideally, is a stimulating environment (Barrett 1989). One of the few anti-poverty programs to continue to receive federal funding support is Head Start because of research which shows its effectiveness for children from poor homes. The program deals with the health, educational and emotional development of the children enrolled. School achievement in early grades is higher for Head Start children, and some results are showing long-lasting effects with more Head Start children graduating from high school.

If **ability grouping** is used by schools, social scientists suggest flexible placements which are reviewed frequently and which differ in each subject area for each child. Thus, a student may be in a higher math grouping than reading group. Teachers and counselors alike should consider factors in addition to test scores in placements. With these cautions, ability grouping can be effective if used for a limited number of courses. However, when grouping locks students into courses and tracks such as college preparatory or vocational, it can have detrimental effects on achievement and equal opportunity (Lucas 1992).

Experts advise early identification of and intervention with at risk students. Some programs, which have proven effective, include: (1) Accelerated academics for students who are bored, after school; (2) Saturday programs for those who need extra help; (3) Alternative programs with different learning environments for alienated students; (4) Laws to deny drivers' licenses to students who are doing poorly in school or who drop out before 18; (5)Programs to get parents involved in the education of their children; (6)Alternatives to suspensions and expulsions such as in-school suspensions; (7)Tutoring, and (8)Rigid work requirements have proven successful in some schools.

Activities in the classroom including assigning special tasks and responsibilities which recognize the strengths of *at risk* students are helpful in providing them with a positive sense of school self.

Equitable funding of schools is an important variable in equal opportunity, yet controversial and hard to achieve. Some school districts have wealthy citizens and therefore have a higher property tax base to support schools, and greater ability to pass community school levies. Attempts to correct the inequalities have reached courts and produced mixed results. Other plans include school partnerships with corporate America. Some corporations promise to pay for the college expenses of those inner city students who stay in school and graduate. Others are sponsoring model schools. Still others are operating schools on corporate premises or bringing students in for courses, training, and internships. Foundations also provide grants to school districts for projects to improve education. Though some fear the influence of the corporate world on schools, local districts can seek the type of involvement they wish from corporations in their area.

Issues of what curricula are appropriate involve communities in controversy as well. For instance, many political, religious, and special interest pressure groups try to influence what schools teach. Some groups challenge choices of textbooks and library holdings; others are concerned about either the inclusion or exclusion of sex education. One example of curricular issues is multicultural education.

Demands for multicultural curricula refer to the teaching of history, literature, and other subjects to accurately reflect the different cultural groups in United States society and the world. Integration of multicultural materials into existing curricula involves inclusion of reading materials by and about minority groups, history which gives a fair and integrated portrayal of all groups, and other themes which promote understanding of all segments of multicultural society in the United States and the world. This movement is attempting to bring awareness of and tolerance for differences and to influence the choices schools and teachers are making about classroom materials and curricula (Ravitch 1990).

What can we learn from this discussion of equal opportunity? Clearly there are many activities that individuals, parents and teachers can carry out to help insure that each child gets the education to which she or he is entitled, and that children are prepared for fruitful, productive lives in society. Awareness of problem areas is the first step in moving toward change. We cannot afford to lose children in the dying school described in the opening case study.

SUMMARY

1. Hopes of parents that their children would have a chance to rise to a higher status have hinged on schools and teachers.
2. Equal opportunity requires removing obstacles to individual achievement such as prejudice, discrimination, and cultural barriers.
3. Two values affect equal educational opportunity: equal access and individual freedom. Equal access means that every individual starts out with the same opportunities. The individual freedom argument is that individuals are entitled to what they have justly earned, regardless of their status.
4. Among those groups most often stuck in the bottom rung of schools and society are racial, ethnic, gender, religious and linguistic groups whose culture and behavior patterns are different from the dominant American middle class patterns.
5. Education serves functions such as passing on to students the culture, knowledge, skills, values and behaviors necessary for society to continue; social control and personal development which helps to maintain order; the selection and allocation function which helps to determine where people are placed in society; and the change and innovation function which refers to creating new knowledge.
6. The emphasis on stability and maintenance of the society by structural functional theory fails to adequately address the qualities between groups in society struggling for equal access and opportunity. This failure leads conflict theory to a very different view of society, which assumes that tension and conflict exist in society between competing individuals and groups.
7. Research from the conflict perspective tends to focus on those tensions created by power relationships that ultimately cause change in the system.

8. Many researchers consider small groups and individuals' interactions in schools and classrooms as their primary interest. Interaction theories focus on individuals in-groups, from teacher-students dyads to interactions in classrooms and schools.

9. To study schools, social scientists combine a theoretical approach with research methods appropriate for gathering needed information. Those are usually national data on schools, systematic observation of educational settings, surveys, and case studies.

10. Children's manners, social class, names, physical appearances, race, sex, language usage, parents' occupation, and children's responses to teachers affect teachers' attitudes toward students. Positive teacher attitudes, approaches, encouragement, and expectations for learning are key to success.

11. The classroom provides very different experiences for girls and boys. When teachers understand these, they can act to reduce those differences which have an equal chance to advance due to methods for placement.

12. Ability groups are a hotly debated practice. Each theoretical orientation provides a different perspective on ability groups. Conflict theorists might argue that not all students have an equal chance to advance due to methods of placement.

13. An interactionist theorist would look at the dynamics of schools and classrooms and the expectations for students from different backgrounds which influence teacher judgments in the placement process. Regardless of theoretical orientation, we know that once a student is placed in a group, change is uncommon unless it is downward.

14. Over 1 in 10 students in the United States will drop out of high school due to factors related to school, jobs, and/or family.

15. Fairness of testing has been challenged on many grounds including cultural bias in questions and problems of comprehension for bilingual students.

16. The 1964 Civil Rights Act required school districts to take action to desegregate and generated much social science research over the past 35 years on its affect.

17. Each new president, each new secretary of education, each new crisis in education brings forth proposals to solve problems in education.

18. The bottom line is that there is little research on school choice that supports improvement in education for low-income youth.

19. Mounting evidence supports the positive effects of parental involvement on student achievement.

20. Early childhood education experiences such as Head Start have proven successful in giving children from less advantaged backgrounds a positive start in school.

21. Flexible ability grouping in which placements are reviewed frequently and differ in each subject area may be beneficial.

22. Early identification of at-risk children allows early programs targeted for these children, such as accelerated academics for students who are bored or denying drivers licenses to students who are doing poorly in school.

23. Equitable funding of schools is very important but controversial and hard to achieve.

24. Issues of what curricula are appropriate involve communities in controversy. Multicultural curricula is just one of the areas receiving attention nationwide.

25. Clearly there are many activities that individuals, parents and teachers can carry out to help insure that each child gets the education to which she or he is entitled, and the children are prepared for fruitful, productive lives in society.

REFERENCES

"America 2000: An Education Strategy" 1991. Washington, D.C.: U.S. Department of Education.

Anyon, Jean 1980. "Social Class and the Hidden Curriculum of Work." *Journal of Education*.

Baker, David P., and Deborah Perkins Jones 1991. "Great Differences: A Cross-National Assessment of Gender Inequality and Sex Differences in Mathematical Performance." unpublished manuscript.

Barrett, Gill 1989. *Disaffection from School? The Early Years*. London: Falmer Press.

Bellisari, Anna 1989. "Male Superiority in Mathematical Aptitude: An Artifact." *Human Organization*. 48(Fall):273-279.

Brookover, Wilbur B., Fritz J. Erickson, and Alan W. McEvoy 1996. *Creating Effective Schools: An In-service Program for Enhancing School Learning Climate and Achievement*. Holmes Beach, FL: Learning Publications.

Coleman, James S. 1990. *Equality and Achievement in Education*. Boulder: Westview Press.

Dornbusch, Sanford M., and Philip L. Ritter 1992. "Home-School Processes in Diverse Ethnic Groups, Social Classes and Family Structures." p. 111-125 in Sandra Christenson and Jane C. Conoley, eds. *Home-School Collaboration*. Silver Springs, MD: National Association of School Psychologists.

Epstein, Joyce L. 1995. "School/FamilylCommunity Partnerships." *Phi Delta Kappan*. (May)701-712.

_____.1990. "School and Family Connections: Theory, Research, and Implications for Integrating Sociologies of Education and Family." In D. G. Unger and M. B. Sussman, eds. Families in Community Settings: Interdisciplinary Perspectives. New York: Haworth Press.

Garcia, E. E. 1993. "Language, Culture and Education." In Linda Darling-Hammond, ed. *Review of Research in Education*. Washington, D.C.: American Educational Research Association.

Garner, Catherine L., and Stephen W. Raudenbush 1991 "Neighborhood Effects on Educational Attainment: A Multilevel Analysis." *Sociology of Education*. 64 October:251-262

Good, T. L. 1981. "Teacher Expectations and Student Perceptions: A Decade of Research." *Educational Leadership*. 38:415-422

Gose, Ben 1995. "Test Scores and Stereotypes." *The Chronicle of Higher Education*. August 18, 1995:31.

Kilgore, Sally B. 1991. "The Organizational Context of Tracking in Schools." American Sociological Review. April 56: 40

Kozol, Jonathan 1991. *Savage Inequalities: Children in America's Schools*. New York: Crown Publishers, Inc.

Levine, Daniel U., and Rayna F. Levine. 1996. Society and Education. 9[th]ed. Boston: Allyn and Bacon.

Lubeck, Sally. 1985. Sandbox Society: Early Education in Black and White America. London: Falmer.

Lucas, Samuel R. 1992. "Secondary School Track Rigidity in the United States: Existence, Extension, and Equity." Paper presented at the American Sociological Association, August, Pittsburgh, PA.

Mitchell, Ann, Michelle Seligson, and Fern Marx 1990. Early Childhood Programs and the Public Schools: Between Promise and Practice. Dover, MA: Auburn House.

National Education Goals Panel, "The National Education Goals Report: Building the Best" Washington, D.C.: NEGP Communications 1993: 3.

Oakes, Jeannie N. D. 1990. "Multiplying Inequalities: The Effects of Race, Social Class, and Tracking on Opportunities to Learn Mathematics and Science." Santa Monica: The Rand Corporation.

Orfield, Gary A., and Associates 1992. "Status of School Desegregation: the Next Generation." Report to the National School Board Association, Alexandria, VA: National School Board Association, 1992.

Ornstein, Allan C., and Daniel U. Levine 1988. *An Introduction to the Foundations of Education*. Fourth ed. Boston: Houghton Mifflin.

Ravitch, Diane 1990. "Multiculturalism Yes, Particularism No." *The Chronicle of Higher Education*. December 12, A13.

Renzetti, Claire M. and Daniel J. Curran 1992. *Women, Men and Society*. 2nd Boston: Allyn and Bacon.

Riehl, Carolyn M., Gary Natriello, and Aaron M. Pallas 1992. "Losing Track: The Dynamics of Student Assignment Processes in High School." Paper presented at the American Sociological Association, August, Pittsburgh, PA.

Schiller, Katheryn S., and David Stevenson 1992. "Sequences of Opportunities for Learning Mathematics." Paper presented at the American Sociological Association. August: Pittsburgh, PA..

Tannen, Deborah 1991a. *You Just Don't Understand: Women and Men in Conversation*. New York: Ballantine Books.

_____1991b. "Teachers' Classroom Strategies should recognize that men and women use language differently." *The Chronicle of Higher Education*. June 19, 1991, B2-3.

Tavris, Carol 1990. "Boys Trample Girls' Turf." Los Angeles Times. U.S. Department of Commerce, Bureau of the Census, Current Population Reports, Series P-20, "School Enrollment." Reprinted in *The Conditions of Education*. 1992. Washington, D.C.: U.S. Printing Office.

U.S. Department of Education, National Center for Education Statistics, "Dropout Rates in the United States", 1997,1999.

U.S. Government Printing Office 1989), Pp.110-11; *Digest of Education Statistics* 1976 (*The Condition of Education 1989*, Vol. 1) (Washington, D.C.: (Washington, D.C.: U.S. Government Printing Office, 1977) p. 40; and *Projections of Educational Statistics to 2000*, (Washington, D.C.: U.S. Government Printing Office, 1989), p.5.

U.S. Department of Education 1996. *The Conditions of Education*.

Useem, Elizabeth L.1991. "Student Selection into Course Sequences in Mathematics: The Impact of Parental Involvement and School Policies." The Journal of Research on Adolescence. Vol. 1.

CHAPTER 14: POPULATION CHANGE
CASE STUDY: PAKISTAN COMPARED TO THE UNITED STATES

Pakistan has half as many people as the United States but could surpass the United States in population within 30 years. Pakistan is one of the world's most rapidly growing countries with an annual population growth rate of 2.9%. This rate of growth results in a doubling of a population every 24 years. Pakistan's population was a mere 32.5 million when it won independence in 1947. In the 50 years since independence it has increased by more than 100 million to reach 134 million people. The current rate of growth for the United States, which is influenced by movement of a large number of people into the country, yields a doubling time of 114 years. For the U.S. and Pakistan, persistence of these same rates of population growth for 114 years would result in a staggering population of 430 million for the United States and an unimaginable population of more than 1.8 billion for Pakistan. At that time Pakistan would have a population that is 3.5 times that of the United States.

Today, Pakistan is one of the poorest countries in the world. Many scientists believe the large population increases that the country has been experiencing have made it much poorer than if its growth had been slower. Many demographers - social scientists who study the relationship between population and other aspects of society believe that the quality of life in Pakistan during the next several decades will be greatly influenced by the extent to which it is able to lower its rate of population growth. They view population and social and economic conditions as bound together in paradoxical ways that make changes in patterns difficult to achieve. Rapid population growth increases poverty and this increase in poverty leads to conditions that sustain rapid population growth.

Pakistan's rapid rate of population change is produced by the large difference between its levels of fertility and mortality. Unlike the United States, many more people move away from than into Pakistan. The average woman in Pakistan has 5.6 children compared to an average of 2.1 children per woman in the United States. This childbearing behavior yields a crude birth rate of 39 for Pakistan and 15 for the United States. At the same time, the two countries have almost equal proportions of their population dying each year, 9 per 1000 people in the United States and 10 per 1000 people in Pakistan. Pakistan's relatively low overall mortality rate exists despite the death of many of its infants. In Pakistan 91 of every 1000 babies die before their 1st birthday compared to 8 per 1000 in the United States. Pakistan's 2.9% rate of population growth is the difference between its birth and death rates, 39 minus 10 per 1000 equals 2.9%. Consequently, reductions in its rate of population growth must come from decreasing the gap between the fertility rate and mortality rate or possibly by finding other countries willing to accept the immigration of millions of Pakistanis.

Controlling population growth requires either a decrease in family size or an increase in the proportion of people dying. Tremendous efforts are being made to lower the country's population growth rate in a context where large families are encouraged by social and cultural institutions. Hence rapid declines in population growth are unlikely. Pakistan's rapid population growth means that its population is considered demographically young. More than 40% of its people are children younger than age 15 compared to 21% of the population of the United States. Having such a large number of young people increases the likelihood of more births in the future because each new generation of people reaching the age of parenthood is substantially larger than the ones preceding it. The tendency for rapid population growth at one point in time to beget rapid growth for many years in the future is called population momentum and works against efforts to slow the rate of population growth.

THEORY BOX by **Michael J. Donnelly** **Chapter 14** **Population and Environment/Human Ecology Theory**

Ecology studies the interrelationships between living organisms and the environment, both organic and inorganic. **Human ecology** is concerned specifically with the interaction and interdependence of human populations with the environment. The key notion involved is adaptation-how humans adapt and thereby alter their environments. Human survival, quality of life, preservation of the environment, all depend upon how humans adapt. Human ecology theory provides a frame of reference for examining how human decisions and actions impact on the environment and how the environment in turn conditions the possibilities for human life and human strategies for adaptation.

Consider how population and environment are inextricably linked. Thomas Malthus proposed long ago that human populations, if left unchecked, would grow rapidly and outstrip the resources (including food) of their environment. Unless checked, in other words, population growth would eventually despoil the environment; by exhausting, polluting, and otherwise undermining its own physical basis, human society would inevitably crash. Modern human ecologists rely on more sophisticated reasoning and modeling techniques, but they have developed a rather similar notion of "carrying capacity"-the upper size limit imposed on a population by its environing set of resources. Estimating carrying capacity is of course a difficult, hypothetical enterprise which requires a variety of assumptions; changes in technology moreover may have difficult-to-predict effects on the system being modeled. Nonetheless, even if not precisely calculable, the idea of an upper limit has been a strong spur to ecological understanding and to practical efforts to devise "sustainable" levels of development into the future.

Controlling the population "explosion" has been one of the key global issues of the late 20th century. It is an issue which industrial nations and developing nations tend to regard rather differently. By and large industrial societies have slowly growing or relatively stable populations (population growth in the United States, for instance, reflects far more the impact of integration than an excess of native births over deaths). In the language of population scientists' industrial societies have completed the "demographic transition." Developing societies on the other hand are still in an earlier growth phase of transition. To see the "demographic transition" in simple terms, think of 3 phases: an original equilibrium or stable population (evident for example in pre-industrial Europe) in which a high birthrate remains high, but the death rate declines, producing explosive growth in population; and finally a 3rd phase, when a new equilibrium is achieved, in which both birthrates and death rates are lower, but the restabilized population is much larger.

Many nations in the developing world are, in the terms of this scheme, in the 2nd phase of explosive growth. It is likely that such societies will eventually complete their own demographic transitions. Much of the contemporary discussion concerns figuring out what factors would accelerate or retard the process.

A young population may also make it more difficult for a country to improve the quality of life it can provide for its citizens. Only 13% of Pakistan's young women between the ages of 12 and 17 and 28% of the young men of these ages are enrolled in school. In the United States 98% of the young women and 97% of the young men between these ages are enrolled in school. The United States was challenged to build enough schools and provide enough teachers and other resources needed to educate the children produced by its relatively short-lived baby boom of the 1950s. Peak fertility for the United States during those years was just over half the fertility levels Pakistan has sustained for decades. Certainly, the inability of the society to fully educate its children will result in parents who are bound to traditions that produce rapid population growth. Finding ways to reduce rates of population growth that are appropriate for the Pakistani social and cultural traditions will be a challenge.

Many social scientists believe rapid population growth has a pervasive impact throughout Pakistani society. In addition to being one of the major causes of poverty, rapid growth contributes to environmental degradation. With its level of development it is difficult for Pakistan to apply the modern technology needed for the establishment of clean industries. Even wealthy countries like the United States find it costly to require industries to adopt techniques that minimize pollution or threats to health and safety of their citizens. The level of air and water pollution in Pakistan are much higher than in countries like the United States, in part because of the pressures associated with efforts to support such large increases in population. High levels of air and water pollution and deterioration in soil quality caused by social and cultural practices as well as by rapid population will influence many aspects of Pakistani society in the future.

Pakistani leaders are committed to improving the quality of life their citizens will have in future years. Like people throughout the developing world, Pakistanis envision a system that provides food, education, and economic opportunities at a level that exists in developed countries like the United States. Leaders want to accomplish these improvements while maintaining many of the society's unique socio-cultural practices: Success will depend to a large extent on how the country deals with its population and environmental dilemmas.

Unfortunately, many third-world countries have high rates of population growth. Indeed, nearly all of the future increase in the world's population, 2.3 billion of the 2.4 billion anticipated increases by the year 2025, is expected to occur in third world countries. Dealing with this social problem from the perspective of these countries and from the perspective of the world's humanity will be difficult.

OVERVIEW OF DEMOGRAPHICS

Problems of poverty, environmental degradation, and even political turmoil are often blamed on overpopulation. In fact, there are several facets of population that are problematic for any society. Population attributes of primary concern are population size, rate of population growth, population composition, and population distribution. Demographers are concerned with a society's levels of mortality, fertility, and migration because these processes, whether stable or changing, are viewed as directly related to the problems of a society. The age and sex composition of populations are also of critical concern in studies of population because they are linked to other facets of population and to many social, economic and political problems.

In modern times, dramatic changes have taken place in virtually all of these dimensions of population, and are considered to constitute problems themselves or to be tied to other serious social problems. Still, the most often talked about population attribute is size and whether there are too many people in relation to the amount of resources available to support them. In the case study, for example, it was noted that many scientists believe Pakistan is much poorer than it would have been if its growth had been slower.

SIZE

The potential for too many people, often referred to as overpopulation, was a concern in earlier times and in Eastern as well as in Western cultures. While some writers have expressed apprehension about the possibility of too few people to make the most advantageous use of land and other resources, it is the potential for overpopulation that has captured the most attention. For example, Plato theorized that a population of 5,040 would be optimal for a city and Aristotle advocated abortion as a means for keeping population from exceeding its optimum size (Keyfitz 1972). Robert Thomas Malthus, a moralist and economist, published his *Essay on the Principle of Population* in 1798. His work brought widespread scientific and public attention to threats posed by the number of people and population growth. Malthus viewed the number of people alive in 1798 as already overtaxing society's ability to provide for the people and as a key cause of hunger and misery. His ideas have been criticized because population has many times exceeded the size one would expect on the basis of his writing. Still, his primary notion that population size will inevitably threaten human society is accepted by many modern analysts known as neo-Malthusians.

Critics of Malthus believe that overpopulation has never been achieved, and some argue that there can never be too many people because societies find ways to support themselves. They point to the fact that the developed countries have food supplies that are more than enough to feed today's population, so that distribution rather than overpopulation is the cause of hunger. Still, many world leaders and scientists from different fields identify overpopulation as one of the most serious problems to persistently challenge human societies. Clearly, the overall welfare of societies is dependent to some extent on the amount of resources available in relation to the number of people who need to sustain themselves as well as to the ways resources are divided within and between societies.

GROWTH

A major emphasis in the study of population, perhaps more so than in any other field in sociology, is numerical measurement. Measures that allow the study of trends within societies and comparisons between countries, cross national comparisons of the levels of births, deaths and population growth have received much of this attention. The crude birth rate and total fertility rate are frequently used demographic measures.

The **crude birth rate** is computed by dividing the number of births in a given year by the midyear population and multiplying the result by 1,000. It yields the number of births per 1,000 people and ranges from as low as 14 for some developed nations to the mid 40s for some less developed countries.

The **total fertility rate** is based on age-specific fertility rates for women of reproductive age, usually age's 15-45 years, and estimates the number of children a woman will have in her lifetime. Currently, these rates range from less than two children per woman in some nations to as high as seven children per woman in others. Recall from the case study at the beginning of the chapter that the average family size in Pakistan is 5.6 children, as compared to the U.S. rate of 2.1. These family sizes are derived using the total fertility rate.

The most basic measure of mortality is the **crude death rate**. This rate is computed by dividing the number of deaths in a year by the midyear population and multiplying the result by 1,000. Life expectancy is a better indicator of overall mortality because, like the total fertility rate, it takes age distributions into account. Life expectancy and infant mortality, two key measures in demography, are among the best overall indicators of the quality of life provided by a society. The subtraction of the death rate from the birth rate gives the rate of natural growth for a population, usually reported as an annual percentage. In the case study, Pakistan had a 2.9% rate of growth compared to 0.4% for the U.S. Migration must be factored into the equation to determine national and local rates of population growth. Official record keeping systems for measuring migration are rare. From a neo-Malthusian perspective fertility levels above replacement level, a total fertility rate of 2.1, will eventually lead to overpopulation. A few societies are now concerned with the possibility of significant population decline as their total fertility rates are now well below 2.1 children per woman. For example, Germany now has a total fertility rate of 1.5 and more deaths than births. This is in stark contrast to the dramatically increasing population in Pakistan.

The rate at which a population is growing is arguably its most important feature. A frequently used and informative measure derived by dividing the growth rate into 70 is doubling time, or the number of years it will take a population to double. Until recent times world population and local populations took thousands of years to double themselves. Now, the doubling time for world population is 47 years and for some nations, like Pakistan, is less than 30 years. When world population growth rates were at their highest point in the 1960s and 1970s, its doubling time was around 33 years. One of the most striking differences between the developed and less developed nations is the difference between their doubling times. At their current rate of growth, the population of less developed countries will double in 38 years compared to a doubling time of 564 years for developed countries. It is the tremendous increase in population resulting from changes in population growth rates, and corresponding shorter time for population to double, that is referred to as the **population explosion.**

Even relatively small populations can reach astounding sizes in a short period of time given the growth rates of today's high-growth countries. The time it takes the world's population to increase by one billion is another reflection of the population explosion. It took from the first appearance of humans until 1850 for population to increase to one billion people. Now, the world's population is increasing by one billion every 11 years. With a growth rate of 1.5 the world's population will increase by approximately 88 million people this year. Put another way, there will be 88 million more births than deaths. From an ecological systems perspective, this is a tremendous imbalance.

POPULATION OF THE UNITED STATES

The United States is the 3rd most populous country in the world with more than 271 million people and it is the most rapidly growing of the world's developed nations. At the time of the country's first census in 1790 its population was just under 4 million and by 1900 the United States had a population of about 76 million. The country's population has grown rapidly throughout this time and continues to grow at a rapid pace (U.S. Bureau of the Census 1995). The United States, given its current rate of increase, will double its population in approximately 70 years with much of the growth coming from immigration.

Admittedly, it is impossible to say exactly what the consequences have been, but it is obvious that the social and economic conditions of the country would be different if population had ceased growing at 4 million or even at a much larger size. For example, the settling and development of the nation's vast territory could not have been accomplished with such a small population also, the existence of modern metropolitan cities is dependent on a large national population. On the other hand, crime, pollution, and other environmental problems would probably be less serious if the nation's population were much smaller.

The New York metropolitan area now has a population of around 20 million. The emergence and expansions of industries and the development of infrastructures such as highways and schools were dependent on population sizes sufficient to build, maintain, and use them. Likewise, future characteristics of American society are likely to be significantly influenced by the size it has reached. In a sense, population size is linked in a Malthusian fashion with the multitude of problems the nation faces in providing opportunities and resources for its citizens. At the same time, it is possible that larger populations spur innovations that improve the overall quality of human welfare.

CENSUSES

The U.S. constitution requires the taking of a census every 10 years in order to provide information needed for a representative form of democratic government. The U.S. censuses also gather valuable information on the social and economic composition of American society. This information is utilized to measure unemployment, poverty, educational achievement, occupational distributions, and a host of other facts about the society.

Population counts are used to allocate congressional representatives among and within states and the social and economic information gathered from censuses is used to identify problems, such as poverty, and to certify the levels of local needs so that federal and state funds can be fairly allocated according to need. Censuses, themselves, are controversial because they require individuals to divulge sensitive information and also because so many important governmental and business decisions are determined by census data. Evidence indicates that census data contains many inaccuracies with respect to being a total count of the population and with regard to accurately measuring the social and economic characteristics of people. For example, the obvious undercount of populations of some areas has resulted in legal challenges. Minority populations are undercounted much more than Whites resulting in fewer population-based resources being distributed to areas where minorities are concentrated, such as in the central cities of large metropolitan areas.

In recent years politicians have debated the way the Census Bureau gathers information and the possibility of placing restrictions on the number and kinds of questions that can be asked. The United States has been a leader in the development of censuses and has taken a census every 10 years since 1790. Restrictions could result in gaps in information on the society and make it difficult to determine differences between the social and economic conditions of states and local areas of the country. Importantly, there would be less factual information to show how the nation's character changes over time.

The Census Bureau is a large bureaucracy with a budget of billions of dollars with the responsibility for gathering information needed in modern societies committed to making decisions on the basis of factual information. In contrast, decisions in non-democratic societies are openly made according to the opinions and wishes of political and other influential individuals. It is important to understand that the collection, analysis, and uses of population data are important aspects of the broader population problem faced by modern societies.

COMPOSITION

Not only does the United States have a history of significant population growth; it has also undergone many shifts in population composition. Two aspects of society that are of central interest in population analysis are sex and age. A basic measure of sex composition is the **sex ratio**. It shows the number of males per 100 females in a population. Every census until the middle of this century recorded more males in American society than females. In 1900 there were more than 104 males for every 100 females in the American population. In 1990 there were 6 million more females than males and a sex ratio showing 95.1 males per 100 females. There are more males born than females, approximately 105 males per 100 females, and males out number females until age 21 after which there are more females than males at each age. For ages 85 and over there are only 39 men for every 100 women.

These shifts in age structure have altered the chances of males and females finding mates of approximately the same age and may have contributed to the emergence and success of the women's movement. In a democracy with a representative form of government the number of people in a movement is of considerable relevance and the larger number of women than men is sometimes mentioned as one reason why more women should be in leadership positions. The fact that women constitute more than half of the population but less than 10% of members of Congress is used as evidence that more needs to be done to promote their greater involvement in politics.

Shifts in the age composition of the population of the United States have been dramatic. The long-term trend has been toward a population with higher and higher proportions of older people. This is reflected in an increase in the median age from 16 years in 1800 to a median age of 34 years in 1996. The **median age** is the age at which half the people in a population are younger and half are older. The aging of the population, or increases in the proportion of people in the population who are older, is mostly a result of decreases in fertility.

From a demographic perspective any age distribution creates a unique set of problems because age composition is related to a host of social and economic factors. For example a young population must be educated and this requires a specific type of resource allocation. The United States had to build additional schools and employ a large number of teachers as a result of its baby boom. A population with a bulging working age population might be challenged to provide enough jobs. A society with an aging population must deal with medical and social security problems, including a declining labor force size. Any age composition places demands on a society's resources and the extent to which any particular composition poses a problem is largely a function of the level of availability of the resources needed by people in the different groups. In this context, the history of America fertility is significant. The United States has experienced drastic shifts in the annual number of births and in fertility rates. The total fertility rate in the U.S. has decreased from 7 children per woman in the early 1800s to approximately 2 children in the 1990s.

The most notable interruption in the historic decline of the American fertility rate was the **baby boom** that began in the late 1940s and lasted until the early 1960s. In the early 1940s the total fertility rate had fallen to an all time low of 2.2 children per woman. In 1957, the peak of the baby boom era, it had increased to 3.8. The baby boom was followed by the baby bust, a sharp drop in fertility rates to their lowest levels in the country's history. This lasted until the mid-1970s when the total fertility rate had dropped to 1.7 children per woman.

The magnitude of the differences between the baby boom, the baby bust and current reproductive rate for American women can be best understood by examining the raw numbers of births and birth rates for selected years. At the height of the baby boom in 1957 there were 36 million women of reproductive age, ages 15-45, in the United States. In that year they gave birth to 4.3 million babies or 119 births per 1,000 women. At the bottom of the bust in 1976 there were 46 million women of reproductive age and they gave birth to 3.2 million children in that year. In 1995 there were 60 million women of reproductive age and 3.9 million births. The total fertility rate for the United States has hovered around 2.0 since the late 1970s.

These numbers show the dynamic nature of reproductive factors. The baby boom is now associated with a decline in the number of births as the oldest of the baby boom generation pass through their reproductive years and the youngest ones enter the lower fertility ages of their reproductive years. With the smaller number of women from the baby bust reaching reproductive age, it is likely that the number of births will remain below 4 million.

It is important to recognize that the shifting numbers of births and subsequent changes in the number of individuals entering the various phases of life have contributed to, if not caused, some of the nation's most serious problems. Just after the baby boom society was forced to expend more resources on education and later to provide significantly more jobs as the baby boomers entered the labor force.

A challenge for the United States in the future is certain to be the allocation of more and more resources to support more and more older people. In 1996 there were 33.9 million people over the age of 64 in the United States compared to a mere 3 million people age 65 and over in 1900. U.S. Bureau of Census population projections indicates the number will increase from 33.9 million in 1996 to more than 69 million by the year 2030 (U.S. Bureau of the Census 1996). The population of people over age 64 itself is getting older as the proportion of the elderly who are over 75 or 80 years increases. Between 1980 and 1996, the number of American 85 years and older almost doubled, reaching 4 million

The aging of the American population is also reflected by the rapid increase in the number of Americans 100 years or older. In 1960 there were 3,000 Americans who were 100 years or older. In 1990 this number had increased to 54,000 and to 60,000 in 1996. Projections indicate that there will be 1.2 million this age or older by the year 2050. Certainly, changes in the number of people at different ages, especially the change in the proportion of people in the oldest age group creates population-based conditions that will challenge the nation's social security system and other institutions.

Not only has fertility impacted on American society, but also patterns of mortality. Mortality, the only process through which individuals are removed from world population, has always been important in understanding human societies. Even societies with the lowest levels of mortality continue to allocate an enormous amount of resources to lower the mortality rate further. Sustaining low mortality rates also requires continued expenditures of high levels of resources.

Numbers of deaths in the United States have increased in recent years despite low mortality rates. In 1996 there were 2.3 million deaths or 8.8 deaths per 1,000 persons. In 1995 the number of deaths was slightly less than 2.3 million. By contrast, in 1960 there were 1.7 million deaths resulting in a crude death rate of 9.5 per 1,000. In 1960 there were 2.6 million fewer deaths than births compared to 1.6 million fewer deaths than births in 1996. The rising number of deaths is due to the fact that population size, the number of people at risk of dying, has increased and that much of this increase has occurred at older ages.

Increasing the number of elderly people, especially the number 85 years old and over, plays an important part in explaining the overall increase in the number of deaths in the United States. It is important to note that the crude death rate and age specific mortality rates have decreased as the number of deaths has increased. Life expectancy at birth increased from 69.7 years in 1960 to over 76 years in the mid 1990s.

Several aspects of mortality make it an important social problem aside from the overall number of deaths and death rates. One of these is that there are inequalities in mortality. One might reasonably conclude that inequalities in mortality are the ultimate outcome of all the other inequalities encountered by certain groups. The close association between mortality and socioeconomic status is exemplified in the proportion of deaths among first class, second class, and third class female passengers on the Titanic (Goldscheider 1971). When the Titanic sank, 4 of the ship's 143 first-class female passengers drowned while 15 of 93 second-class female passengers and 81 of 179 third-class female passengers drowned.

In the United States and other societies similar differences in mortality rates exist between social classes and between minority and non-minority groups. For example, the infant death rate for the Black population in the United States is double the rate for White infants. In 1993, there were 19.6 deaths for every 1,000 Black male infants compared to 7.9 deaths per 1,000 White male infants. Similar differences exist between Black and White female infants. Life expectancy at birth is about 7 years longer for Whites than for Blacks because of overall inequalities in mortality. Eliminating mortality differences that are rooted in social and economic inequity is one of the most compelling challenges facing the United States and other nations.

DISTRIBUTION

The United States' population is diverse. Americans have both gloried in and deplored their role as a magnet for immigrants from many different areas of the world. At the same time, the country has been dominated by Whites of European descent, who have made up 80 to 90% of the nation's population since colonial times. In 1990 the U.S. Census revealed that non-Hispanic Whites still made up 75.7% of the U.S. population and that Blacks were still the largest minority group, 11.9% of the total population. Hispanics constituted 9.0% of the population and Asians made up 3.0%.

The next 5 decades are projected to be much different from the previous 200 years as minority populations rapidly grow and the White non-Hispanic population actually begins to decline after another 30 years of slow growth. By 2050, official projections show a decline in the White non-Hispanic population share of the total minority population from its current 75% to roughly 50% (U.S. Bureau of the Census 1996). The Hispanic population is projected to surpass that of Blacks by 2010 when both will make up about 13.5% of the nation's population, and by 2050 Hispanics will constitute 22.5% of the population compared to 15.7% for Blacks. The rate of growth will be most rapid for Asian Americans as they increase from 7.5 million to 40.5 million and make up 11.3% of the U.S. population by the middle of the coming century. These changes in population composition are relevant to many of the problems the United States is confronting in dealing with diversity. For example, the resolution of debate over affirmative action programs and the establishment of a national or state language are likely to be influenced by changes in population composition. Even more important, the social, economic and cultural character of the nation will change as its racial/ethnic composition varies in the future.

Immigrants, people moving into the country, now out number emigrants by approximately 800,000 people each year. This accounts for about one-third of the country's annual growth. Immigration has been controversial since colonial times. Throughout its existence and despite its identity as a nation of immigrants, the U.S. has had a substantial number of immigrants who have wanted to shut the doors once they were in the country. But many others have promoted allowing more immigrants into the country and some Americans favor no restrictions on who can enter and reside in the country. The debate over the number of people allowed into the country is certain to last long into the future.

The origins of immigrants or the number of immigrants allowed into the country from regions and nations of the world is also controversial. Until this century there were few policies to control entry into the United States and most immigrants came from countries in Europe. The specific origins shifted from northern and Western Europe in the first several decades after 1790 to more immigrants coming from southern and Eastern Europe toward the end of the 1800s. Now most immigrants come from Latin American and Asia. Of the 904,292 immigrants who entered the United States in 1993, Asians made up approximately 40%, Latin Americans made up 37%, Europeans made up 17%, and Africans made up 3%. Government policies now controlling immigration discriminate less against non-European nations but are complex with respect to determining which of the many people who apply from a given country will be allowed to enter. Immigration is almost certain to continue to contribute significantly to the nation's population growth and to play an important role in shaping the future of American society.

WORLD POPULATION

It is the recent enormous increase and expected future growth of the human population, as discussed in the Pakistani case study, that concerns many experts and policy makers. Since 1900 the world's population has grown from 1.5 billion to 6 billion people (McDevitt 1996).

While the time it takes to double the world's population shortened from several thousand years to hundreds of years by 1650, more recently the doubling time has shortened dramatically. Between 1650 and 1850 the world grew by 500 million to reach 1 billion for the first time in human existence. The growth in terms of absolute numbers of people and in growth rates has been explosive since this time. By 1930, 80 years after reaching 1 billion, the world's population grew to 2 billion. World population has nearly tripled in the last 90 years. Many demographers believe that the next century will witness the "second population explosion."

DEMOGRAPHIC TRANSITION

The most widely accepted explanation of these dramatic shifts in population growth is known as the theory of the **demographic transition.** A leading version of the theory postulates that there are 4 stages of population growth. In **stage one** high birth and death rates characterize all areas of the world and growth rates are extremely low. Evidence suggests that the crude birth and crude death rates were above 40 per 1,000 people in this stage. In most years the number of births slightly exceeds the number of deaths but in some years there is a loss of population as the number of deaths exceeds the number of births. Also, the population of some local areas is decimated by famine and disease in some years so that notable increases can only be detected over a long interval of time. No region of the world is free from the Malthusian threats of hunger, disease, and wars and all regions of the world likely experience some years in which there are more deaths than births.

The **second stage** of the demographic transition is characterized by declining mortality and the persistence of high birth rates. It is during this stage when the number of births began to consistently out number deaths. The positive side of this stage is that the decline in mortality signifies an improvement in the living conditions and health of the people. Higher and higher proportions of infants survive into adult ages and have their own children who also survive and reproduce. In a short time, compared to stage one, population begins to grow rapidly. By the end of stage two, population growth is explosive. The negative side of the demographic transition, from a Malthusian perspective, is this rapid increase in population. According to the Malthusian view, improvements in living conditions and health are eventually wiped out by increases in population.

In **stage three** mortality remains low, birth rates decline, and there is a corresponding decline in the rate of population growth. At the end of the third stage, the birth and death rates are approaching equality at low levels and population growth is low. Throughout the demographic transition declines in birth rates are more problematic and less understood than the declines in mortality. Whereas, nearly all cultures are receptive to changes that lower mortality, many if not most cultures resist ideas and technology aimed at lowering fertility rates. The time lapse between declines in the death and births rates may be viewed as a classic example of a culture lag.

The fourth stage of the demographic transition is marked by birth and death rates that are nearly equal, as they were in the first stage. In the fourth stage, both are at low levels, and the rate of population growth, as it was in stage one, is close to zero.

The most serious dimension of the population problem is that the **less developed countries** of the world are in the second stage or early phase of stage three of the demographic transition when population growth is explosive. An example is Pakistan, described in the case study beginning the chapter. Of the 88 million people being added to the world's population annually, more than 77 million or 88% are being added to the populations of less developed countries (McDevitt 1996). Even within the developing countries the poorest ones are growing most rapidly. The developed or wealthier nations are in or approaching stage four of the demographic transition. A few developed countries are experiencing fewer births than deaths, resulting in population declines, accompanied by a greying of their populations. Unless offset by immigration such demographic features may have negative economic consequences, as the dependent elderly begin to out number the employed proportion of the population.

POPULATION DYNAMICS

Although experts cannot be certain that population will grow as projected, there are dynamics on which projections are based that give them a high likelihood of being accurate. One of these is **"population momentum."**

Population momentum refers to characteristics populations have that are likely to greatly influence their future growth. The key characteristic related to population momentum is age composition and especially the number of women ages 15-45. In developing countries, such as Pakistan in our case study, there has been a large increase in the number of women of reproductive age and the number is projected to increase by more than 30 million women over the next 25 years. In the developed countries the number of women in the reproductive ages will actually decrease by 10 million between now and 2025. Even if the number of children per woman decreases significantly, the number of births is likely to increase because of the larger number of women in the reproductive ages. For example, there will be 8 times as many women in Africa in 2025 as there were in 1950.

The tendency for increases in the number of births as the number of births per woman declines is called the **population paradox.** It is the persistence of high levels of fertility and declining infant mortality that has resulted in ever-larger numbers of women of reproductive age in developing countries. In a sense, rapid growth at one point in time causes rapid future growth just as low growth, by producing fewer potential mothers, sustains low growth. Population momentum demonstrates how the different facets of population are linked in a causal network. Many experts believe population growth and other facets of population are also similarly linked with a host of social problems such as poverty. It is just much more difficult to factually demonstrate that poverty or other problems are partly due to the total number of people or to the number of people at different ages.

ENVIRONMENTAL IMPACTS

CONSUMPTION LEVELS

The impacts of population on the environment depend on consumption patterns as well as population size. Many scientists believe the consumption levels of developed countries are doing more harm to human societies and pose more serious threats to the future well-being of humans than the rapid population growth occurring in developing countries. They note that the 1.2 billion people in developed countries are consuming more than twice as much of the world's resources as the 4.7 billion people in developing countries such as Pakistan. The smaller populations of the developed countries produce three-fourths of the world's pollutants and waste. These impacts concern leaders in developing countries when told that the world's resources are insufficient to support their current or future population.

The differences in consumption levels between developed and developing countries point to problems associated with the model of modernization that prevails in the developed countries. If individuals in the developing countries consumed at the same levels as individuals in the developed countries, the world would require up to 30 times the resources now used. The implications are staggering. For example, there would hardly be room for individuals in Pakistan to store one car each much less drive cars on highways. Such increases in consumption in developing countries would result in many times the pollution that now occurs throughout the world. The destruction of ecosystems and extinction of species would increase if patterns that prevail in developed countries come to prevail in developing countries. In essence, the impacts of the population of the developed countries are more harmful than the much larger population of the developing countries.

URBANIZATION

One of the most significant changes in population distribution has been a change from dispersed settlement patterns toward a large urban complex pattern. This dramatic increase in the proportion of people living in cities is referred to as **urbanization.** Prior to industrialization there were only a few cities scattered throughout the world and none could compare with numerous cities of today with respect to size and complexity. In 1800 only 2% of the world's population lived in cities and none of the cities at this point in time had reached a population of one million people. Now, more than 40% of the world's 5.8 billion people live in cities. Projections indicate that cities will absorb nearly all of the world's population growth between now and 2025 as they grow by another 2 billion people compared to an increase of 97 million for rural areas of the world.

The increasing importance of cities is further illustrated by the recent emergence of **mega cities**, cities with a population of at least 10 million people. In 1950 New York was the only city to have a population this large. Now there are 21 mega cities and 44 more (including Karachi, on the Arabian Sea in Pakistan) are expected to exist in 2015. In 1990 the world's largest city, Tokyo, had a population of 25 million, more than twice the population of New York in 1950. From a social problems perspective it is important to understand that urbanization occurs along with the emergence of many of the social problems confronting modern societies.

Some leading sociologists have argued that urbanization is a major cause of modern social problems such as crime. A main contention is that the concentration of large numbers of people from different social and cultural backgrounds disrupts social relationships that underpin social order. In the modern context, urbanization itself is sometimes viewed as resulting from the inability of rural areas to support people. Consequently, cities are often flooded with more people than they can support. The emergence of urban slums and ghettos that are associated with many modern social problems are facets of the massive redistribution of population that has taken place in the last few decades.

POPULATION CONTROL

Finding solutions for population problems may be one of the most serious problems facing today's societies. This is true in part because policies and programs must focus on fundamental aspects of human lives, namely births and deaths. Births and deaths fully determine the rate of world population growth. Simply put, there is no way to slow population growth without reducing the gap between the number of births and deaths. Programs to increase the number of deaths are not acceptable (although failure to introduce programs to reduce mortality may be); and programs to influence the number of children have been frequently controversial. Also, the fact that some people do not consider rapid population growth to be a problem makes the development of policies and programs difficult.

DIRECT AND INDIRECT POLICIES

The linkage between facets of population and other social and economic conditions also makes it difficult to devise population policies. It is possible that successfully changing an aspect of population, such as its growth rate, will have a negative impact on the national economy or some other aspect of a nation. Demographers note that population growth is influenced by many governmental programs because demographic behavior and trends are so closely linked to social and economic conditions. Governmental efforts that promote increased access to education for women are likely to contribute to lower fertility. Tax codes that allow couples with many children to pay less in taxes than those with fewer children may contribute to high birth rates. Demographers refer to policies that influence population although there is no intended influence as **indirect population policies**. Policies developed for the explicit purpose of influencing population growth or some other facet of population are called **direct population policies**.

LIFESAVING TECHNOLOGIES AND CUSTOM

In one sense the population explosion has been caused by the dramatic drop in death rates and the extension of life expectancy by more than 40 years. Improvements in the standard of living and public health programs have played important roles in causing mortality rates to decline in nearly all parts of the world. Programs to save lives have been readily promoted by governments and widely adopted by individuals. Even the most pre-modern societies tend to seek medical and other modern scientific innovations that will save lives.

There are cases in which traditional customs that contribute to high mortality are maintained because of belief systems. For instance, the custom of consanguinity, the marital union of close blood relatives, persists in some societies despite strong evidence that it is the single most important cause of genetically related mortality in developing countries. In Pakistan, the case study beginning the chapter, 50% or more of the marriages are between blood relatives with 80% of these being between first cousins. Lifelong relationships between families, and the flow of resources between them and the rest of society are largely determined by the practice of consanguinity. Belief that marriage to a close blood relative cleanses the bloodline and leads to healthier children has been difficult to dispel.

Still, the adoption of lifesaving technologies and customs has been the rule for people in nearly all societies. Goals and policies to reduce mortality to its lowest possible level exist throughout the world and are likely to contribute to continued rapid population growth well into the 21st century. Certainly, the manipulation of mortality levels to control population growth is not a viable option. New diseases or increases in diseases such as AIDS may have the potential to slow population growth by raising the number of deaths (Olshansky et al. 1997).

LOWERING FERTILITY

Many scientists and political leaders view the population explosion as the result of the persistence of high fertility despite lowering mortality rates. Given the desirability of lower mortality and the conditions that promote it, policy makers and opinion leaders see smaller family size and corresponding declines in fertility rates as the most ethical solution to rapid growth. Until recently, nearly all societies promoted large families. A large population was viewed as an indicator of military power and as a resource for increasing the society's productivity. The important role of children to producing goods in pre-modern societies supported the development of widespread norms and customs that favored large families. In addition, in just about every society children are sources of a variety of social and economic supports for their parents and other family members. Hence, declines in fertility have been slow and policies aimed at lowering fertility have often met strong resistance.

For a program to successfully reduce fertility, it must eventually influence human reproductive behavior. Demographers have identified 3 sets of factors, called the **intermediate variables**, that must be influenced in order to affect fertility (Bongaarts 1982). The first set of factors is **fecundity,** the biological capacity to reproduce. It is estimated that the average woman has the ability to bear 15 children. Some women are capable of having many more than 15 children while others can reproduce few or no children at all. Failure to reach this potential means that other behavioral practices within societies are eliminating a number of births. In the most general sense these practices may be referred to as birth control because they control the number of births occurring in societies.

Hutterite women, who bore an average of 12 children each during the early part of this century are the only population to come close to reaching their maximum level of child bearing. Historically, there has been little variation between societies in the biological ability to reproduce. Policies to lower the biological ability to have children have not been pursued and do not offer a way to reduce the number of births. There have been reports of declines in sperm counts and other biological changes that could lower the biological capacity to reproduce. Obviously, the great difference between fertility rates of populations is due to other factors.

The second set of factors influencing fertility are those that affect the formation and disruption of sexual relationships. Age at first intercourse, proportion of women in a sexual union, and time spent outside such unions are among the most important variables in this set. There is much variation in the relationship between age and sexual activity between societies. A significant amount of the difference between high and low fertility societies is due to a younger age of marriage and entry into sexual relationships for women in high fertility societies. The longer women wait to begin sexual relationships, the fewer children they can have. The delay is a form of birth control.

Women who delay entry into sexual unions until after the end of their reproductive ages have eliminated, on average, 15 births. The low fertility of Northwestern European countries is partly due to a high proportion of women who are still celibate when they reach the age of 45 years (around 18% in

Ireland in the early 1970s). In many high fertility countries, nearly all women have entered and sustained sexual unions as teenagers.

There are many influences on the age of entry and the subsequent pattern of sexual relationships. Social customs and norms that are not necessarily intended to influence family size or birth rates tend to play an important role. In modern societies increases in levels of education and the pursuit of careers by women account for much of the increase in age of marriage or delayed entry into stable sexual unions.

A third set of factors affecting fertility is also of great importance in the formulation of policies to reduce population growth. They largely determine the extent to which sexual intercourse, especially frequent intercourse within sexual unions, result in conception and live births. They consist of the variables that are most commonly referred to as **birth control**, namely the use of contraceptives, voluntary sterilization, and abortion. The use of birth control plays a large role in the achievement of low fertility rates in modern societies where fecundity is normal and a high proportion of women in their prime childbearing years are sexually active.

Policies and programs to increase the use of modern contraception have been heavily emphasized by population scientists and governmental leaders interested in lowering population growth. In developed countries it is common for two-thirds of sexually active women to use modern methods of contraception whereas in less developed countries one-third use a modern method of birth control, such as the pill. In some high fertility countries, less than 5% of sexually active women use a modern form of birth control.

Efforts to increase the use of birth control have sometimes met with strong resistance. Occasionally there is a simple conflict between the social norms that favor large families and the use of any kind of birth control. In other cases religious teachings prohibit the use of any or particular methods of birth control. For example, the Catholic religion prohibits any artificial method of birth control, which includes the pill, intrauterine devices (IUDs), and abortion. This leaves abstinence and the rhythm method as acceptable. Abortion has been the most controversial method of birth control because some people in many societies consider human life to begin at the time of conception. Still, abortion plays a large role in sustaining low fertility rates in many countries. In some societies there are more abortions than births. In the United States about one-third of all pregnancies are terminated by abortions.

SUMMARY

1. More people are being added to the human population in 10 years than were added in the millions of years of human existence before industrialization.
2. It was not until the last several decades that scientists from many fields, political leaders, and the general public have expressed alarm over the tremendous increase in population. Even those who do not consider the present population of about 6 billion to be too large tend to note that such high growth rates will eventually overburden societies.
3. Nearly all recent population growth has occurred in developing countries, and population projections show that nearly all future growth will be in these countries. Developed countries are moving toward slight or no growth, the condition that characterized world growth prior to the start of the demographic transition.

4.   The demographic transition consists of 4 stages: (1) Low or no growth, (2) mortality declines, (3) fertility declines, birth and death rates are low approaching equality in stage 1. Rapid population growth occurs in stages 2 and 3.

5.   Population composition and distribution are associated with an array of social and economic problems. In rapidly growing populations there are many children who do not produce but who must be cared for. In slow-growth or no growth societies there are many elderly people whose needs must be met by the working-age population.

6.   Many experts consider consumption levels to be more important than population size or growth.

7.   The imbalance between developed and developing countries in resources and opportunities has resulted in migration from the developing countries to developed ones and in a massive movement from rural farm land to large urban centers.

8.   The expansion of the number of large cities over the last few decades is perhaps the most significant geographical shift in population in all of human history. About one-half of the world's population lives in cities and there are many more than 20 mega cities, each with a population of more than 10 million people.

9.   Rapid urbanization is occurring mainly in developing societies that do not have the high levels of economic opportunities and facilities to promote the well being of such growth

10. The achievement of zero population growth or other success in population control will not solve all social problems, but the prevailing view is that decreases in the rate of population growth and the eventual achievement of zero population growth will make it easier to solve all other serious social problems.

REFERENCES

Ashford, Lori S 1995. "New Perspectives on Population: Lessons from Cairo." *Population Bulletin. 50: (1)* (Washington, D.C.: Population Reference Bureau, Inc.)

Bongaarts, John 1982. "The Fertility Inhibiting Effects of the Intermediate Variables." *Studies in Family Planning.* 13(6/7): 179-189.

Goldscheider, Calvin 1971. *Population, Modernization and Social Structure.* Boston: Little, Brown and Company.

Keyfitz, Nathan 1972. "Population Theory and Doctrine: A Historical Survey." in William Petersen, ed. Readings in Population. New York: The Macmillan Company.

Malthus, Robert Thomas 1798. *An Essay on the Principle of Population As It Affects the Future Improvement of Society with Remarks on the Speculations of Mr. Goodwin, M. Condorcet, and Other Writers.* London: J. Johnson.

McDevitt, Thomas M. at the U.S. Bureau of the Census 1996. Report WP/96, *World Population Profile.* 1996. U.S. Government Printing Office, Washington, D.C.

Olshansky, S. Jay, Bruce Carnes, Richard G. Rogers and Len Smith 1997. "Infectious Diseases - New and Ancient Threats to World Health." *Population Bulletin.* 52: (2) (Washington, D.C.: Population Reverence Bureau, Inc.).

U.S. Bureau of the Census 1995. Statistical Abstract of the United States: 1995. 115th ed. Washington D.C

INDEX

A

B

C

I

income distribution, 260, 273
independent living model, 165
index of dissimilarity, 187
indirect population policies, 308
inequitable, 118
infant mortality, 141, 212, 213, 214, 215, 216, 225, 226, 298, 306
Infertility, 43, 53
inflation, 185, 231, 269
informal model, 165
instrumental activities of daily living, IADL, 158
Interaction theories, 281, 291
interactionism, 92, 96, 138
intergroup differences in marriage, divorce, and out-of-wedlock
    childbearing, 185
intermediate variables, 309
intervention, 31, 32, 33, 100, 108, 110, 111, 157, 165, 245, 251, 265, 289
intrinsic aging, 157

J

joint household, 138
Juvenile homicide, 107

L

Larceny-theft, 105
Latinos, 23, 56, 76, 178, 182, 183, 197, 242
less developed countries, 297, 298, 305, 310
life course perspective, 140, 149
Life expectancy, 155, 209, 298, 302, 303

M

Male Prostitutes, 61
mandatory minimum sentencing, 109
Marijuana Tax Act, 76
master status, 108
matrix of domination, 64
median age, 146, 148, 151, 301
medical model, 165
Medicare, 29, 153, 159, 163, 164, 166, 167, 168, 200, 222, 223
mega cities, 307, 311
Megan's Law, 103
methodology, 3, 12, 193, 263, 265
mid-level practitioners, 219, 225
minority, 76, 82, 95, 97, 99, 103, 122, 156, 160, 167, 168, 173, 174, 175, 176,
    177, 178, 179, 180, 181, 182, 183, 184, 185, 186, 187, 188, 189, 190, 191,